Emerging Markets in an
Upside Down World

For other titles in the Wiley Finance Series
please see www.wiley.com/finance

Emerging Markets in an Upside Down World

Challenging Perceptions in
Asset Allocation and Investment

Jerome Booth

This edition first published in 2014 by John Wiley & Sons Ltd
© 2014 Jerome Booth

Registered office
John Wiley & Sons Ltd, The Atrium, Southern Gate, Chichester, West Sussex, PO19 8SQ, United Kingdom

For details of our global editorial offices, for customer services and for information about how to apply for permission to reuse the copyright material in this book please see our website at www.wiley.com

Wiley publishes in a variety of print and electronic formats and by print-on-demand. Some material included with standard print versions of this book may not be included in e-books or in print-on-demand. If this book refers to media such as a CD or DVD that is not included in the version you purchased, you may download this material at http://booksupport.wiley.com. For more information about Wiley products, visit www.wiley.com.

Designations used by companies to distinguish their products are often claimed as trademarks. All brand names and product names used in this book are trade names, service marks, trademarks or registered trademarks of their respective owners. The publisher is not associated with any product or vendor mentioned in this book.

Limit of Liability/Disclaimer of Warranty: While the publisher and author have used their best efforts in preparing this book, they make no representations or warranties with respect to the accuracy or completeness of the contents of this book and specifically disclaim any implied warranties of merchantability or fitness for a particular purpose. It is sold on the understanding that the publisher is not engaged in rendering professional services and neither the publisher nor the author shall be liable for damages arising herefrom. If professional advice or other expert assistance is required, the services of a competent professional should be sought.

A catalogue record for this book is available from the British Library.

ISBN 9781118879672 (hardback/paperback)   ISBN 9781118879665 (ebk)
ISBN 9781118879658 (ebk)   ISBN 9781118879641 (obk)

Set in 10/12 Times by Sparks – www.sparkspublishing.com
Printed in Great Britain by CPI Group (UK) Ltd, Croydon, CR0 4YY

Contents

Foreword
by Nigel Lawson

Jerome Booth was a key member of the 1999 buyout team that turned the Ashmore group into a highly successful investment manager specialising in emerging markets. Having made his fortune, he has now left Ashmore to devote his time to building up a portfolio of business start-ups, philanthropy (particularly in the area of music, his great love) and writing this admirable book.

The heart of the book is the case he makes for investing much more heavily than is customary at the present time in emerging markets, and is directed in particular – although not exclusively – to the institutional investor. It is, of course, widely recognised nowadays that for the foreseeable future the growth prospects of much of the developing world are very much greater than those of the developed world. At the very least, they still have a great deal of catching up to do; and the combination of globalisation and the change from top-down planned economies to largely market economies is enabling them to do so.

Yet despite this, Booth observes, a typical Western pension fund might have around 5% of its portfolio invested in emerging markets and 95% in developed world markets. In his judgement, the emerging market proportion should be more like 50% than 5%. So why have Western institutional investors, as he sees it, got it so wrong?

There are a number of reasons, but the most important is the assumption that the emerging world is a much riskier place to invest in. Booth's thesis is that, if anything, the reverse is the case. The disastrous banking meltdown of 2008, following the excessive accumulation of debt of all kinds, sovereign and private alike, within what he likes to call the Highly Indebted Developed Countries, has created a risk of default, inflation (the alternative means of default) and sub-normal growth from which the much less indebted emerging world is largely free. At the very least, in his own words, 'All countries are risky: the emerging markets are those where this is priced in'. In the HIDC, in his judgement, it is not.

You do not have to share his notably downbeat assessment of the likely economic prospect for the developed world at the present time to be persuaded that the conventional assessment of the relative riskiness of investing in emerging markets, as compared with investing in the Western world, is mistaken.

But although the case for investing in emerging markets is at the heart of this book, there is a great deal more to it than that. It is in fact a rare combination of investment expertise and financial sophistication, informed by a thoughtful analysis of the economic and political context in which investment decisions have to be made. In particular, he offers a good account of the causes of the Western world's banking disaster, stressing in particular both the nonsenses produced by the combinaton of the rational expectations hypothesis and the efficient markets theory, and the extent to which banking and finance fell victim to the principal/agent problem (where the client or investor, as principal, is dependent on an agent whose interests and incentives may be very different from those of the principal).

Jerome Booth has written an original, challenging, stimulating and largely convincing book.

Acknowledgements

I would like to thank all those who contributed comments on earlier drafts and with whom I have debated the issues contained in the book. In particular I would like to thank my past colleagues at Ashmore, starting with Mark Coombs, from whom I have learnt more about emerging markets and investing than I could fit into several books let alone one, and my other management buyout partners Jules Green, Tony Kane, Milan Markovic, Chris Raeder and the late Will Mosely. I would also particularly like to thank Jan Dehn, who took over from me as Ashmore's Head of Research and who has given me copious feedback on a number of earlier drafts. I also have benefitted greatly from comments from my ex-colleagues Ousmène Mandeng, Milan Markovic, Tolga Ediz, Cemil Urganci, Kevin Bond, Mark Weiller, Marlon Balroop and Karl Sternberg. I would also like to thank Greg McLeod for the cartoon in Chapter 5. The views in this book are of course my own and do not necessarily reflect the views of Ashmore. I also received detailed comments from Peter Oppenheimer. I am also indebted to my father, Jolyon Booth, for his comments and to Luis Ratinoff for inspiring me many years ago to write a book about money and finance, and for helping round out my education early in my professional career. I am also indebted to my other ex-Inter-American Development Bank friends Michael Jacobs (who, shortly after I had received my economics doctorate, teased me for being too efficient with my education), and Héctor Luisi, both of whom gave me detailed comments on earlier drafts. Likewise I am indebted to fellow emerging market investment guru Liam Halligan. I would also like to thank Adam Swallow for believing in this project, and a number of anonymous academic referees for their valuable comments on an earlier draft. My son Marcus helped me greatly in the preparation of the manuscript, as did Anisha Bansal and Claire Sowry. I would also like to thank all those investors and policymakers I have met over the last twenty years who have stimulated me to write the book. I have had countless people telling me I should write one. Somebody once even apologised to me for not reading it – given the circumstances, I explained that that was quite understandable.

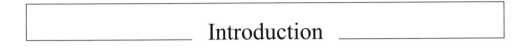

Introduction

'Our comforting conviction that the world makes sense rests on a secure foundation: our almost unlimited ability to ignore our ignorance.'

Kahneman (2011, p. 201)

The world is upside down: the emerging market countries are more important than many investors realise. They have been catching up with the West over the past few decades. Greater market freedom has spread since the end of the Cold War, and with it institutional changes which have further assisted emerging economies in becoming more productive, flexible and resilient. The Western financial crisis which began in 2008 has quickened the pace of the relative rise of emerging markets – their relative economic power, and with it political power, but also their financial power as savers, investors and creditors.

The 2008 crisis also revealed intellectual failures in the way we think about the world: in economics, in finance theory and in the practice of investing. We have known about many of these problems for a while, but the 2008 crisis has exposed them more widely and has given impetus to finding alternatives. This book aims to make a contribution to that search.

The credit crunch and then deleveraging are fundamentally due to excess leverage (borrowing) in developed countries. This excess leverage was built up precisely because risk perceptions were artificially low, in part due to emerging market savings being built up excessively by central banks after the Asian crisis of 1997/8 and then invested in the US, so pushing down the US yield curve. This is the very opposite in the emerging world, where risk perception is higher and leverage did not become anything like as excessive. The deleveraging process can apply only where there is excess leverage, and therefore it is fundamentally a problem of the developed world. Emerging markets suffer from collateral damage because they have economic links with overlevered developed countries, but they don't suffer from the disease itself, and the problems they do have are easier to solve.

This book describes the new world we live and invest in, with particular reference to the role of emerging markets – the new and coming dominant force in the global economy. It also builds the case for an approach to investing that goes beyond the backward-looking asset allocation and investment methodologies currently widespread.

While this book focuses on investment theory and asset allocation in general, emerging markets constitute a common theme due to their central role in the global economy, their richness as a source of prejudices and anomalies typical of current investment practice, but also given my particular expertise and familiarity with them.

The book touches on four topics: the history of emerging markets (sovereign debt in particular); reasons to invest in emerging markets; how institutional investment and the fund management business works; and how financial markets should be regulated. However, this is one book, not four. I have taken the view that the linkages between these topics are sufficiently important to justify touching on all of them, and I have attempted to take the reader on a broad tour of my ideas before presenting some more prescriptive suggestions. If at times the strands appear to diverge, please bear with me. In the interest of space, I have focused on the less well-trodden ground. Hence I have left out many details of emerging market history and current investment opportunities country by country in favour of the bigger picture. That bigger picture is how millions are hostage to prejudice, the grounding of this prejudice in faulty finance theory, and what we can do about this as investors and policymakers.

I.1   UPSIDE DOWN: PERCEPTION VS REALITY

Today's maps typically have north at the top and developing countries at the bottom. What if we turn the map upside down? And what if we mark up the central part as shown in Figure I.1? The emerging markets are mostly within the area indicated at the centre, with developed countries at the periphery. As well as having the south at the top, the map is a Peters projection – an area-accurate map. How should we look at the world today?

Emerging markets are large. They account for over 85% of human population, the bulk of industrial production, energy consumption and economic growth, and around half of recorded economic activity using purchasing power parity. They are anything but peripheral.

The world is also upside down in that many emerging markets are now safer from some of the worst loss investment scenarios than many developed countries. The countries and

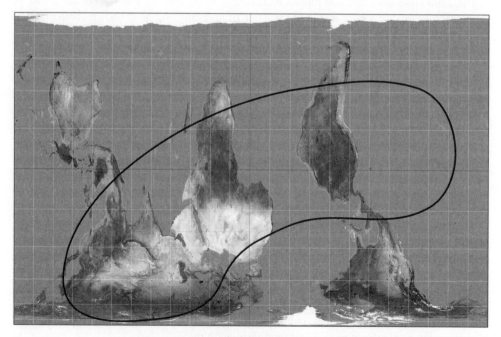

Figure I.1   The world upside down, with developing countries in the middle. Map source: Strebe

investments perceived by many as least risky are often highly risky (in part because the risk is not perceived), and vice versa. This is because the developed world has been borrowing and consuming excessively. Three decades of financial sector deepening has extended leverage (borrowing) to unsustainable levels which will take several more decades to unwind. Many developed countries are facing long periods of work-out and slow growth at best. Not so in the emerging world. Emerging markets are nothing like as heavily leveraged and do not face decades of deleveraging ahead.

Whether we look at a map of the world with north or south at the top seems fairly arbitrary, but is it? Many of us subconsciously associate, rightly or wrongly, the northern developed world with superiority and primacy. This is prejudice – take another look at the map and try to think differently for a moment.

This prejudice is an example of how sometimes we simply don't think consciously about an issue. Our subconscious chooses for us in what Malcolm Gladwell (2005) has called a blink. This is in many cases a desirable efficiency: it makes sense to use models and shortcuts, including subconscious ones, which we have used successfully in the past. Indeed, much of Gladwell's book laments the suppression of our subconscious skills through damaging conscious rationalisations, and we shall join him in that complaint at various points in the book. We also rely on more conscious models and views developed by others: if someone else has thought it through, we don't have to. However, sometimes our gut reactions can mislead us. Sometimes the conventional wisdom can be not merely wrong but dangerous. Sometimes a lot of people can be wrong at the same time.

Finance theory is a relatively new and rapidly expanding area of study which still has serious limitations for guiding the practitioner on how to cope with dynamic situations and structural shifts not previously encountered. Every MBA student should be aware that while finance theory has enabled the growth of financial markets, it has also caused major distortions in the global economy. Macroeconomic factors and more general history outside asset price history are often poorly integrated, belittled, ignored or an afterthought when it comes to investors' allocation decisions. If something is not measurable it may simply not be factored into decisions,[1] leading to risks and lost opportunities for investors, as well as systemic problems for regulators and economies.

Moreover, many institutional investors and investment advisers (and regulators) follow the behaviour of their peers and put up with what they know to be bad theory and asset allocation practices. They have not found better alternative methodologies, and unfortunately the thinking is all too prevalent that, after all, it is not their money. Their own interests, including their reputations and careers, affect investment decisions.

A rapidly changing world needs new investment theory and practices. Emerging economies will increasingly affect developed world financial markets. The savers and investors of tomorrow live and invest in emerging markets. They are younger. Their pension funds are immature and growing fast. Their financial markets, currently puny in comparison to existing GDP, let alone future GDP, will expand much faster than the underlying economies. The investor of today and especially of tomorrow needs macroeconomic, historical, political, behavioural and institutional factors fully incorporated dynamically into their thinking. Non-dynamic models which treat emerging markets as an afterthought are increasingly a dead end for investors.

---

[1] See Wolfram (2002) for a similar critique of traditional mathematics and science, which is biased to study only problems which are simple to model with formulae.

This book is intended primarily for those engaged in financial investment and asset allocation. Their task is much more complex than the academy would have us believe. I suggest
some ways of including a wide range of inputs into investing, even if this amounts to no more
than posing questions for investors and others to consider. This book is also relevant for those
students of finance and economics, international relations and emerging markets, looking for
input from an investor (myself) as to where they might concentrate further research. To this
end, I have attempted to provide an orientation through what I consider the relevant academic
literature, but within the constraints of a book accessible to the general reader. I also hope that
policymakers and regulators both in the developed and in the emerging world may also find
something of use, particularly in Chapter 11, as they ponder how to make sense of the new
upside down world we live in.

I.2   THE STRUCTURE OF THE BOOK

The first eight chapters lay the groundwork for the remainder by discussing the state of the
world and the state of existing theory. Some prescription is included here, particularly in
Chapters 7 and 8, but the later chapters are more wholly prescriptive and targeted at the practical asset allocator and investor (and policymaker in Chapter 11). In a number of chapters
the discussion includes a mixture of history, theory and illustration from emerging markets.

In Chapter 1 some consideration of the history of globalisation leads to the observations
that underpinning technological change is largely irreversible, and that political centralisation efforts are under stress. We discuss how globalisation shapes demand. We briefly cover
the history of commodification. The changing economic landscape of the 20th century is
charted through Bretton Woods to the ideological shift in the 1980s to the period of relative
stability in the early 2000s.

The West was not always economically dominant, and I observe in Chapter 2 that the
growth of debt markets was part of Europe's economic success story. Other countries have
been catching up over the past few decades, and financial markets are playing an important
role in that process. The poorest countries are also catching up, but for them Western defence,
foreign and aid policies also need to adapt.

The bulk of Chapter 1, however, is an introduction to, and history of, emerging markets,
concentrating mostly on the debt markets, and including a description of the major market and
policy developments since 1990. Along the way various crises are discussed but also, briefly:
the role of the IMF, the rise of market economies and institutional change, macroeconomic
shock treatment, the post-Asian crisis build-up of central bank reserves, some thoughts on
fixed exchange rates, and the reduced risk, post-1998, of emerging market-specific financial
contagion. This is from the perspective of an investor and macroeconomist in the markets
and is not necessarily a consensus view. It should convey, though, some of the dynamism
and rapid changes in emerging markets, and give context to policy and investment issues
discussed later in the book.

The superbubble leading to the 2008 financial crisis is discussed in Chapter 3, including the
US housing bubble, the US Federal Reserve's post-2008 challenge and strategy, subsequent
difficulties in the Eurozone, and the unsustainability of excessively large foreign exchange
reserves in the emerging markets.

Chapter 4 reviews the state of current economic and finance theory of relevance for, and as
used by, investors. To spend a few thousand words to summarise an entire academic discipline

(or two) would be rash. Instead, the chapter is necessarily partial and focused on the theory needed to pursue the arguments of the book later on. The discussion does not attempt to be comprehensive in scope or thorough in detail: I highlight some of the main ideas currently used directly or indirectly by investors and allocators in practice and what their limitations are. A cursory history of economic ideas is presented, from classical economics to Keynes, some comments on laissez-faire, and the microeconomic foundations of macroeconomics. Rational expectations theory and the efficient markets hypothesis are introduced and discussed. Much of finance theory is grounded in microeconomics and several of its limitations are discussed, including the fallacy of composition – that what is true for some may not be for all – and that valid theory either has to have realistic assumptions or be empirically testable, which is a problem for parts of finance theory. This brings us to some of the ideas emanating from behavioural finance research. We leave aside some of the details (such as current conventional approaches to asset allocation, which has its own chapter) to later in the book.

Chapter 5 addresses the issue of risk: a subject that deserves its own chapter, as risk management is central to investment and is so much larger a concept than the extrapolation of past volatility. We discuss how risk is not the same as volatility, how risks are different for different people, and how people's decisions are bounded and investors can herd. We criticise the theoretical distinction between specific and systematic risk – a criticism which undermines some traditional thinking about asset classes – and the overuse of data extrapolation in assessing risk. We make the distinction between risk and uncertainty.

How to assess emerging market sovereign risk is then discussed. In the process we discuss rating agencies, formal models, capacity versus willingness to pay, and the importance of trust. I define political risk and comment on its importance for investors, and introduce a three-layer approach to assessing sovereign risk, consisting of a ratio layer, a policy layer and a prejudice layer.

Following from our upside-down-map thinking, Chapter 6, which builds on Chapters 4 and 5 in criticising traditional concepts of risk, criticises our core/periphery view of the world. In the traditional dominant investor's view the core is the developed world, the periphery the emerging world. The core affects the periphery, but too often investors belittle or ignore altogether the effect of the periphery on the core. Challenging this outdated view of the world is necessary to free up our minds, enabling us to see emerging markets and global investing in a new light which better reflects risks and opportunities. In the process we discuss some of the problems facing the developed world which emerging markets do not have. We discuss conditions under which fiscal expansion may be a palliative rather than a cure for slow growth. We also frame the concepts of decoupling, and the spread of a bond above a risk-free rate, as core/periphery ideas. We introduce the idea of a relative theory of risk. Use of GDP weights to allocate investments is also considered.

Chapter 7 argues that the proportions of different types of investors who hold a particular asset or asset class – which I refer to as the structure of an investor base – is an important component of risk. Different investors have different liabilities, beliefs and incentives, and sometimes an overwhelming number of investors who hold an asset may wish to sell at the same time, with very little demand to match their supply at anything but much lower prices, and sometimes none at all. Just as Minsky showed that asset values can collapse, so can liquidity – the amount that an asset trades in a given period. Estimates of future liquidity should not always simply be extrapolated from past liquidity, but take into account the structure of the investor base.

In trying to understand investor behaviour, different notions of what it is to be conservative are identified. Herding and pecuniary and non-pecuniary incentives are discussed. We review some of the limitations of models and approaches which ignore investor base structure and consider some possible future alternative avenues: evolutionary theory, network theory and game theory. With examples from the problem of assessing sovereign risk, I introduce a theory of market segmentation, and highlight three warning signals that a market may be in a bubble, namely: a homogenous investor base, a misperception of risk which may shortly change, and leverage.

Chapter 8 focuses on asset allocation. The purpose of this chapter is to describe and critique existing asset allocation techniques as practised – including the agency problems which drive and constrain many decisions. The definition of asset classes is critiqued further, as is the rise of 'alternatives' to traditional asset classes, mental accounting, and home bias. The Yale model is briefly introduced and its limitations are discussed. Asset/liability management is included in the critique: its lack of accuracy and timeliness as well as other theoretical deficiencies. The benefits and limitations of inflation-linked bonds to meet liabilities are discussed, and also how the traditional efficiency frontier analysis fails to incorporate utility curves to model investor preferences. We also discuss the two-stage process of asset class allocation followed by manager selection, and the assumptions which frame the debate between active and passive management.

Building on our ideas about asset allocation, Chapter 9 turns more prescriptive. We discuss how one might try to incorporate strategic thinking with scenario planning – thinking through the consequences of possible different futures – into asset allocation and investment processes. We include an illustration of how one might think about allocating shortly after being alerted to major possible uncertainties, namely some investment rules of thumb post the 2008 financial crisis. We discuss the importance of thinking broadly about the macroeconomic environment as an input into asset allocation and dynamic portfolio management, and illustrate this with the way Ashmore, the firm whose 1998/9 management buyout I participated in, and which I worked for until 2013, manages funds.

Bringing the preceding ideas together to inform an asset allocator or investor is the task of Chapter 10, ambitiously entitled 'A New Way to Invest'. It takes the form of a list of questions and commentary to enable an investor to manage through periods of structural shift and uncertainty, starting with a questioning of our assumptions. It is an aid to prompt investors and an ongoing work in progress, rather than a finished prescription. I hope it might stimulate more research, but mostly that it may help investors and asset allocators to think about underlying issues and risks perhaps previously bypassed. In any case there is no good substitute for thinking issues through in detail.

Chapter 11 focuses on a variety of policy issues arising from the book's analysis. Crisis brings the opportunity to redesign regulatory oversight. Some new and old but forgotten general lessons about regulating financial institutions are discussed, and then policy responses to systemic risk. Regulation of banks is discussed, but also of other financial markets and institutions. Pension fund regulation could be introduced to tackle money illusion. Regulation should perhaps be better designed to overcome lack of trust and agency problems, including via non-pecuniary incentives and choice architecture. Regulators should perhaps pay more attention to the structures of investor bases and the misperception of risk. Attempts to map investors by both risk perceptions and liability characteristics may prove useful. My theory of investor segmentation may also be of use as a tool for detecting bubbles.

Issues facing policymakers in emerging markets are then more specifically examined, including the opportunities for emerging market banks to expand internationally, the need to avoid dependence on Western rating agencies, the importance of countering core/periphery thinking, and the benefits of building capital markets starting with bond markets (in part to reduce systemic risks). The need to reform the international monetary system is also discussed, as is the challenge of diversifying and reducing excess emerging market central bank reserves. Then there is a section for investors on what to expect from developed market policymakers, and a final section listing some things to expect from emerging market policymakers.

Finally, Chapter 12 concludes with a brief list, complementary to the one at the end of Chapter 11, of further changes investors might see coming from emerging markets in future, summarising some of the arguments referred to in the body of the book, together with some general predictions from my own reading of current trends. I also include a list of possible future research.

1
Globalisation and
the Current Global Economy

'Globalisation should not be just about interconnecting the bell jars of the privileged few.'

De Soto (2000, p. 219)

'The benefits of globalization of trade in goods and services are not controversial among economists. Polls of economists indicate that one of [the] few things on which they agree is that the globalization of international trade, in which markets are opened to flows of foreign goods and services, is desirable. But *financial* globalization, the opening up to flows of foreign capital, is highly controversial, even among economists ...'

Mishkin (2006)

In this chapter we discuss some of the background to attitudes towards money and debt. We explore the historical erosion of despotic power. We aim to understand globalisation, both ancient and modern, identifying the trends most important for current events and policy actions.

1.1   WHAT IS GLOBALISATION?

Globalisation has been through a number of cycles including in the nineteenth century period of free trade.[1] The term requires careful use: its range and ambiguity in common parlance can cause misunderstanding.

Globalisation is both a state and a process. It has an economic facet, perhaps best described as the greater interconnectedness of trade and investment as transactions costs and barriers reduce, but also the idea of lack of constraint on markets by government. It is this element that investors are ultimately most interested in. But globalisation also has a technological aspect (not distinct from the economic aspect), notably as represented recently by innovations and speed in modern communications. And it has a cultural facet, as exposed in the spread of common means of entertainment and ideas. It homogenises, and through standardisation commodifies, but also creates diversity of choice; complicates and simplifies; brings benefits and conflicts; produces winners and losers.

For emerging markets today, globalisation accelerates convergence to the living standards of developed markets. For some, in a world in which the voices of those with something to lose are louder than those who gain, the term is laced with emotive content, often negative, and while it creates jobs and wealth, globalisation is, for many, associated with job losses and erosion of local values.

---

[1] The term has many definitions and while Findlay and O'Rourke (2007, p. 108) argue that globalisation may have begun with the Mongol unification of the Eurasian land mass, that process is a distant shadow of what is called globalisation today.

Ridley (2010) argues that, among other things, it was trade which propagated innovation, technology and civilisation, as do Findlay and O'Rourke (2007). Jane Jacobs in her book *Systems of Survival* (1992) uses a Platonic dialogue to describe the different logics of politics, which is a zero-sum game, and commerce, a positive-sum game. Nations have historically competed for scarce territory, which, if one gained, another must lose; whereas both parties gain from a trade freely entered into.

If we want to avoid conflicts, commerce has a positive role to play. It is no mere historical coincidence that periods of protectionism and limited international trade often precede wars. The failed logic of isolationism and of fighting over land and other limited resources leads from mercantilism to gunboats, to strategic invasions of third countries, and to empire. Empires fall, however, or at best are managed into relative decline. The human tendency to barter and trade is certainly older than recorded history, and has long been geographically broad in extent. Though this is a generalisation, in the progress of greater economic interconnectedness there are waves, affected by human policy and history, as well as trends, driven by technology. Wars of the 'hard' and trade variety, restrictions on economic activity and trade, mass migration and natural disasters have all been disruptive but also sometimes stimulate innovation and new forms of economic activity. In contrast, political stability and incentive structures compatible with innovation have generally nurtured both existing patterns in trade and globalisation.

Braudel (1998) in his history of the ancient Mediterranean world argues that early transhumance (seasonal migration between summer and winter pastures) established a pattern of seasonal trade in the region. The world has clearly seen ebbs and flows in the extent of trade links and civilisations. Toynbee (1946) and others have categorised the rise and fall of civilisations, and with them trade and international links. The story of lack of stability wreaking havoc on economies and trade has repeated itself many times. Globalisation can and does ebb as well as flow. Technology has reversed on occasion as inventions have been forgotten once civilisations collapse. Our European Renaissance is in name a rediscovery. Arguably, however, it takes the destruction of civilisation to reverse technology, and in the modern era, as during periods of stability within earlier civilisations, it has been tenacious and non-reversible.

Technology profoundly impacts globalisation. It can aid economic growth, productivity and, by reducing transport costs, trade. Technology, by changing relative prices, also changes our institutions, as Douglass North (1990) has taught us. For example, technology effects disruptive upheavals in communication from time to time. Neil Postman (1985) has described how the written word, printing and then newspapers changed the pace and nature of interconnectedness. For example, in the 19th century, the telegram helped create the commercial success of newspapers and their news – the interest and novelty of new information from a long distance being of interest primarily, if not solely, because it was new. This 'news' content eroded and then eclipsed more considered thought, telescoping cultural knowledge and political debate to focus more heavily on the near present. Thus with the telegram came the modern newspapers, and with them came trivia, including the invention of the crossword puzzle – to test the reader's knowledge of news trivia.

Subsequently broadcasting has impacted our communication patterns: for example, in the 1850s US presidential candidates would deliver speeches several hours long in public debates, long enough to justify meal breaks. That voters would spend the time to listen to such debates, and that they could comprehend the complex structured paragraphs which were so characteristic, stands in stark contrast to the norm of exchange so typical today.

Have we since 'dumbed down', and does the process of globalisation contain a series of dumbing-down episodes? Not entirely: the telegram, newspapers and then radio and television created a breadth of participation in culture not previously experienced. Political debates became less elitist and more inclusive, with more elite communication and interaction continuing, but less dominantly – less unchallenged.

The perception of dumbing down, and indeed the collapse of our sense of history to a more myopic immediate past, is clearly a strong one but not just a 19th-century one. The impact of television is an issue studied by Postman and especially in the post-Second-World-War US context by Robert Putnam (2000). His book *Bowling Alone* created a vigorous debate about whether television has been the main factor behind the postwar decline of US civic culture (an example of which has been the decline of community bowling alleys). Cries of 'Dumbing down!' go all the way back in history. The move from the oral tradition to the written word was lamented in ancient Greece and seen as destructive of the memory skills developed in the time when Homer's 'Iliad' and 'Odyssey' – arguably still the greatest epics of literature – were related by word of mouth.[2] Broad access to books, particularly the Bible in 16th-century Europe, facilitated religious revolution and war. Dumbing down may look sacrilegious to an elite,[3] but while it may represent a destruction of the means of valuable interchange of ideas, at the same time it can be revelatory and intellectually enriching for many more people not previously communicating with each other.

Technological change in the media has been not only traumatic but also irresistible as old technologies have been replaced. It affects the way newer generations think and interact. There is a feeling of erosive unstoppable destruction of the old as globalisation, via new media, invades. New technologies and the young bring myopia and collective amnesia. Older generations and traditional societies alike feel the tension as their children and communities adopt new modes of speech and ways of thinking and abandon the past. And this is not new. We may fear (or embrace) such change but we can't credibly blame (or give all the credit to) our children. Globalisation may be a more convenient and acceptable receptacle for our emotional discomfort.

Modern communications have massively increased information flow, and the technologies of the Internet and mobile phone have leapfrogged older technologies in many developing countries.[4] As with technological change before, much of this is inexorable and non-reversible. Knowledge of the wider world and aspirations for a better life combine in emerging countries to increase awareness. As populations become more vocal, this leads to pressure on elites for political and economic reform at home.

Economic growth and international competitiveness is in part the result of greater entrepreneurial opportunities. Others leave and migrate to the developed world, competing in labour markets there. Either way, the result is greater economic competition with the developed world, which either has to adapt or face job losses from increased competition. Thus many in the developed world feel threatened by globalisation, while at the same time it opens vast new opportunities to many in developing economies.

Part of globalisation is significant international trade, and also substantial cross-border flows of factors of production (capital, labour, technology). These flows take advantage of

---

[2] See also Gleick (2011) p. 48 for more recent examples of complaints about the loss of oral culture.

[3] See for example Judt (2010, p. 172): "In the US today, town hall meetings and 'tea parties' parody and mimic the 18th century originals. Far from opening debate, they close it down. Demagogues tell the crowd what to think; when their phrases are echoed back to them, they boldly announce that they are merely relaying popular sentiment."

[4] See for example Jeffrey, R., and A. Doron's *The Great Indian Phone Book* (2013).

pricing differences, but in the process, also help reduce them – globalisation helps move the global economy towards an equalisation of returns to factors of production. It also involves multilateral production, and with it the spread of ideas and technology. There is greater openness to foreign inward investment. There is competition between governments for that investment, and for the jobs and knowledge which come attached. Different parts of the same production process may take place in several countries, exploiting comparative advantages. This is made possible by sufficiently low levels of protectionism and reliable low cost transport.

1.2   ECONOMIC HISTORY AND GLOBALISATION

To concentrate on the economic facets of globalisation, it may be useful to consider its historical precedents. Large-scale globalisation is not new. Maddison[5] argues that '[i]n proportionate terms, globalisation was much more important from 1500 to 1870 than it has been since. A great part ... due to gains from increased specialisation and increases in the scale of production'. International trade and capital flows are much larger today, but so is the global economy. There was an interruption as the world went to war in the 20th century, and then protectionism was only reduced gradually, but globalisation is clearly not a novelty.

There are also long economic waves of concern with inflation and deflation. Allen (2005) for example argues that the inflation of the 1970s was partly born from the concern over employment that had previously dominated since the Depression, and similar long waves have been picked by many others since Kondratiev (1925).

Kaplinsky (2005) makes a comparison between the late 19th and early 20th century period of internationalisation on the one hand, and on the other hand the period of globalisation starting in the late 20th century. He comments on the different mix of goods traded, and on the different migration patterns – of the poor in the earlier phase and the skilled and a greater proportion of the monied in the latter.[6]

He also points out[7] that there is a high correlation between effective financial intermediation and economic growth, but that excessive volatility can reduce growth. Hence policymakers often want the competition, ideas and capital which come with openness but are concerned about volatility. Although portfolio investors are not necessarily short term in their outlook, some policymakers – not liking potential volatility in their exchange rate driven by short-term changes in cross-border portfolio flows – are attracted to the idea of discouraging portfolio flows through taxing capital inflows rather than trying to attract more long-term stable investors. Yet trying to prevent inflows rarely has more than a temporary impact on the exchange rate; given inevitable efforts to bypass the restrictions, it can encourage speculative pools of capital and discourage longer-term flows. Hence the simple mantra that characterises

[5] Maddison (2007) pp. 78/9.

[6] He also asserts that the recent period saw short-term as opposed to long-term capital flows. Yet, although the speed at which financial transactions can occur has quickened, there were in both periods crises involving short-term bank loans as well as longer-term bonds. Moreover, after the Brady plans and certainly since the Russian crisis of 1998, as we shall relate in more detail in Chapter 2, the dominant investors in emerging debt moved from those with more speculative motives to those with long-term liabilities making strategic allocations. Markets have remained liquid and on occasion volatile, but both the bonds and the timeframes of the investors are now longer term.

[7] p. 78.

portfolio flows as speculative and thus undesirable may be misplaced. Indeed, efforts to restrict such flows can result in more not less volatility.[8]

1.2.1 The desire to control and its impact on trade

Why do simple policy measures to reduce volatility so often backfire? Today's environment is one of economic complexity, economic liberty and freedom of thought and action. There is a lot of uncontrolled international movement of goods and capital, whereas in the pre-industrial past the movement that did exist was smaller and simpler. The state may have become less able to impose direct control on the mass of individuals and firms, but many have also become more sophisticated at indirect control and at exploiting the behaviour of firms. As Lucas (1976) pointed out in the so-called 'Lucas critique', the use of aggregate macroeconomic data to predict the effect of policy changes can be frustrated. This is due to the behaviour captured by such aggregate data not being independent from policy, but affected in complex ways.

Political control in many spheres has changed. It has been decentralised in some cases as smaller groups have asserted themselves and the centre become less powerful, such as during the fall of Rome in the 4th century, but also due to deliberate delegation of responsibility downwards. In other spheres power has centralised, and many of the problems faced by policymakers today require action above the level of the nation-state to be effective, including some aspects of anti-terrorism and environmental policy. As people's identities and loyalties have multiplied and become more complex and global, identification with the state has also changed, and the degree to which countries can co-opt their citizens in certain ways.

But democracy and well-being are both probably strengthened by this greater complexity. The multiplication of special interests, competing with each other, reaches a point beyond which any central source of political power can command a majority of support whatever mix of policies is chosen. Democratic institutional forms constitute instead legitimising filter mechanisms, the function of which is not merely to create compromises between political groupings but also to allow all politically active groups and individuals to accept and abide by these compromises. Such decentralisation of power is incompatible with authoritarianism. Authoritarian governments fail when their populations no longer acquiesce to their policies.

Today, the freedom of action which comes from the failure of totalitarianism and central power through filter mechanisms such as democracy, erodes national boundaries and creates more scope for globalisation. Competition of ideas and in markets aids creativeness and wealth production.

Let us cast our minds back to medieval Europe, and in particular England. A useful working hypothesis for any government is that it strives to maximise revenue in order, in turn, to maximise power.[9] Medieval monarchs needed revenues for wars, and could often justify taxes to finance them. How they managed this is instructive for how economies, international trade and capital markets developed. A characteristic of England's history is that the king's power, being weaker with regard to the aristocracy compared with that of the king of France, had greater need to legitimise taxation. The Magna Carta of 1215 limited King John's and

---

[8] Li and Rajan (2011) conclude from an empirical study that controls on equity inflows tend to raise the volatility of those inflows, and controls on FDI (foreign direct investment) and also on debt outflows may both increase the volatility of equity outflows – substitution effects. Controls on FDI inflows may also raise the volatility of FDI outflows. Controls on debt inflows tend to raise the volatility of those inflows. See also Frenkel et al. (2001).

[9] See Levi (1988).

subsequent monarchs' powers (weakening under the Tudors and Stuarts in particular), establishing personal and property freedoms and elevating the rule of law above the will of the monarch. Subsequent efforts to raise taxes were notoriously difficult, but this led to an ironic reversal.

'The relatively weaker bargaining position of English monarchs vis-à-vis their constituents led to concessions that French monarchs did not have to make. However, the Parliament that evolved ultimately enhanced the ability of English monarchs to tax. Parliament provided a forum for conditional cooperation. It engendered quasi-voluntary compliance and reduced transactions costs.'

Levi (1988)

Compared to 18th-century France or Rome under the later Caesars, tax farming in England was not widely employed, but rather the taxes collected by Parliament and later the bonds issued involved lower transaction costs, were more legitimate and more reliable.

The range of taxes to finance the monarchs (and their wars) was varied, but was also driven by and impacted the pattern of trade. Taxes needed to be collectible with minimum transaction costs and maximum legitimacy, and hence moved from general levies (amounts collected across the population) to consumer goods to trade to income. But strategic and mercantilist concerns over trade led to developments in policy too. In the mid-16th century the focus of English trade policy was to generate employment and food after the devastating costs of war on the continent (the English were at war for much of the previous 50 years, with a break in the 1530s). The discouragement of domestic production of luxuries including luxury clothing, seen as unnecessary and sapping of the national economy, led to surges of some of these items as imports, and so eventually the reversal of the original trade policy.[10] Then mercantilist and strategic concerns regarding foreign trade started to give way in the later 17th century to the appreciation that 'projects' (schemes of domestic investment for home consumption) were important for the country's overall income and economic health.[11] Patents, starting from the Tudors (the first in 1552 for a technique for making glass, then in 1554 to search for and work metals in England), were established to promote production but often led to the aristocratic holders of such exclusive licences closing down domestic (and less aristocratic) competition. International trade was a small share of the total economy, but it was also clearly impacted by the dominant position of government policy in the national economy. We can say there were periods of great increase in foreign trade, but it was still very much monitored and to a large extent controlled or controllable by governments. Governments in turn acted for a combination of political, strategic and revenue-maximising ways, both directly and through taxes, distorting the incentives to trade.

Today's economic freedoms contrast with more restricted governance structures dominated by guilds and serfdom, tariffs and trade restrictions, economic dependency and personal immobility, and general government heavy-handedness. Whereas the norm in medieval Europe was that companies would seek a licence to engage in certain activities, now companies are prevented from not doing certain things – i.e. they can do anything else. Over time,

---

[10] Sir Thomas Smith listed various imports in his *Discourse of the Commonwealth*, and then sat on a committee in 1559 which framed plans for legislation to promote import substitution for a similar list of goods.

[11] As described by Joan Thirsk (1978).

governments have become less able to ignore the wishes of their citizens. And this is true globally not just nationally.

1.2.2   The influence of money

While our focus is economics, other social forces have also constrained and shaped economic activity. If importation of luxuries was long seen in medieval England as a distraction from more legitimate economic activities, attitudes to money as the medium of exchange take centre stage in the battle between God and Mammon. The history of money is fascinating, as is its sociology and philosophy.[12] The association of money with moral impurity is a common thread from Judas Iscariot to the laws against usury and right up to the present day. In Christian Europe at least, financial market development was restricted by religious mores. However, monarchs still needed to fight, and that cost money. The first banks began in the 15th century, and international loans commonly funded wars between monarchs. Potosí silver fuelled the wealth and power of 16th-century Spain, but the lack of development of a domestic capital market led to Spain under Philip II defaulting again and again to foreign bankers. Florence, Genoa and Amsterdam built their economies on international loans as well as international trade.

Banks were originally a place to secure one's money. Once they started lending out more than they had through issuing notes, there was a risk of bank runs... and the bigger the bank, the bigger the run. Though the Bank of England (1664) and Sveriges Bank (1668) were already established, the mass creation of credit proposed by John Law to the French government, in effect creating a central bank, was initially rejected in 1715, even though the French government was near default following the War of the Spanish Succession (1701–1714) and the Sun King's defeats at the hands of the Duke of Malborough and Prince Eugene. However, Law was allowed to establish the Banque Général, a private bank allowed to issue bank notes in place of scarce gold and so stimulate the economy. The bank in effect became the central bank, and from there Law's scope for credit creation grew and grew in an 18th-century version of our modern-day quantitative easing (QE). Initially providing assistance in financing government, by 1717, Law's notes were legal tender for paying taxes.

The attraction of printing money and credit extension became apparent as a giant means of financing government. Depositors and equity holders came to trust in paper returns. The bank also became an investor in the Mississippi, and shares in the bank were bid up in a financial bubble fuelled by promises of profits which were not forthcoming. It all ended in tears with one of the largest bubble-bursts in history in 1720; but for about 15 months this Scotsman, made Duke of Arkansas but wanted for murder in England,[13] was the most powerful man in France. Love of ingenious financial alchemy (the successful stimulus to the French economy by the initial period of credit creation) was followed by hate (the bursting of the Mississippi speculative bubble); just as today international bank alchemy (a key element of modern globalisation) can create huge benefits but then excessive leverage and crises, followed by public opprobrium.

---

[12] See for example Dodd (1994), Buchan (1998), Galbraith (1975), Shell (1982) and Simmel (1990).

[13] John Law initially fled to Scotland to escape justice, and lobbied against the Union with England, but then had to flee Scotland when the Act of Union (Scotland with England) was passed in 1707.

The closeness of bankers to political power continues to the present day.[14] The Rothschilds' agent in 19th-century Berlin, Gerson Bleichröder, became Bismarck's personal banker but also was central to the finances of the German state and even to foreign policy. Bleichröder provided Bismarck with backchannels via the Rothschilds to the government in Paris and to Disraeli in London. He also was heavily involved in foreign investment, particularly in railways (see Stern, 1977). Likewise in the 20th century, John Pierpont Morgan was famous for playing the role of domestic central bank, stopping the US financial panic of 1907. The associations between finance, international relations and globalisation have long been strong.

1.2.3   Trade and commodification

International trade enables international specialisation. In Britain's case it was the colonies and the ability to import food and raw materials which enabled the industrial revolution. One needs political stability and trust for international trade and globalisation, and trust is personal and built on reputation – hence the growth of family partnership merchant banks, with their own money on the line. These banks had detailed knowledge about others; but, as they lived or died on their reputation, which could be shattered by a single scandal, they kept secrets well.

Globalisation also entails creating the demand for international trade. Trade has existed for centuries, but large-scale trade had to wait for the consumer society. Prior to this, trade was either in luxuries for the few, or in one or two goods for the many. Roman imports of grain from North Africa were clearly considerable in scale, and a staple for the urban population, but the more normal pattern has been of relative self-sufficiency in most staples until the past few centuries, when large-scale trade in grain and textiles resumed. Trade built over several centuries in Europe, but important steps on the way were recognition from the late 17th century of the importance of domestic demand; increasing rural industry and incomes; agricultural enclosure and labour specialisation; and urbanisation.

Commodification – assigning economic value to things not previously so considered – was also a crucial step. London's Great Exhibition of 1851 was a triumph for the establishment of the commodity at centre stage. The exhibits were not explicitly for sale, but rather there for the glorification of industry and the production of items – commodities from soap to tea to heavy machinery – of use to the consumer and society. This was a revolutionary change and to a large extent the attraction of the exhibition: the focus of the commodity from derivative to dominator of human relations (and not just economic relations). Modern advertising and branding were born, and in some of the pictorial advertisements of the time people were in clearly subservient (smaller and not as important) positions to the commodity.[15] Complementary to this radical change was the British Empire, acquired as if by accident for an unknown purpose, but now perceived as having an important role in supplying the growing needs of the consumer (even if the Americas in practice were more important in this role).

If the Great Exhibition drove the desire for domestic consumption, truly dominant mass consumption had to wait for Henry Ford in the US during the early 20th century.

---

[14] In Atlantic Monthly May 2009, Simon Johnson, Former IMF Chief Economist, referred to this banking-politics nexus as a "financial oligarchy that is blocking essential reform" http://www.theatlantic.com/magazine/archive/2009/05/the-quiet-coup/307364/

[15] See Richards (1990).

Commodification continues to this day and is a distinctive part of globalisation, combined with its offspring, advertising and branding.

1.2.4   Nationalism

Interaction between nations has also changed. Nationalism is a fairly new concept in its modern sense, with nation-states developing in the 1700s, as Hobsbawm (1990) has pointed out. It may yet, as a result of globalisation and the political consequences of societal complexity already mentioned, give way to more multinational political structures. It has already changed greatly. No longer (with a few exceptions) is it an extension of a monarch's ego: 'L'état, c'est moi' as Louis XIV, the Sun King, is supposed to have described it. The peace of Westphalia in 1648 after the devastating Thirty Years' War between Catholic and Protestant forces defined the sovereign state and established the principle of non-interference in the affairs of other sovereign states. But as Philip Bobbitt (2002) has described, the state has been through several stages of development since. Most recently, as the 1990s Balkan wars demonstrated, the concept of non-interference established in 1648 is now in conflict with that of self-determination. Having said that, global interference has always been with us: stronger states interfering in the affairs of smaller ones for a combination of reasons: their own (individual or collective) security, economic self-interest and humanitarian aid. In all but the short term, however, self-interest of some description invariably dominates.[16]

What global media and culture have aided is the move to a new reality in which the winning of hearts and minds is central to the modern strategic battleground, and in which traditional armed forces are largely redundant. As a population becomes more educated it will organise and will demand political rights: its voice[17] will be heard and authority perceived to be unjust becomes more difficult to preserve. The days when the 1000-strong Indian Civil Service of British expatriate administrators could run a subcontinent of 300 million is long gone, as was predicted since the British enhanced education for Indians from the 1830s. The values the British chose to spread in India were incompatible with their longer-term presence. Today the spread of these and similar values makes similar long-term passive subjugation of nations quite impossible. In today's world of the Internet and global media, guerrilla not industrial warfare, mass political participation not autocracy, control by physical force alone has become absurdly difficult – even if this is not yet sufficiently understood to have prevented some recent attempts.

Winning minds is the clear preferred route to stable prosperity in today's world, with a more limited support role reserved for physical force. This is in contrast to much of the structure of defence spending, as discussed by two modern generals with recent experience in the Balkans: Clark (2001) and Smith (2005). What has changed is not merely our education and communications technology, but the number of independent countries[18] and also the principle of non-intervention in what were previously considered the internal affairs of nation-states. The principle of such non-interference is now in conflict with the desires, often supported by international opinion, of certain sub-national groups for self-determination. The nation-state

---

[16] So-called humanitarian imperialism is not particularly credible as a justification for armed intervention in a foreign country for the simple reason that it tends not to work.

[17] See Hirschman (1970).

[18] The increase in the number of countries has made international policy co-ordination more difficult. This fragmentation has been the result of the end of empire, decolonisation and more self-determination. These processes in turn have been assisted by globalisation and with it the spread of economic liberty, education and liberal values.

has changed its form several times before. As nationalism is a relatively modern phenomenon in many ways, one should expect it to change further.[19]

Jane Jacobs describes politics as a zero-sum game, but maybe it is even worse: due to fragmentation and more issues requiring international co-operation, states are experiencing shrinking power. Some international problems which would have been resolved by a few countries in the past are now not being resolved. In the wake of globalisation, national politics are becoming less and less autonomous. A number of immigration, environmental and economic issues require supranational governance. In the face of these issues, and in the absence of powerful international institutions, national governments are becoming more impotent; and electorates, realising this, are becoming more frustrated that issues are not being resolved – more apathetic (as shown by voter participation trends), more difficult to please.

Winning minds is about having people agree with you, after letting them freely choose to do so. For the West this freedom or empowerment means allowing people to run their own lives, but also giving up some power – including sharing responsibility with emerging markets. Much more serious reform of the voting shares of the IMF, still heavily dominated by the US and Western Europe, would be a start. The problem is that some Western politicians have great difficulty with implementing this, or giving up their influence, especially when they have little central collective leadership, or are leaders with outdated world views. They often seem oblivious to the observable reality that their policies are getting in the way. Investors, the ultimate pragmatists, have the potential to offset the zero-sum (or all too often negative-sum) logic of politics. Commerce is an important component in bridging conflicts and avoiding them, of getting over ideological prejudices, of creating mutually aligned incentives: in short, of keeping down the testosterone levels in politics.

History can teach us a lot about globalisation but we have to be cautious in interpretation. A reader may misinterpret the values and motives of past decision makers. How do we square Britain's great historical achievements with urban squalor, Irish famine in the 1840s, and Orwell's description of waning empire in Burmese Days? Much of the past has been horrific, and governments have gone to great efforts to rewrite and in some cases to deny history[20], but we also need to recognise that moral values change over time and geography.[21] And values remain different in different geographies today, even if people in distant lands consume some of the same brands and superficially may appear very similar in their values. Also, in the midst of global economic dynamism, there can still be a tendency to be surprised, antisympathetic and hostile to change. The combination of remaining partially myopic yet more interconnected leads to greater risk of sudden uncomfortable change, and indeed conflict.

1.3   RECENT GLOBALISATION

International trade often collapses during war, and economies have struggled with inflation and debts in peacetime. Hence the importance of local and global rules to facilitate trade and capital flows – to facilitate globalisation. Stability matters, as Maddison (2007, p. 111) writing about the period 1500–1800, points out:

---

[19] See Bobbitt (2002) and Hobsbawm (1990).

[20] See for example Paris (2000).

[21] See Harris (2010) for an interesting exposition of how science can determine morality.

'In the UK and the Netherlands, the legal system protected commercial property rights and ensured the enforceability of contracts. State levies were predictable and not arbitrary, and credit for long term ventures was available. As a result groups of capitalists in these countries were able to establish corporations like the Dutch Far East Company (VOC), and the British East India Company (EIC) which could organise risky ventures over huge distances.'

The Bank of England had established the model for central banks up to the 19th century, balancing liquidity needs in the economy with the avoidance of inflation;[22] and the gold standard had emerged to create stability in foreign exchange transactions, with major currencies convertible to gold. This facilitated global trade. The gold standard, however, was vulnerable to supply shocks as new gold deposits were discovered and, in times of war and crisis, countries abandoned it. The Treaty of Versailles in 1919 imposed unrealistically high costs on Germany, which (as John Maynard Keynes warned in The Economic Consequences of the Peace, written in 1919) later forced an exit from the gold standard as their debts became unpayable (and unpaid for their creditors), and set the scene for hyperinflation.

1.3.1   Bretton Woods

The roaring twenties and the stock market boom of 1929 were followed by deflation and depression and then World War II, during which trade patterns were radically curtailed and war economies operated in more planned fashion. Given the strong desire to avoid the inter-war protectionism, and the periods of both deflation and then inflation, in 1944 at Bretton Woods a new global monetary architecture was designed. The International Monetary Fund (IMF) was created to police exchange rates. The main arm of the World Bank, the International Bank for Reconstruction and Development, was tasked to help rebuild Europe. An international trade organisation failed to be agreed to, but belatedly in 1947 the General Agreement on Tariffs and Trade (GATT) was established instead to promote multilateral trade, replaced by the World Trade Organization (WTO) in 1995. An objective was to start to reverse protectionism and promote current account convertibility.

The agenda at Bretton Woods after the inter-war deflation was thus to re-establish some form of managed gold standard. However, there was not enough gold in the world (without a major and geopolitically unacceptable price increase which would have benefitted Russia and South Africa) for full convertibility. Keynes conceived that all foreign exchange transactions would continue to go through central banks, as during the war, and suggested a new international currency called 'Bancor' which would be the unit of account for international transactions, expressed in units of gold. A new international clearing union would facilitate transactions and prevent the build-up of major imbalances. Keynes' design was rejected by the US. This was because, as a major creditor, the US decided not to have penalties imposed on her Bancor surpluses: countries running excessive trade deficits are eventually penalised by being cut off from capital as their credit-worthiness deteriorates, but for every deficit there is necessarily an equivalent surplus somewhere,[23] and so to avoid the build-up of deficits Keynes also proposed that interest be charged on excessive Bancor surpluses.

---

[22] See for example Galbraith (1975) for a history of the development of the banking system and central banking.

[23] Though it is to be noted that for a well-functioning gold standard the converse is not necessarily the case: while there is a surplus for every deficit, there is not always a deficit for every surplus.

Instead of Keynes's plan, a system with an inbuilt tendency towards imbalance was implemented, and still (in 2014) codified in the 'Articles of Agreement Establishing the IMF'. Currencies had fixed exchange rates to the US dollar, which in turn was convertible to gold at $35 an ounce (the official US Treasury price since 1934). Though other countries could have also chosen to have their currencies convertible to gold, none did. Other major currencies were pegged to the dollar.

This led to the so-called Triffin dilemma: a national currency, which is also the international currency, has conflicting pressures of attaining short-term monetary balance nationally and longer-term international balance. Currency and yielding government securities are issued to meet international demand. Otherwise international trade and growth would fall. This, however, creates a tendency towards trade deficits for the issuing country, as the money is printed there and then makes its way into the international economy through being used to purchase goods and assets (as opposed to a more international currency which might be distributed, on printing, more evenly across countries). This in turn builds US debts to the rest of the world. In order to prevent requests that these claims be converted to gold (this leading to an eventual breakdown of the system), the US would either have to raise interest rates on the government securities issued and which are held by foreigners; or to tighten fiscally in order to shrink the economy and its indebtedness, or otherwise reduce the trade deficit. There is an understandable reluctance to do either. They could (as Triffin observed) also allow the price of gold to rise, but this was outside the Bretton Woods agreement and could create destabilising speculative moves into gold by both central banks and private investors – in turn draining US gold stocks and undermining the ability to intervene, and so faith in the reserve system.

The desire by foreigners to offer their goods in exchange for one's currency (in the case of the dollar) can be an attractive alternative to greater domestic fiscal discipline. If, however, there is a tendency to fiscal indiscipline or substantial overseas expenditure, there will be more debt growth relative to the gold supply (eventually reducing the credibility of the promise of convertibility to gold). The problem is exacerbated if the international economy outside the US expands faster than that of the US: then international demand for dollars also expands faster than domestic demand for dollars.

At the end of the war, this system, initially assisted by the Marshall Plan, helped create global stability and the rapid re-industrialisation of Europe and Japan – the (re-)emerging countries of the day.[24] With the US dominating global tradable goods production, European countries bought US goods with the US dollars from the Marshall Plan. The recovery of these economies was successful. The pattern of strong growth in Europe and Japan then continued after the Marshall Plan and the initial period of US surpluses ended. By the early 1960s Europe and Japan had become highly competitive. The fixed exchange rate facing the US had become inappropriately high. The move to current account convertibility in 1958 had put additional pressure on the dollar, as had European concerns about the fiscal policies of the newly elected US president Kennedy. The dollar traded as low as $40 an ounce in 1960. The response was the London gold pool: an agreement whereby the US and seven European central banks co-ordinated sales of gold in the London gold market, buying dollars, which they then invested in US Treasuries. This was no more than a temporary fix, though. In this monetary system the US in the immediate postwar period was doing the rest of the world a

---

[24] The term 're-emerging markets' is from Wolf (2009).

huge favour by creating demand for their goods, but at the cost of building up more and more debt.[25]

As Herb Stein, US President Nixon's adviser at the time, said: 'If something cannot go on forever, it will stop.' Add the cost of the Vietnam War and the unpalatable choice of fiscal adjustment through higher taxes, and the pressure grew. The more aggressive stance by the incoming Nixon administration towards Europe over gold purchases, and specifically the rhetoric of his Treasury Secretary John Connally, backfired and led to market pressure on the gold price. The German mark was floated in May 1971 and then on August 13th the Bank of England asked the US to convert some of its dollars to gold before it was too late. Nixon decided instead to de-link from gold on August 15th, devaluing the dollar, which then rapidly fell from $35 an ounce to $44 an ounce. As the dis-equilibrium had grown to such a level, there was indeed little else he could have done.[26] Sterling floated in June 1972 and some other currencies still pegged to the dollar until early 1973, but the credibility of their anchor had been damaged. Setting a precedent for the more recent build-up in global imbalances in the early 21st century, it was the action of surplus central banks which forced the 1970s crisis. US debts were far in excess of gold reserves. Foreign surplus central banks, wanting to preserve the purchasing power of their reserves, started buying back gold on the secondary market, and eventually asked for gold from the US Treasury in exchange for dollars. Nixon then had a choice: start giving out the gold, run out and then renege on the commitment to convertibility; or renege early and keep the gold. He quite sensibly chose the latter option, although technically another option would have been to raise just the gold price, but that had not been agreed with Europe.

Without the monetary anchors of the Bretton Woods system, inflation became a larger problem from 1973. Oil prices rose as OPEC exerted newfound bargaining power, and food prices spiked due to supply disruption. But the main cause of the 1973 uptick in inflation was arguably the macroeconomic policies in the OECD at the time of loose money which accommodated fiscal deficits. By the end of 1974 gold had reached $195 an ounce, but was volatile, not least due to official gold sales. With inflation, more instability in global (now floating) exchange rates had returned. Countries with large domestic investor bases managed to borrow in their own currencies, which they could then debauch. Without the discipline of the gold standard or fixed parity with the dollar, deficit spending became the norm and inflation became a preferred form of taxation. Gold had been a part of the global monetary system from prehistory to 1971, but has not been since and may never be again. Indeed, in a world of floating exchange rates, inflation may again be used as the principal method of reneging on Western government debt obligations.

1.3.2 Ideological shifts

After World War II, involving as it did enormous state economic planning and mobilisation by all of the major combatants, the consensus was for the state to continue taking a prominent

---

[25] The creation of IMF Special Drawing Rights (SDRs) in 1968 was designed to create a new reserve currency and complement the limited stock of gold to meet growing reserve asset demand, but this need was averted by the growth of the Eurodollar market – private sector borrowing in dollars offshore (in Europe) – which reserve managers could purchase instead of US official debt assets. See Isard (2005), p. 33.

[26] For a more detailed account see Eichengreen (2011).

role in the economy. Added to that were the anthropological[27] and political priorities of building societies with less inequality, leading to the start of the creation of the modern European
welfare state. There were very few economists who thought let alone argued differently.[28] With
state dominance came government control in a wide range of areas, including (and consistent
with the Bretton Woods agreement) European blanket controls on the free flow of cross-border
capital.[29] The modern period of globalisation is thus associated with the period when these
controls came off, which they started to do in 1979 with the lifting of UK exchange controls.

The experience of World War II and the need to rebuild afterwards were clearly behind the
desire for a large economic role for the state, but ideology was also at play. When this fell to
more pro-market ideology in the 1980s, policies shifted dramatically, in some cases with a
slapdash disregard for consequences, in the opposite direction.

Indeed, I experienced the force of an ideological argument myself. Late in George H.W.
Bush's presidency I was working in the Strategic Planning Office of the US Treasury-controlled Plans and Programs Department of the Inter-American Development Bank. Following
a plebiscite in Uruguay against privatisations, a topic which had become highly politicised,
there was concern that privatisations might be stopped in several countries. Hence I wrote a
technical paper on when and how to privatise (and thus by extension also when not and how
not to).[30] It was explained to me officially in a bizarre meeting that, while there was nothing
wrong with the content of the paper, it was inappropriate that it should be seen to be written
from inside the Department. As in Umberto Eco's *Name of the Rose*: knowledge is sin. In
Eco's book the medieval library in which the plot is set is eventually burned down to avoid
the revelations of knowledge in an ancient Greek text. My paper was banned from distribution, which, perhaps predictably, had the opposite effect to that intended.[31]

The 'Washington Consensus' is shorthand for some of the new thinking. The term was
originally coined by John Williamson at a conference in 1989 to describe 10 areas of policy
reform being enacted by Latin American governments: prudent fiscal deficit management,
public expenditure priorities, tax reform, interest rates, the exchange rate, trade policy, foreign direct investment, privatisation, deregulation and property rights.[32] The term was controversial partly because of its name. Frances Stewart has argued, and Williamson did not deny,
that by calling it the Washington Consensus as opposed to the more obvious Latin American
Consensus, the intention was to create US support for what were highly pragmatic and largely
orthodox policies Latin American governments wanted to continue to follow.[33] What started
as a rough pragmatic list of what was happening soon hardened into (right-wing) dogma. And
part of the dogma became free trade and free capital movement across borders: another part
of the story of globalisation's progress.

Globalisation was also pushed in the post-World War II era in the successive trade rounds
of GATT and then (after 1995) the WTO, though, in consequence of (certainly perceived)

---

[27] For example, the Beveridge report on social insurance and allied services can be seen as anthropological in
nature.

[28] See Skidelsky (1995).

[29] US capital controls only began in the 1960s and had limited effect – though one was to stimulate the creation
of the Eurodollar market in 1963.

[30] The full paper can be found on Jerome Booth's blog on newsparta.net.

[31] Distribution of an earlier draft escalated. I have been told subsequently the paper was used several years later as
a guide for privatising CVRD, now known as Vale, one of the largest companies in Brazil.

[32] Williamson, Ed. (1990).

[33] Stewart (1997).

relative bargaining power at the time, with a clear favouritism to the developed world. The emphasis was on free movement of goods, but also capital and (much later) protection of intellectual property rights. Fligstein (2001) categorises three types of globalisation which followed: an increase in world trade, the rise of the Asian Tigers (Hong Kong, Singapore, South Korea and Taiwan) at the expense of the first world, and the growth in financial markets in debt, equity and foreign exchange. We do not live in a world of free trade though, but in a world of more-or-less free trade, except in agriculture and textiles, where protectionism is alive and well – and highly distorting and disadvantageous to emerging countries.[34]

Nevertheless, developing countries have benefited enormously from globalisation. They have taken advantage of greater trade opportunities, grown fast and learnt from their own mistakes and those of others. The sharing of policy experiences across countries should not be underestimated as a great stimulus to better policies. While the bottom billion[35] in failed states in sub-Saharan Africa and Central Asia remain misgoverned,[36] aid-dependent[37] and poor, other economies have grown at the highest rates ever recorded in history. Low-skill jobs have moved to developing countries, but higher skilled ones are moving there too. India and China alone (accounting as they do for 36% of world population) have pulled hundreds of millions out of poverty.

1.3.3   Participating in globalisation: living with volatility

Protectionist sentiment and the import substitution industrialisation (ISI) ideas of Raúl Prebisch and others to support infant industries, popular in the 1960s and 1970s, went out of fashion with the rise of the Washington Consensus in the 1980s and 1990s. Capital accounts started to be liberalised in the Thatcher/Reagan period in a number of countries, both developed and developing.[38]

Countries risk incurring severe costs should they cut themselves off from the outside world. Policymakers are right to be concerned about capital flow volatility, but lack of international competition can reduce both productive and allocative efficiency. Nearly all choose to participate in global markets, but some want to retain an element of control.

No country, once partially liberalised, is currently planning blanket capital controls, but a number of measures have been tried to reduce capital flow volatility. However, while so-called macroprudential policies (not a clearly defined set of policies, but ones focused on reducing financial sector systemic risks) may be advisable to reduce risks of financial contagion and other spill-over effects from other countries' financial systems, capital control measures (as opposed to central bank intervention) designed to affect the exchange rate have no clear history of success except in the very short term. Investors seem always, in time, able to devise structures to get around them. Capital controls in the form of taxes on portfolio inflows can moreover be highly distortionary, and once imposed can create uncertainty over future policy and deter inward investment and damage investor sentiment – so raising borrowing costs for the government. In particular, they can discourage long-term institutional investors and encourage the more flighty speculative investors, and this in turn, ironically, can lead to great volatility. Volatility is often a function of fundamental factors inside or outside the country,

---

[34] See for example Booth (1992).
[35] Paul Collier (2008).
[36] Paul Collier (2010).
[37] See Easterly (2006) and also Moyo (2009).
[38] See for example Allen (2005), from p. 151.

including rapidly changing perceptions of risk, and heightened by significant offshore pools of capital.

We can see globalisation not as the primary cause of contagion or volatility, but rather as the medium. Central bank intervention can reduce volatility, but one needs reserves for that, and the willingness to use them. Beyond that, the way to reduce volatility is to address the fundamental problems, such as fiscal and other domestic imbalances, or factors such as global imbalances or bank deleveraging (a regulatory matter). However, the structure of the international monetary system is in dire need of overhaul and is cause for concern – an issue we shall return to.

2

Defining Emerging Markets

What is an emerging market? There are a number of definitions, but prejudice plays a strong part in determining the universe, and with it, history. All countries are risky. My preferred definition is thus as follows: The emerging market countries are those where this risk is widely perceived and priced in (albeit not always correctly). This is in contrast to a developed country, which is one where a substantial portion of the investor base does not perceive the sovereign risk. To move from an emerging to developed country status is thus not a process, per se, of improved credit-worthiness. If it were, many emerging market countries would be considered developed and some developed ones emerging. Rather, joining the club of developed countries, as with those in Eastern Europe who have joined the EU, is a process whereby the government and the bond market reach a consensus that the country can be trusted – its government bonds are even (by some at least) denoted 'risk-free' as default risk is fully discounted.[1] Risk and changes in risk stop being priced. Volatility falls, which is also by some taken to mean that risk has reduced (though the opposite may be true). Hence the anomaly is not in the emerging markets, but in our misperception of risk in the developed world. It is that which divides the two types of country. Prejudice is a topic we shall return to.

There are alternative definitions, typically a list of countries – maybe 150 of them. Some investors use 'emerging markets' to mean countries defined as middle and low income by the World Bank – but what happens when some emerging markets have higher income per capita than some developed or 'industrial' economies? And, frankly, having high per capita income does not by itself make a country a better credit risk, change economic policy or induce bond markets to ignore sovereign risks.

Another method is exclusive: emerging countries are all countries not in Western Europe, the US, Canada, Japan, Australia and New Zealand. But this definition may also illuminate a prejudice – with the exception of the obviously wealthy Japan, are not all these countries' populations of predominantly European origin? Do we, when we try to think of other criteria, come back to prejudice again?

2.1 THE GREAT GLOBAL REBALANCING

Emerging countries are rising fast after a history of Western domination, and the West is learning to cope with them. The poorest of the emerging countries are still hampered by out-of-date thinking in the West, poor governance and lack of capital and jobs. But they are also emerging.

The World was not always perceived as it is now: with North at the top of the map and Europe and the US the core. The East and Middle East used to be more central. India and China represented the largest shares of global GDP. The European economies, and their progeny in

---

[1] In practice this may give leeway for greater fiscal irresponsibility for a while if they want. The government may have pressing political priorities, and the knowledge that the bond market will allow them greater fiscal laxity often leads to exactly that.

North America and Australasia, often collectively referred to as the 'West', came to dominate the global economy only in the last 200 to 300 years. There are a number of theories as to why this was the case. Maddison (2007) lists four major changes in the West before 1820: the recognition of the ability of humans to transform nature through the application of rational investigation and experiment, including the growth of universities and mass publishing; the emergence of major urban trading centres; the adoption of Christianity as a state religion, leading to changes in marriage, inheritance and kinship; and the emergence of nearby competing nation-states. Earlier focus on moral and religious differences, such as Kant's on the Protestant work ethic and Toynbee's on religion (among many other factors) have given way to more refined empirical understanding of how norms and institutions, including religion, shape economies. Ridley (2010) emphasises, as several others do, the focus on trade; De Soto (2000) focuses on the institutional framework which allowed the creation of capital; Diamond (1999) on guns, germs and steel.

Whatever the exact combination of causes, the expression of aggressive empire building backed by superior military, particularly naval, power led to a significant shift away from Asia to Europe in the 18th and early 19th centuries. The industrial revolution caused, but also was caused by, the international system of trade which enabled greater urbanisation, food importation and labour specialisation. The concentration of the consequent economic power in the West was accompanied by global economic dominance.

2.1.1   Financing sovereigns

Some of the origins of Europe's success lie with debt markets. Early European banks from the de Medicis and the Fuggers onwards lent to foreign kings, often when they could no longer raise more taxes in their own lands. Banks periodically collapsed when monarchs defaulted. With the discovery of New World silver, Spanish wealth made it the most powerful nation in 16th-century Europe under Charles V (also Holy Roman Emperor) and his son Phillip II. Yet Spain depended on foreign bankers and did not develop its own banks.[2] The focus on financing European Christian kings and countries was complemented by investing in overseas settlements and other colonial enterprises, like Elizabethan investments in the Caribbean, but there were also opportunities available to a much broader number of private investors in the form of the English and Dutch East India Companies (originally founded in 1600 and 1602), and later the French East India Company.

England's rise and its victories over its larger, wealthier enemy France, in almost continuous wars through the 18th and early 19th centuries, was a global battle: a) for dominion over territories which in some cases yielded profitable rents and returns on investment and trade (not uniformly: in other cases this proved marginal); b) to secure access to spices, commodities and other trade; and c) in order to prevent other European powers from gaining strategic advantage. The history of the colonial period can be seen as a history of foreign economic ventures, with armies and navies sent to protect investments – Britain's effective colonisation of Egypt in 1882 comes to mind.

The emerging world was on the receiving end of this European competition, from the spice islands (Indonesia) and India and much of the rest of Asia to the Americas, North and South. And today's still-dominant perception of emerging markets comes from this period. Colonies

---

[2] Braudel's *The Mediterranean and the Mediterranean World* describes the repeated indebtedness of Phillip II of Spain to Genoese and other foreign bankers, and the consequent defaults.

tended to be established formally after economic investments, or to secure investments and trade concessions already established. Though European coastal settlements in Africa occurred fairly early on, the big scramble for Africa was relatively late in the 19th century – see Pakenham (1991).

2.1.2 Catching up

As countries have copied European and US success, Western dominance has lessened. Japan was the first to start to catch up, embracing the technologies of Europe before World War II, following its earlier 250 years of isolationism up to 1853. The 'Asian Tigers' followed in the 1960s, then parts of Latin America. China embraced economic reforms since 1978 under Deng Xiaoping. India embraced reforms in the early 1990s. Catch-up has seemed to accelerate since the end of the Cold War, as documented by many, including van Agtmael (2007). Asian and other emerging regions have been learning from the West how to modernise. There is a substantial literature on how developing countries have been catching up.

The shift now underway started with 19th-century migration. This shift is away from a highly concentrated pattern of economic development towards a more diverse (and hence more stable) multi-polar pattern more representative of underlying demographics: a great global rebalancing. This global rebalancing to more stable future follows the violent 20th century and conflict between liberal democracy, fascism and communism. The subsequent end of the Cold War has been of enormous importance for much of the developing world. Vast populations previously treated as pawns in the global power game are now viewed as potential customers and clients (consumers and producers).

The spread of democracy after the fall of communism, but also the replacement of authoritarianism and populism in favour of more independent (from government) opinion-forming processes, has profoundly impacted, and continues to impact, institutional change. Democracy is a process which not only filters the views of many but creates compromises and opinions which can inform government decisions – it disciplines government policies affecting credit-worthiness (as do bond markets). North (2005) describes the process of improving economic performance thus:

$$\text{beliefs} \rightarrow \text{institutions} \rightarrow \text{organisations} \rightarrow \text{policies} \rightarrow \text{outcomes}$$

That beliefs are the starting point is a problem for hubristic centralising policymakers unless they suppress their citizens. Beliefs are in turn determined above all by income, not government actions. Lower middle-income levels constitute the take-off stage for electorates to find their voice and pressure effectively for government policy prudence. If belief systems are static or resistant to change, institutions can be hard to change (and changing one without others can constitute a high-risk strategy). Informal institutions in any event cannot be changed by fiat. By allowing opinions to form and to be flexible dynamically the move to democracy has enabled price (and other) signals to build more effective institutions. Without economic competition or competition of ideas (including those arising from the perceptions and mental constructs of economic actors), many emerging market institutions did not develop well until the end of the Cold War, but have since.[3]

---

[3] For more on the development of institutions, see for example North (1995).

Increased trade and capital market development – specifically the move from personal to impersonal exchange – is key to greater well-being. This move 'always increases total transaction costs but the consequence is a drastic reduction in production costs'.[4] The move to impersonal exchange can be slow, as we have to overcome a genetic motive to defect from those other than our close kin. To do this, we have to see the benefits of impersonal exchange and to create institutions to enforce contracts, including the state, and then see that the state does not abuse its power.

Building such institutions under communism failed. The fall of the Berlin Wall in 1989 and the end of the Cold War with the collapse of the Soviet Union in 1991 were of enormous importance; obviously for Eastern Europe, but also for other countries in the emerging world. And it affected foreign policy: previously the foreign policy of the United States and other developed countries towards the emerging world had been dominated by the bipolar reality. Anti-communist countries, however tyrannical, were supported by the West. Many Western allies as well as Soviet satellites and Soviet-supported countries were less than enthusiastic about building vibrant market economies or societies. The end of the Cold War changed this as foreign policy towards Latin America and Asia focused much more on promoting economic development and increasing trade and investment flows to these regions, to create stability and gain new customers.

Development theory in Latin America was also impacted by the end of the Cold War. Prior to the end of communism, import substitution industrialisation (ISI), as well as other policies to foster infant industries and promote industrialisation, was common. A substantial ideological debate raged over economic theories of development.[5] This is not the place to argue the merits or otherwise of the policies of this period, but to point out the move to a more uniform free-market orthodoxy after the end of the Cold War. Prudent fiscal policy, stable prices, an expanded role for the private sector, reduced government intervention and a number of other policies (ten in all) constituted what became known as the 'Washington Consensus' as mentioned in Chapter 1. This consensus seemed to be given lip service across much of the developing world – although not entirely in Asia. The Washington Consensus, which began as a useful set of descriptions about what had worked in Latin America (albeit simplistic and not uniformly helpful), then turned into a more dogmatic set of prescriptions. However, it did channel energy in the same direction – an improvement on previous patterns of incoming governments' undoing the policies of their predecessors. The political debate largely moved away from how best to create wealth to how to distribute it.

The end of the Cold War did not mean the automatic acceptance of Western values in the form of capitalist liberal democracy. Yet many saw it that way after the fall of the Berlin Wall. This was captured by Francis Fukuyama, whose book *The End of History and the Last Man* (1992) proclaimed the triumph of Western civilisation after the demise of the Soviet Union, while wondering whether the continuing battle between liberty and equality would lead to stability or not. Yet the West did not win the Cold War as far as much of humanity is concerned – the USSR merely lost.[6] We are far from uniformity and ideological battles are not over. However, there are now around 160 emerging markets and the days of the 'one size fits all' view of the world is past.

---

[4] North (2005) p. 91. North also earlier (1990, p. 52) refers to a reduction in political transaction costs, or political efficiency, as being key to efficient property rights.

[5] See Hunt (1989).

[6] This is a view which may aid in understanding post-Cold War Russian politics.

Nevertheless, the West should be flattered that so many countries have modelled themselves on the best they have to offer – i.e. political and economic freedom. Meanwhile the West is watching its own relative economic decline, and clinging on to power and influence for as long as possible. It risks doing so too long and provoking backlashes, some of which have already started. For some, the end of the Cold War has been replaced by other battles. Samuel Huntington (1996) paints China, and in particular Islam, as threats to Western dominance. The emerging world can still learn much from the West, but the financial crisis starting in 2007/8 emphasised elements of weakness. In the West one can of course be in denial about a threat, be aggressive towards it, or try to cope. As Kishore Mahbubani (2008) argues, and I agree, it is better to accept and cope with the rise of emerging countries than to deny it or see it as a battlefield with losers as well as winners.

2.1.3   The poorest can also emerge: aid and debt

Yet there are millions in the developing world in failed or failing states who remain disadvantaged, and are potentially destabilising for others. Economic development is often prevented by poor governance – by despotic rule – a problem in Europe also until parliaments were able to limit the power of the sovereign. A difficult transition lies ahead, requiring visionary leadership and engagement not conflict.

When it comes to relations with the developing world, Western democracies and their politicians often appear more interested in assuaging existential guilt than finding optimal solutions. Electorates' views on aid, often emotive, constrain politicians, not least the ability to focus on achievable governance and institutional development objectives which can allow local financial (but also goods) markets to develop and create jobs. While some aid has been effective at the project level, aid can also create unproductive incentives at both micro and macro level. At worst, the overall impact of an aid programme can resemble a relic from Soviet central planning more than a realistic and optimal proposal to facilitate economic development. Rent seeking[7] is still a major problem in aid politics, corruption a major problem in aid distribution. Implementation can distort markets and create dependency on further aid – see, for example, Easterly (2006).

If Western lobbyists, electorates and their leaders are truly concerned about global poverty, how is it, for example, that agricultural protectionism, which causes massive distortions to global agricultural trade, sustains unassailable domestic political support in many donor countries? Agriculture is by far the most protected area of global trade (we are a long way from living in a world of free trade). The EU's Common Agricultural Policy, CAP, has reduced from nearly half the EU budget but is still around a third. Subsidies to European farmers are an order of magnitude greater than total foreign (non-military) aid, and cause massive distortions to global trade patterns, employment and wealth – much more damaging to the poor than any countervailing benefit of aid. The largest natural resource for many poor countries is their soil, yet many face export pessimism – a situation where there is no point in developing export agriculture. No matter how competitively one can produce food, EU subsidies adjust to ensure that no sales are possible.[8]

---

[7] Economic rent is payment made beyond that necessary to produce a good or service. Rent seeking is the process of obtaining economic rent through influencing institutional arrangements. See Krueger, A. O. (1974).

[8] Booth, J. (1992).

A problem facing some of the poorest countries in sub-Saharan Africa is lack of access to foreign capital at reasonable cost. Aid could be, and in many cases is, productively focused on creating stable governance and the institutional setting to enable domestic capital formation, but this will take many years to grow to an adequate size to meet investment needs. Sovereign and then corporate bond markets could be developed, with foreign institutional savings[9] helping to catalyse them and adding to the available pool of capital, just as in richer emerging markets and developed markets. This is happening already for some countries, but a condition of international aid for some others is that such debt be limited. There is an assumption in some official circles that all government expenditure has a zero return on capital.[10] Some lobby groups believe that debt is simply a bad thing. The surest way to keep countries poor, however, is to keep them cut them off from capital.

2.1.4   From debt to transparency and legitimacy

As touched on in the first chapter, one of the major reasons parliamentary systems came to dominate in Europe was the ability to issue debt. Britain's war with Napoleonic France has even been described by Ferguson (2008) as a victory of one financing system – specifically the one based on a deep credible national debt market – over one substantially supplemented by expropriation in conquered lands. The same was true for the earlier War of the Spanish Succession and for the Seven Years' War. Debt can not only help build needed infrastructure and create jobs, finance companies and help entrepreneurs. It can create an internal political constituency for prudent economic management – taxpayers also lobby their representatives but debt-holders are more concentrated and focused on budgetary prudence. It is part of the mechanism to hold despots to account (albeit that this doesn't work if markets are foolish enough to stop thinking about default risk and lend to profligates, as with the US and Western Europe leading up to 2008).

Following earlier lending to English monarchs from London's merchants and goldsmiths, the Bank of England was founded in 1694 to finance war with France with a loan of £1.2 million. In the subsequent century government dependence on bond financing grew, and bond market prices varied daily. They would sell off, making government financing more expensive, if the government's perceived repayment likelihood fell. A daily and visible barometer of government behaviour had been created.

Having a similar accountability for the world's poorest today is not easy and requires institution building and governance, but most of the larger emerging market countries now have liquid bond markets, and are examples to others. For poor countries, just as for rich ones, the need is for something much more than aid. As Adam Smith taught us in the oft-quoted passage, under the correct conditions it can be that:

---

[9] By institutional savings we mean the funds of institutional investors such as pension funds, insurance companies, endowments and foundations.

[10] Specifically for the Highly Indebted Poor Countries (HIPC) in receipt of official sector debt forgiveness, which as at December 2011 were the following 36 countries: Afghanistan, Benin, Bolivia, Burkina Faso, Burundi, Cameroon, Central African Republic, Chad, Republic of the Congo, Democratic Republic of the Congo, Comoros, Côte d'Ivoire, Ethiopia, Gambia, Ghana, Guinea, Guinea-Bissau, Guyana, Haiti, Honduras, Liberia, Madagascar, Malawi, Mali, Mauritania, Mozambique, Nicaragua, Niger, Rwanda, São Tomé and Principe, Senegal, Sierra Leone, Tanzania, Togo, Uganda, Zambia.

'It is not from the benevolence of the butcher, the brewer or the baker, that we expect our dinner, but from their regard to their own self-interest. We address ourselves, not to their humanity but to their self-love, and never talk to them of our own necessities but of their advantages.'

Adam Smith (1776)

Likewise the best way to help the developing world may be to invest and trade, and by this create jobs and prosperity. Or, to quote the Cambridge economist Joan Robinson (1962, p. 45): '... the misery of being exploited by capitalists is nothing compared to the misery of not being exploited at all.'

If we care about developing countries we should encourage commerce there, invest there and enable markets there to develop (a sentiment at odds with the current failure to achieve progress in multilateral trade negotiations). With commerce comes a lobby for transparency. With local institutionalised savings in local capital markets can come accountability, which at best can be a beneficial restraint on tyrannical leaders.

2.2   INVESTING IN EMERGING MARKETS

As a concept rather than a term, the idea of investing in emerging markets – i.e. new dynamic markets in far-flung geographies – is not new. More recently, the term emerging market was promoted in the 1980s by Antoine van Agtmael, then of the International Finance Corporation (IFC), the private sector lending arm of the World Bank. It described economies between poor and rich with 'investible' (easy for foreign portfolio investors to invest in) publicly listed equity markets. These countries were included in a new IFC emerging market index, and this encouraged institutional investors to start investing in the equity markets of these countries. From an equity concept initially, the term 'emerging markets' now incorporates many different asset classes, and there are a number of different definitions of emerging markets.

As an equity concept the 'emerging' universe is bounded at the top and bottom – markets that are easy to invest in but not those of advanced, developed or industrial countries (we shall use the term 'developed').[11] The border between developed and emerging has been subject to great debate, with graduation from one index to another of defining importance in many eyes. There has even been concern that graduation of some of the larger emerging markets to developed market status could emasculate the emerging equity market. Likewise, at the bottom end, the term 'frontier markets' has been coined to describe another layer of less developed, less liquid equity markets, with less developed institutions. The case for investing in these is one of higher return to compensate for lower liquidity and greater risk – though this risk can be spread and reduced by investing across many such countries.

Relative to other emerging market asset classes, there has been a lot of media focus on emerging market equities, to the extent that the term 'emerging markets' is used sometimes to mean 'emerging market equities'. This may explain why investors have often invested in emerging equity before other emerging market asset classes – it is perhaps strange that investors should choose to invest first in what is arguably the riskiest available asset class. The behaviour is largely just due to the equity bias of investors. Over long periods of time in

---

[11] There are problems with all these terms, but we can think of them as those which are not emerging as per our definition at the start of the chapter.

developed markets (though not during depressions)[12] investors have often made more money from equity than debt investing. However, at early stages of financial market development, risks tend to be highest. The number of risks involved in early-stage emerging equity investing may be compensated by high returns, but sometimes not. Property rights may be insecure; corruption rife; and economic mismanagement and macroeconomic shocks are periodic hazards. These factors have combined to create an impression of high risk and the assumption of high returns to compensate. Attracted by high returns, equity allocators have often looked at emerging equity markets before fixed income or other allocators have looked at emerging fixed income (bonds) or other emerging asset classes. If an asset allocator wants more return, he will often – thinking risk is proportionate to return, and asset classes arraigned on a simple scale of return/risk characteristics – allocate from his own domestic fixed income to domestic equity, and if that is not enough, or within the equity allocation, to emerging equity. Emerging debt is simply overlooked.

At the top, emerging equity countries supposedly graduate to developed country status; at the bottom, equity markets are 'frontier'. In contrast, bond markets have no bottom boundary – they go all the way down the credit spectrum. Sovereign bonds also have a long pedigree. Although there have long been a few listed stocks, including dominant ones like the British and Dutch East India companies', bank loans and then sovereign bonds were the benchmarks of sovereign risks and constituted a broad range of widely available investments from countries in medieval Europe and then in the colonial period. Through the 19th and early 20th centuries, sovereign debt issued by colonies in the British Empire, but also by countries like Argentina and Brazil under British influence, typically traded at a narrow spread over British consols. This was a result of implicit British support for bondholders backed up by the threat of military intervention: they were considered close in risk to that of the British sovereign. There had been defaults and crises, including the famous Barings crisis in Argentina in 1890. But by the early 20th century, to quote Niall Ferguson, 'With the exception of securities issued by improvident Greece and Nicaragua, none of the sovereign or colonial bonds that were traded in London in 1913 yielded more than two percentage points above consols, and most paid considerably less.'[13]

2.3   EMERGING MARKET DEBT IN THE 20TH CENTURY

Through much of the second half of the 19th century, Pax Britannica had been based on an espoused philosophy of free trade and investment by British capital, and secured by the reputation (if not the reality) of military might. Other European countries followed suit, though on a smaller scale. The result was a period of low foreign government bond yields and international trade. However, following the catastrophe of two world wars, and the intervening experience of the Wall Street crash in 1929 followed by slump, unregulated markets and trade openness were distinctly out of fashion and commonly believed by political elites to be undesirable for the conceivable future. The state came to manage a much larger proportion of national economies than in 1913. The trend towards a greater role for the state in social provision preceded, but was accentuated by, the political break at the end of World War II. After the war, the introduction of universal social insurance, education and health provision were on the agenda for war-torn European countries.

---

[12] Depression conditions exist at the time of writing in southern Europe.
[13] Ferguson (2008), pp. 297–8.

In Latin America the depression of the 1930s and disillusion with capitalism led to expropriations, starting in Mexico between 1936 and 1938, Bolivia in 1937 and then in Cuba in 1959 and 1960. In the 1960s and in the context of the Cold War, original investors were not fully compensated and the expropriating countries became more isolationist. As a result they found it difficult to recruit skilled technical and managerial staff to manage the expropriated assets.

After the first oil shock in 1973 and the break-up of the global fixed exchange rate system agreed at the 1944 Bretton Woods conference, there was a period of global inflation. Here was the seed which later was to grow into the Latin American debt problems of the 1980s. Specifically, the proceeds of oil revenues from the Middle East were deposited with Western banks, which in turn lent the money to anyone who was willing to borrow. Real interest rates (after taking inflation into account) were often negative, and Latin American countries were big borrowers. However, a large proportion of the money was mis-invested, leaving unfinanceable future liabilities. This time there were no gunboats to monitor economic management and counter the cyclical euphoria – a euphoria epitomised by a much-quoted sentence from Walter Wriston, head of Citibank: 'Countries don't go bust.'

2.3.1   Types of external sovereign debt

In the second half of the 20th century we can think of several types of developing country debt (see Figure 2.1). Bilateral official debt, lent by one government to another, was and remains often politically motivated – and a long way from being commercial. Some of it historically has been for military hardware, often bought at inflated prices due to corruption, where there was never strong expectation of repayment, even from day one. Some such lending was justified by European governments to attain political influence in ex-colonies and fight the Cold War. But for optical and budgetary reasons this aid was more conveniently deployed not via direct and highly visible budgetary aid, but subsumed under state agency export credit guarantees to private sector suppliers – i.e. via the donor's export guarantee department or agency, funded by the taxpayer through subsidised loans. However, this resultant type of debt is also complemented by debts originating from (the loan as opposed to grant components of) bilateral humanitarian and development assistance.

A substantial subset of this bilateral official debt is 'Paris Club' debt. This has been so called since negotiations with Argentina in 1956 on account of collective creditor positions being put to debtors in meetings held at the finance ministry in Paris. Negotiations have often been conducted in very long meetings where the debtor was not let out of the building until an agreement was reached. Until recently the Paris Club thought in traditional budgetary terms without taking into account a time value of money, and cared more about repayment of principal eventually (for which there is no budgetary accounting loss) than the net present value of a debt restructuring (which is the priority for a private creditor). The important point is that

Table 2.1   Types of external sovereign debt.

Official	Private
Bilateral (includes Paris Club)	Short-term trade finance
Multilateral	London Club

the history of Paris Club and other bilateral official debt is dominated by non-commercial motives, and so is not really comparable to private debt (see London Club below).[14]

The second type of debt is multilateral official debt, lent by international financial institutions such as the World Bank and the regional development banks.[15] Multilateral financing from the World Bank and regional development banks is often arranged on concessional terms, typically with policy conditionality attached. Also in this category we can include the International Monetary Fund (IMF). The IMF is not primarily a development institution, but has a mandate to prevent and help manage balance-of-payments crises. It typically does not lend for specific projects but for general balance-of-payments support.

The financing of the multilateral development banks comes from loan repayments from debtor countries and through bonds which they issue to private sector buyers, backed by the full faith and guarantee of their shareholders – i.e. governments, including all the major Western governments. The paid-in share capital of these institutions is small compared to the callable capital, and their gearing close to or below a 1:1 debt to equity ratio (i.e. they borrow little or no more from the bond market than the callable capital). As well as having to respond to the pressures of Western donor countries and borrowing countries, these institutions are influenced by three other stakeholders: staff, bondholders and non-government organisations (NGOs). The first of these institutions to engage in development banking (as opposed to the reconstruction of Europe after WWII) was the Inter-American Development Bank.

The traditional role of these institutions was to lend for long-term infrastructure, agriculture and other projects where there was little or no private sector borrowing alternative. However, this role has been augmented by more conditional policy lending, increasingly in competition with private financing. As development banks have become more involved in policy-based lending, distinction from IMF activities has also lessened. The IMF, particularly since the leadership of Michel Camdessus (1987–2000), has also moved closer to development bank activities through greater consideration of non-balance-of-payments issues in IMF programme design.

Traditionally, official lenders have insisted on their status as preferred creditors – i.e. the first to be repaid in terms of priority should a country's resources be insufficient to pay all its debts. However, nothing in writing makes this binding. Their ability to achieve this is largely because they have been the lenders of last resort – the source of further near-term funding for a country in difficulty. Interestingly, when they are not the lender of last resort, they can lose their preferred creditor status – even if they don't care to admit this. For example, Nigeria serviced private sector debt for years while in arrears to official creditors. Preferred creditor status is determined not only by the creditor but also by the debtor, as it is the debtor who chooses whom to pay and whom not to. Admittedly, however, debtor countries have often been bamboozled in the past into doing what the Western official creditors want (paying them) rather than acting in their own best interests.

Whereas Africa has been dominated by official lending, Latin America borrowed heavily in the 1970s from private sector banks recycling petrodollars from newly wealthy OPEC countries. Such debt can be split into short-term trade finance (our third type of sovereign debt, vital for a country's trade and very rarely defaulted on) and 'London Club' debt (the

---

[14] See also Caplen (2000).

[15] The main regional multilateral development banks are the Inter-American Development Bank (IDB), Asian Development Bank (AsDB), African Development Bank (AfDB), European Investment Bank (EIB) and European Bank for Reconstruction and Development (EBRD).

fourth type) – in the 1970s and 1980s mainly bank loans to the sovereign. When problems occurred, the London Club of banks (meeting in London rather than the official lenders in Paris) would collectively negotiate a restructuring. Banks would select representatives among themselves to represent all the creditors. This process eventually disintegrated as loan participations were actively traded on secondary markets,[16] resulting in thousands of holders rather than a handful of banks. Also, bank lending was largely replaced by bond issuance, making banks even less representative as creditors. Banks were suspected of trading on the inside information they received from the privileged position of being negotiators inside the 'Chinese wall'. Indeed, the debtor countries across the negotiating table were suspected of doing the same, sometimes in conjunction with disseminating misinformation into the market and trading in the secondary market in their own debt. This process eventually gave way to the bond market preference for greater transparency in negotiations, with a pioneering attempted use in negotiations to restructure Ecuador's debt, after that country's default in 1999. The model is that a country takes views from a variety of creditors (bondholders not only banks) and then makes a public offer with detailed restructuring terms which bondholders can individually choose to accept or reject.

Life is often not simple, however. In the case of Ecuador a bondholder group was formed to present views to the government in a transparent forum, with the outcomes of the meetings being widely available (I was a member of that consultative committee). The complication was that the Ecuadorians claimed to have been advised to default by a senior official from the US Treasury, and Ecuadorian negotiators were unwilling to act independently, blaming Washington for the default decision. Washington officials did not care to participate in the meetings themselves to explain their advice. Whether the Ecuadorian claim was true or not, the evasion of responsibility was problematic to the early re-establishment of trust between the country and creditors (bondholders) and so frustrated the restructuring process, delaying Ecuador's re-access to credit. The restructuring did eventually happen, however, and the transparent model has been used successfully in subsequent cases.[17]

By describing the types of debt we are setting the scene for what has happened since 1990. The point is that in Latin America there was largely private debt – bank loans and then bonds – with some multilateral debt. In Africa the debt was predominantly official sector (bilateral and multilateral), in part because African countries were never considered creditworthy enough to borrow much commercially. Asia's debt markets were less volatile and less internationally traded until the Asian crisis of 1997/8 – prior to that, Asian sovereign debt was predominantly in the form of short-term bank loans. Bonds there were boringly safe and limited in size. Asian companies meanwhile tended to finance themselves through retained earnings and equity, not international debt. Eastern Europe started to borrow private debt just like Latin America, but later – much of it after the fall of the Berlin Wall.

---

[16] A secondary market is a market for securities already in issue, as opposed to a primary market whereby securities are created and sold to an initial set of investors.

[17] The postscript is that Ecuadorian President Correa subsequently deemed the restructuring 'illegitimate' and defaulted again, but just on the restructured bonds.

2.3.2   From Mexican crisis to Brady bonds

Following OPEC oil price rises, and attracted by higher food and raw material prices, foreign investment into developing countries boomed in the 1970s.[18] The funding for the loans, via global banks, came from Middle East oil revenues or 'petrodollars'. Ironically, it was the expectation of future oil revenues that led to funding for huge government investment, and so to budgetary indiscipline, in Mexico. But high interest rates on foreign debt created ever-larger refinancing needs. US and wider inflation in the 1970s was finally reversed after 1979 by US Federal Reserve chairman Volker. His high-interest-rate policy created a global slowdown in the early 1980s which put further pressure on debt sustainability, and in 1982 Mexico announced that it could no longer service its bank loans. So the first modern Latin American debt crisis began. Investor confidence shaken, other Latin American countries followed suit. It was after this that the modern secondary emerging debt market, then known as the less developed country or LDC debt market, really started. This moment may be considered as heralding the birth of the modern emerging debt market. Banks, which had originated the loans, started to swap Latin American loan exposures with each other in order to reduce their concentrated exposures to particular countries. Then other investors also started to participate in this secondary market.

The 1980s were dubbed 'the lost decade' in Latin America by, among others, Inter-American Development Bank President Enrique Iglesias, on account of the low growth and perceived failed economic policies of the period. The Baker plan in 1985, named after the then US Treasury Secretary, attempted to restructure debt but failed due to lack of agreement on which countries to include, and so the region's malaise continued. This was followed by the Brady plan, named after Baker's successor Nicholas Brady. This more successful plan involved a country agreeing to a new set of orthodox economic policies (key to restoring credibility) to be monitored by the IMF, in exchange for a private sector debt restructuring and fresh official financing. Official debt was not restructured.

The bonds coming out of the Brady restructurings were collateralised with special issue US Treasury bonds held in escrow accounts in New York.[19] Collateral typically took the form of 100% principal collateral for 'bullet' bonds,[20] together with up to 18 months' interest rate collateral. Each participating country had its own plan, agreed to sequentially, over a number of years from the late 1980s (see Table 2.2). The restructured debt created Brady bonds much more liquid than the previous bank loans, and much safer, given the US Treasury collateral. Private sector holders of sovereign debt going into the restructuring were offered a combination of several bonds, some collateralised, some not. Although liquid, some of these bonds were highly complex, including for example capitalisation bonds, for which interest payments were initially not paid, but converted into more principal. Others had coupons which increased over time. Yet others had warrants attached, the value of which was conditional on some measure of economic recovery. The collateral also made the bonds complex.[21] However, the large issue size and liquidity created significant investor interest and a large

---

[18] These were essentially 3-month loans, with interest rates tied to LIBOR (London Interbank Offered Rate – the interest rate at which banks lend to each other in the London market).

[19] Bank accounts belonging to the issuing country, containing the US Treasury bonds, with the conditions attached that this collateral would be released to bondholders in the event of default, but if not so used would revert to the issuing government once the debt was either cancelled or fully repaid.

[20] Bonds in which the principal is all paid at the end of the period.

[21] I have memories of building an extremely large spreadsheet to update daily statistics on the whole universe of these bonds.

Table 2.2   Brady plans

Country	Announced	Brady bonds issued	Amount restructured (US$ billion)
Philippines	August 1989	1990	6.6
Mexico	September 1989	1990	47.17
Costa Rica	November 1989	1990	1.61
Venezuela	June 1990	1990	19.01
Uruguay	November 1990	1991	1.6
Nigeria	March 1991	1992	5.34
Argentina	April 1992	1993	29.34
Brazil	August 1992	1994	50
Bolivia	March 1993	None	0.18
Dominican Republic	May 1993	1994	0.8
Jordan	June 1993	1993	0.8
Bulgaria	November 1993	1994	6.8
Poland	March 1994	1994	14
Ecuador	May 1994	1995	7.6
Panama	May 1995	1996	3.94
Peru	October 1995	1996	7.99

secondary market developed, particularly after the New York banks started making markets in these new sovereign bonds. There are no available data for market liquidity before the Brady plans, but see Figure 2.1, which shows the high level of subsequent liquidity.

There were conditions attached to the new flow of official financing: macroeconomic policy and structural reform conditions which had to be fulfilled by the country before disbursements could be made from the IMF, World Bank and IDB. This was comforting to private investors who agreed to the restructuring; they were persuaded that countries would have the resources and incentives to repay on schedule. Typically within a year or two of a Brady agreement, and as repayments were made on schedule, market confidence returned such that countries were able to return to borrowing directly from bond markets at affordable interest rates. Eventually, as economic reforms proved successful and credit-worthiness improved, it was in the interests of both the investors (who did not want their return diluted) and the borrower countries (who wanted to move on from the heritage of restructuring and retrieve the collateral Treasuries in the escrow accounts) to swap Brady bonds into new uncollateralised Eurobonds.[22] Mexico was the first country to retire its Brady bonds in 2003, and others followed. By mid-2006 the bulk of Brady bonds had been bought back or swapped well before their end maturities.

Hence these Brady plans were highly successful in resolving the debt problems of the past. They established sound macroeconomic policies, provided new finance immediately from

---

[22] A Eurobond is a bond issued in a jurisdiction and in a currency other than that of the country in which the issuer is based. The first Eurobonds were issued in Europe in 1963.

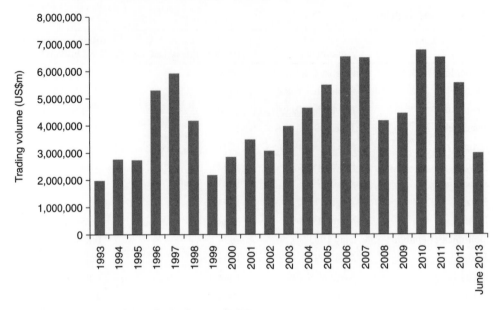

Figure 2.1   Emerging debt is liquid. Source: EMTA

the official sector (the IMF, World Bank, Inter-American Development Bank) and rebuilt trust with the international private sector. After a short period countries were once again able to access international capital markets, and moreover at long maturities – by issuing 30-year bonds rather than reverting to short-term bank loans. And these sovereign debt markets were now highly liquid and easier to access by foreign portfolio investors managing money on behalf of pension funds and other institutional investors.

The move to longer borrowing periods was itself very important. Latin America before the Brady plans had been highly vulnerable to external shocks. Foreign private banks were prone to not roll over short-term loans, causing sudden gaps in external financing. The reasons for not rolling over may or may not have been triggered by a deterioration of domestic credit-worthiness. They could as easily be caused by entirely external factors. Short-term bank loans did not have active secondary markets, hence if a bank was worried for any reason it would simply not renew. With a 30-year bond, however, an unhappy bondholder sells in the secondary market. The transaction can be fully offshore, not impacting the flow of capital to the country. The sovereign, instead of borrowing money continuously for short periods, borrows it intermittently for very much longer periods. Hence there are longer periods between needed refinancing, giving countries more time to make policy changes and reassure markets after an external shock before new borrowing is required. The move to longer-term financing as each country completed their Brady deal was also more appropriate to the timeframe of infrastructure and other development financing needs. The transparency of liquid bonds also helped signal to policymakers market sentiment and reaction to policies. The development of a long-term liquid bond market was thus a major positive development towards stable private sector financing. Although most of the debt problems were in Latin America, a number of other countries also entered into Brady plans or Brady-type restructurings, namely in Bulgaria, Cote D'Ivoire, Nigeria, Philippines, Poland and Vietnam.

2.3.3   Market discipline

The discipline which the market imposed on countries' policymakers was both a burden and a blessing. It could certainly be argued that in the early 1990s bond market participants were often prejudiced and unhelpfully ignorant about countries. But markets also have a strong incentive to (and hence do) learn fast and then act on what they have learnt – faster, typically, than policymakers. Markets cause volatility, but this may be helpful in testing the robustness of macroeconomic policies – better a low level of continuous volatility, than periods of calm interspersed by the occasional catastrophe, as demonstrated by Dehn (2000) with the example of commodity shocks.[23]

Bond markets play a central role in an economy by signalling market confidence and assessing sovereign credit-worthiness, enabling corporate bonds and other markets to factor in sovereign risk. James Carville, adviser to President Clinton, famously said early in the Clinton presidency: 'I used to think if there was reincarnation, I wanted to come back as the president or the pope or a .400 baseball hitter. But now I want to come back as the bond market. You can intimidate everybody.'[24] Sometimes countries have to learn the hard way that pleasing the bond market, but also educating and informing it, is necessary. In defence of the bond market, bond investors created much more transparency (even if derivatives markets sometimes do not). It was now public knowledge what investors thought of particular policies and risks, and it was up to policymakers to react appropriately if they wanted to borrow at low cost from private markets.

Through improving credit-worthiness and so access to capital at low cost, the Brady plans got Latin America on its feet again. This did not stop countries getting into trouble when they experienced external shocks, had balance of payments vulnerabilities or embarked upon imprudent fiscal and monetary policies. Countries were still dependent on foreign financing. Such financing could be withdrawn as a result of a self-fulfilling prophecy: if enough investors, for whatever reason, believed that the country would default, then it was sometimes in the interests of other investors, who initially did not think this, also to sell. The problem of the self-fulfilling prophecy also had a multi-country dimension. If international investors perceived emerging markets to be similar, or even thought that other investors believed them to be similar, or could be expected to act as if they did – and that, as a result, should bonds fall in one country they would also fall in other emerging countries – then there was a risk of financial contagion. The possibility of such contagion increased the risk premiums for all emerging countries.

The high levels of leverage used by many emerging debt investors up to 1998 (borrowing against bonds in order to buy more) led to contagion. As bond prices fell in country A the lending banks made margin calls on the leveraged investors, who raised cash by selling bonds from country B. This then also caused country B's bonds to fall in price. The expectation of this contagion, in the knowledge that there were many leveraged investors needing to raise cash quickly to meet such margin calls, meant other investors also tried to sell country B's bonds.

This risk was also understood by the official sector, with the IMF in the front line of defence against not only individual country default, but also systemic risk across a number of countries. This was because of the collective psychology and behaviour described above, and because crisis-induced losses in one country caused profit-taking in others. The need to

---

[23] See Dehn (2000).

[24] Wessel *et al.* (1993).

contain such contagion motivated the IMF to bail out countries in the knowledge that some of their money would be used to pay bondholders. Bondholders also knew this, creating moral hazard: the incentive to take on additional risk when one has insurance, in this case from the IMF. But this moral hazard was (largely) considered a necessary evil, and a low priority for international policymakers.

This might be explained by the following analogy: the IMF was like a fireman – important for putting out fires, and, if anyone was listening, advising householders how to avoid fire risk. The fact that the existence of a fire service may encourage carelessness by some householders is, correctly, not seen as a good reason to not have firemen. However, some in the official sector were, and remain, aggressively against bailouts in principal, and extremely annoyed that their incentives to bail countries out are predictable and predicted by financial markets, which take advantage of this. The task should be to avoid getting to a position of excessive financial leverage where banks or countries are 'too big to fail' rather than complain that markets can observe this when it is the reality.

2.3.4   Eastern Europe

Though emerging markets were still vulnerable to external shocks, there was a great deal of optimism about the future, not just in Latin America, but also in the newly ex-communist countries in Eastern Europe. With the fall of the Berlin Wall, Eastern Europe and the Commonwealth of Independent States (CIS) became a more prominent part of the emerging debt universe. Following the break-up of the Soviet Union, Russia agreed to take on the bulk of the USSR's sovereign debt in exchange for nuclear defence and other assets from the other new CIS members. Poland, which did have some historic sovereign debt, negotiated a Brady plan.[25] Only 14 months later the country was upgraded to investment grade.[26] The development of the whole region was rapid, as was its financial development.

The new Russian Federation made rapid progress in economic and political development between June and December 1992, but from a history which had gone from serfdom and autocracy to 70 years of totalitarianism with hardly any experience of either liberal democracy or market economy in between. Economic shock treatment was proposed (sudden change in institutions by fiat), and though a market economy similar to those for the West appeared initially to be emerging, mistakes were made (arguably unavoidable ones), and the popularity of such economic policy radicalism declined. The window of opportunity for President Yeltsin and Prime Minister Gaidar to establish democracy and a strong market economy quickly closed. Mass privatisation, though it created a market economy, also expressed itself in corruption, mass thievery and the new oligarch class of super-rich industrialists. Economic reform stalled and the political support for further economic experiments waned.

While dropping the momentum on economic reform is widely seen as a missed opportunity in the West, there is another perspective to this story. There was no Marshall Plan for Russia. Shock treatment (or rather the lack of ability to stop the sudden market changes in the early 1990s) created disillusionment. NATO expansion and USSR break-up put Russia on the

---

[25] Romania and Hungary, which had no Brady plans, took years longer to recover, though admittedly they were also more collectivised than Poland.

[26] Rating agencies rate company, security and country credit-worthiness. Ratings above investment grade are considered (by regulators) without major default risk, and appropriate for banks and the most conservative institutional investors to invest in. Sub-investment grade ratings levels are sometimes denoted speculative grade. Below that are issuers in default.

defensive strategically, and further Balkanisation threatened, particularly in Chechnya. The popularity of Putin from 2000 to 2010 as president and then prime minister can thus be understood: despite his installing ex-KGB officers as business managers, thus consigning much of Russian industry to incompetent oversight, he represented, in the context of a country with a centuries-old sense of vulnerability, strong central rule to create stability. Fortunately there were oil and gas revenues to substitute for other drivers of growth until domestic consumption took off, but more competition and less corruption in the private economy will be necessary for sustained growth.

2.3.5   Mexico in crisis again

US Federal Reserve Chairman Greenspan (who succeeded Volker in 1987) increased US interest rates in 1994. After previous overexcitement about the impact of the North American Free Trade Agreement (NAFTA), the meagre economic benefits for Mexico were much less than hoped for, and this, yet again, was too much for Mexico's finances. Market nerves increased after pre-election fiscal spending at the end of the Salinas presidency in 1994 (an historical feature of Mexico's six-year presidential cycle), and there was particular concern about the costs of Mexico's currency mismatched Tesobonos – government bonds denominated in pesos but indexed to the dollar. A violent uprising in Chiapas in January 1994 and then the assassination in March of the leading presidential candidate, Luis Donaldo Colosio, were not good for market sentiment either. A sharp currency devaluation in December 1994 accompanied increased risk aversion by local and foreign investors. Risk aversion spread further to Argentina and other Latin American countries.

Investors fled Mexico fast, starting with Mexican money. Mexico had suffered a major reversal of investor confidence in what can be described as a case of Micawberism. Mr Micawber is a character in Charles Dickens' *David Copperfield*, famous for his optimism that 'something may turn up', but also his analysis that if one's income is £20 a year and outgoings are £19, 19 shillings and sixpence, then the result is happiness; but if one's outgoings are £20 and sixpence, then the result is misery. Investors focus on balance of payments accounts in Mexico, as in other countries, but have often done so without full understanding of future dynamics. A balance sheet totting up fails to take into account more accurate figures available to a government but not the market, and more crucially, policy choices available to the government to redeem the situation. Moreover, the international official sector often has a strong incentive to avoid systemic risk and to offer a country short-term assistance. The market view taken is too often, much like Mr Micawber's, static and straightforward: if a country is even a little short, then the result is seen as heading for catastrophe. Such an analysis is overly simplistic, but the market has taken time (collectively) to learn this. In 1994 mass panic by bond markets was more common than in 2010. This simplistic all-or-nothing view of default risk was indeed the case with Mexico in early 1995.

The panic increased the size of the problem significantly – the required assistance was large. An IMF member's quota determined, inter alia, its access to IMF financing. At the time of Mexico's bailout (February 1995) the allowed 300% of Mexico's quota amounted to SDR 5.259 million (about US$7.8 billion). The IMF added another US$10 billion to their 18-month stand-by credit agreement, making a total of $17.8 billion. The Bank for International Settlements offered a US$10 billion line of credit, and the Bank of Canada short-term swaps of around US$1 billion. But the US Congress was reluctant to help. The US administration, however, fully understood the risks to other emerging markets, and indeed to the global economy and to the United States, and so used the US Exchange Stabilisation Fund (ESF)[27] to assist Mexico to the tune of a further $20 billion, which did not require congressional approval. The near US$50 billion support enabled Mexico to recover without default on its external debt obligations. No other country defaulted – and the United States made a US$500 million profit on its emergency ESF lending.

2.3.6   The Asian and Russian crises

After a strong market recovery and good investor returns for several years, the next important series of events was in Asia: a part of the developing world not previously prominent in the emerging debt universe due to low dependence on external debt financing and low perceived risk and associated bond investment returns. The Asian crisis of 1997/8 started to bring this region into focus for the emerging debt investor. Indeed, it has been argued that Thailand's excessive reliance on bank rather than bond finance (and hence absence from the emerging debt investor's universe) was a significant cause of their balance of payments problems.[28]

The Asian economies had fixed exchange rates and open capital accounts. Domestic banks borrowed externally in US dollars relatively cheaply and lent domestically at higher interest rates. Although this created risks for the banks – in the form of major losses should the currencies devalue against the dollar – the prospect of their collective failure all at the same time meant the problem was the government's to deal with. This made them more reckless in not protecting themselves from possible devaluation – there was moral hazard. Starting with Thailand, there was also an element of hubris concerning the Asian model of growth, which was considered somehow different. Asia did not completely follow the Washington Consensus and appeared to have a superior way of doing things given its astounding recent track record of economic growth (above 8% per annum from 1986 to 1995).

Building up to the crisis period in 1997/8, several Asian currencies which de facto pegged to the rising US dollar, including the Thai baht, Indonesian rupiah and Korean won, saw strong real currency appreciation. This fuelled imports and construction in an unsustainable fashion. In January 1997 George Soros's fund started selling Thai baht short, but speculative pressure temporarily abated when on May 14th the Central Bank intervened with the help of Singapore (interested in preserving regional currency stability) in buying Thai baht, and on May 15th the Thai government banned offshore baht lending by Thai financial companies. However, this was no more than a reprieve. Market speculation grew too strong for credible sustained intervention, the currency was floated, and depreciated 20% on July 2nd. This was rapidly followed by loss of confidence across other Asian economies, which also experienced exchange rate crises and associated problems meeting debt obligations in foreign currency. On July 11th the Philippine peso was devalued and Indonesia widened its exchange rate band. On July 18th the IMF announced for the Philippines the first use of its 'emergency financing mechanism' of more than US$1 billion. The IMF agreed a US$17 billion assistance programme for Thailand in August and, after a 30% currency fall, Indonesia asked for help on 8th October and agreed a US$40 billion programme on October 31st.

---

[27] This US support took the form of: (i) short-term currency swaps through which Mexico could borrow US dollars in exchange for Mexican pesos for 90 days; (ii) medium-term currency swaps through which Mexico could borrow US dollars for up to five years; and (iii) guaranties through which the United States agreed to back-up Mexico's obligations on government securities for up to ten years.

[28] See Chabchitrchaidol and Panyanukul in Eichengreen *et al.*, 2008.

The crisis then spread to South Korea, which in early December negotiated a $57 billion IMF assistance package – the largest ever up to that time. Intense fears followed about a possible collapse of Korea's banking sector, and international private bank creditors of the government were encouraged to co-operate in a rescue. Consequently an international bank 90-day rollover of short-term sovereign debts was finally agreed on 8th January 1998. A series of further IMF programmes were agreed over the next few months, and while bringing countries back to stability, the dependency and need to comply with its harsh conditionality was resented. The conditionality was complied with, including even through efforts in South Korea to collect donations of gold from the public, but there was regional resolve never to be so vulnerable again.

Following shortly after domino-style problems in Asia, Russia was next. Commodity prices fell following the Asian crisis and in March 1998 President Boris Yeltsin dismissed the government of Premier Chernomyrdin, which had built up an unsustainable fiscal deficit,[29] and appointed Sergei Kiriyenko in his place. By May short-term interest rates reached 150% and on July 13th a $22 billion external support package ($5 billion of which went missing on arrival) was implemented to swap short-term debt into longer Eurobonds. Most commentators at the time thought that it was possible for the country to be bailed out. However, the multinational rescue programme was late and, after Germany (facing an election) pulled out of their contribution to the package, others followed. The package ended up being too small. Its conditionality was also toughened up at US insistence at the last moment (given political opposition in the US Congress) to such an extent that markets saw noncompliance as inevitable. This was what faced newly appointed Prime Minister Kiriyenko, as well as domestic strikes by unpaid workers, and a domestic political scene of corruption and chaos under Yeltsin. On August 17th he declared a default on US$68 billion of domestic debt,[30] currency devaluation and a debt moratorium, all at once. The financial markets might have been able to cope with any one or two of these measures (the situation clearly not being sustainable without some major policy change), but not all three simultaneously.

The background to this was that after the break-up of the Soviet Union in 1991 the new Russian Federation had agreed with breakaway republics to take on all the Soviet-era international sovereign debts. The process of reconciling these debts lasted to about 1994. Then restructuring deals were agreed with the Paris Club (1996) and the London Club (1997). The new London Club debt took the form of principal (PRIN) and interest arrears (IAN) bonds.[31] However, the debt inherited from the Soviet Union was quasi-sovereign – the obligation of the state-owned but not state-guaranteed Vnesheconombank – and the Russian federal government refused to give a sovereign guarantee on this first restructuring in 1997. After the August 1998 default on domestic bonds Vnesheconombank once again defaulted and restructured its inherited USSR debt – the PRINs and IANs. These were restructured in 2000

---

[29] The distinction should be made between the primary or underlying fiscal deficit and the overall deficit including debt service. With monetary policy being tightened, the latter increased especially rapidly.

[30] The instruments which defaulted were zero-coupon Treasury bills – GKOs (*Gosudarstvennoye Kratkosrochnoye Obyazatyelstvo*) – and coupon-bearing Federal loan bonds – OFZs (*Obligatsyi Federal'novo Zaima*).

[31] The London Club deal was slow to conclude, due in part to the long reconciliation process. The debt being rescheduled took the form of bank loans, not bonds. Unlike in the secondary market for bonds where ownership is transferred cleanly, loan documentation retains the original bank lenders as the creditors. The secondary market takes the form of sub-participations – banks sell portions of these loans to others who in turn sell them on, etc. Thousands of transactions later, the chain of who owns exactly what becomes complicated. It was the unravelling of this which took time. In the interim the future PRIN and IAN bonds were heavily traded ahead of the restructuring in a 'when and if' market.

into sovereign Eurobonds. However, as other sovereign Eurobonds issued before the August 1998 crisis never missed a payment, technically the Russian Federation had a perfect foreign debt repayment record.[32]

The crisis then spread to the irresponsibly highly leveraged and massive hedge fund firm Long Term Capital Management (LTCM) in the US. This firm used fixed income arbitrage techniques to identify small market imperfections which it was assumed would be arbitraged out over time. Because the profits on such trades were small, massive leverage was used. At the beginning of 1998 its main fund had about US$4.7 billion of equity capital against which it had borrowed a further US$124.5 billion (a leverage ratio of over 25:1). Losses which had started to build in May 1998 were made worse by the Russian default and then panic buying of US Treasuries, amounting to US$1.85 billion by the end of August. Positions then had to be liquidated, locking in these losses. Investors pulling out of the fund added to the problem, and as the equity shrank faster than the debts, the leverage ratio reached over 250:1 in September. After a failed private buyout offer, and in order to avoid more widespread financial sector crisis, the New York Federal Reserve organised a private bailout by LTCM's creditors of US$3.625 billion.

The contagion also spread to Brazil, which did not default, but did have to leave its crawling peg and devalue in January 1999. Following its successful anti-inflation programme Plano Real from 1994, foreign capital had boosted the exchange rate to unsustainable levels.

2.3.7   Emerging markets grow up

The Russian and subsequent Brazilian devaluations concluded the episode of domino-style contagion across from one emerging country to another. After these events, two important changes occurred at the very end of the 1990s and into the early 2000s. Firstly, country risk improved, and secondly, the structure of the investor base changed from domination by hedge funds and (fast) leveraged money to domination by largely nonleveraged strategic money from pension funds (including local pension funds) and other institutional investors.[33]

(a)   The first change: country and contagion risks fall

Emerging markets learned the hard way, through crises, what imprudent economic policy looks like. In many countries the end of the Cold War has meant a move from authoritarian governments to ones more responsive to electorates. These electorates – many through direct experience, poor and without a welfare state to cushion them – often understand the negative consequences of high inflation and poor macroeconomic management. Government policy has become more responsive to their needs,[34] including the desire to have low inflation and stability, i.e. credible macroeconomic policy. Fiscal and monetary policy improved. Deficit financing reduced. Inflation control improved. Perhaps most relevant for investors, vulnerability to external shocks decreased.[35]

One lesson was not to become as vulnerable again to sudden outflows as in the late 1990s, and this was achieved through self-insurance: the building up of massive foreign exchange

---

[32] The other widely traded Russian debt instruments at the time were MinFin bonds, issued in lieu of confiscated bank accounts.

[33] Author's observation as a market participant. No publicly available comprehensive survey exists.

[34] See for a parallel Sen (1999), who argues that famines are less likely to occur in democracies.

[35] As IMF economists Adler and Tovar (2012) evidence.

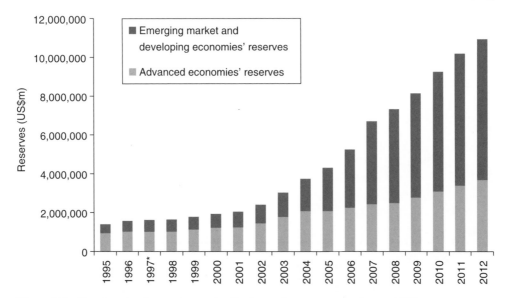

Figure 2.2   Developed and emerging market foreign exchange reserves. Source: IMF

reserves from US$0.46 trillion in 1995 to US$7.26 trillion in 2012 (see Figure 2.2). For the next ten years to the 2008 crisis (and after), Asian countries built these reserves, which also served to keep exchange rates low and support export-led growth. These reserves were largely invested in US Treasury bills and bonds, and the extra demand for these assets in large part led to a mispricing of US Treasury bonds, the yields of which were pushed lower. This enabled cheap borrowing in the US and created a mispricing of many other assets – it fuelled debt creation (leverage) in many places across the US economy, and so arguably helped fuel a series of future G10 bubbles.[36]

As China, India[37] and other emerging countries became wealthier, the impact of global demographics and increased income in the emerging world started to shift global terms of trade. After decades of fluctuation (and following a period of downward movement) commodity prices, not just oil, started to rise in real terms from about 2002 (see Figure 2.3, which shows the CRB commodity price index).

Oil-producing countries in particular started to suffer from what economists call Dutch disease, named in the 1970s from the problem the Netherlands experienced after finding natural gas in 1959. A boom in natural resources naturally results in upward pressure on the exchange rate, and this can squeeze other (non-gas or non-oil) domestic exporters and import-competing sectors as they find it more and more difficult to compete in international markets. If the resource boom, or its pricing, is seen as temporary, the exchange rate can be expected to fall later, when the boom is over or prices fall. When faced with volatile commodity markets, there is a strong desire to try and resist the associated swings in exchange rates. This is done by intervening in the exchange rate markets, building up foreign reserves

---

[36] Emerging economies should arguably instead have invested more in each other's sovereign bonds, but more on that later.

[37] China and India were only marginally impacted by the Asian crisis in large part because they are closed economies but also as they had not liberalised their capital accounts ahead of financial sector reforms as other Asian countries had.

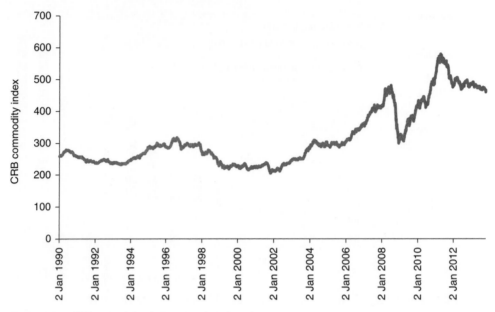

Figure 2.3   CRB commodity index. Source: Bloomberg

when the price of the commodity is high, releasing them again when the commodity price falls or the boom ends, so smoothing the exchange rate and the path of GDP. Central banks can manage this process, or it can be delegated to a stabilisation fund set up for the same purpose, and funded by the central bank or natural resource taxes.

The end result was that both Asian and oil-producing countries built up huge reserves at the same time. This build-up of self-insurance, complemented by greater fiscal and monetary discipline, significantly reduced country default risks but also contagion risks from one emerging country to another.

(b) The second change: the investor base

The structure of the investor base matters to an asset class. Prior to the Russia crisis in 1998, perhaps a third of the investor base in emerging market dollar-denominated debt was highly leveraged and speculative.[38] After the Russian crisis, a lot of this hedge fund money and other speculative investment left emerging market debt. Some funds blew up, as they had in 1994/5. Others, with global mandates, who were not required by their clients to invest in emerging markets, came to the conclusion that emerging markets were not for them. Market volatility and associated balance-of-payments risk reduced as a result of the exit of these investors.

Then around 2000–2001 Western institutional investors started to put more money into emerging debt. Prior to this, whereas emerging equity had been invested in, pension funds took longer to invest in emerging debt. To an extent this was a function of asset allocation biases towards equity markets, and also poor understanding of the risk and return characteristics

---

[38] In the absence of publicly available survey data this observation is based on anecdotal evidence from market makers at the time.

of emerging debt investing. Many institutional investors had not previously invested much in debt outside their own domestic markets, and had to create a new asset class internally in order to be able to allocate.[39] However, the peer-group pressure and demonstration effect in the pension industry is such that once a critical mass of US pension funds and other institutional investors started to allocate, others followed – they realised emerging debt had credit quality, return, volatility and diversification characteristics they liked. This change in investor base from hedge funds to long-only long-term investors[40] added stability to the market, and this in turn attracted more of the same type of investor.

Another change in the investor base has become more and more important: the dominance of the emerging markets' own (domestic) institutional investors. With local liabilities, these investors do not have the same propensity to flee the market when risk perception rises. Indeed, since the mid-2000s local bond markets often rally in most of the larger emerging markets[41] during episodes of risk aversion – because the dominant movement of funds is by domestic investors moving from domestic equities to domestic bonds. At time of writing, local currency debt, largely locally held, is over 80% (and growing) of all emerging markets debt.

2.3.8   Testing robustness: Argentina defaults

The major reduction in vulnerability to external shocks and changes in investor base did not mean that emerging markets were without risk. Argentina has a history of well over a century of defaults, and of unorthodox economic policy.[42] The country has a major structural problem with its fiscal management.[43] From its constitution in the 1850s the federated provinces have delegated the raising of taxes to the central government, while provinces maintain spending prerogatives. The result has been fiscal irresponsibility, with fiscal expenditure difficult to constrain. Political relationships remain strongest in the provinces, and provincial loyalties remain paramount, even for national politicians.

After a series of economic and banking crises over decades and war with the United Kingdom in 1982, the Alfonsín administration again started to struggle with runaway inflation from 1986, culminating in monthly inflation rates over 100% by mid-1989. In part to anchor inflation expectations, the economic team of President Menem in 1991 established a currency board and convertibility plan to peg the peso to the US dollar.

A fixed exchange rate prevents daily pressure by international investors on one's relative prices between tradable and non-tradeable goods, but if domestic inflation is not controlled by fiscal and structural policies, then trade deficits, debts and capital flight may build, and confidence in the ability to maintain the exchange rate may evaporate. Factors which enhance global market volatility, including elements of global capital market development and

---

[39] As we shall discuss and critique in Chapters 5 and 8, pension funds and other institutional investors often invest in a two-stage process of first choosing how much to invest in various assets classes, and then choosing asset managers to manage money in the chosen asset classes. But the set of asset classes is largely considered given – determined by past practice. Changing the conventional consensus of what is an asset class typically takes many years.

[40] Pension funds, unlike some hedge funds, do not use significant leverage. With liabilities often 15 years in duration, and given the nature of their decision processes, they tend to stick to their allocation decisions for years.

[41] But not in those markets, including many in sub-Saharan Africa, where the domestic investor base is still weak.

[42] See for example Lewis (2002).

[43] Booth, J. (2002).

globalisation, may hasten changes in relative prices needed for optimal allocative efficiency. So a fixed exchange rate can provide stability and a respite in order to fix structural problems – but also an opportunity to procrastinate. This respite does not last indefinitely, and in a floating exchange rate world, adopting a fixed currency results in less time available to fix problems than in a global fixed rate environment.

The Argentine convertibility plan can be seen in this context: a creation of breathing space to allow fiscal and other reforms. Such a plan does not however reform fiscal indiscipline on its own. Argentina failed to make sufficient reforms and so entered crisis again, defaulting on its debt in December 2001.

What is interesting in terms of the history of the emerging debt market is that when Argentina defaulted in December 2001, the debt of all other countries in the main emerging debt index rallied within 48 hours. That Argentina was going to default was obvious, and when the event itself finally occurred, it enabled markets to stop worrying and move on. The contagion effect so common in the previous decade did not occur.

2.3.9   The end of the self-fulfilling prophecy

For developing countries, most trade and investment links have been with developed countries, not with each other: north-south, not south-south. This is starting to change[44] (trade with China being the strongest link for many already), and insofar as the previous lack of south-south links was a function of history more than economic logic, and based on now damaged faith in sound economic management in the West, this pattern can be expected to change more rapidly.

Aside from the fact that they may be cut off from capital in a crisis, many developing countries have little in common. One definition of underdevelopment is poor institutional development, and institutions develop only slowly after time – their gaps and inefficiencies are highly country-specific. Hence developing countries are often more diverse economically than developed countries.[45] So a broadly diversified portfolio of developing country sovereign debt should reduce non-correlated risks.

Prior to the end of the Cold War this heterodoxy was suppressed by superpower puppet governments adopting externally dictated policies. And the problem in the 1990s was financial contagion: the common factor was external vulnerability to suddenly being cut off from capital. Financial contagion[46] is collectively irrational, arguably the most irrational feature of financial markets. It may be collectively stupid, but knowing that the behaviour exists, the intelligent act of an individual is to act likewise (and first), in turn strengthening the pattern. Vulnerability is added by the known presence of excessive leverage by non-discriminating speculative investors. Although Brazil and Russia do not trade with each other, when Russia devalued and defaulted in 1998, market nervousness and downward price pressure spread to Brazil and other countries. This contagion was largely driven by margin calls on leveraged investments as described. The same pattern had previously been highly significant when Mexico devalued in late 1994.

---

[44] See the 2013 UN Development Report, which shows trade between developing countries at over 30% of global trade, and growing rapidly.

[45] As Tolstoy puts it in the celebrated opening sentence of Anna Karenina: 'All happy families are alike; each unhappy family is unhappy in its own way.' Likewise, underdevelopment can be thought of as highly heterogeneous.

[46] Here meaning not merely capital flight to reduce risk but capital flight in anticipation of capital flight by others.

The depth of losses in 1998 from the Russian crisis was sufficient to scare off (in some cases put out of business) the leveraged speculators. Many found more fashionable investments elsewhere, especially in the Nasdaq stock market. LTCM should have warned investors off highly leveraged products, yet for many that revelation had to wait another decade (at least) until after Lehman's demise in 2008. However, emerging debt did at last fall out of fashion with the fast money brigade[47] which can on occasion substitute leverage and backward-looking statistical models for any broader understanding. Institutional investors became a more significant proportion of the investor base. Daily asset price volatility of emerging debt instruments decreased substantially just as it was rising in many other asset classes. The remaining investors were largely unleveraged and more discriminating of country risks. Contagion risks reduced as a result.

The first major test to see if contagion would return to emerging debt came at the tail end of the Asian/Russian crisis: the Brazilian devaluation in January 1999. It was well anticipated by many market participants, and the other major emerging markets were not negatively impacted. The exception was Argentina, which, being a major trade partner of and competitor with Brazil, suffered a major shock in terms of trade, not easily adjusted to, given its fixed exchange rate with the US dollar.

The next major test was the subsequent Argentine crisis in late 2001. This was also well understood as a possibility well in advance by many, and was much more severe than the Brazilian problem in 1999. But again, as mentioned above, despite involving default and devaluation, recession and political crisis, there was no financial market contagion – no knee-jerk sell-off in other emerging markets just because they were emerging markets.

The silver lining of the collectively irrational nature of financial contagion is that when it does not exist and is perceived not to exist, it is not automatically expected and is less likely to re-emerge. From 2000, those who previously tried to push the market around by short selling were more likely to get their fingers burnt. The market matured. The general move to floating exchange rates after the late 1990s (not just in Brazil and Argentina but across Asia) also helped to reduce the perception of one-way bets. It was typically through currency markets, speculating against fixed exchange rates as described above in Asia and then Latin America, that macro hedge funds had previously made their returns, and this route to profit was largely shut off.

In 2002, the year after the Argentine default, and in the context of the dotcom bust[48] (which damaged the balance sheets of banks that had provided debt financing to the internet companies and to speculating equity investors), US credit dried up and banks withdrew their exposure to Latin America again. Brazil's economic situation was different from Argentina's. This was not least because it did not have a vulnerable fixed exchange rate to attack, but also because its anti-inflation programme had been successful and in place since 1994 (withstanding the stress of devaluation in 1999), and the country had bit by bit improved fiscal discipline through a series of constitutional amendments since 1988. But it did have an election, and came under speculative pressure. The difference was that this time the self-fulfilling prophecy did not work. This was the view, held by some in Wall Street, that as long as

---

[47] In particular those so-called 'macro-hedge funds' (ones betting long and short on countries), emerging market hedge funds, various other types of hedge fund which use quantitative or arbitrage strategies, and proprietary bank trading accounts which use high levels of leverage and take speculative short positions – i.e. they short (sell assets they did not own) not to hedge risk but for profit.

[48] The bubble in valuations of (particularly US) internet stocks, fuelled by loose monetary policy, peaked in March 2000.

enough like-minded investors sold a country's assets, this would cause a crisis and the fall in asset prices they sought. Brazil's credit-worthiness in 2002 was arguably too strong for this, and the time-frame required for disaster – a year at least – too long.

Brazil in 2002 did not have a solvency problem: the corporate sector was not overly leveraged, the banking sector was healthy, and the country had strong tax revenues and had been meeting IMF agreed fiscal targets.[49] Local bank nervousness about the presidential election caused some initial reluctance to buy government paper. This was fuelled further by the bad-mouthing of the PT (Workers Party) presidential candidate Luiz Inácio Lula da Silva (Lula) by political opponents, particularly to investors in New York. Lula, who won the election, had a history of conciliation and building non-ideological consensus both as a union and party leader, but he was portrayed as an unreliable ideologue of the left. However, the main problem was financial contagion from the US, where banks cut credit lines across the board after the dotcom bubble burst. The reaction of the corporate sector in Brazil was simply to pay off their debt rather than borrow more at extortionate rates. Their demand for dollars to do so then caused a reserves drain at the central bank. This was appropriately and predictably responded to with an extra US$30 billion from the IMF. After this, the markets came up with further 'reasons' for collapse, focusing on local debt servicing sustainability given high domestic interest rates. But these analyses were also partial, failing to factor in the export boom from a weaker currency. Eventually analysts admitted that Brazil was nowhere close to default for a year at least, and those with short positions capitulated.

Nevertheless, Brazilian external debt spreads[50] over US Treasuries blew out to the same as those for the Ivory Coast (in default and with armed rebels controlling the north of the country at the time). One might suspect that, faced with a lack of good reasons, a lot of investors and analysts simply came to the conclusion that they were missing something. The technical arguments[51] propounded at the time for why the country was going to fall apart may have been plausible to many hedge funds, but they were wrong. In large part investors were panicked, driven by severe pessimism in US markets, Wall Street job losses, and facing (many of them for the first time in their professional lives) a secular bear market at home following the dotcom bubble burst.

Events in Uruguay, finally, are of interest for our brief history before we come to 2008, after which the sovereign risk in the developed countries seems far more problematic than that in emerging markets. Uruguay's tourism and banking sectors suffered after Argentina defaulted in December 2001, but Uruguay has a much better credit history. It was determined to avoid a default or a creditor-unfriendly restructuring – which it did eventually through a voluntary market-friendly bond swap. However, this was not before the IMF tried to impose a default, partly, one suspects, to test its new sovereign default restructuring mechanism (SDRM). This was successfully resisted by my own firm, Ashmore, which bought a major proportion of the externally traded sovereign debt and also provided demand to enable the local debt market to reopen, in effect becoming lender of last resort. Uruguay avoided the messy default the IMF seemed to prefer. It is not just the official sector that can be the lender of last resort.

---

[49] The IMF Article IV consultation concluded in January 2002 commended Brazil for its performance, particularly on the fiscal front.

[50] The differences in yields, in this case the additional yields of Brazilian bonds (of various durations) above the yields of (same duration) US Treasury bonds.

[51] Technical analysis focuses on trends and patterns in recent data and, insofar as a significant amount of money is managed by people who follow technical analysis and then trade in ways which amplify the patterns, technical factors can signal the short-term direction of a market.

2.4   THE GROWTH OF LOCAL CURRENCY DEBT

Local currency sovereign debt has two main indices[52] and market segments: one comprising local money market instruments, mainly currency forwards (including non-deliverable forwards); the other, physical bonds with more duration and hence exposure not only to currency risk but also local movements in the government yield curve – interest rates risk. Liquidity has been far greater in the money markets and forwards than in the bonds, but over time, as countries build out their yield curves through bond issuance, the newer bond markets can develop, and this is the priority for many countries.

Why have these markets developed? In the 1990s, after the move from bank loans to Brady and other Eurobonds, the choice for emerging market issuers was often clearly in favour of issuing in dollars – issue, say, 30-year debt in dollars or one-year in local currency at higher interest rates. However, many countries since the turn of the 21st century now have the opportunity and time to change the nature of the choice: they have an ample cushion in terms of reserves, current account and fiscal surpluses. And this is in a global environment of major long-term growth in institutional investor demand for emerging market debt. This environment substantially reduces the vulnerability to and impact from external shocks (such as being cut off from trade finance, or a terms of trade or export market shock) and so creates an opportunity for many countries to take the time to develop local government bond markets. This takes considerable time, as it is desirable not only to issue a range of bonds with different maturities, but also to be seen to replace them successfully as they mature and as time passes and their duration decreases. The whole market may also need to be tested and proved to be resilient to shocks for confidence in its stability to build. Confidence that the yield curve represents sovereign risk in its purest form, without extraneous technical quirks, can gradually be established in the minds of local bond purchasers. Market participants observing this process being well managed over time are likely to become more confident in the future liquidity of the market, and this should help reduce the cost of issuing for the government (the yields). The end objective is to issue long-term bonds in local currency at low interest rates and with local investors being the main purchasers of the bonds – though external investors may play a major part in providing additional finance and in catalysing the development of such local markets. To achieve most of one's borrowing locally in this way is to reduce susceptibility to external shocks and to join the club of rich countries which issue predominantly in their own currency.

In particular, the growth of a local currency debt market can promote domestic savings and development of the banking sector and other financial intermediaries.[53] The development of a series of government bonds with different maturities creates a 'yield curve' which markets use as a benchmark measure of local sovereign risk. This can then be used as a benchmark for pricing domestic corporate bonds, with these priced at spreads above the sovereign curve. Government (and subsequent corporate) bond issues provide investment vehicles for local pension funds. As maturities are pushed out, this can both foster long-term finance for infrastructure projects and help to stimulate the development of mortgage markets.

Owing debt in local currency, not dollars, also allows a government under financial stress more policy choices beyond the decision to pay or not pay. The cost of financing debt can be instead eroded through local taxes, inflation or devaluation. Local currency debt issuance is

---

[52] Indices are commonly used in investment management to benchmark investment manager performance, but more controversially as we shall discuss later, as proxies for asset classes in asset allocation exercises.

[53] For a recent overview of the stabilising benefits of financial deepening, see Goyal *et al.* (2011).

standard for developed countries because investors trust rich-country governments to respect property rights and not to inflate them away – though such trust can be misplaced, as investors are starting to understand again post-2008 (as they did in the inflationary 1970s). As credit-worthiness improves in developing countries, the same becomes true. A country able to issue substantial amounts in its own currency has passed the most important test of capital market development – a degree of market confidence about its 30-year future which significantly reduces vulnerability to external shocks in the nearer term. There are more policy options available to deal with balance of payments crises as they arise – remembering that investors dislike sudden major loss much more than gradual erosion of value. Figure 2.4 shows the growth of these markets as more countries have taken this lesson on board, as well as showing the overall growth of emerging debt.

In many cases dollar-denominated debt issuance should not be totally abandoned, and in some cases it should continue to be dominant for many years to come. One substantial benefit of issuing long-term dollar bonds is that the action of holders of this type of debt in a crisis does not put downward pressure on the currency. In a balance-of-payments crisis characterised by a weakening currency, holders of dollar debt may be concerned about default risk and sell their bonds, but they do so to other investors in the secondary market, with no foreign exchange transaction. In contrast, external investors in local currency assets (debt, but also equity and even unhedged direct investments) will try to reduce their currency exposure, putting even more downward pressure on that currency. Hence for countries that can take the longer-term view, wean themselves off dollar-denominated debt and develop strong local term savings markets, all well and good – although the transition takes years and should not be rushed due to the risk of an external shock during the process. For others embarking on this course without sufficient resource and resolve, a reversal of fortunes may leave them exposed to currency crisis once again. A strong domestic savings base is particularly

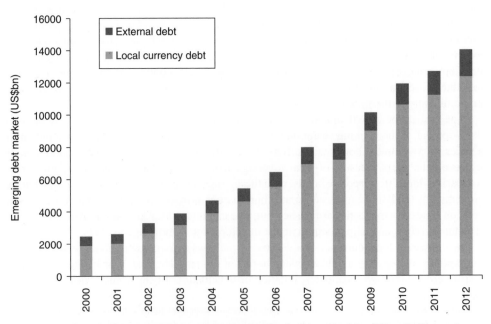

Figure 2.4   Growth of emerging debt markets. Source: Bank of America Merrill Lynch: Size and structure of Global Emerging Markets debt (Jane Brauer)

significant for a country's vulnerability to external shocks. A lack of secondary market liquidity and low domestic investor demand for local bonds can exacerbate a balance of payments crisis. Indeed, having a strong local investor base is a significant watershed, equivalent to the boundary between frontier and emerging market status in equities.

Getting the maturity of liabilities extended is also crucial. The development of long-term dollar bonds – enabling longer-term thinking and investment – was long wished for until they arrived in the late 1980s/early 1990s in the form of Brady bonds. As mentioned, their predecessors were short-term bank loans, which might not be rolled over, or if so only at much higher interest rates, often exacerbating or even creating a balance-of-payments problem for a developing country.

2.5   WHY INVEST IN EMERGING MARKETS?

As with any investment, the reason to invest in emerging markets is to benefit from a combination of future income and capital appreciation. Emerging market economies now constitute the bulk of economic activity on the planet, and for investors to ignore this is to miss out. But the case for investment is not just about return. Emerging markets, through virtue of being different from developed countries, can help diversify risk – indeed, reduce and protect from major risks coming from elsewhere; more on this later.

Investments vary from the highly liquid to the illiquid, with many asset types or asset classes to choose from: sovereign dollar-denominated debt, local money markets, local currency-denominated government bonds, inflation-linked bonds, corporate bonds (already highly significant), equities (shares), small-cap equities, frontier equities, private equity, distressed debt, real estate and infrastructure, to name a few main categories. In many cases investment portfolios can be investment-grade only. They can take local currency exposure or not (if not, currency exposure is still being taken, albeit in, say, the dollar or euro).

Compared to dollar-denominated emerging debt, local currency debt instruments are more exposed to explicit local interest rate dynamics and currency risk. In earlier stages of market development these should be seen as different expressions of the country risk, and as a result investors often might not hedge a currency risk when it is deemed too risky, but rather sell the asset (the bond or equivalent). So the way to manage local currency debt is to be focused on active management of country risk, not just local interest rate dynamics. Then again, in many local emerging debt markets there is a now broad range of instruments to invest in, including the full range of maturities in both domestic and external currency as well as inflation-linked bonds, and a predominantly domestic investor base. The consequence is that whatever one's view there will be a way to express it in the debt market of that country without exiting.

In more recent years there has also been huge growth in corporate bond issuance, offering huge diversification for the investor. Much of this, moreover, is denominated in local currencies, with markets dominated by local investors. Indeed, local currency-denominated corporate debt could soon be the largest debt market in the world (insofar as it is still considered a single market). Financial deepening will no doubt continue in emerging markets as capital markets catch up with the developed world, and approach similar sizes proportionate to GDP.

The fundamental credit-worthiness of many emerging markets is much stronger than in 1990, as should be clear from our brief history. Yet because markets are imperfect, there are information asymmetries, prejudices and agency problems (more on this from Chapter 5 onwards) and returns are often highly attractive – as opportunities have not been properly understood and arbitraged away. Volatilities have reduced since 1990, and risks for many investments have also come down. The prejudices of some create opportunities (market inefficiencies) for others – and as prejudices often only die with their owners, the opportunities are likely to exist for several decades more.

3

The 2008 Credit Crunch and Aftermath

The Five Stages of Grief[1]

(Paper written for Ashmore clients, July 2011)

The well-known Kübler-Ross model of grief has five stages: denial, anger, bargaining, depression and acceptance. Could these five, overlapping, stages be seen in reaction to other psychological shocks, including the prospect of major economic hardships ahead?

The cause of the grief

For there to be a grieving process, there has to be something to grieve. Let us suppose that after three decades of financial deepening, the last of which was excessive, Western Europe and the US now face several years of painful deleveraging. The loss they feel is the death of the levered model, which enabled these developed countries to live beyond their means. Their loss is also a loss of prestige in the world, as their economic models have failed and their policies have created crises. It is a loss which will make the US and Western Europe poorer and more dependent on emerging markets – the part of the world without the 30-year build-up of leverage and without the same problems. National and personal budgets are going to have to be cut. To protect their currencies, several developed economies will need to ask for help from the large surplus reserve countries. Think of the following analogy: many of the developed countries have experienced a death. They have a body on their kitchen floor and there is a lot of blood. Nothing will revive the corpse. We might as economists know how they should react, but… How are they reacting?

Denial: a dead body on the kitchen floor

The UK has its dead body on the kitchen floor, blood everywhere. We are trying to clear up the mess: we can see a policy route to macroeconomic stability and sustainable debt levels which is painful but realistic. In the Eurozone the dead body is not quite as large as in the UK and is around the edge of the room (the Dutch and German parts of the floor are clean). The policy response is akin to covering the body with a sheet and agreeing to deal with it later. Denial is palpable, but the blood is unfortunately spilling out under the sheet and starting to damage Eurozone shoe leather – even threatening a nasty stain on Germany's clean part of the floor. At one level this is not too worrying for Germany, as they have plenty of floor cleaning equipment, but they didn't reckon on cleaning everybody else's part of the floor as well. If they are expected to do that, they need some new rules established. These need to change the antisocial habits (fiscal profligacy, lying about one's numbers) which caused the current (preventable) deaths. And the same old promises to be more careful next time are not good enough. The result is a lot of bickering. The outcome so far has been to come up with larger sheets, without much cleaning up going on. Even with the latest bailout, which buys time, Greece's debt/GDP is unsustainable

---

[1] See disclaimer, p. 235.

under any credible fiscal outcomes without major debt reduction. However, in the US denial is even more pronounced: the cadaver has been placed in a chair, given a cup of coffee and is being engaged in conversation. The US is assumed by many to be zero risk or 'risk free' even when evidence of severe macroeconomic vulnerabilities is plain. In the US especially there are many who think deleveraging and the pain it involves can somehow be avoided. It cannot, and the denial merely allows the problems to fester.

Denial: 'it's just a flesh wound'[2]
Denial is also deviously persistent when faced with the clearest of facts. It morphs into new forms, sidestepping its demise, admitting only the incontrovertible, and then only for a moment and without drawing wider conclusions from the evidence. When faced with a truly awful prospect we explore and then cling to any theory or hope that reality may be different. To the untrained eye it may not be obvious if death has occurred or not. Countries rarely cease to exist, even if they can experience long periods of serious trauma. All financial crises have banks at their core and the normal response is to nationalise them so as to recapitalise quickly and get credit flowing again. Fiscal authorities did not fully capitalise banks in the US though, and Bernanke has instead adopted highly unorthodox policies to help push up asset prices so as to stop and reverse bank balance sheet losses and allow banks to issue new paper and recapitalise themselves. The Fed's two policy tools to achieve this are firstly quantitative easing and secondly rhetoric – talking up the economy to avoid loss of confidence and the risk of a slump-inducing investment strike. In other words, rhetoric is about hiding the full truth for fear the listener will not be able to cope with it, as well as in hope that there may be an improvement. Fiscal policy has also been used to break the news gently to the relatives. Indeed, we can think of the US economy as a patient who, after the Lehman crash, was rushed to hospital and is now on life support: quantitative easing is the oxygen and fiscal policy the drip keeping the patient alive. Nearly three years on, we are removing the drip and have also started to turn off the oxygen. The question is: are we taking the patient off life support because she is healthy or because the equipment is not capable of functioning anymore?

Anger
Greeks are angry with their system; with the lack of fairness whereby the rich seem not to pay taxes. They are antagonistic to their political elite, and many are determined not to co-operate with any austerity measures. Implementation of the fiscal programme in Greece is going to prove extraordinarily difficult. Political anger all over Western Europe and the US is rising, leading to greater myopia and political risk. An angry population is one less likely to co-operate, more likely to smash things, including, if proposed by people they hate, policies they know to be sensible. Blame is directed at bankers, but also to other countries. Eurozone tensions between member states and between their populations are rising, limiting the policy freedom of leaders to reach practical solutions. If we define political risk as politics or policies which adversely affect the economic returns to the foreign investor, then political risk is rising rapidly. With this comes not just the prospect of social unrest and strikes but also maybe more extremism in voting intentions, protectionism and capital controls (not least ones which may be used to 'bail in' foreign holders of Eurozone sovereign bonds facing restructuring). Emerging markets, though innocent

---

[2] The Black Knight's response to Arthur, who has just cut off both his arms, in the film *Monty Python and the Holy Grail*.

bystanders, could also be lashed out at, not least as they seem not to share the loss. They would be wise to create some distance as a result – which they are doing in the form of greater south-south trade and investment, but most importantly by moving away from export dependence towards more domestic demand-driven models of growth.

Bargaining
Bargaining takes the form of offering commitments to stave off loss, which may in any case be inevitable. In September 2008 US Treasury Secretary Hank Paulson went on one knee to implore House Speaker Nancy Pelosi not to blow up his bank rescue deal. The administration was taking fast decisions in a sense of crisis at the time. The aggressive anti-Chinese rhetoric of the past has given way to a conversation of equals (please don't sell Treasuries). Today, pumping more and more money into Greece does not resolve their fiscal imbalances, but buys time. Pumping more money in when fiscal reform is not forthcoming is ostensibly a waste of money, and may be motivated more by political concerns outside Greece than objective economic criteria. Bargaining is an exercise in fantasy about what might be rather than what is likely. Many of the policy responses in the US and Europe in the last three years have been myopic, lacking overall vision.

Depression
Depression involves the giving up of hope. It is the state of great emotional distress. It involves introspection, lack of activity and apathy. Affections are let go and those griev-ing become distant and non-communicative. An economy in depression is one without investment, without hope, without jobs. Unfortunately, depression can last a long time. Moreover, trying to cheer up someone in depression too early may be pointless as it is an important process of reassessment. In an economy, assets need to be written off before new value opportunities can emerge. Deleveraging needs to be substantially complete before substantive sustainable economic recovery can begin.

Acceptance
Acceptance is the final stage of grieving when people come to terms with the new reality. It is the starting point for the rebuilding of lives which remain. Acceptance for Western Europe and the US will come when electoral expectations are realistic, enabling policy-makers to enact structural reforms necessary to delever, and to prevent further imbalances building again. Full acceptance may never happen of course, and even substantial accept-ance is likely to take years.

Where are we now – still in denial?
The Kübler-Ross model has been criticised for being too simplistic, and the stages can over-lap. Such criticism is all the more valid when we think of the economic challenges in the developed world today. But it may help us sift through some of the emotional responses of markets. Markets are not always perfect and do suffer from systemic biases. With different people at different emotional stages, markets can display a combination of all five stages at the same time. But perhaps denial is the most dominant characteristic of developed markets in this crisis so far. Some countries have been through more loss within living memory and are better at grieving, but not so in Western Europe and the US … this may take a long time. Then again, hope springs eternal and there are more positive scenarios – did that body just twitch?

As of early 2014 there is still huge concern among macroeconomists, central bankers and other policymakers – much of it glossed over in public statements – about the economic risks facing the US and Western Europe. The most damaging scenario remains continued deflation, and at worst depression, involving as it does mass misery. Volatile currency movements and major downward adjustments in the deficit currencies may also be associated with global rebalancing. A mishandling of monetary policy could easily lead to inflation – and while some inflation may be desirable to erode debt burdens, it could get out of hand. The biggest risks are clearly in the US and Western Europe.

A number of North Atlantic countries (I have termed them HIDCs, Heavily Indebted Developed Countries)[3] face a painful, wealth-destroying process of deleveraging which will take many years. Among their conclusions Reinhart and Rogoff (2009) find that after a financial crisis the ratio of public debt to GDP rises by an average 86%, growth takes 4.4 years to recover, and real estate takes an average of 6 years. Banking crisis is always at the heart of the problem, but real estate often is too. However, this crisis involves many countries and is large – larger than anything since the 1930s. So perhaps we should not be looking at averages, but at what happened in the 1930s – which was far worse than after 2008 (at least up to early 2014). US GDP halved in four years. Net investment fell 95% in three years[4] and unemployment went from 3% to about 25% in the same period, hitting 50% in urban areas. Growth did not recover until 1941 – largely due to the economic stimulus provided by the build-up to and engagement in World War II – and equities did not recovery their pre-crash peak until 1954. And … there was a Second World War. In other words, we should not be complacent. There was much talk of 'green shoots' in 1930. People often believe what they want to believe, at least for as long as they can.[5]

The good news is that we have two things that they didn't in the 1930s. We have the emerging markets as a potential source of global aggregate demand to supplement US and European consumption while US households deleverage, and to keep commodity prices up; and Keynes invented macroeconomics.

The 2008 and still current superbubble is the result, on the one hand, of lax regulation driven by too much faith in laissez-faire. This, combined with securitisation and the absence of proper self-regulatory systems, led to massive leverage, and to rich countries gorging themselves on too much debt. On the other hand, the crisis was caused by global imbalances whereby emerging market savings were exported to the US (and UK and a few others) through massive build-up of central bank reserves. This pushed the entire US yield curve down, resulting in inappropriate discount factors and measures of risk off which other investments were valued and benchmarked.

3.1   BANK REGULATION FAILURE

Let us quickly review the history of investment banks.[6] Before the latter half of the 19th century, the norm was for company charters granted by the state to allow certain types of activities, with other activities deemed extralegal. With the erosion of this focus in favour of

---

[3] This follows the convention of the IMF/World Bank debt relief programme centred on so-called HIPCs – Heavily Indebted Poor Countries.

[4] Kuznets' data reproduced by Keynes in his *General Theory*.

[5] See Galbraith (1961).

[6] For an institutional history of the investment bank, readers are directed to Morrison and Wilhelm (2007).

greater corporate and individual economic freedom came the ability for capital to combine and recombine in new ways. There was a rise in prosperity, and the conditions were set for the growth and greater sophistication of financial markets which followed. In the United States, in particular, the unfettered agglomeration of companies led to not only greater economic efficiency, but also a concentration of economic power and wealth.

Investment banking grew out of merchant banks, originally international merchants whose competitiveness relied heavily on reputation, who owned the capital deployed, and whose effectiveness relied on strong intra-firm trust. Foreign agents were often family members. The profitability of merchant and then investment banks came from their ability to collect information (assessments of credit-worthiness) on a wide range of economic actors and then pass that on to clients indirectly, via an underwriting or other endorsement, backed by the credibility of their own reputation. A damaged reputation would mean they would no longer be entrusted with confidential information and their endorsements would be discounted. Thus their services would become less useful to potential clients. A reputation for not keeping promises struck disaster for a bank, so they could be relied upon to maintain a reputation for consistent honesty and integrity. To achieve this meant employees needed to think about the long-term reputation of the firm above the benefits of any particular transaction – they had to take a long-term view of what was best for the bank shareholders. The internal incentives to achieve this require management incentives to be closely aligned with, or identical to, the interests of bank shareholders, and for them to have tight controls on the activities of other employees.

Much of the information possessed by these banks was tacit: informal knowledge and specific to the partners.[7] The history of regulation of investment banks is largely one of industry self-regulation: formal regulation cannot access the tacit knowledge and informal norms of behaviour which accompany it. Attempts by the state to enforce tacit contracts are vulnerable to rent seeking and so the well-functioning investment bank is a better alternative for the self-enforcement of tacit contracts.

Because of the benefits of a large network of contacts and confidential information, there are great economies of scale for investment banks, and strong barriers to entry for new would-be competitors. In the first half of the 20th century, because of their dominance in allocating capital across the US economy, there was a backlash against the banks. In part as a result of public outrage at the market abuses uncovered by the Pecora Commission, the 1933 US Securities Acts included the Glass–Steagall Act legislation separating investment and commercial banks. The anti-bank sentiment culminated in the Medina 1950–1953 antitrust trial, in which the US Justice Department charged 17 investment banks with monopoly practices. No convincing evidence of collusion was found, however, and the suit was dismissed with prejudice by the judge, Harold Medina. The cycle subsequently changed direction again: the trial's failure to prove wrongdoing by the banks was followed by a new era of belief in the beneficence of financial markets and their relatively unfettered growth.

This growth in turn adapted and evolved in response to two significant changes: new computer technology and developments in finance economics. Tacit information gave way to mathematical models. The computer displaced trust in many financial transactions: it made the alternative to trusting relationships much cheaper. These developments allowed the commoditisation of financial markets. They eroded the dependence on tacit knowledge

---

[7] The term tacit knowledge, meaning knowledge acquired in practice and only partly communicable, is from Polanyi (1958).

required in much of banking, and reduced the barriers to entry. This changed the incentives and behaviour of banks' management and staff and led to greater competition and risk-taking. The institutional form of investment banks also changed in response to these rapid changes in the marketplace, with all the main US investment banks turning from partnerships (an institutional form conducive to the preservation and passing on of tacit information from generation to generation) to listed companies (an institutional form enabling rapid expansion of the capital base to take advantage of the new economies of scale and commoditisation of financial markets). It was just not possible for the privately held partnerships to expand rapidly enough to maintain market share in the new markets without access to new equity capital via a public listing. The last two investment banks to make this transition were Goldman Sachs (in 1999) and Lazard Frères (in 2005): a reflection of their relative strength in the advisory businesses which benefit most from nurturing tacit knowledge.

This change in the capital structures of banks was in effect a trade-off: more short-term profitability – indeed survival, given what competitor banks were doing – at the expense of the longer-term ability to incentivise management. Management incentives were no longer aligned with the long-term interests of shareholders (they were no longer one and the same individuals). Further, inside the bank, management could no longer as easily control staff, as the size and complexity of the bank meant senior management could not oversee all transactions. And this was exacerbated by the scale and bureaucracy inside these banks.

Deregulation then followed in the mid-1990s. Despite Arthur Levitt becoming head of the SEC in 1993 and arguing loudly for more regulation, the ideological laissez-faire trend was against him, and his budget was cut. Deregulation continued apace, and Glass–Steagall was repealed in 1999.

3.1.1   Sub-prime

The US sub-prime cancer started when securitisation changed the incentives of lenders, reducing their need to understand the credit risk of the borrowers. Loan originators packaged and passed on the risk, so no longer had the same incentive to select only credit-worthy borrowers. Regulation did not keep up. Fallacies of composition were ignored. The volume of sub-prime contracts inflated prices enough to alter likely future correlations assumed fixed, and specifically affected the likelihood of house prices falling and defaults rising across many states at the same time in a way not experienced before.

Housing, as in many crises in the past, played a key role, as Rajan (2010) and others have pointed out. In place of a European-style welfare state, US social stability has historically been achieved through the tax code, but also more than in Europe through upward social mobility and rising income levels. Yet over the last three decades much of American society has experienced static or declining real incomes and lack of upward social mobility. A benefit for the Clinton administration was that, while raising incomes was politically and economically near impossible to achieve, raising consumption was not. But it has the same political result – in the short to medium term at least – of keeping the voters content.

Add Federal Reserve Chairman Greenspan's policy actions: after the dotcom bubble burst in 2000 – a result of overinvestment in internet and new technology stocks, some of which acquired enormous market capitalisations, yet no earnings, let alone profits – he cut interest rates to stimulate the economy. He expected investment to take off, but it did not, as there had been overinvestment prior to the bubble bursting.[8] Instead a lot of the new credit went into housing. The strong demand for housing was in part due to money illusion: people remember the nominal prices of houses more than other goods over long periods, giving them the impression of appreciation when in real terms prices may not have gone up.

There is an observed positive relationship between house prices and consumption. There are several possible explanations, but the most accepted is that of a wealth effect. As house prices move up relative to incomes, this gives the house owner the impression that their net wealth has increased and that in turn leads to higher spending as they cash in.[9] This is particularly intuitive when remortgaging can be achieved so as to release more cash for consumption. The housing boom thus started in the early 1990s, and a series of government initiatives and bailouts helped to boost home ownership.

Unlike other housing markets displaying bubble-type price appreciations, including those in the UK, Spain, Ireland and Australia, the housing market in the US has an added systemically important feature: efforts by successive administrations to keep house prices rising have taken the form of more credit to housing being provided by the quasi-public entities 'Fannie Mae' and 'Freddie Mac'.[10] Problems in the housing market were met with more credit being allowed by the government – government-imposed limits on these agencies were relaxed. These agencies were in effect used to bail out the housing market. These were both then taken over by the federal government (they went into conservatorship) in September 2008 after they suffered major mortgage-related losses. Their liabilities became public sector liabilities – these agencies themselves required bailing out.

Then we have rating agencies, which understated the default risks on mortgage-related financial instruments and those that structured and sold them (the investment banks) and those that underwrote them (the large insurer American International Group, AIG, in particular). They overlooked a fallacy of composition in a big way – believing that risk was additive on a large scale in a similar way to the small scale.[11] But at the large scale macroeconomic factors also come into play. The rating agencies believed quite erroneously that low correlations between housing default rates across the country were stable, irrespective of the amount of paper issued and its macroeconomic impact, or the incentive created by their high demand to originate poor-quality mortgages. Mortgages were bundled and then used to collateralise legal entities called collateralised debt obligations (CDOs). A CDO is an asset-backed security – the first one created in 1987 – which finances purchases of assets (in this case mortgages) through issues of various tranches of debt with different seniorities. Holders of the more senior debt are safer in case of defaults than more junior debt holders, who lose all the value of their investment before the next tranche holders lose any. Rating agencies rated each tranche, giving each what was seen as the appropriate rating. These rating agency

---

[8] There is often little effect of interest rates on investment in practice or theory – see for example Dixit and Pindyck (1994), p13. There are also those who see low interest rates following a dearth of investment opportunities: Martin Wolf, *Financial Times*, 15 December 2010 quoting McKinsey Global Institute (2010).

[9] An alternative explanation is that both house price and consumption increases are the result of a common factor, such as rising productivity. Testing which is a better explanation through different effects on older house-owners and younger house-renters is inconclusive.

[10] The Federal National Mortgage Association (FNMA) and the Federal Home Loan Mortgage Corporation (FHLMC). These institutions borrowed from bond markets at close to the same interest rates as the federal government as they were perceived to have implicit guarantees from the government.

[11] For an account of this, see Tett (2009).

endorsements enabled the investment banks, who structured the CDOs and more complex products from them, to sell them on to end investors.

Incentives of the mortgage originators became corrupted. There is a well-established branch of economics called principal agent theory which studies the behaviour of economic actors with different incentives and information.[12] If a principal (think of an employer) cannot observe the effort of the agent (think of their employee), then the employee may shirk. Principal agent theory analyses this type of problem to help design incentive employment contracts. In other contexts the theory is useful to design optimal regulation structures. In the case of sub-prime mortgages, information asymmetry is created by the process of securitisation. Sub-prime mortgages were mortgages for people, often on low incomes and with limited credit history, less likely to be able to repay than 'prime' borrowers. Before mortgages were securitised they stayed on the balance sheet of the lending bank or mortgage lender. Lenders who originated the loans had a strong incentive to make sure they only lent to credit-worthy householders expected to repay. However, securitisation broke the relationship of trust between borrower and lender. As the mortgage lender could sell all their mortgages, as soon as originated, to a third party – an investment bank who would create a CDO out of them – they had little incentive to check the credit quality of the borrower. Indeed, they had an incentive not to check. The quicker they could generate mortgages and pass them on, the more money they made: taking the time to check credit quality and perhaps having to reject a mortgage proposal inhibited the profitability of the business. The whole exercise was not, as advertised, a way of apportioning risk more efficiently to those who could bear it, but one of concealing or not revealing underlying risks and passing them on to those who could not bear them. The bundling of mortgages and other commoditisation of financial risks suffers from the problems Hayek associated with central planning: the flip side of the economies of scale from centralisation is inevitable information loss and distortion of incentives.

Add to this overdependence on ratings. It seemed fairly obvious to me and my colleagues at Ashmore at the time that some of the structured products being sold around 2004 and 2005 with massive leverage were destined to collapse – rating models were clearly nonsense to any reasonably intelligent bystander. Rating agency incentives were distorted by being paid by issuers. One of the clues to potential disaster was the almost non-existent questioning by buyers of the end structured products concerning the nature of the underlying collateral, beyond its rating that is. Amazingly, though, while some investment banks appear to have understood the risks, including JP Morgan (according to Gillian Tett, 2009), others did not, or seemed not to care. Underwriters pride themselves on understanding risk better than bankers, and arguably for the most part they do. AIG, however, which took on the bulk of super-senior tranches (the top-rated debt issued by CDOs more senior than AAA-rated tranches) from the investment banks, appears not to have done. So the engine of the bubble was fuelled. Where were the regulators? Unfortunately, like a lot of financial market participants, regulators were focused on security-specific risk but not enough on the broader picture of systemic risk. Worse, they embedded rating agency assessments into their own regulatory rules (e.g. Basle and Solvency regulations).

---

[12] An information asymmetry occurs when parties to an economic contract or transaction have different levels of relevant information.

3.2   THE 2008 CRISIS

The problems in the US sub-prime mortgage market became clear by early 2006[13] – the default rates were bound to rise and cause ripple effects across many of the asset-backed securities and CDOs which had been structured. These structured products had been created by investment banks and sold on to institutional investors all over the world. However, the pipeline of new mortgages meant that investment banks also held many of these mortgage liabilities on their balance sheets at any one time. Although some started to reduce their mortgage exposures in late 2006, others continued structuring and selling on mortgages even when they realised a catastrophe was in the making.

US home sales fell steeply in 2007 and house prices fell nationwide for the first time since 1991. Several mortgage origination companies started to go bust from the start of the year, with the largest sub-prime originator, New Century Financial, filing for bankruptcy in April. In February HSBC announced its US mortgage losses had reached $10.5 billion. In June Bear Stearns suspended (i.e. stopped meeting investor redemption requests for) two of its CDO hedge funds invested in mortgage products. As perception of the problem spread, various long/short hedge funds started to experience severe losses from August as market dynamics changed. Also in August BNP Paribas suspended three funds invested in sub-prime debt due to absence of market liquidity, followed by others. The US Federal Reserve, European Central Bank (ECB), Bank of Japan and central banks of Canada and Australia injected liquidity into the banking system in a co-ordinated intervention. In September US unemployment data showed major job losses, bankruptcies and emergency liquidity measures continued and the Federal Reserve started to cut its main interest rate, warning of major falls in house prices. More cuts in interest rates would follow.

At the start of 2008 the stock market started to turn down. In March Bear Stearns collapsed and was bought, with the encouragement of the Federal Reserve, by JP Morgan. Losses mounted in banks globally, and as CDO defaults increased over the coming months, monoline insurers (specialist insurers against bond defaults) were all downgraded from their AAA status, preventing them from writing further business – they all went bust over 2008 and 2009.

On September 7th Fannie Mae and Freddie Mac, which by that time either owned or underwrote (guaranteed) about half the US mortgage market, went into conservatorship – i.e. they were nationalised – adding their liabilities to US sovereign debt. On September 14th Merrill Lynch was sold to Bank of America. On the 15th, and after last-ditch attempts failed to save the bank or sell it, as had been done with Bear Stearns and Merrill Lynch, Lehman Brothers filed for bankruptcy. This event precipitated enormous uncertainty in financial markets and was a watershed for the crisis.[14] The interconnectedness of banks meant that the failure of any one of them had widespread and complex ripple effects. Banks no longer trusted each other and the interbank market seized up. After this, new liquidity for banks had to be provided by central banks.

The next day, September 16th, a money market fund called the Reserve Primary Fund (money market funds were sold to investors as proxies for cash) 'broke the buck' – the value of an investment in this fund fell to below the amount invested. Then on September 17th the

---

[13] Robert Shiller warned of a US housing bubble in 2005 sufficient to cause a global recession and Ashmore's Investment Committee first formally discussed the sub-prime problem in depth in early 2006 – i.e. by that time it was perceived as a threat to global financial markets, not just a problem for the US housing market.

[14] Which is not to say that bailing out Lehman Brothers would have led to a better outcome.

Federal Reserve bailed out AIG by lending it $85 billion to stay afloat. With panic the order of the day, Federal Reserve Chairman Ben Bernanke, who with Treasury Secretary Paulson was arguing for a $700 billion bailout fund for banks, told lawmakers on the 18th 'If we don't do this, we may not have an economy on Monday'. Also in September, Washington Mutual's banking business was absorbed by JP Morgan. Wachovia's – the fourth largest bank in the country – went to Wells Fargo in October.

The US Administration announced the US$700 billion Troubled Assets Relief Program (TARP) in October to help bail out banks by buying their distressed assets. $250 billion of this money was used later in the month to inject money into US banks, and in November it was announced that the remaining funds would not be used to buy distressed assets as originally planned but to bail out financial sector firms. Also in November, the US government injected further capital into Citigroup (whose share price had dropped precipitously), bringing that total bailout to $45 billion.

Central banks of the US, UK, Sweden, Switzerland, China, Canada and the ECB cut interest rates in a co-ordinated action on October 8th. The Federal Reserve started to announce plans to provide large quantities of liquidity to banks, money market funds, Fannie Mae and Freddie Mac and others which it did not sterilise. Before this 'quantitative easing' the balance sheet of the Federal Reserve amounted to between $700 and $800 billion in Treasury notes. In November 2008 the Federal Reserve started to buy $600 billion mortgage-backed securities. Further buying of bank debt and Treasuries led to the Fed's balance sheet swelling to over $3.7 trillion by October 2013. The Bank of England has followed suit in quantitative easing, as has in effect the European Central Bank.

3.3   DEPRESSION RISK

After Lehman Brothers failed there was a sharp fall in trust between financial institutions, and hence an increase in the severity of the financial crisis. The priority under such conditions is to stop a cascade of unmanaged and sudden bankruptcies. Banks are always central to the problem, and action to prevent a cascade of bankruptcies may include organising bank mergers, injections of debt and/or equity capital from the government or central bank, or seizure (majority public sector equity ownership plus the exercise of management control). The banking system provides the lifeblood of credit to a capitalist economy. If broken, it needs to be fixed as a priority of crisis management so that companies reliant on bank credit can continue to function. One may think of a banking sector as a glass of water. For liquidity to flow over the rim into the economy, the glass has to be full. Filling it up halfway – recapitalising it – does not have any impact. The $1 trillion which the administration and Congress put in the banks initially was thus not effective insofar as the shortage was estimated to be nearer $2 trillion.

Ben Bernanke, student of the Depression, as chairman of the Federal Reserve thus had to cope with the banks in the absence of more resources from fiscal authorities. Federal Reserve policy has been confusing to a lot of observers, but perhaps not if one views it from the perspective of trying to recapitalise banks, in the context of a Federal Reserve chairman fearful of deflation and depression, and driven by the realisation that we may have an investment strike under conditions of accumulating uncertainty (as per Keynes's analysis).

The Fed's objective, according to this interpretation, was to push up asset prices through quantitative easing, and so to stop losses on bank balance sheets – indeed, to reverse them.

Pushing up asset prices also enables banks to recapitalise themselves through issuing paper into the environment of rising asset demand. In order to help the banks further, the buying of bonds in the quantitative easing programme was designed to engineer a steepening of the yield curve – a steep yield curve means a government bond market with substantially higher interest rates for longer than shorter duration bonds. Banks can make money from this by borrowing money with short-term repayment schedules and lending longer-term. In a situation of interest rates being artificially low in general (a result of global imbalances and the continued holding and purchase of US Treasuries by emerging market central banks), this was relatively easy for the Fed. Although yields fell across the whole curve, the curve steepening led to long-term borrowing costs higher than they might have been, putting further pressure on the housing market, but that was a medium-term problem, not one of crisis management.

Some of the critics of quantitative easing argue that it has been ineffective, but that judgement should depend on what it is designed for. The extra liquidity drives up asset prices, but a lot of it ends up back at the central bank in the form of excess reserves of US$1.8 trillion (bank deposits at the Federal Reserve in excess of the level required to meet reserve requirements). Hence it does not do much to stimulate the economy. But it does help to recapitalise banks, which want to deposit their cash reserves at the central bank to bolster their capital and liquidity ratios, rather than lend them to consumers and businesses.

Another tool the Federal Reserve has is rhetoric: the objective being to convince markets that everything is fine, and recovery on its way, so that businesses will perceive less uncertainty and invest. One suspects the Federal Reserve has itself been highly fearful of depression, and yet the ability to convince markets otherwise is crucial to avoid it. Ben Bernanke's job has been to convince markets that the emperor has wonderful new clothes. It was thus favourable when many market participants worried about imminent (as opposed to medium-term) inflation soon after quantitative easing started – a sign that the rhetoric is working. One might adapt the words of Franklin D. Roosevelt to summarise Bernanke's policy, thus: 'The only thing to hope for is hope itself.'[15] But some problems do not have solutions. I believe Bernanke's post-2008 policy of a combination of quantitative easing and rhetoric has been the best course of action, but that does not guarantee its effectiveness.

So the strategy is that by recapitalising banks, they will eventually start lending, uncertainty will reduce and investment pick up. Growth will be below par for a few years as deleveraging in the housing and consumer sectors takes place, but consumption will eventually return and once again be a major driver of growth. In the short term, however, asset prices have arguably not reflected the underlying state of the economy. They have been artificially inflated through quantitative easing and are at risk of collapse until the real economy picks up sufficiently to justify them. We are not sure, but maybe the emperor has no clothes. Even if he doesn't, it may still be fine, just so long as nobody points it out too loudly.

There are inflation risks in the US should there be a currency crash, and in the medium term if it is the chosen route to erode debts or if exit from quantitative easing is botched; but in the first few years after 2008 the risk has been still very much a deflationary one. Quantitative easing is not necessarily inflationary, but its exit might be. When banks start lending again, this may lead to a rapid tightening of monetary policy. If so, the policy sequence should ideally be first to sell back the bonds held by the central bank to the market, and when this is complete, start to raise interest rates. Though in a boom this sequence may not be problematic, the difficulty arises of what to do if the bonds are illiquid. One option might

---

[15] From Franklin Delano Roosevelt's inauguration speech: 'The only thing to fear is fear itself.'

be to swap long-dated for shorter-dated bonds that are allowed to roll off, though tightening action may be required sooner than allowed by such a run-off. Alternatively, the Treasury could buy the bonds, but this would have to be funded through fiscal policy, so is likely to be unpalatable; or nothing could be done, risking inflation; or interest rates could be raised while the central bank still holds the bonds. This last option may be fine in small doses, but as interest rates rise, so the value of the bonds will fall, risking balance sheet losses for the central bank. If the losses become big enough, this could threaten the Fed's credibility and require a taxpayer bailout. Given these options, the credibility of the Fed may come into question even before any tightening of monetary policy is required, the incentive simply being to allow this inflation to occur and erode the value of government debt.

3.3.1   Reducing the debt

For many HIDCs it is politically unpalatable to grow one's way out of the national debt overhang – paying back debt little by little over decades, but at the cost of reduced investment and consumption. The likelihood is that a mixture of three strategies will at first prevail. First is some combination of structural and fiscal measures to reduce the government budget deficit and increase the average multiplier on government expenditure. The desired combination of these policies is hotly contended as major distributive consequences arise. Second is financial repression – defined as any policy which captures domestic savings to fund the government, and does so at lower cost than otherwise possible. This takes the form of regulators incentivising/forcing pension funds, insurance companies and banks to buy the government's debt. It was extremely effective after World War II. Third is to convince foreign investors that there is no problem and that government debt is safe, encouraging them to buy it at low interest rates too. Looking tough fiscally and keeping a high credit rating is essential for this.

For as long as the government can sell its debt at very low interest rates, fine. Should this stop, however, another tactic might make more sense. Let us say sufficient growth occurs to cause some inflation, and higher interest rates are expected. Markets may take the view that the government must increase interest rates in order to stem inflation, but that this may reduce credit-worthiness as the interest cost of servicing the debt (which has to be replaced when bonds mature with more expensive debt at the new higher interest rates) becomes unsustainable. Hence, alternatively, they may suspect that interest rates will not be raised sufficiently to control inflation. A central bank, faced with such a market reaction function, may choose not to raise interest rates very much. A period of inflation, as in the 1970s, is a convenient way to erode the debt, but it does make it difficult to sell any debt at less than interest rates which compensate for the inflation – so an inflationary spiral of expectations can take hold quite rapidly if mishandled. Inflation can, however, be used to erode the debt stock over, say, a decade. Then it may be possible, as Federal Reserve Chairman Paul Volcker and other central bankers did at the end of the 1970s and beginning of the 1980s, to tighten monetary policy hard – the reduced debt stock (in real terms) no longer causing huge concerns about debt sustainability. A period of high interest rates to kill inflation and re-establish central bank anti-inflation credibility can then allow interest rates to come down again, ending the cycle. So, will there be inflation or not? It may occur if a combination of structural/fiscal adjustment and financial repression do not do the trick, or if there is a bond crisis for some other reason such that the government faces problems refinancing itself at low interest rates.

Financial repression

Financial repression describes any policy which captures domestic savings in order to fund the government, and at lower cost than otherwise possible. It is a stealthy way to tax savers and investors, with consequent distortions. It includes policies which are ostensibly for other purposes. The main types of financial repression are interest rate caps on private sector lending; regulations which incentivise the purchase of government bonds; the use of moral suasion to achieve the same result; directed lending to the government; the banning of certain other investments; tax incentives and restrictions on cross-border flows. Financial repression has been common in emerging markets as well as in developed markets as a means to reduce debt burdens after World War II. Post-2008, developed countries with unhealthy debt burdens are most incentivised to use financial repression measures to help capture more domestic savings for themselves and reduce the cost of their government borrowing. If they can borrow at less than the rate of inflation, then over time they can erode the real value of the debt burden. The challenge is to sustain a modest but not too high inflation rate and prevent markets from demanding higher returns to compensate for inflation.

The widespread use by regulators of ratings which over-rate developed countries versus emerging ones is a foundation. In the EU, Basle II, Basle III and Solvency II regulations force captive institutional investors to concentrate their assets in Eurozone sovereign bonds beyond levels which otherwise would occur, and indeed beyond levels which otherwise might be considered prudent. Basle II and III dictate different levels of provisioning for assets on bank balance sheets. They use sovereign ratings to do this and, by mandating much higher provisioning, discriminate against government bonds of emerging market countries. Solvency II is designed to reduce insurance company insolvency through a number of measures, and similarly forces greater concentration of insurance sector assets in Eurozone sovereign bonds. Where Solvency II is also being applied to pension funds – which have much longer liabilities – the distortion is even worse, constituting not only a tax on pensioners but also an increase in the risks to their future incomes. Future major macroeconomic risks in the Eurozone may be highly correlated, and from a macroprudential point of view, forcing domestic savings into similar (and similarly currently highly rated) EU sovereign bonds does not look like prudence. The macroprudential motive and the motive for cheap accessible financing for the government are in conflict.

3.3.2 Deleveraging is not an emerging market problem

The credit crunch is fundamentally a problem of excess leverage in developed countries. This excess leverage was built up because risk perceptions were artificially low, in part due to emerging market savings being built up by central banks after the Asian crisis of 1997/8 and then invested in the US, so pushing down the US yield curve. This is the very opposite in the emerging world, where risk perception is higher and leverage did not become anything like as excessive. The deleveraging process can only be a major problem where there is excess leverage to start with, and it is fundamentally therefore a developed world problem. Emerging markets suffer from collateral damage because they have economic links with credit crunch countries, but they don't suffer from the credit crunch disease itself, and the problems they do have are easier to solve.[16]

Across Latin America, Russia and non-Japan Asia, banking systems faced no systemic failures in 2008, in stark contrast to the US and Europe. Collateral damage, however, took four principal forms, the first two acute:

1. Cross-border capital slowed to a trickle.
2. Export market demand fell for developing countries exporting to the developed world.
3. Uncertainty rose, as nobody knew what might blow up next, and this affected consumers and investors temporarily in some otherwise healthy economies.
4. The currencies of countries whose citizens have liquid assets abroad often rise when a crisis strikes at home.[17]

We shall now examine each of these problems in more detail, using examples from Brazil and China to illustrate what happened.

If we think about the first and third of these problems, it is convenient to take Brazil as an example (these were the two main problems facing the country). Brazil is a closed economy, more closed than the United States, and while its export destinations experienced problems and this form of collateral damage was of some consequence, the main problem, although short-lived, was cross-border finance drying up. There was also uncertainty over how policy-makers in the developed world were going to react to the banking sector crisis in their own countries, and this led initially in Brazil, as elsewhere, to economic decisions being delayed. The combination of these two factors caused a reduction in industrial production, unemployment and a reduction in consumption. Interest rates were cut from January 2009, in line with what was going on in the developed world, but more as a prudent measure than as a result of the domestic economic cycle.[18] It is remarkable that in this global crisis emerging markets cut interest rates so uniformly. This was the first time that this has been the case: emerging markets behaved as one expects developed markets to behave when faced with an external shock. Indeed, with the bulk of local stocks and bonds now owned by local institutional investors, the normal pattern has developed across emerging markets that when there is a sudden negative event, local investors switch from equities into bonds and thus bond markets often rally. This is a break from the past, when foreign money dominated and would leave all the local asset markets en masse.

Following the 2008 credit crunch, events in Brazil were very different from those in 2002 described in Chapter 1. There was not the same sense of home-grown crisis or investor concerns about sovereign credit-worthiness. Brazil was self-confident, perhaps even complacent. It did not think it had any of the major problems facing the United States or Europe. When US banks stopped renewing their loans to Brazil at the time of the Lehman Brothers collapse

---

[16] This is generally understood and appreciated in academic circles even if not by financial advisers.

[17] For example, in 1914 at the outbreak of WWI sterling and the French franc rallied (the dollar fell).

[18] Brazil's central bank interest rate decision body, COPOM, cut interest rates initially by 100bp to 12.75% and the meeting minutes refer to the concern of committee members that '… the consolidation of restrictive financial conditions for a longer period should exert a significant contraction effect over demand and, throughout time, a relevant deflation pressure…' In fact such deflation did not occur in Brazil, but that does not argue against the good sense of the decision at the time.

in September 2008, Brazil had over $200 billion in reserves, a level it crossed in June 2008 – more than enough to protect the economy from any external shock.

Faced with a temporary reduction in cross-border finance, a government may naturally consider substituting that finance from domestic resources. That is what several emerging countries did after 2008. What this means is replacing lines of credit to Brazilian exporters, which takes time and is disruptive in the short term. A couple of decades ago, many countries had national export credit guarantee departments and various government-sponsored measures for promoting international trade and financing. Brazil was no exception. The growth of international finance over the last 20 years has made many of these measures redundant, but they could have been resuscitated. It is also the case, however, that Brazilian banks were well capitalised, and they moved into the void left by US and European banks.

After September 2008 there was a major reduction in international dollar liquidity. The US Federal Reserve first extended swap lines to G7 central banks and then, in October 2009, $30 billion lines each to the systematically important economies (and important to the US given the amount of dollars they held) of Brazil, Mexico, South Korea and Singapore. This move was both beneficial to the dollar-strapped recipient countries and self-interested, as without them these countries might have felt it necessary to sell significant amounts of their US Treasury holdings (and Korea had already started to do this). Major selling by a few central banks might then have caused concerns about the dollar among a wider group of central banks, leading to further dollar sales. Such possible concerted selling by central banks risked becoming a flood, and while a fall in the dollar would not have created major problems, a crash (a rapid move of 30% or more in a few days) was possible. Such currency weakness may have unsettled efforts to stabilise the US banking system, for which confidence and stability was deemed necessary.

So in late 2008, Brazilian exporters faced short-term disruption and great uncertainty as to the global future: that was the problem of collateral damage facing Brazil. Yet because there was no substantial adjustment needed in what is a largely closed economy, the business cycle associated with this external shock was always likely to be short-lived (which it was – about a year). And this is in contrast to the problems of an HIDC deleveraging itself, which take many years if not decades to resolve.

China exemplifies the second form of collateral damage: that of a fall in export market demand from the developed world. As with Brazil's foreign bank flow problems, this problem is quite distinct from the credit crunch and HIDC deleveraging. China has two problems: a medium-term and a short-term one. The medium-term problem, well understood prior to the credit crunch as requiring action, is that China would benefit from moving from an export-led model of growth to more of a consumption-led model. It is still a poor country, per capita, which has promoted saving above consumption and built a strong export sector (necessitating significant imports of commodities and intermediate goods) to drive growth. Savings rates are well over 50% of GDP as firms have saved cash and as people save for education and self-insure themselves through high savings against old age, poor health, periods of unemployment and other events which can reduce income. A more comprehensive social safety net would encourage consumption and reduce saving for old age. Greater rural incomes would also boost consumption.

The increase in consumption is much more achievable for China than for an already high-consumption society. When Japan tried to boost consumption prior to the credit crunch in the 1990s and early 2000s, it had great difficulty, given the already high level of consumption. In China, however, there is much larger scope for expanding domestic consumption. Income inequality has been rising since economic reforms in 1978, most notably between rural and urban areas.[19] The building of cities in the hinterland is a policy designed to reduce large income differentials with coastal areas. Rural infrastructure has also been promoted. Unemployment benefits and other social insurance measures have also been designed to move the marginal rate of consumption up.

Though movement could be faster, China is moving to a lower level of personal savings, and so to a consumption-led model of growth, but it takes several years to start to make a significant difference. Developing domestic bond markets is a key component in financial market deepening, which in turn helps reduce the precautionary motive to save. Gross domestic savings as a percentage of GDP peaked in 2009 at over 50%, and while personal and corporate savings subsequently declined, public saving and investment continued to increase to 2012.

Unlike this first medium-term problem, the understanding of which preceded the 2008 crisis, the second problem was that China suffered from an aggregate demand deficiency as the export markets in the United States and Europe, previously so important to Chinese growth, languished. This problem could be repeated.

The Chinese government responded in appropriate Keynesian style in November 2008 with a 4 trillion renminbi (US$586 billion) fiscal package, almost all in the form of additional government spending and largely focused on infrastructure (RMB 2.87 trillion) – construction of railways and mass transit in particular. About half of the total package is likely to have occurred anyway, including the RMB 1 trillion for reconstruction after the Sichuan earthquake, but about RMB 2 trillion, or 3.1% of GDP, was additional. It is also noteworthy that it was financed from cash – unlike in the US and Western Europe, where stimulus had to be paid for by ever-larger borrowings, with the associated risks of creditors' strikes.

The efficacy of fiscal spending in China was greater than tax cuts or much of the government spending in the United States or Western Europe at the same time due to higher multipliers, and the results were very successful. The scale of the stimulus was difficult to gauge, though: too little would result in unemployment, too much in future inflation. The politics of this trade-off were clearly in favour of avoiding unemployment, hence, if anything, there was arguably slightly too much stimulus. As part of the stimulus package China also increased bank credit targets (China still being a country with top-down planning and resource allocation) – not a characteristic feature of bank behaviour in the credit crunch-affected developed world. This did, however, result in companies hoarding cheap money and consequent later difficulties in controlling inflation through credit rationing (as companies still had the ready cash to invest and spend).

Finally, a comment concerning the fourth type of collateral damage – a flight to the currency of a crisis economy as residents bring money back home to cover actual and potential domestic losses. Countries with large central bank reserves and without such a crisis may allow this to happen, i.e. not intervene to stop it. The dollar rose against many emerging currencies after the North Atlantic financial crisis broke in 2008, and many central banks in emerging markets, though quite capable of stopping this move, thought it prudent to save their intervention power lest the situation become even worse, and so allowed the dollar to strengthen. The dollar subsequently fell back, but the initial flight to dollars was widely

---

[19] There are many measures of income inequality in China – see Chen *et al.* (2010). For an analysis of urban savings rates, see Naba (2011).

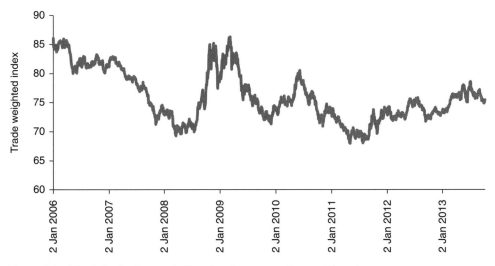

Figure 3.1   The dollar has been volatile rather than strong. Source: Bloomberg

interpreted as a flight to safety rather than a flight to liabilities (including due to so-called 'career risk'). History may yet call it something other than a flight to safety (see Figure 3.1).

3.4   GLOBAL CENTRAL BANK IMBALANCES

Financial markets can overshoot in ways inconsistent with simple macroeconomic theories. Part of the Washington Consensus was that opening capital accounts was generally benefi- cial. While this may often be the case, the context of other policies and global conditions matters. The simplistic pro-free market view of cross-border flows was that if you get cut off from capital temporarily, this should reverse soon enough, albeit at a different cost of capital. Likewise, a currency which oversold would soon attract new capital.

However, reality often turns out to be different, as Latin America experienced in the 1980s. The external environment became hostile as US Federal Reserve Chairman Paul Volker, determined to stamp out US inflation, raised interest rates substantially. Then in 1994 his successor Greenspan again raised interest rates rapidly. These shocks necessarily affected Latin American countries and the price of access to credit, but there was more than just an adjustment in the price of new loans – countries were cut off. Markets overshot and there was no early remission; they were forced to adjust painfully. A developed country, issuing debt in its own currency, can rob its bond holders of value through devaluation and inflation when faced with a credit withdrawal or foreign shock. When debt is in another country's currency, though, there is not the same option. Default and rapid fiscal adjustment are the alternative choices.

For a while Asian economies took the view that this Latin American experience did not apply to them. Asian economies had not followed the Washington Consensus in its entirety, but talked of the East Asian model instead (despite its not being clear what the differences were). To some extent Asian countries thought they were immune from balance-of-payments crises and speculative attacks. The IMF had been warning Thailand months before the 1997 crisis began that the external accounts were unsustainable and that the fixed exchange rate was vulnerable, but these warnings had been ignored. Many market participants were also aware of the dangers of balance-of-payments crises, starting with Thailand. Then the Asian crisis of 1997/8 happened.

After a crisis there are always lessons of experience, yet a remarkable thing is that the lessons after each crisis are often things we already knew. Hence, after the Asian crisis, the World Bank and others came out with their lists of lessons.[20] The new information was not just the detail of the lessons, but also what was included and the relative importance of the different policy issues. Whereas the economic policy establishment knew, before the crisis, that having a robust, well-run and well-regulated domestic banking system was important before opening up one's capital account, it was not realised just how crucial this was. Short-term financing from overseas was seen as a bigger risk afterwards than before. Were economists studying emerging markets thus deficient in their analysis prior to the crisis? Not really.[21] Reality had changed, and it did so in realtime. The relative importance of different policy issues did not emerge earlier, arguably in large part because before the crisis struck and affected market behaviour in novel unpredictable ways, the policy issues were of different relative importance. The problem economists face is that they are frequently analysing the last problem, not the next.

So the world is more confusing than a simple model, a theme central to this book. Also, Asian and other countries discovered something Latin America had already experienced: when the market is against you, it can be vicious. It overshoots. Money can flee the country in a self-fulfilling avalanche. Panic ensues, and this is not irrational: the intelligent investor will do the stupid thing first, before others. A rush for the exit by portfolio investors was not meant to happen in Asia, but it did.

Just as US and European regulators have had their wake-up call about systemic risk and have realised that laissez-faire will not do, emerging markets also had their wake-up call on cross-border flows a decade earlier. After the crisis policy improved, faith in markets declined, faith in the IMF declined and complacency declined. Something else happened, though: the build-up of reserves. The central banks bought dollars and invested them in US Treasuries. In doing so, they put downward pressure on their own exchange rates, consistent with an export model of growth for many of them. The export of their savings funded the negative savings rate in the US and, together with regulators' inadequate attention to the systemic risks in the financial sector which we have already discussed, helped create the North Altantic credit bubble.

Oil and other commodity exporters also built up reserves. Oil dipped below $10 per barrel at the start of 1999, but then started to rally. Indeed, terms of trade for emerging markets, and not just the commodity exporters, started to improve against the developed world, reversing a long period of downward terms of trade pressure since the early 1950s. The terms of trade for Asia had already been improving in the latter half of the 1980s, whereas those for Latin America and Africa had continued deteriorating.[22] From around 2002, though, most emerging markets seemed to experience improvements. And central bank reserves and oil stabilisation

---

[20] For example, Kawai *et al.* (2003). See also Isard (2005), p. 150 as an example of post-crisis identification of vulnerabilities.

[21] Though they were when it came to Northern Rock and sub-prime in the US.

[22] See Allen (2005), p. 144.

funds filled up with dollars as countries intervened to try to keep their exchange rates from rising too rapidly.

The build-up in reserves and global imbalances cannot go on indefinitely. We should remember the Forrest Gump-like wisdom of Nixon adviser Herb Stein already quoted in Chapter 1. It is necessary at some point that emerging market central banks stop buying dollars and allow their currencies to appreciate. There are eight reasons to do so.

1. There is a strong desire (for some of them, not all) to move from an export-led model of growth to a domestic consumption model of growth. Changing terms of trade through currency appreciation (selling dollar reserves) incentivises local entrepreneurs to invest for domestic customers, not export. Undervalued exchange rates have created vulnerabilities to external shocks and also, as before the Asian crisis, may lead to financial sector risks if investment is not channelled appropriately.[23]
2. Secondly, central bank reserve managers have traditionally focused asset allocation to maximise liquidity, and consequently have put around two-thirds of reserves into US Treasuries – seemingly the most liquid asset market in the world. However, emerging central banks – with over 80% of global reserves – are now collectively the dominant foreign owners of that market. One needs liquidity most in a crisis, and a reasonably likely scenario is that of several central banks selling Treasuries at the same time. In this scenario it is difficult to see who might be buying: liquidity could collapse. The US Federal Reserve could buy US Treasuries and so preserve their liquidity, but this would merely hasten the exit of those external investors who wished to sell ahead of the possibility that this exit route might also be closed. As the Federal Reserve is not an external purchaser, its buying of Treasuries would not also entail purchase of the dollars being sold by the sellers of Treasuries. Emerging central bank purchasing of Treasuries has been holding up the dollar for a decade. Domestic buying to meet emerging central bank sales would be unlikely to stop the dollar from collapsing. Hence the liquidity rationale for such preponderant holding of Treasuries is moot. We know that liquidity can change suddenly, and negatively, including in markets where high liquidity has always been the norm before.

    The reaction to this unpleasant thought of panic selling of US Treasuries by central banks and no liquidity is firstly denial. The second reaction is to consider whether another currency, the euro, offers (or could offer if there was a shift in demand for paper) more liquidity; but, given the EU's current woes, the answer is 'probably not'. It may only be at the third attempt to think about the problem that it is realised that the liquidity assumed possible at all times and sought by central banks is not achievable anywhere, and hence liquidity ought to be toppled from its prominent position as one of the principal objectives, or indeed the first objective, against which reserve management allocation is assessed. Although shifting out of dollars may traditionally be considered only as good as the next alternative,[24] it is perhaps more accurate to say that it is only as good as the next set of alternatives once the dominance of a single currency's liquidity seems no longer assured.
3. Reserves are now so large in many countries as to exceed considerably the amount which may be needed for intervention. Hence some of these assets are either being managed with a longer-term endowment-type motive within the central bank, or have been moved to

---

[23] See Eichengreen (2010) p. 31.
[24] Eichengreen (2010) p. 7.

fund separate sovereign wealth funds. Either way, the endowment motive of these funds is incompatible with having the majority in Treasuries: they need to be diversified.

4. Related to point 3, the opportunity cost of holding reserves (in any form) is high, in terms of opportunities foregone from additional consumption or investment.

5. Note that the effect of sterilisation[25] may also redistribute wealth from taxpayers to bondholders, some of whom are not nationals or taxpayers. Holding reserves acts as an insurance policy against external shocks, but one can overdo it.

6. Investing in dollars may be a risky investment. A large proportion of dollar holdings in reserves may not match liabilities, as determined by the relative weights of current and future trade partners. But more than this, addressing the imbalances inherent in global reserves means that currency losses of around 30% are likely in the next few years for surplus emerging central banks holding dollars. If one holds in reserves 25% of GDP which lose 30% of their value, this equates to a loss of 7.5% of GDP. Where does the 30% loss come from? The average yield on the 10-year Treasury bond over the last six decades is around 6.5%. A move to that level from the sub-2% yield in 2013 (ignoring any overshoot) would wipe out about a third of the value of the average US Treasury portfolio. To those who argue that there is a natural demand for the dollar because of its reserve currency status, consider that from its inception as a reserve currency in 1913, when the Federal Reserve system was founded, it only took 11 years (including 1914–18!) for its use in reserves to be greater than that of sterling.[26]

7. There is an optimal level of reserves, and this has arguably been passed for many. Faced with the reality of currency appreciation pressure and of cross-border flows – which can, if allowed, overshoot – the first, best policy is to allow one's currency to adjust in accordance with market forces, but this may be at the cost of excessive volatility and overshooting. Hence the second-best solution is to build up reserves, resisting currency appreciation in the process. Once this is done, however (i.e. sufficiently large reserves have been purchased), rather than resisting further appreciation through capital control efforts, the policy should perhaps be shifted again to allow market forces to determine the exchange rate, but use intervention to reduce extreme volatility and currency overshooting. After 2008 central banks in emerging markets have been slow to make this readjustment of policy.

8. Central banks may need to use exchange rate appreciation to help fight inflation. For example, about half of India's inflation can be attributed to oil import prices, so currency appreciation can reduce this. After Lehman Brothers failed, central banks across the globe, including in emerging markets, faced uncertainty and the prospect of additional international financial sector failures. Many cut interest rates as a precaution, even though they had different economic cycles from the US, and did not have the same deleveraging ahead as the developed countries.

Each country has its own economic cycle and inflationary pressures, but the common effects of loose monetary policy did express themselves in a number of countries. It took a couple of years for inflation to build. Although there was significant concern among Asian central banks about the inflationary cycle, and lessons were sought from the inflationary

---

[25] In order to build up reserves, the central bank prints domestic currency with which to purchase them. This domestic currency then needs to be soaked up or 'sterilised' to avoid inflation by issuing domestic debt – at the prevailing domestic interest rate. The sterilisation cost derives from the difference between the local interest rate and that obtained on the reserve holdings.

[26] See Eichengreen (2011) p. 32.

experiences of devaluations in 1997/8, the first significant signs of inflation were in late 2010 in the form of food price inflation affecting a number of Asian and other countries. However, at that time, central banks were uncertain whether the inflation was likely to pass through and thus whether it warranted policy action.[27] The rationale for using the exchange rate to help fight inflation was because it was considered problematic just to use interest rates should a sudden reversal be required because of further problems in the US and Europe. While central banks could not be certain how markets would react to their efforts to appreciate, the context at the time was one of their fairly continuous purchasing of dollars, building reserves. Merely stopping such intervention, let alone reversing it, could be enough to move the exchange rate. In contrast, raising and shortly afterwards dropping interest rates significantly might constitute a threat to central bank credibility.[28] [29]

We return in Chapter 11 to why, as at late 2013, central bank imbalances have not yet been reduced, and how they might be.

---

[27] If an inflationary episode is seen as a one-off event, not affecting future inflation expectations, then the appropriate monetary policy may be to do nothing.

[28] This rationale was imparted to the author through private conversations with a number of central banks.

[29] In additional to these eight reasons, though not necessarily constituting a reason in itself, in the case of Asia, it has been argued by Kim *et al.* (2008) that the 'tendency of East Asia to invest in dollar-denominated assets may have had a negative impact on regional integration'.

4

Limitations of Economics
and Finance Theory

'... the ideas of economists and political philosophers, both when they are right and when they are wrong, are more powerful than is commonly understood. Indeed the world is ruled by little else. Practical men, who believe themselves to be quite exempt from any intellectual influences, are usually the slaves of some defunct economist.'

Keynes, *General Theory*, Ch 24, V

The ideas of defunct economists have led to misleading, partial or otherwise inadequate investor understanding. In the next two chapters the intention is to focus on those economic ideas that influence the standard thinking of investors but may lead to sub-optimal practical investment consequences.

1. Investors need to assess how financial markets will behave – it comes as no surprise to market practitioners that inefficiencies, market failures, sub-optimal and 'irrational' behaviour, bubbles and crashes exist. What does economics have to say about these, and is it helpful? This is the main focus of this chapter.
2. Investors are interested in assessing risk. So we need to understand what risk is, and this is the focus of Chapter 5.
3. Investors need to appreciate more than market behaviour. They need to understand policymakers, and policymakers need to understand them and be aware of how markets behave. For example, how should we assess sovereign default, devaluation or inflation risks which result from policy decisions? We start to cover that in Chapter 5 with a discussion on sovereign risk.
4. Investors want to know how different financial assets behave when combined. Again, is some of the theory regarding this misleading? We start to discuss the theories underlying this in this chapter and then the risk aspects in more depth in the next.
5. Finance theories have limitations, and if they are misleading it is often the result of practitioners overlooking their limitations rather than due to poor scholarship. This raises a further question: Why are known theoretical limitations ignored? To address this we discuss misaligned incentives and principal/agent problems from Chapter 7 onwards.

4.1   THEORETICAL THOUGHT AND LIMITATIONS

The focus in this chapter on economic theory is necessarily wide: the bigger dynamic picture of the development of theoretical thought, rather than the detail, which can be found elsewhere. The intention is to give no more than an overview of theoretical limitations and boundaries faced by the practitioner. Rather than a repeat of the beneficial aspects of standard finance theory on asset allocation, I hope to show how certain avenues of thought are well explored, and others not; and how this unequal theoretical knowledge may bias our allocation and investment decisions.

First I show, through some brief historical remarks, that the interpretation of economic theory is subject to ideological fashions. Secondly, we notice the trap of excessive confidence given to mathematical formulations and measurable variables. Sometimes observable and quantifiable past patterns cannot be relied on to repeat, and investors need to be cautious with some standard assumptions and models. Thirdly, we discuss Keynes' invention of macroeconomics; fourthly, later efforts to generate microeconomic foundations for macroeconomics and how these may have hidden some of Keynes' insight from view. The consequence for investors is that they may lack the guidance of how to incorporate macroeconomic factors into their decisions. Fifthly, there is an irrelevance to theories which neither have realistic assumptions nor can be tested. Efforts in behavioural finance are attempting to address this through more realistic behavioural assumptions.

4.2   ECONOMICS, A VEHICLE FOR THE RULING IDEOLOGY

Economics has shaped and been shaped by history. There have been writings on economic issues since at least Xenophon and Aristotle. More recently, we can go back to French physiocrats in the mid-18th century (who saw agriculture as the base of the economy) for an overall theory of how an economy functions. Adam Smith's *The Wealth of Nations* soon followed in 1776, establishing the school of thought, including the division of labour and the importance of the 'invisible hand', which became known as classical economics. There has been a huge variety of theories derived since, and this has clearly been important in shaping policies and political ideologies from Marxism to Thatcherism – asset allocation today being small beer in comparison. As Joan Robinson puts it: 'In the general mass of notions and sentiments that make up an ideology those concerned with economic life play a large part, and economics itself (that is the subject as it is taught in universities and evening classes and pronounced upon in leading articles) has always been partly a vehicle for the ruling ideology...' (Robinson, 1962, p. 1).

A common complaint about economics today, particularly as taught at post-graduate level, is the lack of balance resulting from the high proportion of time and effort spent on mathematical techniques. Mathematics, correctly used, can help advance our thinking enormously and aid the teaching and understanding of economic theory. However, to be of contemporary use (admittedly not the only purpose of academic study), it should also, at some point, be grounded in the reality of actual economic problems. Some contemporary critics are indeed scathing about the level of irrelevance of much university economics:

'Indeed, the typical graduate macroeconomics and monetary economics training received at Anglo-American universities during the past 30 years or so, may have set back by decades serious investigations of aggregate economic behaviour and economic policy-relevant understanding.'

Buiter (2009)

How much do we place blind faith in past patterns which can be measured and ignore the possibility of more substantial events which we cannot measure? After a new piece of evidence, many individual investors display what behavioural scientists call extrapolation bias, naively extrapolating existing trends. Then again, institutional investors are more likely to suffer from gambler's fallacy: they are too prone to predict reversals as they misapply the law of large numbers to small samples.[1] I remember attending a conference for institutional investors in the US a few months after Lehman Brothers collapsed in 2008 and being … not shocked (that would imply that it was not expected), but despairing. The cause was a panel of investment consultants with copious advice about asset allocation, including the need for portfolio rebalancing,[2] but with no mention of macroeconomic imbalances or major potential global structural shifts ahead. At the time it appeared (to me at least) that major macroeconomic risks were present in the US and EU equivalent to the period leading to the 1930s depression. We had just seen a major financial crisis, but one which constituted a near miss of something worse, with the risk still of a scenario ahead much worse than experienced for several decades – one which could develop into a 1930s-style depression. If one takes the view that recent events are a poor guide to the future, then portfolio rebalancing is inappropriate. Yet the desire to extrapolate from recent events (but not including as far back as the 1930s) is strong.[3]

4.3   MACROECONOMICS

Macroeconomics is often ignored by investors. It needs to be central to asset allocation, but it is hardly given lip service. The fallacy of composition occurs when one infers that something is true of the whole when it is true merely for some small part. Macroeconomics exists because we cannot always simply infer economy-wide conclusions from microeconomic theory. There are constraints at the broader macroeconomic level which are not experienced by the firm or consumer. When it comes to asset allocation, why are microeconomic ideas generously in evidence but macroeconomic factors often lacking?

There is a view that there is no great distinction between macroeconomics and microeconomics – that macroeconomics is an extension or even a subsumption of microeconomics. Yet, arguably, undergraduate economists go through university learning two distinct subjects: micro- and macroeconomics (in those where they still learn macroeconomics). Many don't realise that the two are at loggerheads, because the effort to make them appear compatible has been so successful. There are related views that macroeconomics is not deserving of separate study in asset allocation, or is a matter largely to be delegated to investment managers after high-level decisions about asset allocation have been made.

---

[1] When there are repeated independent random events, the gambler's fallacy is the belief that after a series of trials with a similar deviation from the expected result, deviation in the opposite direction is more likely – for example, if a tossed coin comes up heads several times in a row, the next toss is believed to be more likely tails than heads. The fallacy can also be expressed as an overinterpretation of the significance of a small recent sample. The law of large numbers is that when a trial is repeated many times the average result will move closer to the expected result. For investors the gambler's fallacy can lead to an overestimation of the significance of a pattern and an underestimation of its duration.

[2] Investors often have target allocations for different 'asset classes'. Portfolio rebalancing is the periodic resetting of these weights – the selling of those asset classes which have performed well over the previous period and buying of those which have performed poorly.

[3] Then again, what I took for extrapolation bias may also be interpreted as modesty – not commenting on the tectonic macroeconomic forces about which they did not pretend to be experts.

John Maynard Keynes created macroeconomics theory where formerly there was just monetary theory. Since then, dominant macroeconomic ideas have been resisted and have shifted over time, and Keynes's insights in particular have also been interpreted and reinterpreted in many different ways. The utility of different theories has changed.

The state of economics before Keynes has parallels with the state of finance theory today – asset allocation in particular. Keynes went up to a Cambridge dominated by Marshall's 19th-century economics and then experienced the failure of the consensus economic theories to explain the Great Depression, or to help policymakers counter it effectively. The result was *The General Theory of Employment, Interest and Money*, published in 1936. Keynes's observation, as one might also easily say of much economic theory today, was that the contemporary dominant theory, while mathematically appealing, was incomplete in crucial respects and flawed in its understanding of human nature.

Interestingly, Keynes wrote his 'Thesis on Probability' in 1919 and only later dedicated his greatest attention to economics. He took a particular interest in the role of uncertainty as an explanation of why investment came to a near halt in the slump. Let us employ the distinction between risk and uncertainty provided by Frank Knight in 1921: uncertainty exists where one does not know the probability distribution of random events and so cannot hedge or insure, whereas risk is where one does and can.

Keynes's insight was that rational entrepreneurs and businesses, when faced with significant uncertainty, will invest nothing. He emphasised the importance of confidence and 'animal spirits' in determining investment decisions by entrepreneurs and business leaders. If others are not investing, this will depress economic activity, increase uncertainty more and further reduce the incentive to invest.[4] If there is a high level of uncertainty in an economy, there will be sub-optimal investment. Lack of investment causes unemployment and more uncertainty, and so a positive feedback loop is established and a slump can occur.[5] Hence the need for government investment instead to counter the downward spiral in confidence and boost Keynes's new concept: aggregate demand. That, in a nutshell, is his General Theory, and much of the book is spent demolishing classical economic thinking to make way for what is at heart a simple idea.

Keynes' ideas of aggregate demand management through government fiscal policy (taxes and expenditure) were seemingly effective in the years following World War II, after his death.[6] They were subsequently arguably overused, and applied excessively to situations which were not threatening slumps but were more normal business cycle recessions. If there are unemployed factors of production lying idle for want of aggregate demand, fiscal stimulation makes more sense than if there is near full employment, in which case additional stimulus will create inflation. And if stimulus is used to try to regulate a business cycle and is

---

[4] Investor behaviour faced with risk is quite different. Because risk can be quantified and hedging/insurance is possible, an optimal investment may be calculated.

[5] There have been other depressions, for example the so-called 'Long Depression' 1873–96. A slump of the scale of the 1930s was avoided, however, arguably because monetary growth in previous depressions was either deliberately expansionary or did not contract as significantly as in the 1930s. The idea that markets should clear without government help was less entrenched in the minds of policymakers. Also, by the 1930s banks had become more dominant in the economy than before and their rapid deleveraging was on a larger scale than experienced before.

[6] However, arguably Keynesian policy was not necessary in this period. Demand conditions in postwar Britain were very different to pre-war conditions of suppressed demand when Keynesian polices were more appropriate. Postwar labour was scarce relative to capital. And investment, partly maybe assisted by government policy, was a major source of demand growth. See Matthews (1968).

then not withdrawn, or not withdrawn in time, when the cycle turns more positive, then the result is again likely to be inflation. Indeed, a trade-off between unemployment and inflation – the Phillips curve – was purportedly observed in 1958 from a long series of past British data, and subsequently elsewhere.

Government expenditure may be appropriate to address aggregate demand deficiencies and market failures but can also be inefficient and a source of rent seeking. The call for minimal government has long been in tension with Keynesian theories of aggregate demand management. The stagflation of the 1970s[7] was arguably due in part to excessive use of fiscal rather than structural policies to address unemployment, leading to the build-up of structural rigidities. The economic policy of Reagan's and Thatcher's governments was decisively away from government intervention.[8] Theories stressed the importance of supply-side economics.[9] Friedman and Schwartz (1965) argued from US historical data the importance of monetary policy in managing the trajectory of an economy, at the start of a returned ideological preference in the Anglo-Saxon world for the dominance of the liberalised market economy with a reduced role for the state – though what was achieved in practice was more a cap on the growth of government expenditure as a percentage of GDP rather than a significant reduction.

This ideological shift applied not just to the use of fiscal policy to manage aggregate demand but to government regulation of the economy in general. Markets were in more respects seen as self-regulating, including financial markets. Capital controls were relaxed in several countries and restrictions on the activities of banks were relaxed, which increased competition and allocative efficiency but, without sufficient changes in oversight, also led to problems apparent since 2008. Milton Friedman famously even called for the abolition of central banks and replacement by a simple monetary rule.[10]

4.4   MICROECONOMIC FOUNDATIONS OF MACROECONOMICS

From the 1950s the neoclassical synthesis tried to square the insights of Keynes' general theory with neoclassical economic theory: the tradition which began with the marginal revolution of the 1860s and 1870s. The first step was earlier, though: the codification of Keynes's macroeconomics, most famously by Hicks into the IS-LM model in 1936–7.[11] This is a simplifying device which describes where two curves intersect to establish a general equilibrium between national output and (real) interest rates in the absence of inflation. The first curve represents the relationship between investment and saving (IS) and the second between liquidity preference and money supply (LM). The model has been of huge use heuristically, but is necessarily a demand-side-focused simplification and has several deficiencies, not least

---

[7] Stagflation is the condition of high and persistent unemployment in combination with inflation. The origins of stagflation can be a supply shock, inappropriately loose monetary policy or labour market or other structural rigidities in the economy.

[8] Nigel Lawson, a UK Treasury minister in the first Thatcher government and later her longest-serving Chancellor of the Exchequer (Finance Minister), argued that monetary policy should be the main policy instrument to control demand, while the stance of fiscal policy should shape the pattern of that demand. See Lawson (2010, p. 76).

[9] It is noted that neither using monetary policy to manage the economy, nor for that matter, supply-side policies are either inherently contrary to demand management, or non-Keynesian.

[10] Interview with Reason magazine (2006), quoted in Cooper (2008).

[11] Axel Leijonhufvud (1968) argued that Hicks's IS-LM analysis fails to represent the disequilibrium dynamics of Keynes' theory.

that it fails to capture Keynes' analysis of investment under uncertainty. The labour market is not explicitly shown, and involuntary unemployment and disequilibrium phenomena and dynamics cannot be adequately captured. But it and other formulations enabled models to create microeconomic foundations of macroeconomics.

The Keynesian model has since been reinterpreted by Lucas and others who created rational expectations theory (RET). Before Lucas it was assumed in economic theory that investment decisions were made on the basis of current data. Lucas' contribution was that investment decisions are based on what future conditions will be. But this is achieved through a leap of faith that fully predetermined models can predict markets – in order to be compatible with microeconomics, which assumes competitive markets[12] and supply and demand clearing in equilibrium conditions – conditions absent in a depression. Non-clearing labour markets (resistance to lower nominal wages) and other factors have been used to explain aggregate demand deficiencies and depression economics rather than Knightian uncertainty.[13]

Rational expectations theory (RET) assumes that, on average, economic agents (individuals and firms) are not systematically wrong in their decisions over long periods of time.[14] They, on average, understand the way the economy works and are 'rational' in that the result for the economy as a whole tends to equilibrium – equilibrium here meaning mutual consistency of agents' decisions. It is this which challenged much of the disequilibria thinking of Keynes and others. It is RET which assumes that supply-side economics is overwhelmingly dominant and breaks with Keynes in assuming away uncertainty and the need for a separate study of macroeconomics.

RET forms a basis for much of finance theory. It may have led to investment behaviour which contradicts RET's basic assumption of random expectation errors: if markets are not systematically wrong, there is no need for research beyond observing past market prices. This is not the only example in finance whereby a theory, if it is believed and employed widely, ceases to be true.

Microeconomic and finance theory assumes that asset prices behave just like goods markets: namely that when the price of a good goes up, demand for it falls.[15] However, when the price of an asset goes up, people, companies and especially banks often want more, not less, of it due to asymmetric information patterns and tendencies to herd.[16] And they can go on wanting more for months and years. This creates bubbles and, if these are large enough, disruptive market crashes when they burst. Such crashes almost invariably, when large, result in government or central bank intervention, effectively bailing out at least some of a bubble's speculators. Because intervention is on the downside and not the upside, an asymmetry is created, and so a secondary cause of bubbles is the creation of moral hazard: the expectation

---

[12] Though it is understood that there are monopolies, externalities, public goods and other market deficiencies and failures.

[13] Sticky expectations have also been used: see Roberts (1998) and Mankiw and Reis (2001).

[14] Keynes famously said in the long run we are all dead. In practice, many RET models assume the long run is not very long.

[15] The rare exceptions being luxury status items which become more desirable the more expensive they are (the utility function shifts positively with price) and 'Giffen' goods where the utility function is given, independent of price but the cost of buying the good dominates disposable income, and the income effect (higher price reducing purchasing power) dominates the substitution effect. The only known example is the potato during the Irish famine: as potatoes were scarce and rising in price, demand actually increased because consumers were so impoverished by a rise in potato prices that they could no longer afford to supplement their diet with more expensive foods.

[16] For evidence of momentum causing bubbles, see Vayanos and Woolley (2008).

of future bailouts may lead to ever bigger crashes and ever bigger bailouts, until eventually we have a situation when the required bailout is too large to fund.

Did we not know all this before 2008? Yes and no – we knew it and forgot it. History is littered with financial crises. The savings and loan crisis in the US was quite recent: it destroyed roughly a third of all savings and loan institutions between 1988 and 1991. Then again, a lot of the economics and policymaking establishment really believed in laissez-faire when it comes to markets, including financial markets. They believed in the neoclassical model with ideological zeal. Now that it has all crashed, we are rediscovering what was known all along. The Federal Reserve system was created in 1913, not primarily to control inflation, but in order to avoid a repeat of the asset bubbles of 1893 and 1907. Economists through history have largely had little time for laissez-faire. The growth of vigorous market capitalism in Victorian England was accompanied by new laws to protect the process of competition. Even von Hayek in the first chapter of his famously pro-freedom 1944 book *The Road to Serfdom* says:

'There is nothing in the basic principles of liberalism to make it a stationary creed, there are no hard-and-fast rules fixed once and for all. The fundamental principle that in the ordering of our affairs we should make as much use as possible of the spontaneous forces of society, and resort as little as possible to coercion, is capable of an infinite variety of applications. There is, in particular, all the difference between deliberately creating a system within which competition will work as beneficially as possible, and passively accepting institutions as they are. Probably nothing has done so much harm to the liberal cause as the wooden insistence of some liberals on certain rough rules of thumb, above all the principle of *laissez-faire*.'

Though he immediately goes on, and remembering the context of arguing against fascism and socialism in 1944:

'Yet in a sense this was necessary and unavoidable. Against the innumerable interests who could show that particular measures would confer immediate and obvious benefits on some, while the harm they caused was much more indirect and difficult to see, nothing short of some hard-and-fast rule would have been effective. And since a strong presumption in favour of industrial liberty had undoubtedly been established, the temptation to present it as a rule which knew no exceptions was too strong always to be resisted.'[17]

Thus in a single paragraph is captured both the inadequacies of an ideological view of market freedom and an example, from time to time, of its political and practical attraction. Karl Popper, echoing Adam Smith's comment that businessmen collude given the chance, also commented that a free market is paradoxical and that if the state does not interfere, then other organisations may do.

We have known how to regulate banking systems for decades – at least since Bagehot (1873) – and been more or less on our guard since at least John Law's escapade with credit in 1720. Yes, financial markets have become more complicated, but the real problem is that regulation has simply not focused properly on systemic uncertainties and risks.

---

[17] Hayek (1944) p. 17.

4.4.1   Efficient market hypothesis

The academic theory behind the consensus view of how to invest is anchored by RET and the efficient markets hypothesis (EMH). Assuming RET, the EMH, developed by Eugene Fama, postulates that market prices at all times fully reflect all available information. The model assumes that investors' behaviour is collectively unpredictable and distributed normally. However, while EMH may be a good description in all but a few examples in goods markets, there is plenty of evidence that this is often not a convincing description of reality in finan-cial markets. Also, the normal distribution assumption is often difficult to square with asset price data. It is a bell-shaped curve describing the probability distribution of random events around a mean. The standard deviation of the distribution scales it – 66% of the distribution lies within one standard deviation for example. Reality in asset markets is, however, deeply non-normal, as Mandelbrot pointed out in the early 1960s, most typically with larger extreme events or so-called 'fat tails' (see Figure 4.1). There are, as a result of assuming normality when it is not present, systematic biases in investor behaviour.

RET and EMH are not without empirical backing. This includes evidence that mutual fund managers cannot beat the market (outperform the index they are measured against), yet there are also studies with evidence that they can. Friedman pointed out that theoretical complete-ness (concrete rules) can only exist in a conceptual world. If there are instances where EMH does not apply, we should try to find out why rather than carrying on using EMH regardless. The search for a better model based on RET to fit the data is a highly active one. However, the assumptions of human behaviour in RET are simplistic and constitute an imperfect model of reality. That in itself does not invalidate their use, but, combined with the observation of more complex behavioural motives, and with contradictory empirical evidence, it should at least urge caution not to be overdependent or focused on them. This means, at a practi-cal level for an investor, one should not leverage (borrow) massively to exploit automated arbitrage strategies while believing you do not face the risk of losing all your money one day. One might have thought that obvious, but it isn't always so to people highly trained in these matters … and who sometimes have different incentives from the owners of the capital.

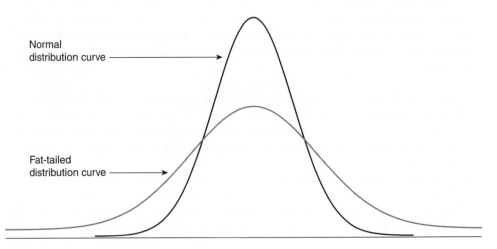

Figure 4.1   A normal and a fat-tailed distribution curve

The history of quantitative trading is the history of stunning success interspersed with disaster. On so-called 'Black Monday' in October 1987[18] there was, assuming a normal distribution, a 27 standard deviation event. That is an event which has a probability something like 1 over 10 to the power of 160 ($1/10^{160}$) – this compares with there being only something like 10^{80} atoms in the universe – not very likely, in other words. Another such unlikely series of events wiped out LTCM in 1998, and still more failures ensued in 2007 and 2008. Financial asset markets are simply not normal, and these 'impossible' events (according to some quantitative analysts) demonstrate this as clearly as is possible.

Let us tarry again over one of the consequences of RET and EMH: the impossibility of bubbles.[19] If investors were not systemically wrong in their predictions (i.e. RET holds), then as many betting on a change away from the 'true' value one way should be balanced with others betting the other way. So bubbles could not grow, even though experience shows that they can and do grow, and moreover can be observed as bubbles even before they collapse. Having said that, there has been much research trying to square this circle – 'limits to arbitrage' models which assume that though there may be (correct) naysayers otherwise willing to bet against misinformed speculators in the act of creating a bubble, the naysayers' risk aversion and knowledge of the presence of less informed investors reduces their willingness to participate. So this type of amendment qualifies RET by, in effect, highlighting conditions for its suspension or, if used merely to explain short-term aberrations, buttress it. Either way, this supports the argument that EMH is wrong. And RET does not offer a convincing explanation of herd behaviour and of the empirical reality that large bubbles can form over long periods.

Frydman and Goldberg (2011, p. 114) criticise both RET but also behavioural bubble models insofar as they explain upswings as being due to market participants downplaying fundamentals, so that 'fluctuations in asset markets are disconnected from movements of fundamental factors for long periods, implying that markets often grossly misallocate society's scarce capital.' However, while they may not find this credible, my experience in emerging markets is precisely that. While fundamentals normally impact the dynamics of financial markets, markets can, even for decades, misallocate society's scarce capital. As at early 2013 far too much money is being invested in the US and EU, for example, relative to emerging markets, and this has been the case for a long time. It goes against EMH and RET, but that a lot of people do a stupid thing does not make it intelligent (or efficient) – it just means there are a lot of people doing a stupid thing.

Moreover, the presence of momentum investing, herding and market inefficiency makes much of finance theory impotent. Minsky's explanation of how asset prices can fall precipitously is a well-known example of reality contradicting traditional efficient market theory. As Woolley in the London Stock Exchange Report on the Future of Finance (Woolley, in Turner et al., 2010, p. 113) reports:

'The fact and scale of mispricing invalidates much of the existing toolbox of fund management. Security market indices no longer constitute efficient portfolios and are no longer seen as appropriate benchmarks for either active or passive investment. Risk analysis based on past prices and used to assess the riskiness of portfolios and the basis

---

[18] Some crises are more predictable than others. Having climbed 40% in nine months for no good reason between January and September 1987, the US stock market then shed these gains in two weeks in October in a predictable collapse, but one which did not go on to cause widespread contagion.

[19] For a fuller coverage of some of the arguments referred to here, see Cooper (2008) and also Frydman and Goldberg (2011).

for diversification will be seen as flawed. Risk analysis has often failed investors when they needed it most, but now the reason for this can be seen. The risk that is being measured in these models is based on market prices, which are driven by flows of funds unrelated to fair value.'

Moreover, the efficient market hypothesis is found to be impossible in a famous paper by Grossman and Stiglitz (1980). They point out that if all market participants had the same level of understanding of the market and the process impacting prices, then there would be a free-rider problem and no one would have an incentive to bear the cost of collecting any information – they would just observe the price instead. Hence all available information will not be priced in, hence no EMH. Again Buiter (2009):

> 'Even during the seventies, eighties, nineties and noughties before 2007, the manifest failure of the EMH in many key asset markets was obvious to virtually all those whose cognitive abilities had not been warped by a modern Anglo-American Ph.D. education.'

In response to these weaknesses, efforts to preserve the RET while jettisoning the need for the EMH have relied largely on the existence of asymmetric information, and on the distinction between fundamental information on the one hand, and on the other, the knowledge, including informal knowledge, on which investors base their decisions.

As mentioned, RET does not assume short-term financial market efficiency, only that expectations are not systematically wrong over the long term – but how long is that, and how useful is it to ignore the short term? Many of the approaches to keep RET but not EMH still downplay systemic biases in financial markets. (One view is that if regulation could somehow correct the systemic biases identified, there would be market stability.) They underplay the tendency of financial markets to create positive feedbacks, and they fail to capture medium- to long-term but identifiable macroeconomic imbalances. They are not good at explaining sudden market falls and structural shifts – defined as discrete non-reversible changes in economic behaviour or economic conditions. Yet structural shifts do occur and to understand them requires some knowledge of macroeconomic imbalances and policies or what used to be called political economy. And short-term events do not always wash out in the long term but can define the long term. History can be path dependent.

There has been work done to incorporate structural shifts within finance theory, but it involves ditching RET. Frydman and Goldberg (2011) analyse changes in the market's forecasting strategy, as well as valuation changes using them, because of new information. They propose the contingent market hypothesis, which ... 'supposes that:

> The causal process underpinning price movements depends on available information, which includes observations concerning fundamental factors specific to each market.'[20]

However, in sharp contrast to the efficient market hypothesis:

> 'This process cannot be adequately characterised by an over-arching model, defined as a rule that exactly relates market outcomes to available information up to a fully predetermined random error at all time periods, past, present, and future.'

---

[20] This can include the structure and behaviour of market participants as we shall discuss in Chapter 7.

It would certainly appear to be consistent with empirical observation not only that structural shifts do occur, but also that it is unreasonable to expect any fully pre-determined model to predict financial markets when they do.

4.4.2 Modern portfolio theory

A standard investment tool has been modern portfolio theory (MPT), which selects, from all allowable combinations, the optimal combination of assets or asset classes to produce a portfolio which maximises return for a given level of volatility (called risk) – or minimises volatility for a given level of return. To compute this, one needs expected future volatilities (standard deviations of returns, or their variances),[21] expected returns and expected co-variances (or correlations)[22] of different securities or of (somehow pre-defined and pre-selected) groups of securities or asset classes. Model results are typically highly sensitive to assumed co-variances, and the number of co-variances needed may be very large (ideally those between each possible pair of securities). Markowitz (1959) showed how it was computationally easier (note: not necessarily according with reality) to assume that the co-variance between two securities could be explained solely in terms of their co-variances with an index, dramatically reducing the numbers of co-variances required for anything but small investment universes. This simplification is a great convenience in practice, but it may render the model results meaningless, specifically where a group of securities are significantly correlated together independently of variations in the index (for example in a particular industry sector or sub-sector).

Markowitz showed how linear programming and Monte Carlo simulations can be used to calculate efficient portfolios. Together these form an efficiency frontier – a locus of points, each one representing a possible portfolio. Which portfolio is preferred can be determined by an investor's utility function – their preferred combination of expected variance and return.

Markowitz's choice of variables is somewhat arbitrary. For the inputs to the calculations, for example, one might use other measures of centrality than the mean (e.g. the mode or median), and more interestingly, other measures of risk than variance from the mean. Semi-variance (which only looks at variances below a certain level) or maximum loss can be substituted for variance. In theory it is also possible to input changing future co-variances, volatilities and returns.

However, even expected co-variances to an index are often near impossible to estimate with any accuracy. A typical approach takes the set of possible assets or asset classes as finite, given and static. Computation uses past standard deviations, returns and index co-variances. Securities are assumed otherwise independent, normally distributed and with unchanging characteristics. The results from such studies are often meaningless in changeable macroeconomic and policy environments. Guesstimating future volatilities, co-variances and returns different to those simply extrapolated from the past may do little to improve matters because models are often highly sensitive to these inputs. Simulating various different scenarios for the expected variables can prove more useful, may involve more sophisticated assumptions and, much more onerous, requires far greater efforts in defining the inputs.

---

[21] The variance of a data set is normally defined as the average squared difference from the expected value of the variable (normally the mean). The standard deviation is the square root of the variance.

[22] Co-variance is related to correlation. The co-variance between two variables, x and y, $S_{xy} = r.S_x.S_y$, where r is their coefficient of correlation and S_x and S_y the standard deviations of x and y, respectively.

MPT literature, as for much of finance theory, typically employs the word 'risk' to mean standard deviation of returns – volatility – and so is useful primarily to those asset allocators who care overwhelmingly about the combination of return and volatility. Markowitz did look at other measures of risk, notably semi-variance, and utility theory. His preference for variance over semi-variance largely came down to computational ease (this is before the era of the personal computer). In market environments without major structural shifts, where volatilities, returns and co-variances can be expected to be stable, standard MPT is a powerful tool for investors with short-term liabilities – i.e. ones who care strongly about volatility. It is a much less useful tool for those with long-term liabilities, for two main reasons. Firstly, one cannot generally assume that past co-variances, returns and volatilities will remain stable over the longer the period of time under consideration. Secondly, volatility is of less concern to those with long-term liabilities than those with short-term ones, especially when set against non-normal extreme types of risk not captured by the model, many of which we care about much more than volatility.

4.4.3   Investment under uncertainty

Knightian uncertainty is also largely ignored by much of finance theory in favour of the analysis of economic decisions in the presence of Knightian risk (i.e. where probability distributions are known). Without known probability distributions, of course, neat mathematical models are not possible. The Bayesian approach to probability has been neglected. In many models systematic deviations from equilibrium are incompatible with the theory, or in other words assumed not to exist. The so-called 'complete markets paradigm' denies the possibility of macroeconomic phenomena like depressions. In Buiter's words again:

> 'In a world where there are markets for contingent claims trading that span all possible states of nature (all possible contingencies and outcomes), and in which intertemporal budget constraints are always satisfied by assumption, default, bankruptcy and insolvency are impossible.'
>
> Buiter (2009)

Is it prudent for investors to use theory which assumes this?

However, there is also a considerable literature both on the 'economics of uncertainty' – which is really about risk – analysing investment decisions where investors try to optimise in the presence of uncertainty; and the economics of information, where the emphasis is on finding out more information before taking an investment decision. Dixit and Pindyck (1994) and others have refined the analysis of investment theory to incorporate the irreversibility of investments and the ability to wait while one obtains more information. They use options theory to price the option of delaying and investing later. Also, Kahneman and Tversky (1979) developed their behavioural prospect theory, which describes decisions between risky alternatives: people have been observed, using experimental data, to base decisions on potential losses and gains rather than expected outcomes (see Figure 4.2). In a two-stage process, people first edit the choices – they order them, determine a neutral outcome and consider those with better outcomes as gains and those with worse outcomes as losses. In the second stage, evaluation, people behave as if they have computed utilities associated with different outcomes' gains and probabilities, and then maximised their utility. Beyond certain points they value additional losses and gains less. They also weight gains less than losses. In both

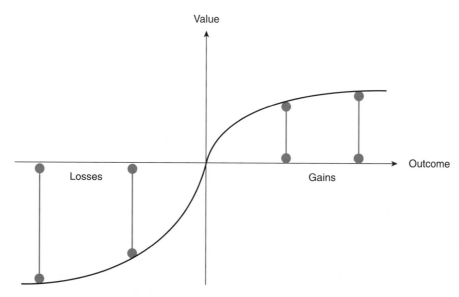

Figure 4.2   Prospect theory: gains and losses are valued differently

cases the bulk of research has had a strong mathematical component with formal models focused on risk where the probability distributions are known. The focus of these approaches is primarily microeconomic.

More recent macroeconomic literature on investment under uncertainty, such as the book *Animal Spirits* by Akerlof and Shiller (2009), and including some valuable empirical research, has arguably only confirmed how little we know – not much in addition to what we know from Keynes' insight, i.e. not a lot more than that confidence is really important. Akerlof and Shiller's descriptive (i.e. non-mathematical) book observes several different aspects of animal spirits: confidence, fairness, corruption and antisocial behaviour, money illusion and stories. They summarise their view in the introduction:

- 'The cornerstone of our theory is *confidence* and the feedback mechanisms between it and the economy that amplify disturbances.
- 'The setting of wages and prices depends largely on concerns about *fairness*.
- 'We acknowledge the temptation toward *corrupt and antisocial behaviour* and their role in the economy.
- '*Money illusion* is another cornerstone of our theory. The public is confused by inflation or deflation and does not reason through its effects.
- 'Finally, our sense of reality, of who we are and what we are doing, is intertwined with the story of our lives and of the lives of others. The aggregate of such *stories* is a national or international story, which itself plays an important role in the economy.'
(their italics)

They then go on to describe how these ideas can help us understand a number of real economic problems. This approach intuitively seems realistic and useful, but is in a different language from Dixit and Pindyck and the world of the mathematical economists.

The fallacy of composition is at work: what may be true at a micro level is not true for the economy as a whole. However, the intellectual desire to find microeconomic foundations for macroeconomics (or equivalently, that microeconomic factors 'aggregate' to macroeconomic results) has led as mentioned to a reinterpretation of Keynes, a fudging of his insight: assuming that sticky wages and other rigidities can lead to slow adjustment and so to sub-optimal demand in the short and medium term. Not just the Chicago School but New Keynesians[23] have adopted such thinking.

For several decades this has not mattered much, but maybe it does now (since the financial crises of 2008) as we face a similar potential for mass uncertainty delaying investment as in the 1930s. The consequence has been little business investment taking place in the US in the five years since 2008, but there are two interpretations of this. The common one is that as investment opportunities clearly exist, then investment is sure to pick up strongly shortly, and this will help drive economic growth. This is the more necessary for eventual economic recovery in the context that the US consumer – the previous driver of US demand – faces several years of deleveraging and fiscal adjustment (itself a cause of uncertainty) and so less consumption ahead. The other interpretation is that investment is suppressed because of widespread uncertainty. This can create low confidence and feed on itself and create, particularly in the absence of a significant boost in consumption (or other means to boost aggregate demand), a deflationary spiral and a depression.

4.5   BOUNDED DECISIONS AND BEHAVIOURAL FINANCE

Given the computational impossibility of the human brain analysing every possible choice and optimising continuously, we all take daily shortcuts in our thinking. Indeed, intelligence can be defined as the selective destruction of information. The constraints of computation can also be seen in economic theory. Adam Smith's 'invisible hand' is an example of the argument for bounded decisions, the opposite of the impossible dream[24] of central planning as a holistic optimisation of economic resources (also see Hayek, 1944). Likewise in investment, we institutionalise a delegation of thought, with separate decisions at the levels of asset allocation, manager selection and security selection. In risk management we have automated our thinking. We have graded risks, and invented risk budgeting behind which we assume stable correlations between investments and asset classes.

Bounded rationality, a concept propounded by Herbert Simon whereby people are seen as satisficers, not maximally rational as defined by RET, is a central tenet of behavioural finance. We also know that the neural networks in human brains appear to work through pattern recognition, not logic. Consistent with this, human learning occurs through familiarity, which leads to the development of implicit knowledge which has never been reasoned out. This starts to explain herding, biases and so-called irrational behaviour in investment behaviour. If we want to learn more about new things, we have to make a special effort to focus on

---

[23] The Chicago School of economics rejected Keynesian demand management for monetarism and then in the 1970s turned to New Classical Macroeconomics, with its focus on rational expectations and efficient markets. Partly in response to criticism of Keynesian economics from the Chicago School, New Keynesianism was coined to describe efforts to defend Keynesian ideas through finding microeconomic foundations which also assumed rational expectations but giving greater weight than New Classical Macroeconomics to market failures and imperfect competition.

[24] Actually a dream only ever harboured by very few.

them. This echoes what we know about herd behaviour in animals, which presumably learn in a similar evolutionary way by instinct. Herds are easily led astray, and when they get it wrong they can get it wrong spectacularly – even discounting their own informational cues, they will follow others (see for example Miller, 2010, pp. 207–208). Good leadership is thus essential. This has parallels and consequences in the investment universe. Herd behaviour by institutional investors, for example, can create incentives for herd fund management by those they employ – benchmark hugging.[25]

Supermarkets understand and exploit bounded rationality well. When we learn where our preferred products are shelved, we speed our shopping by going just to those shelves. But shoppers unfamiliar with the supermarket layout tend to spend more as, in looking for products, they notice the wider range on offer. Some supermarkets, making more money out of less knowledgeable shoppers, alter the layout now and then, just enough to distract regular shoppers and so encourage more impulse buying, but not enough to upset them so much that they shop elsewhere. Companies but also policymakers and investors can pay attention to such 'choice architecture'.

Supermarkets change the environment in a way often incomprehensible to the shopper. Likewise, global investment opportunities and risks change in unpredictable ways. Shoppers faced with a changed product location can look elsewhere or ask for assistance. On the next visit an experienced shopper will remember the new location for the product. If our investment and risk universe change, do we also adjust quickly? Arguably not, because we often do not know we are allocated poorly and do not know when and how to adjust. We tend not to change our assumptions of the nature of the investment opportunities we face and what constitutes risk, but perhaps we should. We are like blind shoppers with nobody to ask for assistance. Our bounded rationality goes from being an investment and risk management aid to being a hindrance, especially if the environment is changing fast.

Since the seminal body of work by Kahneman and Tversky on the psychology of decisions,[26] so-called behavioural finance has grown rapidly. The starting point for analysis is an empirical understanding of human biases and the way decisions are made, which may not only vary at the individual level from those assumed by the rational expectations assumption of unbiased expectations, but also, more importantly for economic analysis, may do so in aggregate. The economist is interested in the aggregate behaviour of many people, not of individuals per se; and economic assumptions of behaviour do not require that they be complex or accurate to achieve acceptance, merely that they have predictive power. Moreover, given the choice between models with the same predictive power, the preference is for the one with the fewest and simplest assumptions.[27]

Behavioural finance models are built to explain actual observed individual, and aggregate, economic decisions. These models can be seen as modifications and/or challenges to RET. They have been criticised by upholders of RET as failing to do more than explain some

---

[25] Nofsinger and Sias (1999) present evidence that equity market herding is caused by institutional more than retail investors. One suspects agency problems affecting institutional investors may outweigh the relative informational disadvantage facing retail investors.

[26] See Kahneman, Slovak and Tversky (1982).

[27] Occam's razor is the parsimonious principle of selecting hypotheses which, otherwise equal, have the fewest assumptions. A related concept is that, from among available choices which yield the same predictive power, the assumptions chosen for an economic model should be as simple as possible.

anomalies.[28] Perhaps taking that on board, much of the work in behavioural finance has been to take empirical findings and adjust RET models to incorporate them.

An alternative conclusion is that no easy or useful way exists to adjust RET to incorporate some behavioural findings. The evidence to back this up is the evidence that financial markets, not just individuals, can display biases and not incorporate all available information – the evidence, for instance, that major bubbles exist. This conclusion however is seen by some on both sides of the debate – pro-RET and pro-behavioural finance – as unpalatable. Vested interests by academics schooled in nothing else no doubt also play their part, a phenomenon not restricted to the finance or economics disciplines. The world without RET is a much more complex one: one in which structure matters and a priori assumptions about financial markets alone may blind us to major risks. If the assumption of rational expectations constitutes a good rough guide to reality, and there is none better, then analysts and investors should perhaps stick with it. But if it is no more than a rough guide, we should perhaps also be on the lookout for where its application is least appropriate as a model for reality. That a theory works well most of the time is taken by some to constitute empirical evidence indicating its relevance.[29] Yet if some of the rest of the time it fails not by a little, but spectacularly, then we also have empirical evidence that it requires selective application.

What then is the basis of behavioural finance? There are numerous taxonomies, but most of the work so far has tried to classify a series of empirically observed biases in decision-making which vary from the supposedly rational – i.e. from what we would expect if we assume rational expectations. So-called rational behaviour is often held up as a mythical standard of perfection; yet it is important to note that RET theorists do not suppose that the bulk of, or even any, individuals actually behave rationally as so defined, merely that there is in aggregate no major and systemic difference between actual behaviour and the behaviour which would result if all were rational.

Note also that so-called rational behaviour is not only not always how people behave, but often not even what we might otherwise define as rational in a broader sense. Rational investors are assumed to maximise their utility, but utility is often used as a catch-all term, and has little specific content beyond the tautological 'what one chooses'. People often maximise economic gain or utility in complex ways not captured by simple assumptions. People not only display satisficing rather than optimising behaviour, they also have what has been called visceral emotions: worry and fear can impact behaviour. Having said that, and for the sake of convention and ease of understanding, we shall continue here to employ the terminology of describing decisions which follow from rational expectations theory as rational, and others as irrational.

Many cognitive biases have been identified. Those of most relevance for investors have been categorised variously by different authors, but three common aspects included by behavioural finance are:

- The presence of biases in investors' decision making. For example, optimism, conservatism in adapting one's judgement to contradictory evidence and 'overreaction' to exciting, but rare, events.

---

[28] See for example Fama (1998).

[29] Then again, does it work most of the time better than the alternative explanations? The hypothesis for example that market sentiment drives markets – as monitored by momentum and technical analysis (driven in turn by psychological biases) – would appear in many instances at least as good a predictor as theories based on fundamental value.

- The use of mental 'frames' to simplify complex decisions or learning 'heuristics' to characterise and simplify data used in decision making.
- The presence of time inconsistency in choice, inducing a need to distinguish between the 'planner' and 'doers' of some proposed course of action.

From *Forbes* (2009), p. 7.

There has been a wealth of research on biases, including institutional investor biases, resulting in commonly observed over-reactions and then corrections, for example to earnings results.

Mental frames include various sorts of prejudices, models and shortcuts which we use to aid us in making decisions. Rules of thumb, or heuristics, can be helpful in making decisions but also lead to systematic biases. Tversky and Kahneman's (1974) initial work on rules of thumb concentrated on three of them: anchoring (for example, guessing a city's population by adjusting from the known population of another); availability (for example being more concerned by more familiar risks); and representativeness (making a judgement based on how similar a thing is to our stereotype). Some familiar concepts called primitives are also well-recognised devices acting as shortcuts, and, according to Shiller (2003, p. 84) include: 'private property, government, law, family, parents and children, kindness, sharing, charity, gift exchange, social hierarchy, religious symbols, honour, obeisance, leaders, heroes and fairness'. They are familiar categorisations that provide well-established frames of references for our thinking, enabling us to reach conclusions and solve problems more easily but also channelling our thoughts in well-established patterns.

By way of explaining the difference between the 'planner' and the 'doer' in us in the third bullet point above, Thaler and Sunstein (2008) describe the planner in us as the *Star Trek* character Mr Spock, the far-sighted rational thinker, and the doer as our instinctual Homer Simpson.

Dan Gardner (2008) further observes how our instinct kicks in when we have a prejudice. MRI scanning has shown that a different side of the brain fires when instinct is at play than when making rational decisions – prejudice takes physiological form inside our heads. Some have argued this has evolutionary roots. On the plains of Africa thousands of years ago, if we saw a potential danger we did not waste time trying to verify it; we ran. Perhaps, since we know this, professional investors should compensate, but one suspects this does not happen for the most part.

Investors treat potential gains and losses differently, are sensitive to absolute and relative differences in payoffs and engage in mental accounting by putting different sums in different mental boxes. They savour some things and dread others, both of which can alter their behaviour. Their consumption is often closely in line with income, which may explain an otherwise seemingly irrational concern about market volatility by individual investors. They often misinterpret probabilities from observed data (causing both momentum and over-reaction). They can be risk seeking in certain situations and risk averse in others.

Behavioural finance is a broad church at the moment, but also has linkages to the past. Keynes was quite aware that psychological factors could move financial markets – his famed 'animal spirits' – and for sustained periods, but also that such movements were based on fundamental factors. Specifically, he was very clear that goods markets do a better job than the state when it comes to allocating resources in an economy, but he also lived in a world where unregulated financial markets could overshoot, crash and cause severe disruption to the economy. Efforts have been made, as with the adaptive markets hypothesis (AMH), an amendment to the efficient markets hypothesis (EMH), to integrate behavioural finance into the main body of accepted investment theory through evolutionary concepts – see Lo (2005). Lo introduces bounded rationality and, following the work of Herbert Simon, assumes the objective is not to maximise gains but to survive, and lays importance on understanding the populations of different species of economic agents (the structure of a market). One hopes more accurate modelling of behaviour will yield more reliable and useful tools for asset allocation.

However, while there is a tendency among many to fit in with, and alter, EMH, others reject not only EMH but RET altogether. Shiller (2003) sings the praises of new information technology, comparing economics today to astronomy when the telescope was invented or biology when the microscope was invented (p. 81). He also, however (p. 270), makes clear our inability so far to look at large long-term risks:

> 'Persuading the public of the other, bigger, long-term economic risks that remain unmanaged today will take some work. … Public leaders must be willing to talk about longer-term risks that we all face.'

This includes, as Shiller says, using risk management devices to reduce longer-term risks such as unemployment, bankruptcy, home price falls, inequality and intergenerational inequality. It includes, also, knowing when to dispense with inappropriate theory and replacing it. It means investors should look to the long term and not be anything like as concerned as many of them are about short-term volatility. Volatility is not risk, as we shall explore in more depth in the next chapter.

Some of the divisions in economics discussed in this chapter have clear implications for finance theory, and the purpose here has been to flag some of the theoretical problems which we see causing confusion and systemic problems for investors:

1. We have noticed that economics has not escaped shifts in ideological fashion.
2. The invention of macroeconomics should be a comfort for policymakers, especially post-2008, but is a far country for most in finance and investment – a state of affairs glossed over by Chicago but also New Keynesian economists.
3. Finance theory is rife with false assumptions, starting with Markowitz's 1959 assumption that most co-variances between securities in an asset class can be ignored – leading to a (rich and complex) mathematical cul-de-sac.
4. EMH seems highly misleading and is widely discredited.
5. EMH, RET and mathematical alterations to them fail in times of great macroeconomic and historical moment.
6. Uncertainty is largely ignored.

5

What is Risk?

A Martian falls to Earth[1]

Say a Martian, disguised as a human, falls to Earth and becomes a trustee of a pension fund. He is concerned not to invest in markets which are too risky. Unfortunately, he likes abstract models, and rapidly takes to the mathematical beauty of RET and EMH. He sees no reason why people would not have identical preferences expressible via smooth fully differentiable mathematical equations, have perfect information and maximise utility – or at least most of them. He believes in the law of one price and that observed market clearing equilibrium levels must be optimal – traits that perhaps caused problems on his own planet. Perhaps he and his peers there argued that there would always be optimal equilibrium in the long term, but other equilibriums kept getting in the way, so they imposed a different type of equilibrium to take care of the short-term anomalies. Equilibrium, the tendency not to move, in biology is called death: hence the need to move planet.

He makes two errors in his new job. First, he assumes that there is no Knightian uncertainty, only Knightian risk. Risk can be managed and hedged: he assumes that the more he can analyse something, the more he will understand. As everybody else is doing likewise, the better populated an asset class, the lower the unmanageable risk. Unfortunately there are too many things to analyse and not enough time. Plus, anyway, it's just a job and this is not even his planet.

Secondly, he assumes all his human peers concentrate their portfolios the way they do for good reasons. If he thinks differently for a while, it must be that they know something he doesn't. When he has doubts, he reminds himself that, according to RET (and EMH), there are no systemic errors in the collective expectations of his peer group in the long term (and the short term). As there are a lot of professional investors, they must collectively have understood the risks everywhere, not just where they have traditionally invested. It is a bit odd, though – they tend to invest the vast bulk in the US and Europe.

This gets him thinking, and he asks a colleague about it. He was expecting a wealth of detailed arguments about the high risks of investing in emerging markets, but the answers he got were rather different and appeared as a sequence of arguments as below:

1. There is a list of established asset classes, and it does not include emerging market debt any more than Martian debt (was his disguise not working, he worried?).
2. Asset classes are defined by indices. If there is not an index, then it doesn't exist as an asset class. Even if it has an index, that doesn't mean it is an asset class.
3. Most investment added value is obtained from asset allocation, so one really has to look mainly at allocations across the available asset classes. If what you want to invest in is not in an established asset class, then tough – it's going to have to compete with a huge

---

[1] See disclaimer, p. 235.

number of wacky ideas fund managers tout all the time for the small amount we leave to one side for non-conventional allocations. Everything else, including manager selection, macroeconomics, politics and so on is subsidiary to getting the right asset class mix.

4. Oh ... and the starting point for deciding the relative weights of asset class allocations is the market capitalisations of the indices, which are themselves market cap weighted.

He thinks to himself 'So the allocation weighting is driven by index weightings; index weightings are driven by market cap; market cap is driven by ... investor demand – i.e. by us, institutional investor demand. But isn't that circular?'

Still bemused, as there does not seem in practice to be a tie-up between market size of indices and global allocation (some things are just excluded, emerging market debt accounting for US$14 trillion for a start), he asks the advice of another colleague, who answers that it's perceived not actual risk that counts; and if we invest in emerging markets and it goes wrong, we look foolish and get fired.

The more he thought about objections to emerging markets – political risk, macroeconomic management, reserves, fiscal positions, debt, etc. – the more he realised that none of the standard objections to investing, at least in the relatively safe investment grade debt of these countries, stacked up. The developed countries in all these categories often had similar or worse problems. And these risks were simply not priced in in the developed world. And then there was all the leverage in the developed world!

Especially now that we are in a world of major macroeconomic challenges should we not think of emerging markets as capable of reducing risk? And some of the managers in emerging markets were clearly more experienced at analysing sovereign risks than their colleagues floundering about and failing to understand the current Eurozone crisis. Our Martian asked about active managers and how maybe they could reduce risk to less than that represented by the indices. The stock response was as follows:

5. There is a list of established asset classes, and it still does not include emerging market debt any more than Martian debt. It might include emerging equities, but they are very risky.

Once he had repeated the question, and had suggested that to reduce risk he was thinking about emerging sovereign debt, not equities, and wondering if active managers could reduce the risk of major losses in the future (as distinct from short-term volatility), the response was:

6. Once you have set your asset allocation, you might want to have some asset classes actively managed (as opposed to passively buying the index components). Some say this is a waste of money – we don't really know why, but yes, it can work in practice.

7. If you do want to hire active managers you must ensure they manage to an asset class benchmark, because otherwise you have no idea what they are up to. You measure their performance relative to the benchmark using three main sorts of measure: excess return, tracking error (standard deviation of excess returns) and some measure of fit to the index (beta or correlation).

8. Managers can only add risk to the benchmark (hopefully in combination with higher returns): benchmark risk is by definition always positive. If you don't like the risk

characteristics of the index, then don't invest, because you can't (at least in theory) reduce the risk below that of the index.

Initially that seemed clear enough – a categorical refutation that his active emerging debt manager proposal could reduce risk. The more he pondered it, though, the more he wondered if his question had really been answered. Eventually our Martian friend worked two things out and suspected a third. Firstly, he worked out that humans with finance training talk about risk constantly, but do not mean risk in a broad sense at all – they misapply the word to mean short-term volatility. Secondly, they didn't know how to cope with unquantifiable uncertainty, and so they just assumed it away. He suspected that some of them found it much more attractive to do what everybody else did than to reduce risk in its broader sense.

Despite all the equations, he realised that habit and faith was driving investment decisions not science. Were the others, like him, all really Martians in disguise?

'In January 2008, there were 12 AAA-rated companies in the world. At the same time, there were 64,000 structured finance instruments, such as collateralised debt obligations, rated triple A.'[2]

We start this chapter with a discussion of some of risk's broader aspects. We then criticise the distinction between specific and systematic risk as being dependent on the existence of clear boundaries between known asset classes, despite such boundaries being arbitrary, changeable and unclear. We also discuss the tendencies 1) to extrapolate, 2) to ignore uncertainty and 3) to focus overly on volatility. We then discuss risk in emerging markets – how to assess sovereign risk, which necessitates analysis of macroeconomics, policymaking and market behaviour. I introduce a three-layer approach to thinking about sovereign risk.

It is easy to criticise our Martian as seeing the world in simplistic terms. A lot of investment professionals are fully aware of the issues highlighted and are trying strenuously to compensate for them. Even so, and as Goldman Sachs head Lloyd Blankfein's quote above illustrates, the outsourcing of critical analysis and risk management, not only to rating agencies but perhaps to the boxed-in safety of a quantitative analysis in general, needs to be rethought.[3]

Risk management is central to investment. All investments have risks and uncertainties attached. Some of these have been ignored for a long time by many investors. Too often they have been seen as exogenous and static in their characteristics. Lack of perception of risk has created its own (vulnerable) stability in many developed and other accepted markets – volatility being endogenous to the behaviour of the investor base.

So what is risk? Slovic has challenged the objectivity of risk: 'Human beings have invented the concept of "risk" to help them understand and cope with the dangers and uncertainties of life. Although these dangers are real, there is no such thing as "real risk" or "objective risk."'

---

[2] Lloyd Blankfein, "Do not destroy the essential catalyst of risk," *Financial Times*, February 8, 2009.
[3] The outsourcing of thinking in the form of passive index investing, including in 'tracker funds' and passive exchange traded funds (ETFs), also poses dangers.

He further argues that 'defining risk is thus an exercise in power.' (quoted in Kahneman [2011, p. 141]). Is it the West's power over emerging countries that denotes them as risky?

We talk of risky assets – but as opposed to what? All investments are risky to a greater or lesser degree. There are also different types of risk. Where sovereign default risk is small because countries issue debt in their own currency, there is still the risk of losing economic value, through inflation and devaluation, and this applies to all countries, not just emerging markets. Other types of risk include credit risk, currency risks, tax or capital control or other policy risks, regulatory risks, political risk, interest rate risk, duration risk, volatility, liquidity risk, counterparty risk, operational risk, legal risk, hedging or other basis risk, residual model risk, securitisation risk, reputational risk, market risk, leverage risk and mark-to-market risk. Many of these overlap, and risk is categorised differently by different institutions. For example, from the perspective of an institutional investor (Logue and Rader, 1997, quoted in Muralidhar, 2001) one might categorise under the headings 'investment risk', 'surplus risk', 'sponsor risk' and 'concentration risk'. There are many others.

Niall Ferguson (2006) in his book *The War of the World: History's Age of Hatred* argues that war may be caused in part by volatility in economic activity. Though small changes may be stimulatory, large changes in economic fortune can be disruptive, for individuals as well as whole societies. Stability is a comfort in and of itself, irrespective of income levels. Extremely volatile economic periods (both up and down) are often associated with income redistribution, typically a concentration, in turn generating a sense of injustice among those who lose out relatively. Income distribution probably has an optimal distribution for growth maximisation in a given economy at a given time (though this is quite likely impossible to calculate), but it is perceived by many, and most of the time, as a zero-sum game: if the rich are getting richer, and particularly if the articulate middle classes are not getting richer at the same time, there is often resentment. All the more so if it is happening quickly. With economic bubbles come economic crashes. With crashes come ample scope for policy mistakes, the politics of envy and hatred, and raised potential for manufactured disasters of the worst types.

So 'risk' is a word which takes on different definitions depending on how wide one casts one's imagination. A wide definition is 'future randomness of all types'. Extreme economic volatility (in GDP, employment levels and turnover, inflation, etc.), for example, is a concept of risk which should clearly be a concern for investors if Niall Ferguson is right. Then again, in a much narrower sense, modern portfolio theory (MPT) defines risk as standard deviation of expected portfolio returns – and in practice the 'expected' typically gets dropped in favour of backward-looking extrapolations. MPT has limits defined not just by its assumptions, but also because it provides answers to a limited type of question. It, and many other measures of risk and processes for managing risk, is a useful tool for thinking about risk once we are comfortable about the over-riding or bigger issues – when a simple extrapolation of the past is a good guide to the future. Yet that is not always the case.

Traditional concepts of risk are also framed at the individual level. Loss is not perceived symmetrically with gain, and the magnitude of potential losses matters. People can be risk-averse in certain respects and risk-loving in others. Tolerance for risk increases after big gains and after losses when there is a chance to break even. Career risk may impact investment decisions for one investor very differently from that for another. Incentive structures and behaviour can vary and are thus important for understanding risk management and investment behaviour in practice.

5.1 SPECIFIC AND SYSTEMATIC RISK

Our Martian was told (wrongly) that one could not have less risk in an asset class than the index risk. How did such an idea so easily falsifiable empirically become accepted? Modern portfolio theory (MPT), introduced in the last chapter, is used by asset allocators to construct portfolios with optimal combinations of securities – or of asset classes – to maximise return for a given volatility, or minimise volatility for a given target return.[4] To increase computational ease, the many necessary co-variances (between all possible pairs of securities) are replaced by a lesser number of co-variances, namely those between individual securities and a market index. But this is only valid if the securities can be assumed otherwise independent from each other.[5] For this to be valid, securities in an asset class should rise and fall together or otherwise rise and fall completely independently from other securities in the asset class – i.e. there should not be discernible sub-groups. If not, then one can try remodelling using smaller groupings of securities – smaller indices and factors[6] – such that the behaviour of such a grouping of securities can more realistically be assumed to be captured by the co-variance with the broader index and assumed otherwise independent from other securities or groups of securities. This is rarely even attempted. Moreover, such grouping can be problematic: chosen groups of securities may yet have strong dependencies with each other. And, making attempts at better representation more difficult still, such relationships – and so valid factors or sub-asset class groupings – change, sometimes unpredictably.

Mirroring Markovitz's assumption about index co-variances being sufficient to model the behaviour of large numbers of securities in a portfolio, MPT classifies 'risk' (defined as standard deviation of returns) into two component categories. Specific risk relates to individual assets and can be reduced through diversification. Systematic or market risk consists of risks inherent to a whole market which cannot be reduced through diversification within the market concerned. Relationships between securities which may help reduce risk are deemed irrelevant. Risk is (often incorrectly) considered binary – security-specific or index-related. Other risks, reflected in other co-variances, are ignored – for instance, a sub-group of companies may similarly be affected by an oil price change, or other (sub-index) sector-specific factors.

By focusing overly on the relationships between individual securities and indices one also solidifies the perception of clear dividing lines between asset classes (as represented by such indices). In practice these are typically not as clear-cut in terms of behaviour of the underlying securities, especially in times of market stress. At such times, the underlying fundamental risks of a security – not which index it happens to be in – may dominate asset price behaviour.

Most practitioners simply ignore these problems. They ignore types of variation and risk other than specific and systematic risks, and by ignoring measurable aspects of market reality they not only make sub-optimal allocation decisions but suffer from a false sense of security – they may underestimate risks, especially in periods of market stress. However, the dominant Markowitz view described does affect market price behaviour, itself reinforcing the apparent distinctiveness of asset classes and the adequacy of the simple systematic/specific risk distinction.

---

[4] We discuss this again in Chapter 8, together with some alternative approaches.

[5] Markowitz (1959, p. 99) assumes this.

[6] Rather than grouping individual securities, factors, such as macroeconomic factors, can be used to capture relationships between securities not otherwise captured by index co-variances.

The distinction between systematic and specific risk is also one which can operate at multi-asset class levels. One can have a portfolio of securities in a single market – a single market portfolio – and at a higher level a portfolio of these market portfolios, in which case we treat the characteristics of the single market portfolio as we do those of individual securities at the lower level.

Some of the systematic risk at the lower level then becomes specific risk at the higher as we pool risk from a larger universe. It is fairly crucial therefore that we have a clear idea of the boundaries between markets, and indeed that there be clear boundaries – for without such clear distinction it is no longer straightforward to split risk into systematic and specific categories and the analysis loses validity. But there are not such clear boundaries. For example: What is an emerging market? There is plenty of debate and not much consensus on even such a large-scale delineation.

The assumption of there being clear boundaries has driven much of the traditional approach to institutional asset allocation. Indices have solidified these boundaries. Yet the definition of where one market ends and another begins is largely arbitrary, a function of convention. As more asset classes have been discovered, so boundary problems have increased. And as markets have grown and changed, the evolution of the accepted boundaries has lagged.

Why should this matter? Let us consider what for convenience we can call the traditional approach to asset allocation. We assume for the moment that markets are all distinct and the boundaries known. If we want to construct a portfolio for, say, a pension fund, we can then use a comprehensive index, including all or nearly all the investible securities, to represent each of the markets. When an index is comprehensive it is often thought that investors cannot beat it on average: it is a zero-sum game[7] for them. Hence asset allocation (choosing which asset classes to select in what proportions) takes precedence over manager selection.

However, when the boundaries are unclear, and moreover when they change, and some or even all managers invest across boundaries, this simplification breaks down. One could simply tell one's managers not to do this, but that may mean attractive investment opportunities are missed.[8] Some managers can and do consistently outperform the indices used as benchmarks for their performance (the same indices whose volatilities are used to represent the systematic risk, and as inputs into asset class allocation exercises). This would be inevitable in a large sample of asset managers anyway. However, some of these managers not only have consistently outperformed but can be reasonably expected to continue to do so as a result of some market imperfection they are exploiting, including stepping out of the index-defined universe. And outperformance can mean not just higher returns but less volatility too. This tendency is all the more marked in fast developing new and less efficient markets – ones which are less accepted as major asset classes.

At a higher level of choosing not securities but asset classes, the same pattern emerges. Tactical asset allocation across asset classes can, and sometimes does, both reduce risk and add returns. Also, the lagging acceptance of the existence of a new asset class disadvantages those investors slow to recognise it and invest.

The reason for the breakdown of the traditional approach when boundaries are unclear is also in part down to the difference between optimisation in one stage and optimisation in

---

[7] Where no one can gain more except at the expense of somebody else.

[8] Just as managers' skills may cross traditional asset class boundary definitions, maybe systematic risk can be seen as doing the same. This, however, might lead us to define asset classes as contiguous with the things our asset managers invest in, and so the distinction between asset class allocation and manager selection evaporates – they are one and the same.

several stages. A multi-stage decision process may not factor in the way risks are correlated across asset classes – co-variance awareness is low.

The way portfolio diversification is modelled is also problematic. Markowitz assumed that the average of security-index variances of a portfolio reduces as more stocks are added. Consistent with this, there is research showing that randomly increasing the number of stocks in a portfolio beyond a certain number adds little value.[9] But such research is not particularly relevant to the question of how many stocks might be appropriate for a manager applying some analysis on which stocks to add.

Diversification, in accordance with EMH, can be considered a largely random process of adding more stocks. Although stock-picking is in practice widely seen as a valid source of return (relaxing the contrary assumption of EMH), managers are assumed incapable of re-ducing volatility in any way which exploits the co-variances between stocks, only those with the index. Focusing just on stock-picking, it is common to assume that for everyone with a bargain there must be a loser. Hence, for the average manager, diversification is assumed to be mostly unintelligent, and if stocks are chosen with less volatility than the index, then, on average, this is at the cost of less return than the index – exposure to the index being the key relationship of a stock to all others in the asset class. This is consistent with assuming there is only systematic and specific risk.

In such a world there is no value added from understanding different groups of companies, their different industries and sectors, different exposures to macroeconomics, policy or other factors. Reality is, of course, different, and managers can often, and if they choose, reduce volatility and risk to less than that of an index. If they can achieve this without giving up any return relative to the index, this is evidence that systematic risk, if it is represented by such an index, is a concept of doubtful validity. Being able to escape the trade-off between risk and return as measured by the index volatility and return is, on average, assumed impossible, and, employing the strict EMH assumption, due to luck not skill in the short term.

But managers can achieve this, contradicting EMH. Moreover, if they can achieve this on average, then not only is EMH disproven but also there must be variance due to more than just specific and systematic risk, or the index must be an inappropriate measure of systematic risk. Yet if systematic risk is not represented by an index then by what is it represented? Not something measurable. Being unmeasurable, it loses all practical purpose.

One of the reasons this problem has been hidden (until 1977 to academics and to the present for many practitioners) is that standard MPT is untestable. It suffers from circular logic. Roll (1977) proved that the selecting of efficient portfolios by MPT is no more than a mathematical consequence of its assumptions and the definition of efficiency.[10]

Yet from MPT we have the idea of beta (β) as a measure of a security's or portfolio's rela-tionship with an index – as shown in Figure 5.1, β is the slope of a simple linear regression line of best fit. But what if the relationship is non-linear? Or, even less tractable, one needs more variables and cannot usefully dispense with co-variances with other securities? Testing

[9] See, for example, Statman (1987).

[10] Specifically, Roll showed that the two-parameter asset pricing model of Black (1972) can only be tested for mean-variance efficiency, nothing more. Black's model is that the expected return for a security

$$E(\hat{R}_i) = R_f + \beta_i[E(\hat{R}_m) - R_f]$$

where R_f is the 'risk-free' return of holding cash, $E(\hat{R}_m)$ is the expected return of the index, and $\beta_i = \text{cov}(\hat{R}_i, \hat{R}_m)/\text{var}(\hat{R}_m)$, i.e. the co-variance of the security with the index divided by the index variance.

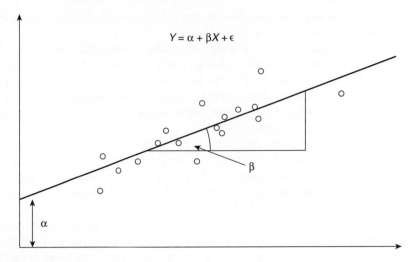

Figure 5.1   Linear regression: where α and β come from

the theory on these issues is impossible because of the circularity of the model's assumptions with its supposed findings (including that there is a linear relation between expected return and beta).

Ignoring co-variances – assuming only security relationships with an index are important – leads to a false importance given to indices as representative of asset classes, indeed of the usefulness of asset classes (so defined) as units of portfolio construction. The capital asset pricing model (CAPM) is also based on MPT and is a standard model for assessing if a security should be included in a portfolio – or indeed, in the world of corporate finance, whether a company should be acquired or not. It assesses a hurdle rate of return for portfolio inclusion of a security given its non-diversifiable (i.e. systematic) risk. A simple trade-off is assumed – so much extra return to compensate for extra volatility – often represented by a 'security market line' on a graph between these two variables. And different securities/ companies are compared with different indices.

Our argument so far has highlighted the arbitrary boundaries imposed by indices, and the circular logic which has obscured the importance of this oversight. The 'market portfolio' used in MPT and CAPM in theory encompasses all possible investments everywhere, which is totally impractical, as pointed out in the critique by Roll (1977). In practice divisions are made and only subsets of available assets are considered eligible to be part of market portfolios. A consequence is that the 'beta' of a security (its co-variance with the market return) is unmeasurable, and the CAPM model is untestable. Yet it is still widely used in practice. And its widespread use creates some of the market behaviour which in the short term appears to justify it.

So arbitrary delineation between asset classes – and the systematic risk concept – has consequences for our Martian's grappling with whether one can have less risk than the index. As mentioned, it is often assumed that one cannot, while staying in the asset class (or set of asset classes) concerned, reduce volatility (risk) below that of the index. This is valid if one adopts the following assumptions: that fund managers are mandated to be 100% invested in the market all the time; that they are not permitted to hold anything other than assets included in the index; and that the market is efficient according to EMH and hence there is no 'skill' possible to enable him to beat the market. This last assumption is crucial and provides a circular logic – if one assumes no skill is possible and so one cannot beat the markets, then … one cannot beat the market. It is simply assumed that they cannot reduce the impact of systematic risk on the portfolio. If, say, the systematic risk takes the form of a change in interest rates which impacts the asset class negatively but their portfolios less, then this is assumed to be the result of chance. They are assumed not to have reduced risk, but, indeed, to have added risk (called 'tracking error' or sometimes, confusingly, 'benchmark risk')[11] by straying from the index – a risk which (in this instance) paid off – but one which is added to, not subtracted, from the volatility of the index in assessing performance.

There is a further problem when managers stray outside the boundaries defined by an index. The moment any assets are excluded from asset allocation studies, as they always are in practice – including the most obscure private assets in the most isolated country, but also derivatives on instruments which are included in accepted asset classes – there is a possibility of a manager doing something outside the universe: outside the asset class or set of asset classes. This also breaks the fictional divide between systematic and specific risk.

What modern portfolio theory does is restrict the investible universe to the most understood and efficient markets. These may be where there is least opportunity to make excess return over the average. However, as shown by events after the 2008 financial crisis, asset classes which are apparently well understood and perceived as low risk can also see highly correlated selling in extremis as investors behave uniformly.

5.2 LOOKING BACKWARDS

There is a further problem. Simple quantitative analyses which try to find patterns in past data and extrapolate are blind to structural shifts in the relationships between variables over time. Theoretical models are meant to be calibrated with expected returns, expected volatilities and expected co-variances, but these are commonly no more than past extrapolations. Risk analytics, like econometrics and modern portfolio theory, is overwhelmingly backward-looking. They are useful but not complete tools. We can illustrate this again with reference to emerging markets.

Emerging market sovereign debt is a good example of an asset class (arguably several asset classes) often impacted by structural changes: this includes strong political dynamics (political events can significantly change asset prices), economic and other trends (such as the growth of local pension funds) and discrete policy choices which can significantly affect credit-worthiness and so asset values. In this environment, analysing sovereign risk is more of art than science, and the past is only partially useful for predicting the future. Indeed, knowledge of political history, understanding policy frameworks, incentives facing key decisionmakers and the structure and behaviour of investor groups are typically more important guides than formal modelling. There is no shortcut to obtaining this type of information – to do it well often requires building relationships with policymakers and local institutional investors over many years. But the very fact that such experience does take years to build is the

---

[11] Excess returns are the geometric differences between a portfolio's percentage returns and those of the benchmark index in the same period. A portfolio's tracking error is the standard deviation of its excess returns.

reason why there are strong barriers to entry facing money managers new to the asset class. This keeps up the advantage, the alpha,[12] for those who do have such experience.

One can think of many types of modelling, whether so-called 'fundamental' (based on some analysis of underlying causes) or technical (which try to predict the behaviour of other market participants), as attempts to identify patterns in historical data and extrapolate. In assessing sovereign risk, fundamental modelling typically focuses on identifying balance of payments or other macroeconomic disequilibria, but cannot normally indicate when a problem may become critical. As such, it may have explanatory power only after the event.

5.3   UNCERTAINTY

Keynes argued that under conditions of uncertainty as opposed to risk, the rational individual response is not to invest at all – an observable phenomenon and totally at odds with rational expectations theory. Keynes' insight has major consequences for economic prospects and policy, but also for market perceptions. In the face of uncertainty, behaviour becomes conventional – people simply do not assess, are unable to assess, all the facts.

However, North (2005, p. 14) follows Heiner's (1983) analysis that uncertainty is also the origin of predictable behaviour. When we are faced with complex situations and a large gap between the agent's competence and the difficulty of the decision (the C-D gap), we build rules to restrict decision choice, and these rules constitute our institutions. This does not mean, however, that we construct them in an ideal or optimal way, as our perceptions of appropriate rules may be misplaced. To explain how institutions change, we should understand the C-D gaps. For example, the difficulties in asset allocation have led us to define asset classes, amend and add to them too slowly, employ staged processes in asset allocation and manager selection, use mental accounting in portfolio construction and regulate financial institutions using crude and inadequate techniques.

We may perceive uncertainty as risk. Weak statistical relationships have often been assumed stronger than they are; robust when they are not. Importantly, structural shifts have been ignored or downplayed. For example, in late 2008 as the credit crunch was starting, there was a problem for assets, otherwise independent, which had leveraged (highly indebted) investor bases, and where correlations, previously low and reasonably stable, consequently moved close to one as the investor bases deleveraged. The common factors were the leverage and the similar motives of investors.

Financial markets also tend to overcompensate for perceived uncertainty: where we believe there is uncertainty we underinvest compared to where we believe there is risk. Unanticipated negative shocks have been found to have large negative effects on growth, as for example Dehn (2000) has shown with his work on commodity shocks. Historically, sovereign default risk has been much tougher to quantify than, say, US corporate default. There is thought to be more uncertainty versus risk in the former. This is reflected in ratings being unjustifiably low for emerging sovereigns historically on the basis of actual investor losses compared to

---

[12] Looking again at Figure 5.1, the term alpha (α) is derived from a simple linear regression of a fund's (monthly percentage) returns (Y) versus index returns (X) defined thus: $Y=\alpha+\beta X$. It is hence the amount of return expected from extrapolation of the past pattern, should index returns be zero (i.e. from the above $Y = \alpha$ when $\beta = 0$). A regression finds the line of best fit for a plot of XY data points. The best fit line is defined as the line with the minimum possible sum of squared error terms (the distance from the data points to the lines). Alpha is often confused with, but is not the same as, excess return (see previous footnote), defined as $(Y+1)/(X+1)-1$.

US corporate bonds, and unjustifiably strong for EU country sovereigns facing high debt burdens. In short, emerging markets have traditionally been seen as very uncertain – though in truth this perception may have much more to do with lack of familiarity than the existence of the unknowable. However, when there are big structural shifts coming in the global economy, then we find it difficult to quantify them: risk gives way to much greater uncertainty everywhere.

A further complication is that the distinction between risk and uncertainty is not as pure as first appears. You take less risk when you have more information and know what you are doing. One person's uncertainty can be another's risk. This applies to the understanding of emerging market politics, for example. The degree of information asymmetry in a market is another way of expressing this (the degree to which not all market participants have the same or nearly the same information relevant for valuing assets). In emerging markets, much of the information asymmetries which could be reduced through some fact finding and analysis is often instead preserved by prejudice. Also, uncertainty may not only be converted into risk through finding out more information but by aggregating and so revealing statistical probability distributions.

5.4   RISK AND VOLATILITY

The finance theory literature (and many investors) tends to equate risk with volatility. Yet the risks most investors want most to avoid are not volatilities but large non-reversible losses. Also, unlike volatility, risk is not additive because risk from identical investments is different for different people because of different liabilities, different information sets and different speeds of reaction.

A liquid instrument is one which can be sold fast, and is typically seen as less 'risky' than an illiquid one. But if everyone else sells as fast, this may not give much comfort, only visible losses. A liquid asset may be more volatile than an illiquid one over certain periods of time, and this may negatively impact one's ability to fund other things compared to a less liquid investment.

Then again, illiquidity can allow imbalances to build up for a long time, followed by catastrophe. Extreme event risk may be a larger problem for less liquid assets if risks go unnoticed for longer and so prices drift further from equilibrium. Hence liquidity, and the

mark-to-mark volatility which goes with it, should not be equated to risk in a simplistic way. Having liquidity means one has the ability to exit and avoid even greater risks. Volatility, by signalling possible problems early, can also help reduce risk, for example as policymakers take corrective action to mitigate investor concerns. On the one hand, a lock-up on a fund can allow it to buy into panic-induced market weakness where open-ended funds are unable to do so as they face redemption requests. On the other hand, you cannot easily get your money out of a fund you believe to be mismanaged, and this can lead to major losses.

Another sense in which risk and volatility differ is where there are significant information asymmetries in a market. The greater the asymmetric access to information (having earlier and more reliable information than other investors, enabling one to buy or sell before them) or greater asset manager skill compared to peers, the lower the risk for that manager in buying assets compared to risks facing the less skilled or less informed manager investing in the same assets. When one has more information, one is taking less risk; one is also less likely to panic-sell – whence the anomaly that confident and capable managers often wear through volatile market periods, making money as a result, but doing so while fundamentally taking less risk than managers with less information or skill.[13] In the process, the better manager can experience more mark-to-market volatility. So volatility often diverges from risk and may do so more, the greater the range of investor skills or information levels in a market. Another way to say the same thing is that low tracking error managers, in an asset class characterised by the ability to increase returns and reduce risks through active management, may be signalling to prospective clients that they have low skill levels and may not always achieve the best results.

To summarise the problem so far: the traditional approach (arbitrarily) defines the investible universe in terms of discrete asset classes. These asset classes, though they should be characterised in terms of future expected parameters, are in practice characterised by past returns, past volatilities (assumed to be similar to, indeed even called, risk), and a selection of past correlations/co-variances (confused with causalities) to other asset classes similarly defined. A multi-stage optimisation process then takes place, sometimes with reference to the structure of current liabilities, to determine asset allocation – i.e. the weights to be assigned in the portfolio to different asset classes. Past index returns are used in this process, not actual or expected manager returns, because it is assumed that managers cannot be chosen who can be expected to outperform consistently. Yet this is contrary to fact and theory in less efficient markets, and where index boundaries are unclear, as they are. So a bias is created, herding investors to indices and more established markets, and often also to more passive index-following managers. This consequently increases risk per unit of return, particularly major event risk where herding is most dangerous.

5.5   RISK IN EMERGING MARKETS

When it comes to sovereign borrowers, there are a number of difficulties in measuring default risk. Having tried to come up with predictive models for over four decades we have not found a model. So-called 'new models of currency crises'[14] tell us crises can happen

---

[13] Skill in portfolio management might be described as the ability to collect more information, process more information or discount it better than the average manager. This may involve using quantitative models but it may also mean not using them.

[14] See for example Isard (2005), p. 129.

suddenly, happen unpredictably to countries with some vulnerabilities, and that balance sheet mismatches reduce the effectiveness of fiscal and monetary policies. Unfortunately, one cannot easily model investor behaviour leading up to and in crises, and such models are of little use to the investor. But this alone should tell us something. There is, as already mentioned, a difference between risk, where the statistical properties of a distribution are known, and uncertainty, where they are not (even though they are sometimes thought to be). In the case of sovereign default we are more in the territory of uncertainty than of risk. This is in contrast to, say, US corporate debt in the absence of major macroeconomic problems, where, given enough companies and certain standard financial data, one can have a firmer idea how many will default.

The best that can be said is that when variables (for example debt/GDP or current account deficit/GDP) exceed certain safe ranges they indicate heightened risk.[15] This includes not just macroeconomic variables but also financial market factors (debt types, maturities and currencies), the reason being that the behaviour of investors is what matters. Liquidity measures such as daily traded volumes and simple 'risk aversion' measures – such as indices of market volatility or measures of interbank lending rates – have lost much of the advantage they had for a while in the 1990s for heralding financial market-driven crashes when emerging debt was highly leveraged, herd mentality dominant and emerging country finances precarious enough to tip countries over the edge.

If macroeconomic modelling is impotent, statistical modelling may be dangerous. At one level, statistical analysis of market behaviour can be useful, but is often conducted without understanding the causes of such behaviour. But behaviour in an inefficient and fast growing market is subject to sudden change. Arbitrage opportunities may be small (as we saw in Chapter 2, LTCM's response was to lever massively, with unpleasant results). Long-short and hedging strategies which depend on hedging risks and statistical relationships holding have often underestimated 'basis risk' – the risk that the instrument one uses to hedge a position does not behave as one expects under stress.

Models appear to have two problems when it comes to their practical usefulness to an investor. Firstly, there are timing problems. Identifying that a crisis might develop over three to five years is of no use in an environment where a whole range of major events can occur within six months. Models that conversely focus on the very short term are typically not helpful either – if something is critical, the market will already know about it. Secondly, even if one could find a model that identifies a problem developing in a three-to-six-month period, it still will not tell you the thing you really want to know: what will be the nature and timing of the government's policy response? To model that, one needs to get inside a premier's or finance minister's head.

What is the alternative or complement to models? There is no substitute for understanding the details of sovereign risk, the relevant history, politics and the policy dynamic and investor structure and behaviour. This may require experience and a wide variety of contacts and information sources, often built over many years. It requires not only the recognition of instability in market behaviour, but an ability to predict how that behaviour may change under different scenarios. In other words, rather than searching statistical data for correlations and then assuming they will hold when in fact they can break down, one needs to think through

---

[15] There is no consensus about what this level may be. Moreover, different debt/GDP levels seem to apply to developing and industrial countries (variously around 90% and 40%, respectively). The level of debt/GDP required in order to sustain investor confidence even in the same country can also vary widely.

scenarios under which correlations may change, how they may change and what triggers could lead to such changes.

We thus enter more explicitly the world of psychology or behavioural finance but also of political economy and history. To achieve our objective we need to be well acquainted with other (often local) financial market participants' positions, their thoughts on local politics and policies, and form views on how they might change positions in different policy/political scenarios. We need to understand the behaviour of different international investors, market makers and policymakers and regulators, and the interdependence of different variables.

5.6   RATING AGENCIES

Many formal models[16] of sovereign risk have focused on ability to pay, and hence the balance of payments – though there have been some studies of willingness to pay following Eaton and Gersovitz (1981). While some have predictive power, they have been of limited use to investors. They have explained events after they have occurred. Identifying disequilibrium may not be much use if it is sustained for years, and by the time something is critical there is typically no need for a model. Also, insofar as simple ratios, such as debt to GDP, reflect sovereign risk, several developed countries have fared much worse than emerging countries for years.

So what do rating agencies do? They traditionally try to estimate the risk of sovereign default by scoring countries under a number of headings including political risk, economic vulnerability, fiscal and monetary policy performance and external vulnerabilities. Ratings matter and do have an impact on price, particularly at the sub-investment grade level, and most of all when a country either crosses the investment grade line or defaults. Ratings do not change as rapidly as investor perceptions of risk, or for that matter the actual risk.

Also, investors (including those with long-duration liabilities) are often focused on shorter-term risks than rating agencies' medium- and long-term assessments. This is not to say that they are not interested in investing for ten years, or even in locked-up investments for ten years. Rather, they are often judged on short- not long-term performance. Even if invested in long-duration instruments, there is often a way to reduce exposure or hedge risk in a shorter timeframe.

Ratings also affect bond prices due to regulation, particularly Basle II and Basle III rules, which force banks to hold more capital against lower rated credits. The fact that ratings agencies continued to give high ratings to HIDC government bonds after 2008 has been a convenience for HIDC governments trying to fund themselves. Indeed, ratings agencies are part of the mechanism of financial repression. It also creates major agency problems that they are paid by those they are rating (this was not always the case). There is also evidence that ratings agencies do not invest enough of their own resources to enable them to assess sovereign risk in poorer countries (Ferri, 2004), and that they overestimate sovereign risk in developing countries (Collier and Gunning, 1999).

Emerging markets should follow China, who established her own Dagong rating agency (see Table 5.1). As emerging market pension funds venture abroad, it would be a travesty to employ Western rating agencies which encouraged investments into HIDCs rather than safer but traditionally lower rated sovereigns. Dagong's ratings frankly look more realistic to me.

---

[16] See for example the literature review sections of Manasse *et al.* (2003), Peter (2002) and Aylward and Thorne (1998).

Table 5.1   Long-term foreign currency ratings

Country	Dagong rating	S&P rating	Fitch rating	Moody's rating
Argentina	B–	CCC+	CC	B3
Australia	AA+	AAA	AAA	Aaa
Belgium	A+	AA	AA	Aa3
Brazil	A–	BBB	BBB	Baa2
Canada	AA+	AAA	AAA	Aaa
China	AAA	AA–	A+	Aa3
France	A+	AAA	AA+	Aa1
Germany	AA+	AAA	AAA	Aaa
Greece	CC	B–	B–	Caa3
Hong Kong	AAA	AAA	AA+	Aa1
India	BBB	BBB–	BBB–	Baa3
Ireland	BBB	BBB+	BBB+	Ba1
Italy	BBB	BBB	BBB+	Baa2
Japan	A+	AA–	A+	Aa3
Korea	AA–	A+	AA–	Aa3
Mexico	BBB	BBB	BBB+	Baa1
Netherlands	AA+	AA+	AAA	Aaa
Nigeria	BB+	BB–	BB–	Ba3
Portugal	BB	BB	BB+	Ba3
Russia	A	BBB	BBB	Baa1
South Africa	A–	BBB	BBB	Baa1
Spain	A	BBB–	BBB	Baa3
Switzerland	AAA	AAA	AAA	Aaa
UK	A+	AAA	AA+	Aa1
US	A–	AA+	AAA	Aaa

Data as at December 2013. Sources: Dagong, http://en.dagongcredit.com; S&P, http://www.standardandpoors.com; Fitch, https://www.fitchratings.com; Moody's, https://www.moodys.com. Both the Fitch and Moody's sites require logins to access.

5.7   CAPACITY, WILLINGNESS, TRUST

In practice there are many complexities and structural shifts in the relationships between causal factors. Estimating default risk in the short to medium term comes down to understanding the capacity and willingness to pay, and in the very short term the timing is largely driven by politics. Capacity is normally the more straightforward (though can be the less decisive in practice where the will is stronger than the means). To assess willingness to pay, one first needs to assess the motives of the key decisionmakers – their rationality and their incentive structures. If incentives are aligned with the best economic interests of the population (not always the case), one then has to make an assessment of what they are. Countries sometimes have a strong incentive to default, most typically when they have done so recently, face high costs of servicing debt and have limited prospect of accessing new financing. Conversely, as building a reputation as credit-worthy can take many years, a good payer, with a lower cost of finance, has an incentive to keep paying.

However, while past history may be indicative, it is the expectation of the future which is most important to an investor. John Pierpont Morgan was asked when testifying before Congress:

'Is not commercial credit based primarily upon money or property?'

'No sir,' replied Morgan. 'The first thing is character.'

'Before money or property?'

'Before money or anything else. Money cannot buy it … Because a man I do not trust could not get money from me on all the bonds in Christendom.'[17]

Previous good behaviour does not necessarily create trust, neither does bad behaviour preclude it.

Moreover, an overfocus on legal mechanisms of default or too much interference by regulators or other third parties may reduce the ability to create trust between borrower and lender – an illustration is that whether sovereign bonds are under US or English law has made little difference to restructuring outcomes. This point is all too often missed by those wanting to use formal and legalistic routes to restructure bonds. If trust cannot be re-established, then the country will not regain access to bond markets and has little incentive to strike a deal – they might as well stay in default. If they can regain trust, they are not going to do so as a result of legal wording in the documentation or the mechanism used for processing the restructuring, such issues being entirely secondary.[18]

5.7.1   Rich countries default by other means

So assessing sovereign risk is complex. But there is more than sovereign default risk to consider. When a country issues debt in its own currency some of the default risk is replaced by inflation and currency risk. In the spirit of Clausewitz, who described war as a continuation of politics by other means, we might say inflation and devaluation are default by other means. Either way, investors lose value on their investment. Having said that, currency and inflation risks are default risks a little bit at a time rather than all at once, and behavioural research confirms that this may be more acceptable to some investors. Given the choice of losing the same amount of money (particularly if it is somebody else's) gradually or all at once, it is human nature to choose the former: maybe this is more acceptable for reasons of reputation.

Emerging markets are often perceived as 'risky', yet objectively the risk is overcompensated for in the price. When one compares US Treasuries with a portfolio of, say, 25 emerging countries' sovereign debt (see Figure 5.2), emerging debt is less volatile (remembering that this is the comparison typically faced – not US Treasuries versus the bonds of a single emerging country). This is understandable as the local investor bases are multiple and different, as are the interest rate, business and political dynamics.

The fact that emerging markets are perceived as risky – and hence have to pay higher bond yields to investors – is part of their attraction. Investors who have overcome (or never suffered from) prejudice about emerging market risks rarely change their minds. But changing prejudice takes years if not decades – so the arbitrage opportunity of buying at higher risk-adjusted yields than the developed world equivalents is set to continue. The gradual trend for Western institutional investors to invest in emerging market debt since speculative

---

[17] Testimony of J.P. Morgan before the Bank and Currency Committee of the US House of Representatives, December 1912.

[18] This is largely from the author's observation as a participant in the sovereign debt markets. However, so long as there remains an absence of clear empirical studies demonstrating that formal sovereign debt restructuring mechanisms are counterproductive, they will no doubt continue to be propounded by some policymakers.

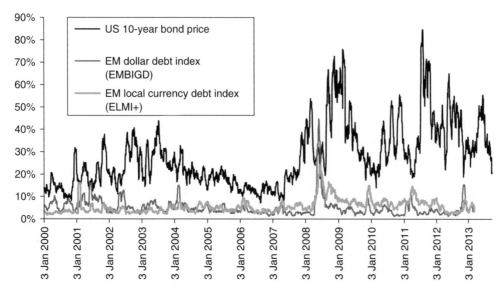

Figure 5.2   Fact vs prejudice: US Treasuries are more volatile than emerging debt. Source: Bloomberg, JP Morgan

money was replaced by institutional investors after the later 1990s is not so much cyclical as an uneven upward trend, as prejudice is eroded only gradually.

5.7.2   Two sets of risk in emerging markets

There are many risks in emerging markets, just as there are in the developed world. The main difference is that they are perceived better, even overcompensated for. Prejudice pervades our thinking. The idea that corruption or political risk (see box on 'Political risk') is greater in emerging markets should not lead us to think that these risks do not exist elsewhere. They often can be avoided or mitigated, and one may be compensated for them or can diversify and pool the risk.

As discussed in Chapter 2, the investor base in emerging debt changed in the early 2000s to a less leveraged, more institutional one, and sovereign credit-worthiness has improved substantially. The end of the Cold War has released countries from the imposition of outside uniform polices. Governments now reflect local culture, preferences and history, each one unique. The common factor of low income prompts macroeconomic prudence. Though there are groups of emerging countries sharing similar problems, there is plenty of diversity for an investor to take advantage of. Given the disappearance of factors which caused very heterogeneous countries to be similarly vulnerable to external speculative attack, we are arguably in a world with two sets of major risks for emerging markets, not three. There are those global risks which can affect all markets and which emerging markets cannot escape. There are those which are country specific and can be avoided in a multi-country actively managed emerging fund. But there is no major collective risk to emerging markets alone. That is an empty set.

Political risk[1]

Political risk is a component of sovereign risk. It exists in all countries, but is perceived (maybe overperceived) as a major problem for investors in emerging markets and often completely ignored in the developed world. And it is thus in the developed world where a political risk event is often a major surprise.

Political risk v. noise

Political risk takes different forms and is not the same everywhere. The occurrence of violence and regime change is higher in many emerging markets than in the average developed country. Yet that may or may not be important for an investor. Some countries in the emerging market category have experienced high levels of violence for many years, such as Mexico, without preventing continued investment in non-affected areas of the economy, and without a deterioration of sovereign risk. Northern Ireland is a developed world comparison for long-sustained violence. Likewise, fraud may occur in Enron or WorldCom just as it does in some emerging market companies, and political corruption is not an exclusive phenomenon of emerging markets.

Developed countries do differ in having much stronger institutions, more accountability of politicians and less violence than the average emerging market. We can hardly compare Berlusconi's alleged activities with those of the Ivory Coast's Gbagbo. Yet political risk takes different forms in the developed world and is often not priced correctly. Economic policy can expropriate value from investors. Retroactive impact from legislation is not uncommon in developed countries. And investors may have much less ability to resist politically motivated measures which penalise them in developed countries than in contemporary emerging markets.

So we need to separate what is important for the investor from what is not. From the investor's viewpoint we can define political risk as 'politics or policies which adversely affect the economic returns to the foreign investor'. For every hundred significant news items from a country, 97 might be noise, of no fundamental importance to an investment. Very few items of news impact sovereign risk. To the three remaining we might also add the impact of some of the 97 on the temporary behaviour of other investors, but these we can exclude from our assessment of fundamental risk.

Stability v. adaptability

Developed country institutions are stronger and older than in many developing countries. This has clear and major advantages but also disadvantages. Stability can also lead to an inability to adapt. If you are in a dark alley late at night facing thugs, you prefer someone next to you who has been in a few scraps. Emerging policymakers can be more practised and better at responding to severe shocks than some of their developed-world peers. The lack of speed in dealing with Northern Rock in the UK was really quite shocking (from an emerging market investor's perspective at least). Regulation to cope with systemic risk looks positively sclerotic in places in the developed world. In Brazil, which has sophisticated and complex capital markets, every derivative is registered – the central bank can identify pools of capital quickly and accurately if there is a systemic threat, and thus where and how much to intervene. What hope of such protection from systemic risk in the developed world?

---

[1] See disclaimer, p. 235.

Electoral responsibility

As mentioned in Chapter 2, the most important political event in many senses in the last half century has been the end of the Cold War. Since then there has been a widespread trend to market competition in domestic markets and to democracy. The poor in countries without welfare states, when they get the chance to vote, tend to vote for economic prudence – for growth and stability. The Indian and Indonesian elections after the onset of the Western financial crisis in 2008 are both illustrations of electorates voting for pro-reform incumbent administrations as a result of the uncertainties caused by the external shock. After the crisis in 1998 in South Korea, people were queuing to give their gold rings to help the state. Could that happen in the Eurozone?

There is no substantive ideological debate about the economic model in Latin America any more outside Cuba and (made possible because of government oil revenues) Venezuela. There is a more than 20-year-old Latin American pattern of politicians being elected on left-wing or populist rhetoric and then implementing more or less the same economic policies that their more (politically) conservative opponents would have. This should reassure us that rhetoric is often simply that. Economic policy is widely considered as too important to mess up. The political argument is no longer about how to generate wealth, but about how to distribute its gains. In Brazil, however much the political opposition and press argue otherwise, economic policy in its implementation is largely non-ideological. In Colombia the electorate voted for the less popular of the two main presidential candidates in 2010 because he had the majority in Congress to pass the prudent economic reforms both candidates agree on.

This latter example is in stark contrast to developed rich electorates voting in line with their often highly varied interpretations of events. People in rich countries vote more in accordance with the version of reality they prefer. There is arguably more denial in developed world politics about unpleasant economic realities and about the economic challenges ahead. There is certainly a lack of consensus on how to respond. The risk is that, as deleveraging and deflationary conditions persist for several years more in Western Europe and the US, so political myopia becomes a greater constraint on economic policy.

In the developed world, not least due to entrenched beliefs and vested interests in social welfare, political risks are correlated to economic stress. As job losses build so will political pressure in favour of economic short-sightedness.

Emerging markets have lots of political risk which the developed world does not, both in that certain types of political events (involving violence in particular) are more common, and there is often more political instability. But, and it is a big but, it is perceived and priced. This creates both market volatility (and the ability to take advantage of such volatility) but also reduces the chances of major unanticipated political shockwaves.

If we are concerned about risks in Western Europe affecting our investments in emerging markets, we should be more concerned about risks in Western Europe affecting our investments in Western Europe. If we are concerned about economic growth, we should be more concerned about the prospects of near-zero growth in the HIDCs than a possible scenario of only 4.5% growth in emerging markets. If we are concerned about inflation, we should be most concerned about it in countries with a pile of debt to erode and electorates protected from the ravages of inflation by welfare states. If we are concerned about China, as the largest emerging market, having a major impact on the global economy, then this is not an emerging market-specific concern. If we are concerned about protectionism, then we should be most concerned about the overindebted HIDCs most likely to start and participate in trade wars rather than emerging countries which have incentives to retaliate, but also to trade more among themselves.

5.8   SOVEREIGN RISK: A THREE-LAYER APPROACH

One can, for illustrative purposes, think of the market pricing of sovereign risk as having three component layers. The perception of risk builds from the bottom layer upwards.

The first layer, which I call the numbers or **ratio layer**, consists of macroeconomic ratios such as debt/GDP, fiscal deficit, etc. These are seen by many as the obvious components of sovereign risk. However, four observations are in order. First, formal modelling efforts concentrating solely on ability to pay have not (at least yet) been able to generate useful predictive tools for the investor, except perhaps for those who only make decisions very intermittently.

Secondly, many of the countries with the worst ratios today are developed countries. And Reinhart and Rogoff (2009) conclude that financial crises are just as likely in developed as developing countries, but also that the level of debt/GDP ratio above which default risk starts to rise noticeably is very low, at around 30%. This is not much more than telling us that default risk is low when countries don't have much debt – hardly revelatory.

Thirdly, sustainable levels of debt/GDP, for example, can vary enormously from country to country and over time. Britain's estimated debt/GDP of around 240% in 1820 was paid off.[19] Japan could maybe credibly sustain a level of 300% in the 2010s as its own domestic institutions can be expected to continue to be the dominant buyers of government debt at low interest rates, but for Greece in 2013 a level of 60% looks more like the credible limit. The question of what is a government's credible debt/GDP ceiling is a function of several things, including deficit and debt levels and the economic growth rate, but it is not easily calculable. Its determination is similar to the assessment of what reserve ratio is credible to sustain confidence in a bank. It is that amount which inspires financial market confidence, and is a function of financial market expectations. If a country appears to be a possible defaulter, the limit falls, making matters worse.

Fourthly, the set of measures which we think matters changes. The ratio of bank assets to GDP, for example, went largely unnoticed until 2008. As the ECB has pointed out, in the euro area this ratio went from 145% in 1992 to 331% in 2007 (Gonzáles-Páramo, 2011). Although we might make some credible guesses, we cannot know in advance those ratios which financial markets do not worry about today but will worry about tomorrow.

The second layer may be called the **policy layer**. Crucial factors in this layer are the ability of policymakers to implement sound economic policy and engender the spread of a market economy, and for policy to react in an intelligent and timely manner to events. These policy factors can collectively be considered as more important than simple (inherently more static) starting ratios. One could easily extend the definition of the policy layer to include many sublayers comprising different institutional arrangements. However, the point is not to define the problem of development in detail, but rather to emphasise its complexity and the importance of dynamic human agency in determining credit-worthiness. One of the impacts of the North

---

[19] This debt came down gradually to 100% of GDP in the 1850s and to around 60% of GDP by 1872.

Atlantic credit crunch starting in 2008 has been to raise policy risk considerably in developed markets.

Analysing the statements from central banks and linking this to changes in policy is an example of understanding the second layer. This can be combined with analysis of underlying economic data to give a much better picture than the data alone. In this way participants in financial markets have become used to analysing these two layers, giving credible explanations of events most of the time, and occasionally being able to predict the future.

Unfortunately for them, there is a third layer above the other two which they are often not aware of. It is like the atmosphere – large and taken for granted most of the time – except when there is a storm. The human brain will see patterns where there are none, for example in scattered iron filings, but not necessarily the same ones.[20] When the patterns observed in financial markets are so confused the third layer, normally quiescent and unnoticed, may be stirring.

This third layer pays even more homage to the power of ideas and may be called the risk perception or **prejudice layer**. In emerging markets this layer has arguably been highly significant for many years. It can also be thought to exist for developed markets, but much thinner or negative. To some extent this is equivalent to saying that the market has long overestimated risks in emerging markets if one looks at the quality of the macroeconomic numbers and quality of policymaking. If prejudices are stable, it may appear they have an impact on market prices but not changes in prices. However, the layer can nevertheless be seen as real, and a function of prejudice. Risk perception concerning distant countries can be greater than for closer countries or one's domestic market. It can be more vivid, often not evaluated with reference to probabilities, and often social – it is easy for a whole society to be prejudiced against a distant country they have little to do with in daily life. Prejudice can also be highly resilient to outside challenge – and so, while it may not be a good explanation for short-term swings and bubbles, it can explain long-term mismatches between risk and return.[21]

Indeed, because prejudices are normally static, those analysing just the ratio and policy layers can convince themselves that they are seeing more of what is relevant for sovereign risk than is in truth the case. But at times when prejudices are challenged, and investor and policymaker behaviours change, such analysis starts to flail.

Prejudices towards emerging market risk can be viewed as wrong because they are irrelevant or incorrect. They can be irrelevant insofar as they do not affect the investment concerned. For example, poor corporate governance may be a significant risk for equity investors but irrelevant for sovereign debt. Much of the news coming out of a country is irrelevant for most investments except insofar as it impacts investor sentiment in the short term. In many cases this means that a 'bad' but irrelevant piece of news – i.e. one which has no lasting impact but causes some investors to sell – can be seen as a buying opportunity.

Prejudices which are often incorrect rather than just irrelevant concern (among others) corruption and political risk. They are often real and substantive, and impact investment returns. The prejudice is to overestimate their impact and to do so relative to similar risks in developed countries. Corruption and political risk are everywhere, not just in emerging markets.

---

[20] This has been coined apophenia, of which the gambler's fallacy is an example.

[21] Somewhat similarly, North (1981) bases his theory of institutions on three pillars – a theory of property rights, a theory of the state and a theory of ideology. It is in this last pillar that he discusses changing perceptions of objective reality.

They are often ignored in developed countries – investors pay the cost without noticing – but sometimes are revealed and come as a great surprise.

The layers of risk in emerging markets are changing in two important ways as mentioned in Chapter 2. First, at the policy layer there has been very substantial progress – on fiscal policy in particular – and this has led to many improvements at the ratio layer and prejudice layer. Arguably more important, however, has been the impact of change in the structure of the investor base (the types of investors holding the assets) with profound associated reduction in the size of the prejudice layer. With the move since 1998 towards local investors, and towards non-leveraged external institutional investors, not only has the perception of emerging risk changed dramatically but so has actual risk. Prejudice can still price assets, but it has less ability to affect underlying risk.

5.9 PREJUDICE, RISK AND MARKETS

Do financial markets know which countries are risky by some sort of instinct, price them accordingly, and then come up after the event with arguments as to why they are priced that way? Or do market participants objectively assess all countries according to the same criteria? The former would be prejudice of course, but rather a self-sustaining one for all that if enough investors share the same prejudice. After all, and as already mentioned, the rational investor does not strive to avoid stupid decisions, but, where the market is expected to be collectively stupid, to do the said stupid thing first, before everybody else does. In this sense, at least for a while, possibly a long while, perception becomes reality – this insight is not exclusive to political spin doctors.

Prudent long-term investors will want to avoid such prejudices, but with the proviso that collapse of the said prejudice is likely within the timescale of their liability structure. Hence pension funds, with an average liability of 15 years, are going to be more averse to prejudice-driven investment views (short-term behavioural trends might be another name for them) than a hedge fund manager.

A further observation about prejudice – the good thing about it – is that it is asymmetric. Once lost, it is gone forever; unlike knowledge, which if lost can be re-acquired. The consequence for an asset class affected by significant prejudice is that as investors see the light and shed their prejudices, they tend not to become disillusioned again (or not for the same reasons).

However, prejudice tends to be slow to change. This can offer long-term arbitrage opportunities for those not so prejudiced, but also can be a frustration. People guard their views, including their prejudices, carefully; even nurture them. The vulnerability of prejudice to fact is often understood implicitly, and those with strongly held prejudices often prefer to stuff their ears full of cotton wool at the first sign of oncoming knowledge. Then again, people have often simply made up their mind on a subject already and don't have the time to reconsider it. However, another possible reason for intellectual stubbornness is that, for some of us, our prejudices help define our sense of self, both to ourselves and others.[22]

---

[22] For example, consider someone who enjoys telling a group of friends that she has never watched a certain trashy but popular television show. She manages to display, consistently over many years, ignorance of any of the main characters. She perhaps, in a small way, is pleased not to have wasted her time watching it and can signal this to others. She has only to watch the programme once (and admit to it) and her prejudice (and her ability to boast about it) is gone, never to be retrieved. Is this a common type of behaviour? Does it apply to many investors' views of emerging markets?

Everybody 'knows' that emerging markets are risky, which is precisely why, in price-adjusted terms, they are less risky than many developed markets (where people often assume there is little or no risk). We create investment principles which structure and so guide our decisionmaking. Common examples include:

'Emerging markets are highly risky.'

'Equity outperforms debt.'

'Investing at home is less risky than investing overseas.'

'Doing what peer group investors do is safer than doing something different.'

'Delegating asset allocation advice to traditional experts will reduce risk.'

'Past volatility is a good measure of risk.'

'Asset class distinctions, justified by lack of correlations between them, are stable.'

'Asset class valuations revert to the mean, which justifies portfolio rebalancing.'

'Getting asset class allocation right is more important for returns than manager selection.'

A moment's reflection will show that while these principles may have been helpful props to our thinking in the past, they are not necessarily true. Arguably, in a crisis situation as in 2008 characterised by big structural shifts, all the above are false, and at the same time.

At times of major structural changes, one should question asset allocation and risk assumptions. Yet this is difficult, and particularly during a crisis fear drives us to what we know or think we know. Our natural urge is to reduce risk, but we tend to do so in a systematically biased way which seeks the comfort of familiarity. We become more myopic and more consensus-driven. Joining the crowd works well in many situations, but not too near a cliff edge. Being conservative and reducing risk are different concepts.

The way we perceive the world drives our investment decisions and risk perception plays a large part in what is and is not acceptable as an investment destination. We tend to think in a binary way however: something is either risky or it is not. More precisely, we think in a lexicographic way: first is whether something is risky or not, secondly, for those investments we consider risky we try to rate or rank them. This is sub-optimal, even irrational.

5.9.1   When you have a hammer, everything looks like a nail

The largely traditional view of risk as an add-on process to investment, an afterthought, is one of risk as purely exogenous and thus quantifiable. It is a world of risk budgeting (choosing investment combinations so as to limit expected future portfolio volatilities) and compartmentalisation. It is also the world of assuming certain risks to be independent, with low correlations, because they had low correlations in the past. Yet if there is no stability in the relationships between variables over time, then time-series analysis has little predictive power.

To assess and manage endogenous risk is not easy: hence bean-counting and box-ticking are more popular. Investment views and reactions becoming more homogenous (and therefore problematic from a risk perspective) may be a reflection of the globalisation of finance but also of media and cultural components of globalisation. One needs to consider the dissemination channels of information and views, the degree of homogeneity of incentives, and hence the likely collective behaviour of investors. This may be more achievable in some markets than others, and requires active focus on market 'technicals' (behaviour) as well as 'fundamentals'.

When catastrophe hits, as with LTCM in 1998 or the financial crisis in 2008, and markets have behaved in direct contradiction to the expectations of many market participants and to the theories they adhere to (such as EMH), there are two responses: adjust or deny. It is perhaps surprising that many people now are unapologetic and just cling to their long-held views despite the most dramatic contrary evidence.

Risk perception needs to change. Unless we see a change in herd behaviour and a change in the idea that some investments are 'risk-free', then we will continue to have major risks build unnoticed. We may experience more avoidable bubbles and crashes, indeed more superbubbles.

The misallocation of emerging market savings to the developed world since the Asian crisis in 1997/8 as emerging countries decided to insure themselves and build up huge reserves has, in part, been a result of emerging market central banks' misperceptions of what is safe. As mentioned, these allocations pushed down the whole US yield curve artificially, and so, together with lax regulation, helped create the superbubble and credit crunch.[23]

---

[23] See Altumbas *et al.* (BIS Working Paper, March 2010), which concludes: 'Low short-term interest rates may influence banks' perceptions of, and attitude towards, risk in at least two ways: (i) through their impact on valuations, incomes and cash flows which in turn can modify how banks measure risk; (ii) through a more intensive search for yield process, especially when nominal return targets are in place. These two ways may be amplified if agents perceive that monetary policy will be relaxed in the case of decreasing asset prices in a financial downturn (the so-called insurance effect) causing a classic moral hazard problem.'

6
Core/Periphery Disease

Our view of the world matters. Our perception of the world is a simplification, a model – and none of our ideologies, as Greenspan calls them, can be accurate.

There are different views of reality. Is spin reality? Is perception sometimes more important than empirical observation? Clearly some powerful people think so. A senior adviser to former US President George W. Bush told journalist Ron Suskind (2004) that Suskind lived 'in what we call the reality-based community', where you 'believe that solutions emerge from your judicious study of discernible reality.' When Suskind started to respond, the aide cut him off: 'That's not the way the world really works anymore. We're an empire now, and when we act, we create our own reality …'. Power is to a certain extent the ability to ignore the reality of others; to create new dominant thoughts which others follow and so to create new realities.[1]

Markets are their own empire. They are self-referential in that the beliefs of market participants determine patterns of market behaviour which in turn appear to validate the beliefs. Risk perception, for example, is self-referential. Perceptions of risk (not merely independent events) determine patterns of market behaviour which appear to validate the risk perceptions, and so reinforce them. Such risk perceptions can drift a long way from objective likelihoods of loss. This is backed up by what we know from behavioural finance. People's perceptions are biased by overconfidence and optimism and people often believe in 'hot hands', which results in rhetoric and sentiment trumping empiricism and careful judgement. Consequently, for an investor it is often more important, at least in the short term, to predict market perceptions and consequent behaviour than any more fundamental reality.[2]

Without getting too philosophical about reality, and the structure of thought and the media, suffice it to say that our perception of reality often differs from that of others. We all rely on mappings and models of reality; some more and some less useful. Dominant views emerge – but can also be proved wrong and can change rapidly. Even with something as seemingly objective as hard science, a new paradigm, such as Einstein's relativity, takes a long time to gain widespread acceptance and supersede a preceding paradigm such as Newton's. Merely explaining more phenomena and describing reality better is not enough. Eventually a critical mass of followers is reached and a rapid 'paradigm shift' occurs. The ability to solve major new problems helps. Having said that, there are always diehards. Near-universal acceptance has literally to wait for older scientists to die. Likewise, a full and genuine rerating of emerging markets in institutional portfolios will have to await a change of guard at the top of these institutions.

Why rethink a basic concept, like the shape of the (investment) world? I argue that our mental map needs radical change in relation to emerging markets and the role they play now and will do in the near future. Neuron-based intelligence and experience grow through use and empirical testing: through the development and growth of some connections but not others. The structure of our thoughts is thus largely conservative, based on past ways

---

[1] After Deutsche (1963).
[2] As Keynes pointed out in Chapter XII of *General Theory*.

of thinking – as are our institutions. We all need shortcuts to be able to think constructively, and these evolve to include various strongly held views, robust after long testing by human experience (not just our own): principles and theories, rules of thumb, but also a wide variety of prejudices, many of which have been valid in the past, some of which are no longer valid. We need to challenge these from time to time – such is the nature of progress in human thought. Reality changes, and with it we may need to employ different, more appropriate, models and views.

At times of big structural changes in the global economy, we should re-examine the validity of key assumptions about the structure of the global economy. The post-2008 credit crunch and deleveraging challenge is a North Atlantic disease, not one that primarily afflicts emerging markets. The huge reserves in emerging market central banks can work as self-insurance policies. The so-called 'Great Moderation' is over and global rebalancing is coming.[3] The world is upside down. What was perceived safe is now risky or uncertain, and what was considered risky is relatively safe.

6.1   THE CORE/PERIPHERY PARADIGM

Our mental maps have changed in the past. The medieval European map and concept of the universe with its celestial spheres was very different from the one we have today, for instance.[4] Those who make maps have the prerogative to place their nations, or the places they consider most important at the centre, as for Jerusalem in the English Mappa Mundi (created around 1300 and reflecting the spiritual thinking, not just the geographical knowledge, of the medieval Christian church). Today, for all our ability to measure accurately, we also have a distorted mental map of the world. I call it the core/periphery model or the core/periphery disease, given that it is so deeply engrained into many people's brains. The core is the developed world, and the periphery is the emerging markets. The essence of the idea is that the core affects the periphery, but we can ignore the effect of the periphery on the core. Those in the core don't think much about the periphery, except as a source of stories to bolster their existing prejudices. Those in the periphery also defer to the core, suffer from inferiority complexes, or, even if they have a high opinion of themselves, look down on others in the periphery. And having a high self-opinion typically takes the form of trying to be more like the core – which may not be in their own best interests.

The core strongly affects the periphery, which is an appendage: the periphery follows the core, is secondary to it, of minor importance. Those in the core may find it diverting to think of the periphery from time to time, but it is not vital to them. A thousand deaths in a foreign land may compete with one local death for media airtime.

Yet this is changing as the average geographical scope of our communications with each other increase, identities become more global and we become more empathetic. If we accept that human capacity for empathy or understanding of complexity is bounded by the physical constraints of our brains, then discounting distant events and issues may be rational, not simply a matter of ignorance. Rifkin (2009) argues that empathy is on the rise. Clearly it differs across countries. In the US there is more inequality than Sweden, where arguably equality

---

[3] The Great Moderation, a phrase coined by Ben Bernanke in 2004, refers to the pre-2008 period of reduced volatility in the business cycle since the 1980s.

[4] See Lewis (1964).

is valued more than individual success.[5] Maybe empathy grows with income, maybe with education, maybe with technology and media, or maybe with borders and common problems.

In the meantime we are stuck with core/periphery thinking. This powerful prejudice originates at least from the historical period of European empire and colonialism, when all reference was to the centre, and replaced other core/periphery views in China, India and elsewhere. Not only did Europe see itself as central to the world, but other regions perceived Europe as central too. Emerging markets historically were locations on the outskirts of European civilisation, where natural resources were first plundered and then traded back to the centre of empire. Transport networks were built for this purpose. The location of cities, often on major rivers or coasts or other export transport nodes, was likewise dominated by the logic of international trade, rather than fostering and catering to domestic demand, particularly in those parts of the world less hospitable to European settlement, such as much of sub-Saharan Africa. More recently there came dependency theory (after Prebisch and Singer) and the sub-discipline of development economics, within which the concepts of core and periphery were strongly ingrained. To this day the global monetary system (the set of institutions which govern currencies and cross-border capital flows) is dominated by developed world currencies (making up 98% of reserves at end 2012, according to IMF data). This dominance is an aspect of core/periphery thinking, and a long way from representative of global economic activity and linkages. The idea of a core and a periphery also remains imprinted deeply in how we view emerging markets as investors. This view of the world is out of date and deeply misleading.

6.1.1   Core breach?

It is a feature of the core/periphery model that when there is a problem in the core nobody thinks very much, at least initially, about the periphery. And if one does think about the periphery, the natural assumption is that it suffers from the same problems as the core. If, added to that, there are obvious problems of credit crunch in specific countries – for example, initially in Eastern Europe and Russia in 2008 – and moreover signs of distress elsewhere in emerging markets, or then again sell-offs in 2013 in emerging markets triggered by fears of US interest rate rises, this is seen as corroborating evidence to the thesis that the periphery is bound to suffer, possibly more so, from the disease at the core. Academics and the media ask questions about the vulnerabilities of the periphery (e.g. concerning the effect of being cut off from international capital, of facing major inflationary pressures, of uncontrollable debt dynamics, of inability to sell sovereign bonds, or of a major devaluation) which are simply not asked about the core. The bias is subconscious, and conclusions drawn about relative risks thus often both false and widely held. Where there is evidence that the causality is from the periphery to the core, the reaction is often surprise.

The scope for effective fiscal stimulus five years on from 2008 is still much less in the core than in the periphery. Should there be a messy exit from quantitative easing, a bond crash in HIDC sovereign bonds or an extended slump, then not only are potential economic consequences much worse than those of the collateral damage affecting emerging markets,

---

[5] Why might this be so? One might argue that part of being Swedish, being a relatively small nation, is fear of the outside, leading to a greater desire to engage and co-operate with the outside world. Nordic countries also give more foreign aid than the average developed nation.

but the policy tools available are necessarily different and far less adequate: they may simply not work.

The main problem facing developed countries in late 2008 was arguably the recapitalising of their banks. Rather than seize them, this is still at time of writing being done piecemeal, requiring stability in financial markets and time for the banks to rebuild their balance sheets. During this period policymakers have tried to avoid major uncertainty – which might induce a greater investment strike and so a slump. Hence it has also been a priority to avoid a disruptive currency devaluation crisis severe enough to create further financial market uncertainty. However, the ostensible main focus of developed market policymakers in early 2009 was fiscal expansionism. This was appropriate for China in 2009, facing a temporary shortfall of aggregate demand as the country moves from an export-oriented to a consumption-led model of growth, and being a high savings, high growth, low debt (by HIDC standards) economy. But the problem in much of the developed world in 2008 was the opposite: not too little aggregate demand, but too much. Excess leverage in financial and housing sectors and excess consumption (in the US certainly) needed to be reversed. Expansionary fiscal policy in this context is a palliative, not a cure. It is the drug fix that the addict takes to make the pain go away, with an associated cost to pay later.

Developed world fiscal policy has been used to reduce hardship in an economic slowdown, not simply to adjust macroeconomic balance as fast as possible. For this legitimate reason, and given the political difficulty of major structural change in government budgets at the time, fiscal policy in the post-2008 period has been inefficient – its multiplier impact is low (for a survey of multipliers see Ilzetzki et al., 2011). Keynes referred in *The General Theory* to the multiplier benefits of digging holes in the ground (gold mines). The digging may have no direct economic benefit, but those employed consume more than in the counterfactual case of their being unemployed. This consumption stimulates the creation of more jobs and in turn more consumption, and so on. This multiplier effect is greatest where part of the workforce is unemployed beyond normal levels and other resources are underutilised, but weak when there is little spare capacity in the parts of economy being stimulated – then one gets 'crowding out' instead. Where the economy has been leveraged and there has been overconsumption, such stimulation by fiscal expenditure is not very useful except in delaying the day of reckoning.

This is especially true if the expansionary fiscal policy is wasteful – a multiplier of less than one from government expenditure is entirely possible – notwithstanding recent research that multipliers when cutting expenditure may be larger than previously thought.[6] Such waste may occur when government expenditure is not only less effective at creating jobs than the private sector (quite believable for most developed economies) but is a net destroyer of them. Absurd though this may at first sound, it is entirely possible if, say, the bulk of fiscal expenditure goes on transfer payments which distort employment market incentives and on employing public servants who create job-destroying regulations and tax cuts which increase savings but not consumption. Indeed, one of the conclusions of Ilzetzki et al. (2011) is: 'During episodes where the outstanding debt of the central government was high (exceeding 60 percent of GDP), the fiscal multiplier was not statistically different from zero on impact and was negative (and statistically different from zero) in the long run.'

If that is not bad enough, fiscal expansion can come at an additional cost. Insofar as higher expenditure is not funded by higher taxation, the government has to borrow in order to spend,

---

[6] Blanchard and Leigh (2013).

and the national debt goes up as a result. At some point this may significantly increase the marginal cost of financing the government, as investors in government bonds start to price in the extra inflation/devaluation/default risks associated with a great national debt by demanding a higher interest rate on the bonds. Some recent authors have belittled this. Hence while there are legitimate reasons to avoid a reduction in aggregate demand in credit crunch countries, the case is not a simple one. Design matters: where the expenditure occurs and what its multiplier effects are. Also, a government's credibility that it will revert to stricter fiscal discipline in the future is important, possibly to the extent of being critical to financing expansion today.[7]

Therefore we have a problem in the 'core' countries. I put it that the problems faced in the periphery are not anything like as worrisome as in the core and are much more manageable. The range of policy instruments at the disposal of emerging market central banks and other policymakers (use of reserves, interest rate cuts, bank supervision changes, moral suasion on key private sector actors, extending taxation, greater prudence in expenditure, structural and sectoral reforms, state-sector investment) is much greater than for their peers in the developed world. From an investment and asset allocation point of view, emerging markets are much safer places to invest than the core countries in the worst-case developed world scenarios, depression being the worst (short of war, to which one can ascribe a much lower probability).

Global economic growth no longer depends – and hasn't done for about 20 years – on the developed countries alone. Whereas threats to that growth in the 1990s often came from emerging countries, since 2008 they decidedly are coming from the developed world. Even if one still considers emerging markets peripheral (let alone if one doesn't), there is now a strong case that emerging market asset classes are collectively safer than Western Europe and the US (see Figure 6.1).

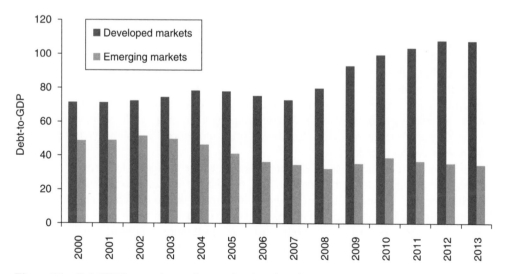

Figure 6.1   Debt/GDP: emerging markets vs developed markets. Source: IMF

---

[7] For a recent survey, see Spilimbergo *et al.* (2009).

6.1.2   Another core/periphery concept: decoupling

The theory of 'decoupling' is an unhelpful derivative model of core/periphery thinking. In a globalised world with numerous complex interactions, it is simplistic to think of 'decoupling' – the word 'couple' denotes two things to some: a core and a periphery. Much worse, though, the concept is used in a misleading way. Through association of the periphery with additional risk, it fails to help us register that in the worst-case scenarios (in the core) the periphery, though negatively impacted, becomes a considerably safer investment destination. Think of depression in the US with all that entails versus an associated major slowdown in growth in the emerging world.

Due to prejudices and some of the problems of risk perception we have discussed, when developed world investors become concerned about problems in the developed world, they sell supposedly 'risky' assets. To them, this often perversely means emerging markets rather than the markets which actually have heightened unpriced risk nearer home. They also assume that all other investors that matter are like them. Yet emerging market investors are significant global creditors, especially central banks – holding over 80% of global reserves and as a result core to the stability of developed countries. Emerging market central banks can be expected to react, possibly very destructively, to seriously bad news in the developed world, even if they do very little in reaction to only moderately bad news (and allow their currencies, bond and equity markets to sell off a bit due to Western investment portfolio outflows). It is a core/periphery conceit of the West that their capital flows to emerging markets are more important than emerging market flows to them, and when the opposite may prove more pertinent.

6.1.3   And another: spreads

The language 'risk-free' used to describe US Treasury curves and their equivalent government yield curves in developed countries is misleading. The HIDC debt overhang means there is significant risk of loss from holding dollars, euro and sterling. Deflation and devaluation risks dominate, but there is also a risk of inflation in a few years as a means to reduce debts, or if exit from quantitative easing is mismanaged – possibly sooner if devaluation occurs uncontrollably fast. There is rising political risk (defined previously), operational risk (loss from an internal process failure), counterparty risk (the credit risk of a contracting party such as an investment bank), basis risk (from imperfect hedging – defined previously), and various forms of market risk (loss from asset price movement) including yield curve risk (risk from a shift in interest rates).

The notion of (peripheral) sovereign credit spread above the (core) US Treasury curve is another core/periphery derivative concept. The spread is the amount of additional yield above the 'risk-free rate' the market requires from an investment due to its default and other risks. Yet emerging market sovereign default risk is very similar to, in some cases less than, that for many 'risk-free' countries. Some other risks are much more significant than default risk, especially currency risk. No investment is risk-free. The 'risk-free rate' is a fiction and can be more volatile than the supposed credit which trades above it.

Once we dispense with the idea of a core or risk-free rate, the concept of a spread changes radically. It becomes merely a yield difference as opposed to an objective or absolute risk measure. Negative spreads become possible. Indeed, negative emerging local bond spreads have already been common in the mid-2000s.

An illustration of the absence of solidity at the 'core' is currency markets. Globally currencies are a zero-sum game: all defined in terms of each other. Gold used to be a core, a global basis of value, but we now live in a multi-currency world, especially since the US dollar stopped being convertible to gold in 1971. We should replace our core/periphery model with one more akin to a hydraulic network in which pushing liquid down one piston merely forces it up another. Some pistons (currencies) may be larger or more important than others, but none are independent of the others – none are core. Given the state of the US and European economies in the crisis post-2008, and that emerging currencies have been kept artificially low for over a decade through excessive reserve accumulation, we expect significant dollar, sterling and probably euro depreciation against surplus countries in the medium term. This is arguably the essence of global rebalancing. Indeed, HIDCs can arguably only reduce their excessive debt burdens in a politically acceptable timeframe – starting with a reversal of quantitative easing – through a combination of inflation and devaluation.

If a Brazilian investor sells reals to buy dollars and invests in US Treasuries, and has a larger chance of losing 10% in a year than if he simply keeps the money in cash at home, then, rather than complaining about the risk of Brazilian real appreciation, he can equivalently conclude that investing in the US is risky. The same logic applies to a US investor. Investing in Brazil is likely to return more, and there is an opportunity cost or risk in not doing so. The response to this argument is that a US investor's liabilities are in dollars, and that risk can be defined to an extent as occurring when one moves away from matching these liabilities.[8]

Many emerging (and developed) currencies have tended to move up and down against the dollar at the same time since 2008, demonstrating that it is the dollar which is unstable. Yet this is not perceived when the 'core' dollar is the reference point. For emerging market-based investors it is the US which is risky. The insidious core/periphery virus, often most ingrained in the periphery itself, has blocked out such thinking too often. Emerging investors have, from central banks to individuals, perceived US Treasuries as safe – a bizarre perversion of current if not past reality and a triumph for core/periphery-induced mass delusion. This money illusion – confusion between nominal and real value – may stem to some degree from lack of self-confidence, bolstered by groupthink and incentive/agency problems.

6.2   BEYOND CORE/PERIPHERY

6.2.1   Towards a relative theory of risk

Recall our definition of emerging markets from Chapter 2: all countries are risky. Emerging markets are those where this risk is priced in. Developed countries are where a significant portion of investors do not perceive sovereign risk. Greece and other countries joining the EU were given licences to be fiscally irresponsible. Developed countries have built up excessive leverage after two to three decades of financial deepening which has not occurred in emerging markets. So I define emerging markets not by risk, but by risk perception.

The perceptual flaw is with the core, not the periphery. A more objective view of the world should perceive risk much more broadly, and especially where the greatest deficit of risk perception is: the developed world. In an hydraulic system all is fluid. Nothing is fixed; everything impacts everything else. We need a relative theory of risk. Just as physicists were very reluctant to accept that there is no ether; so it will take time for people to accept that

---

[8] We shall argue in Chapter 8 that liabilities are not this simple.

there is no risk-free rate; no safe investment (including, and at times especially, previously assumed safe investments such as money market funds or cash in a vulnerable but dominant currency). What appears safe is only relatively safe ... for the moment.

A relative theory of risk might not mean doing away entirely with any hope of measurement, but it does do away with oversimplification. One could consider a non-investible concept of the risk-free rate – one that actually means what it says and so is non-achievable in practice. The obvious proxy would be to call a non-investment risk-free,[9] and so the risk-free rate might mean either a zero real return or a negative one. It might be negative, to take account of money illusion in its inflation and currency forms, but also to pay for the costs of insuring against loss, as nothing is a perfect store of value. But the insurance market is not perfect, and information asymmetries are everywhere. One could not borrow at such a rate. It would not be useable to leverage investments in theory or practice – so useless in forming the capital market line used in the capital asset pricing model (CAPM).[10] Such an amended concept seems perhaps a dead end.

More practical might be to use a proxy for the risk-free rate as now, but be prepared to abandon it if its properties stray significantly from representing something risk-free.

When such a proxy for 'risk-free' is rejected as highly distortionary, we have to think about relative risk, and crank out our assessments of risk a bit more manually. Without a concept of 'risk-free', even theoretically, we have to measure our risks by thinking them through in the context of other risks. We weigh the risks of one course of action against the risks of alternatives. How much more risk, say, of a 30% loss in a year's time, might there be of choosing investment A compared to B? Risk – a manufactured concept – is perceived as always relative to an alternative, and we have to accept that our risk assessment will vary as we choose different alternatives for comparison. In thinking through such risks scenarios we have to take account of the interconnections of all the other factors and participants. A relative theory of risk requires constantly reassessing where we are. It challenges us constantly to re-assess what our comparator should be. It is specific to our existing portfolio, but also to our liabilities and capacities.

6.2.2   GDP weighting

With substantial investment risks emanating from the developed world, we need to re-assess our global investment map and move to GDP weights. None of this will be easy if we remain wedded to core/periphery prejudices, and a binary view of risk.

The most accepted valid ways for valuing equities are Tobin's q ratio (the ratio of the market value to replacement value of a physical asset) and the cyclically adjusted price/earnings ratio (CAPE).[11] The west of Ireland is very beautiful, but there are thousands of empty houses there. How should one value them – on the basis of replacement cost or income? What most

---

[9] This is not without difficulties. A non-investment of capital arguably destroys that capital, which is more a process of replication, a set of social relations, than something more material. A non-investment is also not possible, or rather if it is and if capital is so destroyed completely, it can be said to have an infinitely negative return.

[10] This is the line drawn from a tangent to the efficiency frontier (the efficient frontier being a curve representing the set of portfolios with the highest possible returns for lowest possible volatilities) to the point where return equals the risk-free rate. The capital market line is supposedly an improvement on the efficient frontier as it allows for inclusion of a risk-free asset, and enables a portfolio beyond the efficient frontier insofar as an investor can hold some 'risk-free' assets or borrow at the risk-free rate (i.e. have a negative quantity of the risk-free asset).

[11] See Smithers (2009).

investors want is future income. Yet market capitalisation often reflects replacement costs as much as or more than any income stream. How to measure future income, though? One of the best measures is past income, which at a national and international level is GDP. One might want to take into account variability of GDP, look at recent trends and factor in that some economies are prone to boom/bust dynamics. In contrast, market capitalisation, commonly used in index construction, is not as good a measure of future income, especially when bubbles and largely wasteful economic investment have occurred (like the dotcom bubble where market capitalisation bore no relationship to profitability or income). Yet market-cap indices are what most asset class allocators and advisers use (we explore this in more detail in Chapter 8). We should move to GDP weighting in country asset allocation. The main consequence would be much higher emerging market allocations.

The existing norm for indices is that they are market-cap weighted, 'investible' and cover specific well-defined asset classes. The assumption of what is investible is problematic. It is possible to invest in non-public instruments, and it is possible to alter one's investment weights to favour larger economies rather than larger public equity markets. Thus by 'investible' we actually mean something more restrictive than 'can be invested in'. We mean 'easy to invest in': liquid and accessible through recognised exchanges or other liquid (including over-the-counter – OTC) markets. Measurability of components is important, as is transparency, so that indices can be created and decisions justified.

But why should the inevitably somewhat arbitrary, and fairly static, rules of an index provider define either the asset class or useful investment allocations? Aside from the circular but compelling logic that they replicate what others do, in turn because others also follow indices, they arguably provide no guarantee to optimal allocation (as our Martian noted in Chapter 5). At best they might constitute a good guess.

The inclusion of a country in an index arguably does not make it more attractive as an investment. It may represent an underlying improvement in investment attractiveness, but often not one that justifies the resulting price rise caused by index trackers and other passive and index-focused investors – the price premium resulting from index inclusion often reduces risk-adjusted returns.

However, we observe that volatility and hence even risk can be partially endogenous to the index inclusion decision: that others use the indices naturally appeals to our conservative investor, and also helps generate greater liquidity and scrutiny and hence lower risk. More likely, if a country is included in a widely tracked index, it may (depending on the flightiness of the investors who use the index) become less volatile rather than less risky, and more investible purely because of the changed liquidity. In other words, we have a positive feedback loop.

The ostensible case for much of the toolkit we use in asset allocation is that it is better than any alternative. Yet this is arguably not the case when it comes to global country weightings. There are systematic biases in the existing market-cap approach specific to the weighting of countries. Market cap favours economies where firms are financed more through publicly quoted stocks and bonds (which are included in indices) than via retained earnings, non-quoted private equity or debt, or bank loans (which are not).[12] Where investors additionally have an equity bias, the result can also be a further discrimination against economies where public debt finance is relatively dominant over public equity issuance. The status quo favours

---

[12] This distorts allocations even within the developed world – comparing say Germany and the UK, where company capital structures vary.

markets which are considered advanced and capitalist by many because they have well-developed public markets. Yet there are lots of variants as to how companies are financed, lots of forms of capitalism.

Following 2008 those economies with more public securities as a percentage of investible assets were those with overleverage; those with greatest systemic risk of a major 1930s style collapse; those with, we would argue, the greatest currency and inflation risks. This is not coincidental, and it is at least in part a reflection of the liquidity, transparency and measurability of these markets which have favoured their inclusion in indices. The experience of many asset allocators such as US endowments and foundations who moved to 'alternative' asset classes by the early 2000s is salutary here: they tended to diversify, but almost all to developed countries where the common factor of excess leverage was present, causing a correlated decline across many developed world asset classes when credit crunch hit in 2008. Effective diversification needs to avoid such leveraged markets and economies, which means avoiding some of the traditional tools which favoured them.

Investors have a big bias towards the core. Pension funds are often only 5% or less invested in emerging markets, 95% in developed country markets. A move to GDP weighting would argue for 38% of total portfolio assets in emerging markets if we use current market exchange rates, 50% if we use purchasing power parity (PPP).[13] There are three reasons why we should indeed favour closer to 50% than 38%: first, because emerging market exchange rates, kept low against the dollar through massive intervention by central banks for over a decade, may be about to move up, moving market prices and PPP more in line; second, even using market prices and without any currency appreciation, emerging market GDP is headed for 50% of global GDP within a decade, especially given even more divergent growth rates as a result of the credit crunch; and third, because of the technical move expected as investors move from deeply underweight positions over the next several years.

For those who have not fallen off their chairs at the thought of a 50% or even 38% allocation to emerging markets, there needs to be a strategy to achieve such an allocation. As some of the largest and most progressive Western pension funds and endowments are already targeting 30–35% (most emerging market pension funds are near 100%) we can observe how they have approached the problem. First, there are many asset classes in emerging markets – not just debt and equity. Second, it requires specialists to get access to many of these markets and assets. Third, one can use existing allocations more effectively to increase emerging exposures: invest in emerging markets within international sovereign allocations, within corporate credit allocations, within private equity and real estate allocations, etc., though do so strategically and employ specialist skills as needed. Fourth, use proxies: invest in developed world companies which have strong activities in emerging markets (not ideal, inasmuch as downside risk is likely to remain at the developed world level). Fifth, invest in non-listed assets such as real estate, infrastructure and private companies.

Global GDP indices are now available (which adjust country weights in proportion not to market capitalisation but to GDP), but they still take as their underlying components so-called 'investible' (i.e. easy to invest in) assets. This poses the problem that they are not universally usable – if all those currently using market capitalisation-weighted indices tried

---

[13] Purchasing power parity (PPP) does not use prevailing market exchange rates to calculate prices, but exchange rates which makes purchasing power equivalent. Market exchange rates tend to underestimate incomes in poorer countries, and can be more volatile than actual purchasing power. The relative prices of equivalent baskets of goods are used to calculate PPP exchange rates.

instead to use these GDP indices, investors would not find enough assets to buy. Then again, given the slow change in thinking on asset allocation, such a rush is unlikely. So long as allocation growth is no faster than the growth of these asset classes – up to the point at which they represent about the same share of GDP as their equivalents do in the developed world – then this objection evaporates. Nevertheless, the argument for GDP weights is a fuller one: it is an argument for gaining access to the hard-to-invest (i.e. so-called 'non-investible') assets – the real estate and private companies, infrastructure and the full range of income-generating assets – not merely waiting for these businesses to issue securities in more accessible forms (publicly listed stocks and bonds).

In my view, global GDP weighting offers investors an improved risk-adjusted return stream over market-cap approaches. But GDP weighting may also be the thin end of the wedge for much of the traditional toolset for asset allocation. It challenges the bias in investing towards the developed world. It challenges prejudice about emerging markets. It challenges the home country bias. It challenges some of the thinking surrounding traditional approaches to asset/liability management. It challenges the psychology of preferring the static, known and measurable to the dynamic and difficult to measure. It challenges the idea of an asset class, not least by questioning index-defined boundaries. It challenges some parts of the investment industry with vested interests in the status quo. It challenges core/periphery disease.

Shocks also challenge the status quo, lead to re-evaluation and distinguish truth from prejudice. Shocks prompt paradigm change, and the period of shocks the global economy has been going through since 2008 will surely reveal emerging markets as strong; for shocks, to my thinking, are positive for markets held back by prejudice. But the realities of global imbalances mean emerging market central banks are overexposed to the developed world and need the core/periphery paradigm to erode slowly in order to preserve their own macroeconomic stability.

It is no longer useful to ignore the emerging world or think of it as an appendage. It is impossible to understand the shape of the global economy or policies to right it without an understanding of emerging markets. It is impossible for investors to be optimally allocated without emerging markets. It is imprudent to ignore emerging markets if one is concerned about sovereign risk in the developed world.

7

The Structure of Investment

We have discussed limitations to our understanding of economics and finance, and some of the distortions in how we look at the world. Our current view of the world is out of date and far too static. It would be peculiar if this did not also affect how we invest, and indeed it does. To a large extent, economic theory is not useful in informing investment except for the principle of diversification. Much of the theory we do use does not stand critical scrutiny. Our view of the world has not kept up with the rapid pace of change, and in particular the new prominence of emerging markets.

This chapter looks at how the structure of an investor base impacts market dynamics. This is a topic largely ignored to date both in the literature and in practice but of huge importance for our understanding of markets once we can wean ourselves from fictitious models of how markets should work in theory. By 'structure' we mean the populations of different types of investors holding or potentially holding an asset or class of asset. Investor populations may be differentiated by their geographic base, institutional form (private investor, pension fund, central bank, etc.), regulatory framework affecting their objectives and incentives, liabilities and decision processes. Of particular interest is their likely behaviour in future scenarios. We introduce a description of market segmentation and other observations with regard to incentives to describe how investor base structures can form the way they do. Once we can admit that perfect competition is an ideal not normally achieved, and once we start to appreciate that different investors face different risks and liabilities, and that they have different world views, then we realise that the structure of an investor base, particularly in crisis, is crucial for our understanding of future possible scenarios.

We also continue to explore the idea that our inherited bias towards the developed world has created new and large systemic risks. The blindness of markets and the overallocation to the developed world rests on outdated views. There will be dynamic risks as these ideas fade in the minds of market participants in the years ahead and are replaced by ideas more in balance with global economic reality – i.e. ideas that accord emerging markets more importance. If we can better understand some of the contours and distortions which exist in the structure of investment, then we can try to think about ways to compensate for them in our thinking and investment behaviour, to reduce risk and improve performance.

We should be on the lookout for potential structural shifts in the asset allocation decisions of others, in turn driven by the strategies and models they employ. These distortions help shape the growth of financial markets and hence markets for goods and services in path-dependent ways. This is clear in emerging markets where the existence of a corporate bond market, say, can for companies make the difference between international competitiveness or not and for people jobs or poverty.[1]

Our existing science is static in a dynamic world, ignoring changing perceptions. We have mentioned the difficulty of fully pre-defined models. As Frydman and Goldberg (2011, p. 87)

---

[1] While financial markets in the final resort are proved right or wrong by markets for goods and services, they in the meantime also change wealth distribution, and spread markets and associated efficiencies in path-dependent and non-uniform ways. They can shape which markets for goods and services exist, which market gaps are filled first.

say: 'By insisting on fully predetermining their models, economists ignore any revisions to forecasting strategies that they cannot pre-specify.' Changing views and strategies creates in part, on both a small and a large scale, potential for exchange. But they also create volatility, which we like little and often, but not a lot all at once. Moreover, our current misperception is so large that we can expect big swings (overshooting) with big changes in views and investment strategies. Investors and policymakers need to be prepared.

7.1   MISALIGNED INCENTIVES

The structure of investors matters because different investors have different liabilities and preferences but also different information sets and incentives. We turn first to incentives. Coase (1937) has taught us that when there are transactions costs, institutions matter. When institutions matter, principal/agent problems matter, as misaligned incentives can create sub-optimal investment decisions. Specifically, a delegated investment decision creates a relationship between the 'principal' (the beneficial owner of the capital) and the 'agent' (the manager or adviser making investment decisions on behalf of the principal). There may be a chain of delegations: for example pensioners, the beneficial owners of a pension fund, delegate management of the fund (typically they are legally obliged to do so) to a board of trustees or another form of governing body with fiduciary responsibility. This body, advised by a permanent staff, may then delegate, in whole or part, asset allocation and fund manager selection to outside pension consultants, as well as the assessment of liabilities. In a further delegation, investment management firms are employed to manage portions of the fund. Incentive structures may be used to incentivise the investment management firms, but incentive contracts are rare elsewhere in the chain. Such a chain is not only normal but can be justified by the desire to take advantage of a fuller range of skills than accessible by fewer individuals, for the greater benefit of the pensioners. It can also reduce costs.

Agency problems may encourage defensible rather than optimal decisions. Trustees, pension fund staff and consultants can to some extent blame the investment manager if performance is bad (and can sack them), but the crucial issue of asset allocation is often left in their hands, and they do not face as much competition as the manager, or have incentive contracts. Also, their roles as agents are often not easily observable by their ultimate principals (the owners of the capital: pension plan participants). The problem is well understood and widespread across a range of institutional investors, but measures to mitigate the incentive misalignments are often impractical, and untried at a regulatory level. Liabilities may be very long term, yet contracts short. An agent's time preferences (most simply expressed as the per-unit-time discount that they apply to money received in the future such that it is valued equally with money received today) may differ from those of the principals or beneficial owners (e.g. the pensioners). Preferences and risk taking also vary with income level. Incentive contracts may cost more, to compensate for the uncertainty of variable remuneration, but not produce noticeably better results. It may simply be unpalatable for the beneficial owners to see large sums going to those working for the pension fund.

Without mitigation, this all leads to a type of conservatism which, at worst, amounts to herding. The word 'conservative' is self-applied, one suspects, to the majority of institutional investors if not individual investors, but it means different things to different people. It may thus be useful to distinguish several types of conservatism:

- *Prudence*, an informed mitigation of risk;
- *Ignorance*, which derives from lack of information;
- *Prejudice*, which panders to a strained model of the world;
- *Denial*, related to prejudice, refers to a temporary lagged interpretation of immediate events;
- *Dynamic conservatism*, the view that the future will be the same as the past; and
- *Peer conservatism*, which is the desire to do what your peers are doing.

The last in particular, peer conservatism, stems from misaligned incentives and causes herding. But it is particularly dangerous when combined with dynamic conservatism in the presence of structural shifts. Peer conservatism exists for many types of investor, but most particularly for institutional ones where we can identify principal/agent structures and misaligned incentives.

There are potential mitigations to reduce herding. Consider doctors who daren't save costs on superfluous tests in case of being sued, leading to unnecessary costs and stress for patients – a solution is to limit the legal opportunities for patients to sue them. Likewise for investors: misaligned incentives – including public and peer group pressure emanating from prejudice and fed by the media – may prevent investment professionals making the right investments. To counter misaligned incentives, as for doctors, there could be legal protections from being sued. But further, one needs to battle underlying group prejudices and incorrect perceptions of risk.

The perception of risk is often binary – that some things are risky and others not. Investors did not check whether Bernard Madoff, who perpetuated an enormous financial fraud for years until 2008, had an accountant. What is remarkable is that simple due diligence (in this case little more than trying to visit his auditor as stated in his public accounts) would have identified him as a fraud. Likewise, institutional investors in the UK and the Netherlands invested in Icelandic bank paper in 2008 despite the available warning signals: a brief look at the IMF's website or a cursory look at macroeconomic data, or, if that was not enough, observation that Iceland's currency fell by 30% in the first half of 2006, leading to the fall of the government in elections mid-year. The interest rates offered and the clearly unsustainable scale of, and increase in, bank liabilities would have dissuaded an intelligent teenager not to invest. But ... just as 'everybody else invested with Madoff, so it must be safe', lots of other institutions were depositing with Icelandic banks, so that must be fine also. And Iceland is somewhere near Sweden, isn't it, and a developed country? For all the fancy investment theory, we know this genre of thought motivated many investment decisions.

So here is an idea: institute a regulatory principle such that no fiduciary, if they have lost money, should afterwards be able to claim in their defence that they were only doing what everyone else was doing. Using such an excuse should lead to disapprobation of some description. This is in stark contrast to what actually happened to UK local authority officials after losing money in Iceland – viz., very little, except that the government was blamed for encouraging these institutions to obtain the best returns on their money. In fact, the lack of punishment creates moral hazard – the incentive to herd all the more next time in the context of an apparently spineless regulatory regime.

Of all the distortions in the investment industry, misaligned incentives is perhaps the worst. And the worst part is that herding does not simply apply to a subsection of investment decisions, but to the widespread adoption and use of faulty theory, which many know to be faulty, but use anyway because it is what everybody else uses.

7.2   CONFUSED INCENTIVES

We sometimes herd despite, not because of, our economic incentives. We have non-economic incentives, and our preferences can be manipulated. We suffer from groupthink. In part this occurs because we take shortcuts. People, being mortal, have limited time for spending but also limited time to think about money, have other concerns aside from money, and worry about some of the moral associations money brings with it. Of course there are obsessive individuals, and money is most important when it is scarce. To some, making money is an excitement of more interest than spending it. But this is not even a possibility for most people, and money is generally viewed as primarily a means to other things. One set of such shortcuts is to use standard finance theory. Another is to trust the decisions of other people. It is when nobody checks the basis of this trust that Madoff-type scandals can occur. Trust is a form of delegation. As emphasised in Chapter 5, with the quote from J.P. Morgan, trust is the basis of all credit: without an assessment of a man's character which he could trust, Morgan would not lend. But how do you assess someone's character if you have not known them long, or even if you have, but have not seen them in a situation of stress? The problem would seem to worsen as financial complexity grows and contact with the end customer or contractor becomes more impersonal. Sometimes people may appear to be of good character, but are simply acting. In the attributed words of Groucho Marx: 'The secret of business success is integrity. If you can fake that, you're made.'

People often care more about other things than money, but have strong emotional responses to it. Money is a personal topic, taboo in polite conversations in some societies. There is also a deal of deliberate mystery about the subject, and with that comes difficulties in understanding and pretence. This is ripe picking for prejudices, rumours and, worse, deliberate efforts to create counterproductive common views about what is appropriate investment behaviour.

Is it legitimate for UK local authorities to excuse themselves from their decision to invest in highly rated Icelandic bank paper on the grounds that the government suggested they find the highest interest rates? I think not, but that this was reported in the press as a legitimate response to abrogation of fiduciary duty is evidence of how political views can obscure reason and how powerful groupthink can be.

We also sometimes choose the warm mantle of ignorance in preference to stark reality. In the UK as in many developed countries, ignorance about basic financial matters is astounding.[2] Perhaps this is representative of wider ignorance about everything else, but it is certainly a state which encourages herding and is attractive ground for mass marketing of standardised financial products with high fees, sold on brand recognition, often by individuals receiving commission, not solely on objective assessments of performance or capability. It is also perhaps a reflection on the modern nanny state, in which personal responsibility has been replaced by state responsibility, and where if investors lose money they might appeal to the state to bail them out: a form of moral hazard. People do not want to think about their pensions as they feel inadequate when they try to, and because nobody else they know does, and because if something goes wrong they expect, or at least hope, to be bailed out.

Hence the problem is not just one of analysing misaligned incentives using principal agent theory. Our principals not only cannot observe the efforts of those employed on their behalf to look after their savings; worse, they don't want to. They instead assume government will monitor their agents for them. Where the savers and pensioners are also the electorate, they

---

[2] I sat on a table at an investment conference in the US in the late 1990s and a trustee of a multi-billion-dollar US state pension plan asked what a bond was. Ignorance is not confined to either the UK or to retail investors.

have invariably got their wish, and governments have indeed tried to take responsibility in monitoring retail investment in great detail. The result is a ham-fisted regulatory approach along the lines of central planning in an area of choice where decentralisation is called for to achieve optimal investment results.

We do not live in a world of optimal decisions easily analysed by models with simplistic assumptions about our behaviour and easy-to-identify asset classes. We do not live in a world with risk but no uncertainty. We live in a world with numerous blinkers and filters on people's eyes. We live in a world of powerful myths and mythmakers, of secrecy, manipulation, self-imposed ignorance and deceit. And the myths change. We may consider political and economic conditions stable, but we only have to cast back a few decades to observe how reality can change or be revealed to be very different. In the late 1940s the consensus in Western Europe was that market economics without overall monitoring and planning, or at least management of aggregate demand through fiscal policy, was finished: the battle of state capitalism against fascism may have triumphed, but only after the bloodiest half-century in the history of mankind. After winning such a battle, allowing markets to reign free was not on the agenda in a number of Western European countries for fear of the counter-reaction being further support for communism.[3] And then the iron curtain fell: again, free markets were not on the agenda. In the West from 1980 the ideology changed again to be more pro-free market (even if a large degree of overall macroeconomic monitoring if not planning still persisted). What is remarkable is not that any of this has happened, but that investment theory and many investors seem oblivious to it. All countries have sovereign risk, and yet in the West part of the public myth is that there is much less risk at home than abroad: bizarre.

7.3   EVOLUTIONARY DYNAMICS, INSTITUTIONAL FORMS

We have explored why investors have different incentives, why they herd and why they may not behave in accordance with their incentives. But groups of investors also change and evolve: relative population sizes change and so do population characteristics. Of particular note is that groupthink and therefore group behaviour can change, sometimes rapidly, triggered by a new idea or event.

A criticism of standard finance theory is that it uses static techniques to explain a dynamic reality, and moreover one in which the observer is part of the system, and the system as a whole evolves. Compare Kepler's and Newton's conceptualisation of planetary motion, as compared to Darwinian evolution of an ecosystem. Kepler's laws describe planetary motion and Newton's explain them with reference to his law of gravity and laws of motion. In this area of study, equilibrium is something to be calculated, more or less accurately.[4] Planetary bodies move but in line with theories which can be calculated. The laws of nature are immutable.

---

[3] See Skidelsky (1995) on the debate between Keynes, Hayek and other economists in the mid-1940s. A parallel is also the move towards political reform in Great Britain in the early 19th century, partly motivated by concerns about conditions in France leading to the 1789 revolution.

[4] With the emphasis on 'more or less': in Waldrop's book *Complexity* (1992) he describes the meeting of economists and physicists at the Santa Fe institute, including two Nobel Laureates each. The physicists were impressed with the strong mathematical competency of the economists, but it was pure maths. The economists were slightly shocked at the physicists' use of applied not pure mathematics.

Much of classical and neoclassical economics similarly focuses on finding equilibrium market solutions where supply equals demand, albeit incorporating dynamic complications, where there is no tendency to change relationships between variables, or for the pattern of development over time to change suddenly. In contrast, in an ecosystem we have Darwinian evolution and path dependency (hysteresis) – it is important to know the state of the relationships between different species before we can understand an observed change. Relationships between species are not described as laws and are not immutable. The system is complex: predicting change is highly problematic. Moreover, the population of a species matters. An external shock may have only a temporary impact; alternatively, it may cause a permanent structural shift in the relative populations and relationships between species. Markets would appear to be more like ecosystems than planetary motion. And so perhaps we have a deficient tool set.

The word 'institution' has several meanings. We use it here to define the customs or norms of human interactions, and they too evolve. Institutions govern economic relations as they do non-economic relations. To think of our ecosystem parallel: a species has certain mating rituals and eats some, but only some, other species. These relationships can, of course, change. Institutions also vary from human society to society and over time, and on the whole they change gradually: they evolve. A difference between Darwinian and human institutional evolution is arguably the intentionality of the players, though echoing the debate over free will, this distinction may be less important than some think. North (1990) argues that human intentionality is crucial for institutional development while also insisting that relative prices dominate how institutions form. The evolutionary idea has also been extended by Dawkins (1976) and then more comprehensively by Blackmore (1999) to the behavioural concept of memes: intellectual viruses with evolutionary characteristics. A meme could be a tune we cannot get out of our head to investors' rules-of-thumb. Whether or not memes are a useful way of describing certain phenomena, we can agree with both North and meme adherents that evolutionary-type path dependence occurs as institutions develop. However, while institutions constrain interactions, memes populate far afield and create innovation (even if what they, over time, create includes new institutional forms). Memes can be fast-changing, or slow-changing like institutions. Culture can be defined as the cross-generational transmission mechanisms of modes of thought which constrain us – again, these are describable as memes. In turn North (1990 p. 87) observes culture (we could say cultural memes) constrain institutional development: 'The persistence of cultural traits in the face of changes in relative prices, formal rules, or political status makes informal constraints change at a different rate than formal rules.'

The result can be complex and varied. For example, the buying of a glass of wine is governed by certain rules, some legally binding, others social rules. In some societies buying any wine is simply illegal. In others wine cannot be carried in a glass or bottle in open view in public. In still other societies it may be legal but frowned on to drink wine mid-morning in public. Buying a glass of wine in a restaurant will not only have a different price per unit than buying a bottle of the same wine in a supermarket, but is covered by different rules and taxes and expected behaviour patterns. So it is with other markets: haggling is expected in some, frowned on in others. The attitude to wine drinking (or haggling) clearly differs across society and time, but cannot be separated from the historical development and aspects of the society beyond economics. Likewise with money. Money is moreover the great neutral intermediary between human values and desires, and institutions/norms governing people's use of money vary enormously.

Moving to modern bond markets, for example, there is also a role for the anthropologist: there are agreed rules, from how interest is calculated to settlement practices to conditions under which a bond trade can be invalidated or reversed, to the process of how to deal with late or nonpayment of interest or principal. Sovereign borrowers who get into difficulty are treated differently by bondholders depending on a whole range of issues, most notably those pertaining to trust and good faith, but also differentiating between reasons for nonpayment. An external factor like a natural disaster devastating the economy will often be treated more leniently than a reduced willingness to pay when the capacity to do so is unchanged. At a given moment in a given market, the range of such reactions may often be predictable. Such norms or market institutions cover all markets and affect the behaviour of sellers, buyers, intermediaries, policymakers and individuals as well as media observers. They are not unaffected by institutional setting. Likewise, governments may also have different conceptions from markets about what should happen, and can try to change behavioural norms through formal legal and organisational changes but also through the media. Our risk perceptions are governed by institutions/norms.

7.3.1   History matters

Because of institutional context, history matters. There are some differences of opinion on this, as evidenced for example by the varied attitude of economists to so-called 'shock treatment'. The first case of the term being used in recent times refers to a sudden implementation of a wide range of economic policy changes, administered by a team led by Jeffrey Sachs in Bolivia in 1985, to achieve macroeconomic stabilisation. It was seen as highly successful. In essence, a badly run economy was turned round rapidly through a top-down implementation. Though a generalisation, the concept of shock treatment has an important characteristic which distinguishes it from more context-specific and/or gradual reform: the goal of the end design of certain institutions and arrangements features large compared to the path by which to get there. Conceptually, extreme shock treatment can thus be seen as a black box: it doesn't matter what is inside just as long as the outcome is clear.

Bolivia proved a simpler economy to fix than Russia, which became a less successful recipient of the treatment after the break-up of the Soviet Union – arguably there was more of a collapse than anything else in Russia, with attempts at design (shock or otherwise) failing comprehensively. To this day many Russians resent how mass privatisation (the shock) enriched a very few 'oligarchs' and how, for all the rhetoric, there was not much benefit seen for most of the population. Political opening was associated with this period of economic chaos, and the reaction was support for a return to more centralised power under Putin. There could have been many different outcomes for Russia's economy and politics. Similar sudden-change policy attempts in Bolivia and Russia had very different impacts.

We are also part of our ecosystem, not observers of distant planets. Our actions in markets, and even shaping thoughts about markets, are internal to the system. The Lucas critique (after Robert E. Lucas) is that it is naïve to expect relationships observed in historical economic data to be usable in a policy context, as the policy may affect behaviour. In the area of monetary policy Goodhart's law is a related if narrower idea.[5] The self-fulfilling prophecy, called the 'Oedipus effect' by Karl Popper and 'reflexibity' by his student George Soros, describes a self-referential or circular system where effects are also causes and vice versa: reminiscent of an evolving ecosystem. Reflexivity in economics is widespread and discussed by Taleb (2007).

7.4   NETWORK THEORY

Which techniques can we use to understand a Darwinian evolving world? We need to think about how economic agents interact, for which a branch of mathematics called network theory may help.[6] In any network there are nodes and links. We can define the degree of a node as the number of links to it from other nodes, and hubs as nodes with many links. We can describe a network by the pattern of concentration of links – the distribution of nodes' degrees. These degree distributions are often non-normal and commonly display power law distributions. This means the sizes of the biggest hubs increase as a power of the size of the network, leading to large networks having some vast hubs, yet the majority, as for smaller networks, still having just a few links. In many systems, some hubs are much larger than would exist in a randomly generated network. As for the World Wide Web, many financial markets share this power law distribution.

This pattern can develop if a network grows through 'preferential attachment'. This is the phenomenon that as the network grows (think for example of people building websites and then creating links to other sites), the preference is to link to existing nodes with a large number of links already. Older nodes can be favoured as a result, leading to first mover advantages.

Hub-based networks have high connectivity and display the so-called 'small world' effect: a fraction of dominant hubs leads to shorter average distances (minimum possible number of links, not geographical distance) between different parts of the network than would be the case if new links were created more randomly. Such systems can be very robust to random events (those where all nodes are equally likely of being disabled), but fragile to targeted attack on the hubs. Networks can also display robustness up to a threshold of debilitation and then experience cascading collapse.

Many financial markets also display hub-network characteristics (the largest global investment banks have grown as hubs serving global customer bases with positive economies of scale), and also most of the time are very robust. But they can fail under targeted attack, experiencing cascading collapse. Also … markets do attack. They go short, as George Soros did the pound, leading to its exit from the European exchange rate mechanism (ERM) in September 1992. Liquidity can dry up very quickly in particular markets. Banks in particular can fail and cause cascading failure. In behavioural finance the term 'information cascade' has been coined to describe when members of a group ignore their own independent evaluation because they take the view that the majority cannot be wrong (i.e. herd behaviour). Shiller (2008, p. 104) describes 'attention cascade' as a condition where an issue becomes more and more dominant in the media until it dominates public thinking. Older observations on how propaganda can feed on fear are also illustrative of how fast and effective negative

---

[5] Goodhart's law is that if a particular definition of the money supply is used as a target of monetary policy, its statistical relationship with spending in the economy will break down, and the policy will become ineffective, because economic actors will behave differently once they know the central bank rule. This does not mean that monetary restraint will not prevent or cure inflation and so is not of interest except for those attempting to target the money supply.

[6] See Barabási (2003) for an introduction.

cascades and mass behaviour can be – see for example Chakotin (1940), who describes the seductive power of Hitler's propaganda. Also, as Shiller (2008 p. 62) observes: 'Most people … try to think of speculative events as rational responses to information, for they do not understand the contagion of thought.' Fads and memes exist and can be highly destructive. Yet the structure of bank and other financial networks may not be well enough understood for regulators to be certain of how vulnerable the whole system is to systemic failure as a result of hub attack[7] – not that this is an excuse for regulatory failure.

Certain markets can be observed as prone to such problems, but such backward-looking observation does not help us understand future vulnerabilities when markets evolve to new structural forms. Regulators have started to think about such issues, but this area of study is still new, and the structure of financial markets requires more investigation. It is not clear what makes systems vulnerable: complex systems can display emergent behaviour (i.e. new behavioural patterns which develop as systems evolve) and regulatory authorities are particularly constrained by overlapping jurisdictions (across countries and markets) which mitigate an overall perspective on, and response to, systemic risks.

For investors the consequences are firstly that there needs to be a shift in risk perception to take account of the catastrophic risk scenarios that follow from hub failure. Secondly, should financial networks evolve to become more interconnected but less dependent on a small number of hubs, the robustness of the whole to random events may improve. Thirdly, less leveraged, less connected subsystems, such as the financial system in an emerging market, can be safer than highly leveraged developed country markets, especially banking systems.

7.5 GAME THEORY

Another area of theory which may help us understand the evolution of investor bases is game theory. Much of finance theory and microeconomics consists of simplified mathematical models, constructed to describe the relationships between economic agents by way of mathematical formulae. These can struggle to describe complex systems with emergent behaviour. An alternative starting point for modelling is simulation: using computer simulations in repeat interactions or 'games'.

Computer simulations have been used for over 30 years to test the efficacy of different behavioural strategies. Robert Axelrod (1984) famously held two tournaments around 1980 to test competing behavioural strategies in a computer-simulated iterated prisoner's dilemma.[8] In an iterated prisoner's dilemma the agents (prisoners) interact in pairs to co-operate or defect with each other and win points as a function of their behaviour and that of the agent they interact with: for example, if both co-operate they may gain three points each, but if one co-operates and the other defects, the defector gains five points and the co-operator zero; whereas if both defect, they both gain one point each. A simple strategy would be 'always defect' or 'always co-operate', but the winning strategy, i.e. the one which ended up with the most points after many iterations, was 'tit-for-tat'. Tit-for-tat co-operates in the first interaction with

---

[7] But see, for example, Gai and Kapadia (2010) and Jae Hyun Jo (2012).

[8] The prisoners' dilemma, from game theory, describes two criminals being interviewed in separate cells by police who suspect them jointly of a crime, but have little evidence. The prisoners cannot communicate with each other. Both are offered deals of a light sentence if they give evidence against the other, but not if they both implicate each other, in which case they get only slightly shorter sentences than if they don't talk but are implicated. The best solution for them is to remain silent, in which case they both go free. Assuming no loyalty between thieves, though, if one prisoner assumes the other will talk, then he has an incentive to talk too, so they both talk and both go to prison for a long, if not the longest, stretch.

a specific opponent, but then remembers the opponent's behaviour and the next time copies whatever the opponent did in the previous interaction between the two. Tit-for-tat appears to be successful because it co-operates if not provoked, retaliates and forgives; and works best when there is a good chance of meeting the same opponent many times, not just a few.

We might think tit-for-tat a good strategy for co-operating in international diplomacy and bureaucracies where the same people interact with each other again and again and have long memories, but less so in more anonymous interactions in markets. A market-maker or someone whose reputation for not defecting is important for future business may be more likely to use 'tit-for-tat' or a strategy with similar characteristics than someone effectively playing a once-only game of prisoner's dilemma. Trust can be analysed as an emergent characteristic from such game theory, as can altruism and other behavioural characteristics.

Such games can and have become much more sophisticated since Axelrod's tournaments. Multiple simulations with slightly different starting populations and rules can be used to test how stable simulation results are. Instead of simple strategies like 'tit-for-tat', we can observe actual behaviour of economic agents or analyse incentives to derive expected behaviour; and then, given an observed market structure of different economic agents interacting with each other in different ways according to certain rules, try to replicate the actual behaviour observed in real financial markets. If we can do this in sufficient detail to produce a simulation which fits past aggregate market behaviour, we can also test that market's vulnerability to external shocks or changing conditions in a way which can help us understand systemic risks. However, as North (1990, p. 12) points out, the conditions under which co-operation is predicted by game theory are not that common: 'One does not necessarily have repeated dealings, not know the other party, nor deal with a small number of other people.' Game theory appears better suited to bilateral oligopolies than competitive markets.

Trying to construct a map of institutional structure may also be immensely difficult. But we can perhaps identify large misperceptions and use simulated games to gauge the dynamics of potential structural changes not factored in by market participants. However, more sophisticated simulations, based on much better understanding of investor base structures, may yield useful results in future. Wolfram's work[9] on cellular automata can for example be extended to financial markets. His work challenges traditional model-based approaches to science and instead investigates the complex patterns which can be generated by simple rules repeated many times. If observed market behaviour is approximated by such simulations we may be able to discover some underlying truths of how markets operate and make better predictions about the future.

7.6   INVESTOR STRUCTURE AND LIQUIDITY

Having discussed in general terms how structure matters, we now turn to a more specific issue where structure is highly determinant: liquidity.

> 'Of the maxims of orthodox finance none, surely, is more anti-social than the fetish of liquidity, the doctrine that it is a positive virtue on the part of investment institutions to concentrate their resources upon the holding of "liquid" securities. It forgets that there is no such thing as liquidity of investment for the community as a whole.'
>
> Keynes (1936, Chapter 12, part V)

---

[9] Wolfram (2002).

A liquid market is one where large transactions can be executed rapidly with a small impact on price. This is a forward-looking concept, but in practice an asset's liquidity is normally measured by the amount of face value traded per unit of time in the past: a market may have so many billion dollars' worth traded in a day, or an instrument (individual bond or stock) so many million dollars' worth. Chabchitrchaidol and Panyanukul in Eichengreen *et al.* (2008, p. 206) further elaborate four dimensions of liquidity: tightness (measured by bid-ask spread), the related measure of depth (amount of trading possible without affecting prices), resiliency (speed at which price impacts from trades are dissipated) and immediacy (the time from order placement to execution). Market liquidity can vary over time of course, as it is a function of the behaviour of market participants. In particular, as another example of the fallacy of composition, and as indicated in the latter part of Keynes' quote above, it can dry up when there is nobody on the other side of the trade – when everybody wants to sell at the same time.

Is liquidity a good thing? Turner in Turner *et al.* (2010, p. 52) notes 'The dominant ideology of financial liberalization and innovation has ... argued that increased liquidity is wholly beneficial in all markets ...' The reasoning is that transaction costs and (due to arbitrage opportunities) volatility are both reduced, and allocative efficiency increased.[10]

Markets can of course be inefficient, overshoot and be impacted by agency and behavioural problems. So liquidity might be excessive and momentum-driven, and greater liquidity might increase systemic risks and volatility. As Forbes (2009, p. 106) points out:

'Central elements of any financial speculation are financial innovations designed to facilitate an increased volume of trade. New conceptualizations of the allocation of ownership rights facilitate growing volumes of trade. Very often these new strategies come down to exercising the magic of leverage on a portfolio, which in a rising market appears to offer far greater return without any apparent risk.'

This is a fiction, of course – why would anyone lend as opposed to borrow in such a world?

As we know that liquidity conditions can change and, moreover, in a crisis fall rapidly, one practical and defensive approach, which Ashmore has taken for many years, is to try to reduce dependence on past liquidity patterns and be more forward-looking. In order to understand how liquidity may change there is no shortcut. One has to understand the structure of the investor base in the particular market, and the belief systems of the various types of holders of the paper, and relevant policymakers, and so how they might change their behaviour in given future scenarios (we might call these their reaction functions). One needs to understand which scenarios might cause sudden changes in behaviour. This is clearly a very different process from merely working out what liquidity has been, even in previously bad patches, and extrapolating. It is a complex and difficult task, requiring the ability to glean views from a wide range of market participants. It also reflects a now familiar theme of this book: it may be easy to look backwards and extrapolate, but it is not always the right thing to do. The alternative is typically much more difficult. In the famous words attributed to Niels Bohr: 'Prediction is very difficult, especially about the future.'

So the structure of an investor base can impact liquidity of an instrument (as well as vice versa), indeed a whole market, or markets. This is most likely to be missed by analysing past data when one faces different scenarios to those faced in the past, but also where the structure

---

[10] The link to volatility is that volatility typically increases bid-offer spreads and so transaction costs, reducing liquidity. The ability to hedge volatility thus facilitates greater overall liquidity.

of the investor base is different. This may pose particular problems after a period of marked development and change in investor bases in general – i.e. of strong growth in financial markets, as in the last 30 years. As Turner again (2010, p. 53) points out: you can have too much of a good thing (or declining marginal utility) including too much liquidity.

One aspect of this has come to the attention of central banks in recent years, as mentioned in Chapter 3. They hold around 60% of their reserve assets in US Treasuries,[11] motivated by the desire to invest in the most liquid market in the world. And according to past liquidity data the US Treasury market is highly liquid. Central bank reserve managers' first priority is to have liquid reserves which they can sell and use at very short notice for the purpose of intervention to control domestic monetary conditions and the exchange rate. Acceptability of the currency is key as well as liquidity. However, given the size of their reserves, they collectively hold a dominant share of non-US-held US Treasuries. Some of them are starting to factor in not only the risk of loss of value, but the possible lack of liquidity for their 'community as a whole' as Keynes puts it. They are thinking through scenarios where liquidity might disappear, and in the context of the need for global rebalancing, they are becoming concerned.

The worrying scenario today is that one or a few central banks initially, but then possibly more, might start selling US Treasuries aggressively, trying to sell before others do so. With or without this scenario actually developing, central banks with large reserve surpluses currently invested in US Treasuries (and in other US investments for that matter) do face a collective action problem akin to the prisoner's dilemma. A dramatic fall in US Treasury bond liquidity is possible.

7.7   MARKET SEGMENTATION

Following on from the observation that investor base structure is important, and sudden drops in liquidity are possible in certain circumstances, we develop a theory of market segmentation. We arrive at this via an analysis of sovereign default risk.

The law of one price (LOOP) is that in an efficient market identical things will have the same price. However, not all markets are efficient, not least because people have different views and information. One consequence is not two prices for an asset (which one can get when there are high transaction costs and so different geographical markets for the same goods) but an exit from the market by many who value the asset much lower – because they see a risk which those who remain do not.

> 'In physics, one of the trademarks of a phase transition is increasing synchronization … In financial markets, crashes occur because of increasing synchronization of the individual market participants … by local self-reinforcing imitation between investors.'
>
> Montier (2002 p. 141)

In 1996 Thailand's macroeconomic fundamentals indicated a systemic problem building up: the exchange rate was unsustainable. This was clearly visible to IMF officials and emerging debt investors (like me) experienced in balance-of-payments crises. Yet investors active in Thai bonds had a different perspective, and it was they who kept Thai bond prices up until the moment of crisis. Hence one could read years later in the academic literature that, as

---

[11] Bills and bonds issued by the US government through the Department of the Treasury.

indicated by bond spreads, the market did not foresee the crisis. Yet this is not my recollection. Some investors did understand and foresee it, but they avoided participating in the market. In the case of Thailand many traditional emerging debt investors were simply not invested in Thailand prior to the crisis.

As risk-aware investors exit, this need not drive prices down so long as other investors, with a completely different perception of the risk, take their place, attracted by the marginal arbitrage opportunity occasioned by the exit. In other words, bond spreads need not indicate the risk perception of the broader market if significant potential investors and opinion leaders are not active participants in the market, or indeed even if they exit but their place is taken by others seeing an arbitrage opportunity from their exit.

The process of perception change can be seen as Kuhnian precisely because people cling to beliefs long after the world around them and the appropriateness of their beliefs change.

Similarly, in Greece after 2008, spreads did not move to reflect default risk adequately for many months: some investors 'got it', others did not. We know from behavioural finance that when an event is of very low probability we often assume its probability to be zero and then stick with this assessment (as a result of confirmation bias). In the Eurozone government bond market pre-2008 the implicit assumption by many was that default risk was zero – a view aided by the ratings agencies. Having assumed that, they adopted a methodology to value government bonds – including those issued by Greece – which ignored default risk. Typically this involves observing the spread (additional yield) of Greek bonds over the German government bond benchmarks. Assuming a normal or similar stable distribution, if the spread moves excessively – say to two standard deviations above the average historical spread – then the Greek bonds could be said to be undervalued, and the recommendation was to buy them. If others were selling, pushing spreads higher, the incentive to keep buying for those using such a model merely increased. From their perspective they were taking advantage of a temporary arbitrage opportunity. They continued buying until they held more and more of the bonds, and so one has a segmentation of the investor base, with more and more exiting.

Should the prospect of sovereign default become significant, the first reaction is denial: market participants are reluctant to alter their habits and model for assessing sovereign bond prices. When change of model comes it comes piecemeal as individuals have their 'Eureka!' moments at different times. Once default risk is significant and has to be factored in, the model just described becomes meaningless.

Once the model is perceived as broken, the market participant needs to talk to someone like an emerging bond investor with experience of how to value sovereign bonds when there is a default prospect. The answers they get are very alien to their traditional approach, and might roughly follow the sequence below:

Q1: What is the sustainable debt/GDP for this country, bearing in mind this will be very different for different countries and at different times?

A1: For Japan it might be 300%; for Britain in 1820 it is believed to have been 240%; but for Greece in 2008 a figure of around 60% seems about right.

Q2: Can a credible fiscal adjustment together with other policies, particularly structural measures to increase growth (e.g. more flexible labour laws) get the country from where it is to the target specified above?[12]

---

[12] This needs to take account of: (a) political resistance and implementation problems, plus (b) the risk of a negative spiral in the economy as adjustment shrinks the economy and so tax revenues, implying the need for ever greater adjustment.

A2: In Italy's case in 2008: Yes; for Greece: No.

If the answer to the second question is No, then there are two, and only two, sustainable policy tools:

P1:   Default or restructure sovereign debt to reduce debt repayments;
P2:   Devalue or allow depreciation (possibly covertly) to re-establish competitiveness.[13]

It is important to note that being bailed out by the EU is not a sustainable solution unless transfers are to be permanently recurring (and keep growing).

Such a choice of policies above leads to estimates of possible losses for investors through nonrepayment, debt restructuring and devaluation, in turn determining valuation of bonds today. This is not only radically different from the mean-variance normal distribution model we discussed first, but leads to much lower bond valuations – valuations which may be way below market prices. An investor, having had a 'Eureka!' conversion to the new assessment of value, may wobble: there is no question of going back to the old mean-variance view – they have shed their previous prejudice and prejudice once shed is never reacquired. Rather, should the market price be much higher than implied by the new model, they can come to two conclusions: that others have not yet had their 'Eureka!' moments, and/or that somebody in Brussels or elsewhere knows something they do not. The second interpretation is most probably incorrect, but to think it is also to have the confidence to ditch yet another deep-seated idea (meme) that markets are efficient.

The end result is our model of market segmentation: segmentation occurs gradually in a market where new (more representative) thinking of how the market operates spreads as, little by little, more people 'get it' and exit, and those left behind buy more and more. The views of those remaining become more and more homogenous, raising the risk for them that when they exit market collapse will occur and there will be no one on the other side of the trade willing to buy – a liquidity crisis. Observing the belief systems of others is important. We should pay attention to investor base structure lest we be caught out in the endgame.

7.7.1   Warning signals

Having described the broad characteristics of our market segmentation model, we can be a bit more helpful to investors and policymakers by suggesting some of the conditions precedent for a liquidity crisis. The important ones appear to be threefold. They are: (a) investor homogeneity; (b) an event which may change the view and behaviour of investors (possibly on account of them being under some false impression); and (c) leverage (at the security, but also wider asset class and economy levels). These three interlinked conditions may be seen as blow-up risk indicators.

Let us consider the three a little more. The investor homogeneity we care about most may be defined as the existence of a homogenous desire to buy or sell in a crisis. A homogenous investor base is a blow-up precondition; whereas a diverse investor base is less likely to

---

[13] Another possible option, inflation is not open to countries which cannot borrow in their own currencies. For those which can, inflation can have the effect of solving indebtedness over time, but is not normally considered a positive policy choice given the amount of inflation typically necessary to erode the value of debt and given its negative side effects.

change its mind simultaneously. For large investor types like pension funds and in particular central banks, it may be possible to reduce investor homogeneity by insisting on low percentage participation by one's peers in an asset class before investing – a central bank could for example refuse to buy more US Treasuries if global central banks collectively own above a certain percentage of foreign-owned Treasuries in issuance. Pension funds or their regulators could take a similar line. For all investors, the structure of an investor base in an investment is a component of the investment's risk, not just for those who happen to form part of the homogenous group.

Investor base structure as a source of risk is not captured by conventional measures of risk as it relates largely to future one-off events not previously measured. It is not extrapolated from past volatility. To illustrate this think of another self-fulfilling risk – a bank run. If a large number of depositors were to withdraw their money simultaneously from almost any deposit-taking bank, it would without external assistance face a liquidity crisis. The risk for a depositor is a function of the behaviour of other depositors. The rules a regulator devises to prevent a lack of confidence leading to a bank run are necessarily more art than science. What may seem reasonable and sufficient one day may not the next. After financial crisis re-establishing a bank's credibility, and that of whole banking systems in the developed world, has been uncharted territory.

Investor homogeneity can exist at the same time as high levels of liquidity. This may be the case with new markets which have grown quickly, and those which have attracted only a few types of market participants. Credit default swaps (CDS)[14] would be a case in point – a highly liquid market, but in 2008/9 one in which liquidity in parts of the market became very low and prices became highly distorted.

For many of these CDS markets the underlying credit risk was not the problem. The problem was the investor base. The bonds of which CDS were a derivative did not come under the same amount of stress as the CDS themselves because they had a more heterogeneous investor base.[15]

Our second warning signal is an event which may change the incorrect views, and so the behaviour, of investors. Having a distorted view of the world and risk – having core/periphery disease – opens up an investor to a sudden change in view. Calling something 'risk-free', for example, is a signal, not that it is risk-free (there is no such thing), but that risk is not perceived. The presence of investor homogeneity makes such changes of view potentially more pertinent.

For a really big bang, the third factor is essential: leverage. This can be either in the market being considered or in other markets but employed by the same investors – hence overall economy-wide leverage is a danger even in a relatively non-levered market. Bank credit is a form of leverage: a banking system creates money by lending more than it has; and banks and other forms of credit are at the centre of a developed market economy. Credit creates value by enabling other factors of production to be employed. Financial engineering in general creates

---

[14] A credit default swap (CDS) is a financial derivative which is referenced to an underlying security. The holder is paid only if the underlying security defaults. The CDS price should in theory thus move with a similar dynamic to the underlying security, but as CDSs were often used for hedging or as proxies for the underlying by similar types of investor, and as the market size of these derivatives had in some cases come to dwarf the underlying issue size, so in crisis they saw larger price swings than in the underlying. This phenomenon, whereby a hedge does not function in a crisis as it should in theory, is also called basis risk. Also, CDS involve counterpart risk.

[15] It would be possible for regulators to collect holding pattern data from market makers. The observation is, however, made from personal conversations with market makers and investors.

allocative efficiency whereby the extension but also the withdrawal of credit can allow more efficient combinations of factors of production to emerge. But you can have too much of a good thing. Avoidance of bubbles and consequent crashes is one motive for regulating banking systems (or should be).

How much financial deepening is too much? The amount of sustainable leverage is a function of trust, stability in what has been sustained in the past, faith and regulation. It is not quantifiable. What we can do though is identify pockets of leverage which are dangerous. Banks, highly leveraged quantitative hedge funds and structured products are candidates for examination. On banks there has been a great deal written, including on staff incentives and lack of risk budgeting for investment bank units, including and notably those within large commercial banks.

All too often it is a particular market or instrument type which is the target of regulators' ire, when looking at the underlying investor base and their leverage may be more illuminating.

Quantitative models suffer from failing to account for fallacies of composition. If a market pattern, particularly one which takes the form of an arbitrage opportunity, can be identified, then 'quant' funds can make money out of it. However, the profit may be very small in proportion to the market positions needed to be put on, so leverage is often employed. If the trade works, more capital can be put into it until the volume of such transactions dominates the holding structure, and this affects market dynamics – the statistical relationships between the variables break down. A single fund may understand this, but others may also crowd into the trade with the same strategy in mind, creating a highly homogenised investor base. What works for a small bet does not work for larger amounts. Ignoring this fallacy can create hubris followed by surprise, as seen with the collapse of LTCM (as described in Chapter 2), with similar psychology repeated a number of times in 2007 and 2008.[16] Financial markets sometimes 'don't behave as they should'.[17]

After LTCM the consensus regulatory view on hedge funds was to monitor the counterparties – the banks – more closely. Every hedge fund trade has two parties – the hedge fund and normally an investment bank – so if the leverage and exposures of the investment banks were better monitored, the regulator could have a better picture of the overall structure of the market, and thus of potential problem areas and their magnitudes. They could compare the similarities of investment bank exposures with each other to stop another LTCM – not that this stopped subsequent faulty assumptions about correlations of house prices and the subprime exposure build-up. Highly leveraged quants apart, other less leveraged hedge funds, despite some popular antagonism, were seen by regulators as stabilising after previous crises, including in 1998. When other investors have panicked, a regulator wants to see markets pick themselves up and trading start again. After a fall the best thing is for money not likely to cause systemic risk (i.e. not bank balance sheet money, but owned by wealthy people who can afford to lose it) to start buying and change market sentiment as others see prices begin to level off and then rise.

Structured products (packaged financial investments typically including derivatives, typically created by investment banks) can be dangerous because they are often bought by similarly minded investors, have not been properly understood by their buyers – not least because

---

[16] The book *The Quants* by Scott Patterson (2010) is a source of anecdotes about some who play this game very profitably for the most part.

[17] I am thinking here in particular of a quant fund manager, described in Patterson (2010), who smashed several computer screens during periods of particular market tension, and later affirmed that the computer screens deserved it.

they took rating agencies' assessments seriously – and are often highly leveraged. In other words, they had all three of the ingredients for a potential blow-up.

Widespread confusion in the design of these products between correlation and causation expressed itself in assumptions that correlations between variables that had been stable (such as low correlations of mortgage default rates across different parts of the US) would continue to be stable irrespective of financial market activity to exploit these relationships. Moreover, correlations were seen as a function largely of non-financial market activity, and so it was assumed that if correlations changed it was certainly not conceived that that they would do so all at the same time in the same way. Yet correlations can and do move to unity when leverage is the common factor – because of homogeneity in investor behaviour. There may be some institutional investors scratching their heads after 2008, thinking that diversification doesn't work after all, but by just diversifying within economies in Western Europe and the US they did not diversify against the key common risk factor: leverage. If they had invested more in non-leveraged markets and economies without systemic banking risks (i.e. emerging markets), they would have seen more diversification benefit, and as these economies and markets diversify further this will become even clearer in the years ahead.

The opacity of the products also created plenty of misaligned incentives and agency problems along the way. And the sudden growth in many of these products and the amount of leverage employed did not create warning signals for many because such factors are not in the standard text of how to assess risk or how to invest.

7.8   INVESTOR BASE STRUCTURE MATTERS

The realisation that other investors behave with some homogeneity may be a comfort in stable markets, but in a period of structural change a source of risk and a reason to be some distance from the crowd. Structure matters, as do the beliefs of other investors, and how these might change.

> '… professional investment may be likened to those newspaper competitions in which the competitors have to pick out the six prettiest faces from a hundred photographs, the prize being awarded to the competitor whose choice most nearly corresponds to the average preferences of the competitors as a whole; so that each competitor has to pick, not those faces which he himself finds prettiest, but those which he thinks likeliest to catch the fancy of the other competitors, all of whom are looking at the problem from the same point of view.'

> Keynes (1936, Chapter 12, part V)

Just as in Keynes' beauty contest, the beliefs of others matters. As Frydman and Goldberg (2011, p. 125) point out, the cultural backgrounds of the other beauty competition judges also matter. Keynes took the view that psychological factors affecting individual decisions do not amount to irrationality, and mass irrationality could not sustain for long swings in asset prices. Most economists follow this line – supply and demand for goods and services are assumed largely independent from short-term financial market gyrations. This is despite our knowledge that psychological and cultural factors (and regulations) can exist for more than the short-term. However, even sticking to Keynes's view, what if psychological factors or cultural backgrounds do on occasion have a large impact on decisions in the short term, and moreover that there are long-term path-dependent outcomes from these short-term decisions? Then, and contrary to rational expectations theory, the structure of an investor base matters, and may create risks not apparent using traditional backward-looking analysis. Understanding of institutional structure is important: economic models are specific to particular institutional forms, and ideas and ideologies are also shaped by institutional form.[18] Thinking of scenarios, and insuring against the negative consequences of some of these scenarios, may make more sense than purely focusing on more traditional concepts of risk management.

Structure also often changes faster than risk perceptions. Emerging market debt is a good example of this. In the 1990s maybe a third of the investor base was highly leveraged and this, combined with substantial country default risks and contagion risks, led to high risk. However, as described in Chapter 2, after the Russian crisis in 1998 leveraged hedge funds became much less prominent. Non-leveraged institutional investors, with different motives and beliefs, started to shed their prejudices about emerging markets and came to dominate the asset class. Just as US pension funds did not invest in international equities at the start of the 1970s, but almost all did after five years, so with emerging debt. And this is happening in different countries' pension markets (and among other investors) starting at different times. Many investor bases have hardly started yet and are a long way from expected future allocation weights. The whole process is lagged, but gradually investor base structure impacts risk and in turn attracts greater stable long-term investors, and so feeds further allocation in a virtuous circle.

As well as having seen a major change in the type of external investor, today we are in a world where emerging markets have a much more reliable and heterogeneous investor base because it is mostly made up of local institutional investors in the various markets, as mentioned in Chapter 2.

The developed world has plenty of the toxic triple mix of investor homogeneity, events ahead which may change investor views and behaviour, and excessive leverage. In contrast, emerging markets today face two not three sets of risks, as we mentioned in Chapter 5. Firstly, there are those negative scenarios emanating from the developed world – in the worst of which emerging markets can be hit badly but not on the whole as badly as the developed world itself. Secondly, there are country-specific risks which an active manager can avoid. Thirdly, the set of risks that affect emerging markets but not developed markets is an empty set. This heterogeneous group of countries is no longer linked by a shared dependency on foreign capital – only by a shared prejudice about how risky they are, especially compared to the developed world. They may well face similar shocks but their policy reactions are likely to be very different, and their investor bases are diverse and not particularly overlapping.

---

[18] North (1990, pp. 110–11).

8

Asset Allocation

'We tend to get it wrong when the accumulated experiences and beliefs derived from the past do not provide a correct guide to future decision-making. There are two reasons ... not correctly comprehending what is happening to us ... (and) an inability to make the necessary institutional adjustments.'

North (2005, p. 117)

Our Martian friend whom we introduced in the box at the beginning of Chapter 5 reached some conclusions about risk but also about asset allocation, which is the high-level process of how we decide what sort of things we are going to invest in and in what proportions. He noticed several things about how asset allocation is often practised:

1. Risk is poorly understood.
2. Uncertainty is ignored.
3. Herd mentality is rife.
4. The set of asset classes is fairly arbitrary and static.
5. Indices dominate thinking in defining asset classes and asset allocation.
6. There is a circular logic to investing in line with (market-cap weighted) index weightings: the more investors invest in an asset class, the bigger the market cap of the index, the greater incentive they have to invest there.
7. Asset allocation is given a high degree of prominence over manager selection by many institutional investors – the theory to back this up again has a circular logic as EMH is assumed (i.e. that managers cannot beat indices consistently) to lead to a conclusion that ... managers cannot beat indices consistently.
8. The debate over passive versus active management is further confused by the two-stage allocation process of asset class allocation then manager selection, with risk at the second stage defined with reference not to the whole portfolio but in terms of variance from a benchmark index representative of the relevant asset class only – in effect the ability to have lower risk than the benchmark is (incorrectly, since Markowitz's simplification) assumed to be impossible and the impact of active management on the whole portfolio is often not properly taken into account.

Just as we explored in the last chapter, several of these errors are a result of incorrect assumptions about the simplicity and efficiency of markets, and also due to substantial principal/agent problems in asset allocation. Having discussed the importance of institutional structure, and more specifically an asset class's investor base structure, we now look at how asset allocation is conducted.

Anybody who makes a series of investments is, whether consciously or not, making asset allocation decisions. The individual investor may manage his or her own assets from a certain restricted knowledge base and not venture very far from the familiar. The institutional investor need not be so essentially random and restricted, but suffers from more agency problems.

The institutional investor's process of asset allocation is often quite formalised and in many instances follows common patterns of thinking. In part this is to make the process of investing more reliable and measurable. As Forbes (2009, p. 333) says in describing the case studies and field work of John Holland and others on how investment and asset allocation decisions are made: 'One thing that this literature makes clear is the intensely personal and at times heated nature of relationships that produce these decisions.'

Good investing often requires holistic overview and understanding of complex narratives, as well as elements of the immeasurable if not ineffable, including judgements of human character. Much of this research Forbes refers to has been on fund managers. Good asset allocators understand that they can never comprehend all the details of investment decisions made by their better managers, but also that the same immeasurable aspects of decision-making apply to themselves. Having formal processes for both investing and asset allocation makes sense to try to measure, understand and justify what is being decided, but it needs to be recognised that changing and constraining an investment process to make it more measure-able and standardised may be at the cost of performance.

Systematic patterns, and biases, in asset allocation are the norm. These can be reasonably stable over time, often changing only gradually, or at least, in aggregate, at a rate and with a momentum which can be observed and anticipated. Conformity is not only common and psychologically desirable: brain-imaging studies have suggested that people often see things as they know their peers do – differently from how they perceive the same thing without peer input.[1] In the last chapter we noted North's point that informal constraints can change at different rates from formal rules. Investing institutions may change more slowly than the economic environment. Consequently the structure of asset allocation across a whole class of investor may find itself outdated – not in line with new realities of the economy and marketplace, and this can increase collective risks, even to the point of enhancing the chances of catastrophe – i.e. a major discrete event causing major sudden investment losses such as a systemic banking crisis or sovereign default. Traditional following of old approaches can aid mass delusion. More specifically, it can create collective blind spots with regard to low-probability but high-risk scenarios.

To really avoid significant losses in the catastrophe scenario may require allocations far from consensus, possibly further than peer or hierarchic pressure or regulation may allow. Also, in a world where gambling is penalised only when it doesn't pay off, risk reduction for risks which then don't materialise often goes unrecognised. The prospect of relative under-performance of peers if the catastrophe does not occur, but still massive investment loss and the same job and personal loss (career risk) if it does means many choose to follow Chuck Prince's line of reasoning below to ignore catastrophic risk:

'When the music stops, in terms of liquidity, things will be complicated. But as long as the music is playing, you've got to get up and dance. We're still dancing.'[2]

---

[1] Thaler and Sunstein (2008, p. 57).

[2] As reported by the *Financial Times*: http://www.ft.com/cms/s/0/80e2987a-2e50-11dc-821c-0000779fd2ac.html#ixzz1CK5gE4Fs

8.1   ASSET CLASSES

As mentioned in Chapter 5 in the discussion of specific and systematic risk, there are problems with asset class delineations. There is seemingly endless debate on what is and what is not an asset class, and many different opinions. A simplified version of how thinking on the issue has developed starts with only two asset classes: debt and equity. In this most simple schema there is no international investing. Debt is domestic government bills and bonds; equities are only publicly listed domestic equities. Bonds are assumed to match liabilities best and are assumed to be less risky than equities. The case for investing in equities is that the total return to the investor should be higher than from bonds over the long term, as recompense for greater risk (an assumption not always true). Bonds may be less risky and match future liabilities better. Hence the distinction between asset classes rests on a distinction between the types of instruments and consequent characteristics. There has since been proliferation of asset classes, and it is not at all clear which set of potential asset classes and sub-asset classes to adopt as eligible for allocation.

We can trace a historical development of asset classes from the perspective of Western institutional investors, their consultants, the dominant financial firms, academic journal literature on asset classes and press coverage. It starts, as mentioned, with bonds and equities. International investing in (developed market) equities and in bonds has typically been added, as have a number of sub-asset classes in domestic equities and bonds: mid-cap, small-cap, corporate investment grade and high yield bonds, real estate, private equity. But do commodities constitute an asset class, or covered calls?[3] How do hedge funds and structured products and currency overlay programmes fit?[4] What makes an asset class? Emerging equity has been added in many instances, but emerging debt not so often. Many ignore emerging debt and many see emerging equity as a part of global equity. Other emerging market asset classes or sub-asset classes like local currency sovereign bonds, money markets, real estate, private equity and corporate bonds are often not considered.

Also, does it matter where you live? Are Brazilian investors in a different universe from US investors? If not, then presumably they should invest in European and US asset classes before neighbouring countries or large trading partners like China – but is this wise? Probably not.

Swensen (2009), from the Yale endowment, includes a list of asset classes for example, but there are obvious gaps, not least the $14 trillion emerging debt market (as at 2012, and growing fast). Muralidhar (2001, p. 53) suggests three criteria for denotation as an asset class: that the market must be sufficiently large for the investor to make an allocation equivalent to 5% of their assets; secondly, that assets should be sufficiently different to the assets in other asset classes to result in a correlation less than 0.9 (one suspects, disappointingly, that past correlation is being thought of here rather than future correlation or causation), and thirdly, that investment managers must offer products in the asset class. He also refers to Sharpe (1990), who adds criteria that asset classes be easy to measure and not too many of them – which

---

[3] A covered call is where the seller of a call option (who receives a premium for agreeing to sell a security to a counterpart – the call option's buyer) also buys some of the underlying security to 'cover' what would otherwise be the loss incurred if the security price rises beyond the option's strike price and the option is exercised (obliging the call option seller to buy the security in the open market at a price higher than the delivery price). The result is an income enhancement for the covered call holder at the cost of losing some of the potential upside from holding the underlying.

[4] A programme of currency risk management conducted by large institutional investors either internally or outsourced.

perhaps makes a lot of sense if the objective is to theorise and justify one's actions, but less sense if one wants to take best advantage of what the investment universe has to offer. Muralidhar also states:

'The definition of any investment opportunity as an asset class is subjective, and practitioners must use good judgement and common sense to identify asset classes. Classic candidates include domestic equities, domestic bonds, international developed market equities (hedged and unhedged), emerging market equities (unhedged), foreign bonds (hedged and unhedged), real estate (domestic and foreign), and private equity (which incorporates many variants).'

Appeals to common sense (not just as that above in choosing asset classes) should perhaps be treated with suspicion. Muralidhar's list of asset classes is arbitrary. One suspects that to a large extent the tail (the third criterion above: products investment managers offer) is wagging the dog (the denotation of asset class status). The names of asset classes are also often implicitly US-centric or developed world-centric. This channels our thoughts within the prevailing core/periphery view of the world.

We have seen an early primitive taxonomy give way to a range of candidates for the status of 'asset class', and indeed 'sub-asset class', including, inter alia, international and global equities, small-cap equity, international bonds, real estate, corporate bonds, high yield bonds, emerging equity, emerging debt, private equity, hedge funds and commodities. But a consensus on taxonomic criteria is still lacking, and common ground on what is and what is not an asset class remains amorphous. The general trend, however, has been towards proliferation.[5]

The case for adding an asset class is not driven by some objective academic discourse, but is a matter of opinion for thousands of market participants who choose to have a view and act on it. The formation of views is nevertheless led: led by market participants with inherent structural biases which are not uniform across types of market participants. Pension fund consultants, rating agencies, index providers, established financial firms and large public pension funds often have biases to preserve the status quo. Conversely, an individual investor or pensioner typically may not start with such bias, but is not as influential in the debate of what defines an asset class.

We can see how views on asset class taxonomy have lagged reality, and then, realising the error, caught up in surges. We mentioned at the end of the last chapter that in the 1970s US institutional investors did not invest in emerging equities. Indeed, they did not invest much outside the US, but after five or so years many did, and 'international' equity investing became the norm in a relatively short period, lagging behind the reality that institutional investors could have invested overseas years before.

Biological scientists' personal biases may affect biological taxonomy – they want to be right and have their views accepted.[6] With asset classes, however, there is more involved than just personal interest. Bias is a function of the interests of the dominant market participants who frame the debate (investors, consultants, fund managers). Most importantly, their collective views are largely resistant to challenges. Peer review is weak, unlike in the academic world. This is not to deny a lot of useful and objective academic work on asset

---

[5] Further future proliferation can still be expected, even though, post-2008, we may see the decline, even extinction, of certain product groupings if not asset classes.

[6] See Gould (1981) for examples of data being fudged to fix the taxonomy.

classes (established ones at least), but where theory conflicts with existing practice, theory tends to be the loser: its impact on behaviour is minimal. Academic work on asset classes tends to follow rather than lead consensus[7] and arguably has a much more limited impact on taxonomy actually used by practitioners when compared to the influence that objective observation has on how we classify animals. Defining asset classes is not a science. It is the evolved way investors have come to classify types of assets, under the influence of past and current conventional wisdom, without much interference from objective criticism along the way.[8] Yet we do not allow drug companies to define diseases to suit the medicine, so why do we allow classification of asset classes to suit the industry providers? Maybe, however, drug companies do define diseases to some extent.

Current approaches to asset taxonomy suffer from four overlapping objections: 1. missed opportunities due to a reduced universe defined by standard indices; 2. missed opportunities from limiting asset class diversification, 3. missed opportunities because allocation is slow to adjust; and 4. problems arising from many investors investing in the same things.

1. There is a bias towards the assets included in standard indices and easiest to invest in – there is a positive feedback loop driven by market capitalisation indices being used for asset allocation. As discussed in Chapter 6, this results in a perceived investment universe very different to the universe of actual investible economic activity globally. Many smaller or less liquid asset are excluded.

2. A common argument is that one should not have too many asset classes. The logic is that one only needs a few to achieve diversification – having more takes extra resources to analyse. However this is in part based on the questionable assumption that one can achieve maximum diversification with few investments. This argument may be false when the diversification process is not random but intelligent. Starting with a portfolio of one security and gradually adding more randomly selected securities, volatilities of equity portfolios have been shown to converge very quickly to that of the asset class benchmark index from which the securities are selected.[9] Unfortunately, the generally held conclusions emanating from this research do not consider the possibility of having lower volatility than the index (which is often possible). Also, it ignores the impact of risky events not experienced before which might impact all the assets one is invested in but not others. This is particularly pertinent when one uses the same logic for asset allocation – selecting a few asset classes may appear sufficient to reach maximum available diversification based on past volatility, but this may be an illusion. If you choose five asset classes, all in the highly leveraged developed world, then you are not going to get much diversification benefit in a 2008-style credit crunch, which you may be able to do with a different or broader set of asset classes – at least in the medium term once any short-term market contagion gives way to market appreciation of fundamental economic differences.

---

[7] Asset classes are largely taken as given, merely their characteristics explored, and I am unaware of studies which both go further in proposing new taxonomies and which have had a noticeable impact on the asset class taxonomies actually used by institutional investors.

[8] The term conventional wisdom, now common parlance, was coined by the economist John Kenneth Galbraith in his 1958 book *The Affluent Society*. His definition is as follows: 'It will be convenient to have a name for the ideas which are esteemed at any time for their acceptability, and it should be a term that emphasizes this predictability. I shall refer to these henceforth as the conventional wisdom.'

[9] Statman (1987).

3. There is a bias against the new which comes from too much influence from the incumbents, too much status quo. Investors may lag reality unnecessarily, and in dynamic times this may be particularly inappropriate. Emerging market debt is for example still at zero weighting in many institutional allocations. Moreover this is in many cases not a result of an informed decision about its merits, but too often based on next to no examination at all.
4. Similar types of investor can end up investing in the same few asset classes, which can result in homogenous investor bases and so systemic risks as discussed.

Keeping things simple is often attractive, but unfortunately life is becoming ever more complex, and it behoves investors to do more than just ignore this reality. Darwin noticed how selective breeding radically changed species. Deliberate intelligent financial product development and market behaviour has, over the years, complicated the simple split between equities and bonds. There are derivatives which sometimes look like bonds, sometimes like equities. There are many new instruments we are not sure about. Should emerging market private equity fall under 'private equity' or 'emerging markets'? Often opportunities categorised together employ different skills and display different return streams. For example, financial engineering and leverage may be key characteristics in US private equity, whereas emerging markets private equity often employs little or no leverage and is dependent on strong local relationships which take years to develop. The returns and the skills to obtain them are markedly different.

US sovereign bonds are perceived as low risk. Emerging market equities are perceived as high risk – a simplistic characterisation as discussed in Chapter 3. Therefore emerging sovereign bonds are low risk or high risk? Which if any preconception takes precedence in describing something outside our established taxonomy?

The question of where to place, if at all, an asset class in a portfolio often falls within the following (and flawed) staged process:

(a) Define the investment universe to be traditional asset classes, in the process excluding large segments of the investible universe.
(b) When faced with opportunities outside the commonly used benchmark indices, nevertheless categorise them according to the existing set of indices wherever possible.
(c) Otherwise (for those new opportunities which really do not fit) consider adding a new asset class if there is an appropriate benchmark index which can be used as a proxy – this process can only happen occasionally as it may necessitate rethinking the whole portfolio allocation.
(d) Another route for inclusion, possibly pending a review of new asset classes as at (c) above, is to put it in an 'alternative' allocation.
(e) Otherwise ignore the opportunity.
(f) Select a combination of asset classes on the basis of their commonly used benchmark indices.
(g) Select managers to manage assets in the selected asset classes.

8.1.1 Alternatives

One method to deal with the plethora of new investment opportunities is to call anything unconventional – i.e. anything not deemed an asset class – 'alternative'. This gets over the frustration with the inadequacy of the traditional taxonomy in its exclusion of some valuable investment opportunities, while still paying lip service to the traditional process of asset allocation whereby overall portfolio performance is driven by the major allocations among traditional asset classes. The introduction of alternatives into the asset allocation process is often an example of mental accounting – in many cases a compromise between the desire to conform and the desire to invest well. Yet many institutional investors are now over 50% allocated to alternatives (and some others are still at zero). Having that large an alternative allocation bucket is subversive of the traditional taxonomy. If minimum allocations to traditional asset classes are maintained, then sub-optimal allocations can be expected. If alternatives are in practice put through the same optimisation process as traditional asset classes, for that optimisation process to work all should be treated equally, with traditional asset classes as easy to exclude as any alternative. If so, then everything is actually an 'alternative', and saying otherwise is possibly little more than semantics, presumably to avoid objections from traditionalists. If alternatives are to be significant, it raises the question: If one is so dissatisfied with the traditional approach, why stop at 50%? Why not allocate 100% differently? Otherwise the delineation of what is and what is not an asset class appears to be getting in the way.

8.2 HOW ASSET ALLOCATION OCCURS TODAY

Asset allocation has been shown by studies in behavioural finance often to be a stage or pyramid-building process where investors assign different functions to certain allocations, or layers in a pyramid.[10] First is the goal of safety, and assets are allocated in the base of the pyramid to supposedly 'risk-free' assets or to ones ostensibly matching liabilities. Next, on top of those, may be assets geared towards generating income, then growth assets to counter inflation and then higher-risk higher-return assets at the top of the pyramid. We can see how investing in alternatives fits into this schema of mental accounting, but mental accounting is broader than just the distinction between traditional asset classes and alternatives. The end result is a series of mini-portfolios and to quote Nofsinger (2011, p. 72): 'Investors tend to overlook the interaction among mental accounts and among investment assets. As a result, investor diversification comes from investment goal diversification rather than from a purposeful asset diversification, as described in Markowitz's portfolio theory.' This amounts to a self-imposed constraint on how a portfolio is managed, which, if binding, reduces the ability to achieve its objectives. Another way to put this is that asset allocation is, for many, not a universal optimisation process, and the results are consequently sub-optimal.

There is also overwhelming evidence of home bias, but also of foreign bias – foreign investment by developed country institutional investors is predominantly into nearby developed countries with similar culture. Indeed, there is no getting away from behavioural 'irrationalities'. Markowitz has even explained that his personal investment choice was not optimal but designed to minimise future regret.[11] Framing is widespread in investment, and loss aversion, including motivated to reduce regret ('minimax regret'), is common.

The main objective of an institutional investor is often expressed simply as a target rate of return over a certain time period. Objectives may be more complex, designed to meet the flow of future liabilities. We have discussed that there is evidence of pyramid building

---

[10] Shefrin and Statman (2000) and Statman (1999), both quoted in Nofsinger (2011, p. 71).
[11] In Shefrin (2002, p. 31).

and objectives can also include shorter-term as well as longer-term return targets, volatility targets, liquidity targets, and there may be regulatory, tax and other constraints.

Now for the theory: the purpose of asset allocation is to meet the portfolio's objectives. The basic approach is to define asset classes or investment opportunities (the default typically being to use indices as discussed), explore their characteristics, find out their relationships with each other historically, make assumptions about these characteristics and relationships in the future, and then optimise (for example using a mean-variance optimiser) or use a simulation technique so as to draw conclusions about optimal allocation in order to meet portfolio objectives. Looking forward requires observing how asset classes, sub-asset classes and more specific opportunities correlate historically and in different types of historical market conditions, but then considering in what ways this may all change. As previously discussed in Chapter 4, this is a tall order: optimisation techniques are typically highly sensitive to small changes in assumptions about asset class characteristics.[12] Reality is complex. Standard finance theory models can on occasion help us understand bits of it well, and, if there are no big structural shifts, the whole of it with some degree of accuracy. But the toolset we have does not perform well when faced with structural shifts and new evolving situations.

The 'Yale model' pioneered by Swensen (2009) goes some way in improving on more traditional asset allocation approaches and in particular emphasises diversification, including across alternatives. It has also managed to break from the common fixation with liquidity: Swensen favours significant allocations to less liquid long-term investments. These are both positive developments, although the 'Yale model' generally did not fare well in 2008. It still has a static view of what is and what is not an asset class, suffers from core/periphery disease if not home bias, has an equity bias, and has no clear place for macroeconomic analysis to drive strategic allocation dynamically: target allocations are largely fixed and reviewed at regular periods rather than with decisions timed to occur in line with changes in the economic environment. In a rapidly changing world the unrepresentative limited asset allocations, and static nature of the approach, interspersed with ad hoc changes to allocation, are always lagging behind reality.

8.2.1 Investor types

We have mentioned how investor base structures matter in the last chapter, but asset allocation approaches also vary by type of investor, depending on, among other things: investment purpose and liabilities, size, agency issues, governance structure, legal/regulatory environment, tax treatment, political context and peer group characteristics. Having said that, there are commonalities, presented below as stylised facts, though with significant exceptions not covered. Similar investors may have very different concerns. Also, the same type of investor in different countries may have very different characteristics, and not just due to regulation, tax or liabilities. Typical US pension fund trustees may have a very different concept of Russian equity risk from their Dutch equivalents. Even within a country, perceived political and public relations issues may vary enormously. A private (company) pension fund does not normally face the degree of political pressures a public fund does, but even within the set of US public pension funds, the staff of a West Coast State or Teachers' pension fund may

---

[12] For example, Swensen (2009, p. 120) illustrates this with a discussion of real estate, in which unadjusted non-realistic extrapolated projections for returns and correlations led to high allocation recommendations from an optimisation.

have very different constraints from those of a police and firefighters' pension fund in Texas. However, traditional categorisation of investor types is useful, not least as it helps us define peer groups. Hence we can think of investor types engaging in asset allocation to include public and private pension funds, endowments, foundations, family offices, private banks and high net worth individuals, insurance companies, corporate treasuries, sovereign wealth funds, central banks and retail investors.

Pensions can be funded or unfunded (i.e. 'pay-as-you-go' from future government revenues), defined contribution or defined benefit.[13] In the US, public sector workers typically contribute to a state pension fund, a state teachers' fund, a city or county fund or maybe a police and/or firefighters' pension fund,[14] and these are all typically defined benefit plans. The governance structure normally consists of a trustee board with fiduciary responsibilities, and this can include political appointees or elected officials, worker representatives and financial experts. Investment staff normally report to the board or an investment subcommittee, and this staff can vary considerably in size from pension fund to pension fund. Some investment management may be conducted by this staff directly, most often in US government bills and bonds, but much, and often all, investment is outsourced to private fund management firms. The main functions of the investment staff are thus liability assessment, asset allocation and manager selection. The staff may commission consultants to assist in these tasks. Employee contributors and pensioners have representatives on the board, but delegate the investment decisions, and judge the pension fund primarily on overall investment performance. Trustees want to optimise the benefits for retirees but are often peer conscious and sensitive about possible public or press criticism. Investment staff may also reflect these concerns in asset allocation, and may not have the resources to investigate new asset classes very much. Consultants want their clients to outperform but, like them, often have more incentive to avoid losses, particularly if not shared by other peer-group pension funds, than promote innovative allocations which may lead to better performance (a principal/agent issue).

Private pension funds typically differ from public funds in that they face fewer political pressures, and have a less layered governance structure. Staff incentive pay may also be more common, and with fewer agency problems, private pension funds often have more diversified asset allocation than public funds. In the case of a company pension, the ability to meet private pension fund liabilities is linked to the prospects of the company, and thus the ability to continue making employer contributions. The separation between company balance sheet and pension is regulated differently in different countries, and a matter deserving of oversight given past abuses by the likes of Robert Maxwell.[15] However, the fate of the two is connected. Particularly for listed companies providing quarterly earnings reports to investors, which thus have an incentive to maintain steady valuations on corporate balance sheet assets, it would seem logical to put low volatility investments in the corporate treasury and longer-term but possibly more volatile assets in the pension fund which may have a 15-year liability structure.

Though similar in many ways, endowments and foundations often have very different asset allocations from private pension funds. They have different liabilities: more typically an absolute or percentage annual amount is required for spending, whereas pension liabilities can vary with pension system maturity, the age structure of employees and retirees and

---

[13] A defined contribution pension is one determined by contributions and investment returns. A defined benefit pension is determined by a formula including such items as age, number of years of employment and salary history.

[14] Sometimes called 'guns and hoses' funds.

[15] Robert Maxwell, who died at sea in mysterious circumstances in 1991, was a UK publisher and newspaper proprietor who got into debt and stole £440m from the pension funds of the companies he controlled in the 1980s.

other actuarial assumptions, as well as corporate developments. But even the approach to the payout level can differ: a university endowment for example may have very different levels of flexibility on spending levels (i.e. the liability structure for the fund) than a neighbouring peer. While many university trustees may be conscious of the need to adjust new building plans to the financial health of the endowment, there are those who would spend all the endowment to build first-rate facilities to attract students and top professors and then later ask alumni for more money.[16] Sovereign wealth funds are much like large endowments, albeit owned by governments and all that implies. Central banks, as discussed already, typically manage a core of reserves, if not the entire amount, with a big focus on liquidity.

Though family offices can be quite sophisticated, individual investors sometimes depend on advisers, who may have incentives to recommend particular products and so asset allocations, but lack the expert knowledge to make prudent investment decisions on their own. Regulators may try to protect non-expert retail investors, but in doing so pander to existing prejudices of what is and what is not safe. Banks also have agency problems in managing the capital of their own shareholders, and may have a very short time perspective.

So there is quite a range of investor structure and incentive/information problems. But for certain types of investor, before we consider asset allocation further, we need to have a better conception of liabilities. For pension funds and insurance companies in particular, asset/liability management is commonly a determinant for asset allocation.

8.2.2   Asset/liability management

Investors have liabilities. For a defined benefit pension plan, actuaries can work out the likely future payments required to provide pensioners and future pensioners their formulaically agreed pensions. The retirement dates, monthly payments due and life expectancies can be estimated and consequent liabilities summed across the pension plan participants to give the stream of payments the fund has to come up with in the future. This is a rough science and re-estimation is required periodically – not least as life expectancy changes. From this can be derived a required target rate of investment return the pension fund has to earn on its pool of assets to meet its liabilities. This may be easily achievable or unrealistically high. If persistently higher than actual investment returns, then the pension fund can be said to be underfunded, and if it in effect eats into capital (besides spending income) to meet current obligations, then its funding status will deteriorate.[17] The liabilities and expected returns can change, however, depending on factors other than investment returns (expected returns are more frequently adjusted than liabilities for, on the whole, legitimate reasons given asset prices tend to move faster than liabilities). If interest rates rise across the government yield curve (i.e. not just short-term interest rates), then available investment returns may also rise and liabilities, which are typically discounted by a rate linked to prevailing interest rates, will fall (as long as they are not index- or inflation-linked). The degree to which assets and liabilities both move in line with each other if interest rates change is a very rough function of how the duration[18] of the portfolio matches the duration of the liabilities. A pension fund, which

---

[16] From comments at a private conference by the CIO of a major US university endowment.

[17] 100% funded means having the assets to meet all liabilities as conventionally calculated; above 100% more than needed; below less than needed.

[18] Duration is the average term of the payments of a bond, expressed in years, and weighted by the size of the payments. A discount rate (the interest rate) is applied across the life of a bond to estimate the current price – the sum of the net present values of the bond's stream of future payments. A bond's duration is thus also the percentage change (one year equating to 1%) in the value of the bond caused by a 1% move in the discount rate.

has to make payments many years into the future, may have an average liability of 15 years. If the duration of the investment portfolio is less than this[19] and interest rates rise, then the financial status of the fund vis-à-vis its liabilities will improve as the values of liabilities and asset fall, but liabilities more so. But if interest rates fall, the funding status will deteriorate as liabilities will rise faster than the value of assets.

However, life is not that simple. Unfortunately assets cannot always predictably match liabilities, not least because assets do not always deliver (they can default or lose value in other ways such as by being taxed), and liabilities typically change more often than they are measured or estimated. Also, we could say that the first law of asset/liability management is to have some assets. In 1977 Venezuela was AAA rated. If a fully funded Venezuelan pension fund had then invested 100% in Venezuelan sovereign bonds to match liabilities perfectly, they would have since found, all else being equal, that 30 years later it was massively under-funded. They would not have met their liabilities for the simple reason that some of the bonds defaulted.

Whereas Venezuela has defaulted in the past, rich countries, as already mentioned, default principally by other means. Both inflation and devaluation reduce the value of money relative to the prices of other things. To ignore this effect, and assume that money will retain its value, is called 'money illusion'. From the analysis of asset/liability management above, if a pension fund has an asset pool with a lower duration than the duration of the liabilities, and interest rates rise, the pension fund may become less underfunded (or more overfunded) even though the net asset value of the fund has fallen. This is because the liabilities have fallen. In other words, it is because the values of the pensions which have to be paid out in the future have fallen. The pensioners, and future pensioners, may not immediately notice it, but they are worse off. Having said that, if interest rates go down again they will be better off again, and it may be quite acceptable for them to ignore such fluctuations in the short term. Another way of looking at it is that if the fund was really underfunded to begin with, then the participants were just fooling themselves about the value of their future pensions.

Such calculations can go awry. The most obvious scenario is that greater longevity increases liabilities. The next most obvious is because inflation is high for a sustained period, robbing savers of value, denuding the value of bonds, reducing the purchasing power of pensions. In such a scenario a pension fund can meet its liabilities but shrink in real terms (i.e. relative to the purchasing power of its assets). In the context of a long period of high inflation it is quite possible that electorates will demand legislation to index pensions to inflation or other changes to retain purchasing power. Furthermore, the likelihood is that such legislation would affect existing not just future pensioners. With such risk of regulatory rule changes with retroactive impact, perfect asset-liability matching which ignores purchasing power can become an exercise in fiction. Should pension funds assign a zero probability to the likelihood that they will experience a serious bout of inflation over the next couple of decades? Should they also discount the possibility that regulation may force them to wake up from their money illusion and take account of purchasing power in the future? To do so might be imprudent.

And should they not be looking after the best interests of pensioners by targeting purchasing power anyway? There may be a different attitude to inflation/devaluation from public and private pensions. If a pensioner is not able to buy the goods and services they expected 20 years before, a private pension fund may just think: 'Tough.' The fund's legal obligation was

---

[19] All portfolios have a duration insofar as they all can be expected to change value should interest rates change, even an equity portfolio.

for a fixed nominal stream of payments, no more. However, a public fund, whose pensioners may, through consequent poverty, be foisted on another welfare arm of the state to supplement their now inadequate pension, may care to take a view more in line with the interests of the pensioner. Such a prescient view is even more likely for an endowment or private individual who clearly should care more about purchasing power than nominal amounts. The contrast is that pension funds, and other investor types with agency problems, are less than fully attuned to the interests of the beneficial owners of the capital they manage (the pensioners in this example).

Taking domestic inflation into account helps stem the gap between nominal values and purchasing power, which an investor can do by buying inflation-linked bonds. But (a) such bonds may not track the basket of consumption goods that a retiree wants; (b) while inflation linkers can protect against short-term spikes in yields they, like other bonds, do not protect against sustained higher real yields, including those associated with high inflation periods; (c) the market for these bonds remains small relative to other government bonds; and (d) were the market much larger, then the government's ability to manage its debt service would be reduced creating a credit deterioration and higher yields. This fourth argument is a macroeconomic one – governments use inflation to erode their debts but cannot do so if the debt is all linked to inflation. The objective of creating a larger inflation-linked market to protect savers may come into conflict with a country's ability to afford paying for the standard of living its retirees want. It won't happen, in other words.

In periods of deflation an additional problem is that financial repression and irrational perceptions of risk may result in artificially low yields (including on inflation linkers). This reduces returns on these investments. Additionally, if the net present value of future liabilities is calculated using government bonds (mandated by regulators), there is an additional negative impact on pension funds.

Devaluation is an alternative (and complement) to inflation, and has similar effect. For example, if the dollar halves in value but global supply and demand conditions for oil do not change, then the price of oil, in dollars, will double. So US pensioners wanting to buy fuel for their cars will be worse off. If they live in a closed economy (one where imports and exports are a small share of GDP) they can be more isolated from the domestic currency devaluing than if they live in an open economy. However, even in a relatively closed economy they should worry about who has global pricing power. As the emerging markets become more dominant in setting not just global commodity prices but goods prices, then emerging markets are becoming a larger part of the pensioner's liability and the pension funds' liability in purchasing power terms. Instead of thinking of liabilities in dollar or euro or sterling terms, we should think of them in terms of the underlying trends in the domestic and international economy. Thinking about liabilities in domestic nominal currency terms may be more convenient, but it is a shorthand, a fiction. In many scenarios the approximation may not matter much, but it does matter in extreme scenarios where inflation and currency shifts may be significant, and it does matter when one considers liabilities longer than a few years, as with life savings or pensions.

So a pension fund should perhaps re-evaluate liabilities in terms of prices of goods and services which make up the basket of goods their pensioners will want in the future. That is not an easy thing to do, and involves recognising global relative pricing power now and in the future – about 15 years in the future for most. For many pension funds asset/liability management is often seen as a reason to stay in domestic government bonds. Yet if money illusion is overcome, the same desire to match assets to liabilities could result in zero allocations to domestic government bonds and tenfold increases in allocations to emerging market asset classes.

Asset/liability management is much more complex and difficult than it first appears. But there is something else. At the start of this section we referred to trying to work out liabilities, and from them deriving a target rate of return. Then what? Does this mean we should not invest in higher return investments once the mix of investments we already have are expected to meet the criteria? Or does it mean we should separate the portfolio into two parts in a mental accounting exercise again – one, presumably the bulk, to match liabilities and the rest to try and gain extra return for a rainy day? Both approaches are advocated and used by some institutional investors. Governments have also been known to tax away any apparent or temporary 'excesses' above those needed to meet liabilities,[20] all resulting in a satisficing not optimising approach. If working out liabilities and investment are such imperfect sciences, should we not try to do better than just match liabilities – so that we have some cushion to fall back on if things don't go as planned? A future unforeseen risk is a potential liability too.

8.3 FROM EFFICIENCY FRONTIERS TO REVEALED PREFERENCES

We have discussed the efficient market hypothesis (EMH), the capital asset pricing model (CAPM) and the market portfolio. We have also discussed the limitations of fully predetermined models and how they may fail to work in a world of large uncertainties and structural shifts. A world running in accordance with fully predetermined models is a world where highly centralised economic planning works well – a world inconsistent with Hayek's insight that central state co-ordination of economic activity is inferior to a liberal system of many economic decisionmakers. Optimisation models can still have a role to play, as can simulation models, and many are available.[21] Models are typically highly limited: many not only ignore macroeconomic risks but assume fictitious 'risk-free' investments, and may allow leverage and hedging without factoring in fallacies of composition which might affect future correlations and basis risks in highly leveraged environments. Many statistics and models used are not realistic or dynamic enough to be relied on for long. The main difficulty with formal modelling though lies with the model inputs: the expected future returns, future volatilities and future co-variances of different investment opportunities. We might guesstimate returns, but the other two are much more difficult.

A widespread and sometime erroneous assumption is that investments with low return are low risk and ones with high return are necessarily high risk. Risk is not as straightforward as often assumed, and is not the same as volatility. It is not additive, as risks affect each other and interact in non-linear ways. Hence risk budgeting is largely nonsense, little more than short-term volatility budgeting assuming the past is a good indication of the future. Risk is not even the same for different investors invested in the same investment: they may have different degrees of information about the investment or control over it, propensities to act differently in the future, different other investments and different liabilities.

---

[20] For example, the removal of UK advanced corporation tax relief in 1997 was a case of money illusion (or tax illusion) by the government. It transferred what appeared to be pension fund surpluses to the government only for the pension funds to experience significant consequent underfunding a few years later.

[21] See for example Muralidhar (2001) Appendix 3.1.

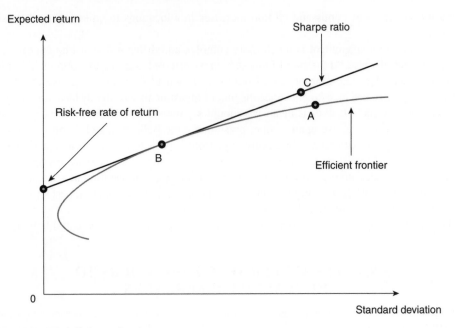

Figure 8.1   The efficiency frontier

However, let us for the moment continue with the convenient and for the most part empirically correct assumption that high volatility investments are less attractive to investors than low volatility ones. We can also, less controversially, assume investors want higher rather than lower return. The efficiency frontier (see Figure 8.1) is the boundary of the set of achievable combinations of volatility and return an investor can achieve through different allocations to eligible asset classes or assets (with assumed future returns, volatilities and co-variances).

The theory goes that we should invest in the combination of investments (the point on the curve) which gives us our preferred mix of volatility and return. We can perhaps also improve on this portfolio by use of leverage or cash. This is provided courtesy of the Sharpe ratio, represented on the graph by the upward sloping straight line. The Sharpe ratio is the expected excess return (i.e. expected portfolio return above the 'risk-free rate' or benchmark return) divided by portfolio standard deviation. The 'risk-free rate' is the rate on domestic government bonds, or, assuming perfect access to fully scalable bank credit, the interest rate at which an investor can borrow or deposit cash. It is thus also the return where the straight line crosses the Y axis (with zero 'risk'). Hence the Sharpe ratio is the slope of the line. If we can borrow or deposit as much as we want, we can, with a combination of cash/leverage and the tangential portfolio, then invest anywhere along the line. And this line becomes our new efficiency frontier. Say we like best the combination of past return and volatility represented by point A on the curved efficiency frontier, we can do better by investing at B and then borrowing to move to C, which has higher return and less volatility.

In microeconomics there is a similar graph called the production function, showing the possible combinations of factors of production which can be employed to produce a certain output (good or set of goods). However, in micro-economics there also are indifference or utility curves imposed on top to denote the preferred combination. The indifference curves

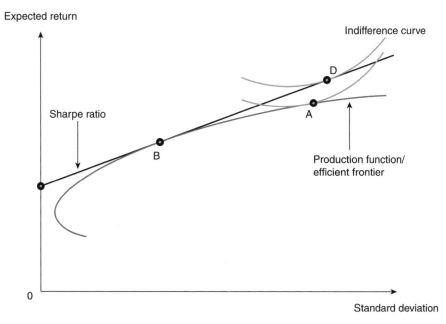

Figure 8.2   Adding utility indifference curves to the efficiency frontier

furthest to the top denote higher utilities, with utility levels equal along each individual curve. One locates on the production curve where it intersects with the highest indifference curve – at point D in Figure 8.2.

But where are the indifference curves above our efficiency frontier? A Sharpe ratio is not an indifference curve but a way to extend the production function. We need to know what combinations of volatility and return a fund prefers, and not a simple fixed trade-off as defined by the line. Yet the standard approach is not to optimise at all, but to work out the percentage return target needed to meet the liabilities as discussed, then gear up, through borrowing, until this return is reached, and accept the associated volatility and no more.

However, the work of actuaries is complicated in practice, and we have more objectives to think of optimising than just volatility and return (the graph becomes multidimensional). A pension fund has choices: whether to risk various levels of underfunding in the future, whether to cut benefits (or increase them) now or in the future, and whether to alter contributions up or down now or in the future. These preferences could be expressed as time vectors and a carefully crafted questionnaire may even be able to reveal the trade-offs in preferences (of trustees, sponsors, plan participants) between them. Directly asking trustees what their utility function is may be less than successful. Rather, questionnaires might include the following sort of question: would you prefer a 5% risk of being 10% underfunded in three years or a 1% increase in contributions today?[22] If, and it might be a big if, such questionnaires produced meaningful results, one could indeed create multidimensional indifference curves which might help complement the efficiency frontier model we have discussed above.[23] And

---

[22] Muralidhar (2001, p. 50) includes an example of a questionnaire for a policy oversight committee which could be elaborated further.

[23] And Lagrange multipliers could be used from this data to calculate optimal allocations, in theory.

even if such questionnaires prove impractical in defining indifference curves, there may still be heuristic benefits from posing such questions in helping pension fund trustees and managers thinking through their options.

8.4   ASSET ALLOCATION VS MANAGER SELECTION; ACTIVE VS PASSIVE

'Absolutists erroneously jump from the virtually incontrovertible evidence that it is hard to outperform the market to the erroneous prescription that all efforts to evaluate the correctness of market prices are useless.'

Bhidé (2010, p. 113)

Indices, which are often weighted by the size of the component's market capitalisations, are often unnecessarily risky ways to invest, and hence easy to outperform, both in terms of risk and return. Sovereign debt provides some good examples, both in developed and in emerging markets. For example, if a country is mismanaging its fiscal balance it may borrow more. By borrowing more, its debt stock and ultimately also its debt/GDP ratio expand. Thus its debt becomes a greater share of capitalisation-weighted indices, while the risk of default increases sooner or later. Moreover, before catastrophe strikes, the problem is visible to all concerned and the government may try any number of policies to avoid default, devaluation or inflationary exit from the commitment to repay the real value of the debt to investors. In such markets the first role of active management is to reduce risk, and one of the worst ways to invest is through passive following of the index. A good example is Argentina, which had built up larger and larger debts ahead of its default in 2001 until its debt instruments comprised a fifth of the JP Morgan Emerging Markets Bond Index Global Diversified (EMBI GD) index, which is market capitalisation-weighted (and so raised its weighting for Argentina as the debt rose). That Argentina was going to default was fairly easy to predict, if not the exact timing. Hence many active managers simply held none of its debt going into the default, whereas the passive index funds suffered serious losses when the default occurred. Conclusion: active management can reduce risk.

While many believe that active management adds fees but, on average, no additional performance, this does not apply everywhere. In the case of emerging debt, and after 2008 European sovereign debt, we can resolutely claim that passive investing is much riskier than active investing. It is less expensive in fees, yes, but driving a car with one's eyes closed also requires less energy and effort – not an argument on its own to recommend it. The active versus passive issue is linked to the debate on the relative merits of asset allocation versus manager selection, and so too to the struggle between consultants and fund managers on who should do what. Our analysis here is linked to our earlier discussion of delineation of asset classes as well as the inadequacies of defining an asset class by an index.

To begin our illustration, let us define an asset class as including no more or less than the components of an index with 100 stocks. There is no change in the market participants or in the index or thus the asset class components over the time period we are considering. Fund managers own 100% of the asset class – i.e. all the available stocks – throughout the period. They can trade with each other, but every purchase has a counterpart sale. The index is market capitalisation-weighted. In this example it is easily apparent that, barring transactions costs, the index will perform identically to the aggregate of all the assets in all the portfolios, as both have exactly the same relative weights and individual performances. For every loss there is a gain, and vice versa. The sum of all active managers cannot beat the (passive) index.

We can then expand the argument to a higher level, defining the whole global investment universe in terms of a global index, including within it many indices or sub-indices representing different asset classes. There is a widespread understanding that asset allocation can improve portfolio performance significantly, but there is also a widespread but questionable assumption that a simple combination of the set of available indices in a global index is a reasonable benchmark.

There is research both to support the view that active managers on average cannot beat the index and that they can. Underlying the debate are concerns that it is difficult to identify good managers from bad, good managers may just have been lucky in the past and may not repeat the outperformance, bad managers go out of business and are no longer in databases (this is called survivor bias), and fees and transaction costs are higher for active managers than passive ones.

A well-known paper by Brinson *et al.* (1986) showed that asset allocation can explain around 93.6% (the R^2 result of the study) of the variability of pension fund returns over time. For pension funds the argument often drawn from this, though it does not follow, is that asset allocation policy is much more important than manager selection. The 93.6 R^2 says nothing about relative performance, merely that on average the good performers and the bad moved in line with the strategic asset allocation. Other studies show that active management can add hundreds of basis point excess return over this. The Brinson result is simply consistent with pension funds sticking to strategic allocations over time. Focusing more on return, Ibbotson and Kaplan (2000) have shown around 40% of the variability among funds of the sample they used was caused by asset allocation policy – a far cry from 93.6%. Yet this still tells us little or nothing about the potential to do better from active management. It merely describes the consequence of past asset allocation and manager selection decisions. If, however, asset allocation is so important in explaining returns relative to other factors it is likely that one could do even better by having a more inclusive universe of asset classes to choose from.[24]

Also, when is moving away from a benchmark an asset allocation, and when is it portfolio management? If managers are given little leeway to move off benchmark in allocations, but this freedom is allowed to the asset allocator, then asset allocation may add more return. If the same flexibility is allowed to the manager, the result may reverse.

Revisiting our simple index and asset class with 100 stocks, we can quickly see how a manager may outperform an index. Outperformance need not result simply from going off benchmark. Firstly, the universe may expand or contract with index weights not adjusting instantaneously to composition and weight changes.

Secondly, it may be possible to identify good managers. There is typically a lot of focus on doing exactly that. Different investors active in a market have different skills and knowledge bases. The question for the pension fund is: who is best placed to understand the market and make excess returns from changing positions? This question, moreover, informs not only manager selection, but also asset allocation in the broader sense of who should be employed to manage what assets.

---

[24] This is not the standard interpretation. The frame of debate is normally restricted to whether active managers can add value. One sub-plot of the debate is whether consultants, who advise on asset allocation, are more valuable to a pension fund client than the fund managers employed to invest the assets.

At an emerging markets conference a few years ago[25] a large pension fund made a presentation on the relative merits of employing specialist emerging equity managers versus allowing their international (i.e. non-US developed world) equity manager the tactical asset allocation discretion to dip into emerging equities from time to time. Their own experience and evidence suggested that when the international managers invested in emerging equities they added value versus their (international) benchmark index, but the selection of emerging equities they invested in underperformed the emerging equity benchmark index. Their conclusion was that tactical asset allocation worked but specialist managers also added value, so they should both employ specialist emerging equity managers and allow the international managers to dip in. However, this assumes that the emerging equity manager is not as capable as the international manager at actively going over- or underweight the emerging asset class.

The evidence presented indicated two things: first, that tactical asset allocation adds value, and secondly that the international managers in question were not good at managing emerging equities. The next question would have been: are the emerging equity managers (or possible replacements) as able as the international managers to make the decision when to go longer or shorter the whole asset class? If yes, then what was an asset allocation decision (if and where to deploy tactical asset allocation to emerging equities) has to some extent become a manager selection issue. The tactical asset allocation can be delegated to the emerging equity manager. Determining when to move in and out of asset classes is an asset allocation decision, whether temporary (tactical asset allocation) or more permanent. It makes sense that those with the skills to do that best should be the ones doing it, and that may or may not be asset class specialists, depending on specific circumstances.

So rather than always rigorously following a structured decision tree of asset allocation followed by manager selection, the manager selection process can also inform the asset allocation decision, depending on what one finds in one's manager selection process – in this case, if the manager has better ability to allocate tactically to their asset class than a global manager or consultant or the pension fund.

Another feature of this emerging equity story is that emerging equity managers in the room at the time thought it controversial if not unreasonable that they be delegated tactical asset allocation. To some extent this may be because the particular managers in the room at the time who spoke out were not macro specialists but more bottom-up stock pickers, and felt they were not best placed to execute tactical asset allocation. But an additional argument made was that their clients (the pension funds) would not want them to use leverage or cash and that such behaviour would compromise their performance statistics. This hierarchical view – that it is fine for developed world equity managers to asset allocate tactically, but not emerging managers – can be categorised as a case of core/periphery disease.[26] It is also perhaps an example of the desire for measurement potentially getting in the way of performance.

Thirdly, there may be other holders of the stocks, with other liabilities and frames for judging performance. For example, from the perspective of a US investor think of gilts: sovereign bonds denominated in local currency (pound sterling) issued by a foreign country (the UK). If the pound falls significantly against the dollar the US investor overweight gilts may make a loss against their (US-centric) benchmark. And if all gilts are owned by similar US investors

---

[25] Author's personal experience.

[26] It inspires me to desire a 'core plus' emerging market fund: one which invests at least 80% of assets in emerging markets and tactically invests some money in the peripheral (and presumably riskier) developed markets from time to time. As GDP weighting would indicate a 50:50 split and it will take a few decades for the core-periphery prejudice to erode, during which risk-adjusted returns in emerging markets will be higher, this may not be so far-fetched.

(i.e. none are owned by anyone in the UK – remember, this is a thought experiment), then, compared to the index of international bonds of which gilts are a part, the losses of some investors who are overweight gilts are matched by gains elsewhere for those who are underweight gilts. So if we again assume away our ability to select good managers, we are back with an argument for passive over active management (because active fees are higher).

But now we relax the assumption that only US investors own gilts, and assume that UK investors, with a different UK-focused index benchmark, now own some. Assume that gilts do better than other UK bonds. The UK investors who are overweight gilts may not consider they have made any loss in absolute terms or versus their benchmark. Having different liabilities and expressing this by simply employing a different benchmark can change perceived performance. The overweight UK investor made money (in sterling). The underweight US investor made money (in dollars). The assumption that there are as many losers as winners in any market evaporates once we define gains and losses in terms of different benchmarks. What is important, though, as we covered in Chapter 7, is to understand the structure of the investor base and their different liabilities and motives, and to be aware of the macroeconomics and have a view on the exchange rate.

8.5   ALLOCATING AT SEA

We thought we were on dry land, measuring investments from a fixed point called 'Risk-free Point' in a world without weather systems clouding our vision. But we now realise that we are on a ship, previously becalmed but now in a storm. Contrary to a simple world of two asset classes and some neat theory about a uniform market portfolio which can then be leveraged up in accordance with the Sharpe ratio, we live in a financial world of complexity, dynamism, information asymmetries, agency problems and other behavioural constraints. The fixed reference points, not only of 'risk-free' but also of credit ratings and indices, are not as reliable as previously thought – in fact, they may be misleading. Macro-hedge funds and bank proprietary trading books, CTAs,[27] CDOs and ETFs, the growth of derivatives and the globalisation of finance now present investors with a large number of ways to invest into markets which are no longer as distinct as previous choices. Correlations were never fixed, but now we are starting to factor in what that means. Asset allocation as a traditional ordered set of decisions – defining liabilities, defining asset classes, finding benchmarks, allocating target weights to asset classes, selecting managers to manage within those asset classes – is being questioned. The sub-optimal alternative of ignoring the seemingly inadequate process of formal optimisation in favour of mental accounting and pyramid building is also being questioned, as it is hostage to prejudices and also may lack ways to cope with a rapidly changing world. Hierarchical decisionmaking too is under attack: managers' skills do not fit neatly into separate categories any more, and the distinctions between (strategic) asset allocation and tactical asset allocation and manager discretion are becoming blurred.

The investor wants to take best advantage of what is on offer, but the traditional classifications of asset classes leaves too many opportunities unexplored. An investor's peers may not be invested in such new areas, returns may be high and the opportunities may increase diversification, particularly in environments of macroeconomic stress at home. In this environment

---

[27] A Commodity Trading Fund (CTA) is a hedge fund (or their adviser) regulated by the US Commodity Futures Trading Commission (CTFC) typically investing in a wide range of commodities and futures and often employing automated quantitative trading strategies.

there should be divergence not convergence of asset allocation approaches. Pride is taken, correctly, from doing things slightly differently which leads to outperformance. But for many the asset allocation process remains traditional yet.

At the back of our minds, we know that we should really avoid becoming myopic. We need to start thinking about asset allocation in a more dynamic way, with more focus on the macroeconomic environment and the wider world. We should perhaps search for systemic biases and watch out for specific tail risks, such as a dollar crash or HIDC depression. We should maybe move to GDP weighting. We should consider factoring in how others are invested and how asset class characteristics can change – not just their income streams but the possibilities of defaults, currency movements and sudden liquidity changes.

9

Thinking Strategically in the Investment Process

9.1 THINKING STRATEGICALLY

Much of our discussion so far in this book has concerned problems with standard thought and theories. The next chapter will draw together many of the threads we have been weaving to create a checklist for investors. Our last thread before that concerns strategic thinking, scenario planning and some pointers on when and when not to use standard techniques and analysis. Frydman and Goldberg (2011) have noted how investors change views and strategies, and how traditional finance theory does not typically factor this in. How should investors think about change, and alter their investments and allocations?

There are existing techniques which should probably be used more frequently by investors, such as Monte Carlo simulations. However, strategic thinking – seeing the big picture – is essential. It starts by challenging some traditional assumptions about what the context is. Most of Keynes's General Theory is a critique of the relevance, in certain conditions, of the neoclassical economic theory dominant when he was writing. Likewise, we need to spend time questioning our existing approaches to investing in order to locate weaknesses where we need to employ new or different methods. This includes stepping back and considering how our collective beliefs might be biasing us. Historical perspective often helps us in this, by thinking of past occasions with similarities to today's conditions.

Importantly, strategic thinking should not be static. There is a tendency all too often to see strategy as something to be reviewed only very occasionally. One suspects this is largely a reflection of a static view of the world, aided and abetted by static economic and finance theories. Yet to be most effective, strategic thinking should be constant, potentially impacting investment and asset allocation at any time. Should events unfold rapidly, then strategic thinking should be engaged at the same time to advise us of portfolio alterations.

9.1.1 Thinking strategically: appropriate discounting

A goal of this book's early chapters has been to show the importance of global macroeconomic issues and risks, and the relevance to investors of having a view about them. There are, of course, many other readings of recent history, the state of the world and globalisation. Some of the views expressed are necessarily partial and subjective, but, one hopes illustrative of how important these issues are, and of how one may think about them.

One may choose not to spend any time thinking about global economic imbalances and risks, but by doing so one is by default accepting the (often conventional consensus) views of others. Moreover, the view you receive may have gone through some very selective filtering and contextualising, a result of the agency characteristics of the information trail before it reaches you. Only a small proportion of stories and the slants taken by the media have real informational benefit, not already captured by the market, and few are also designed primarily to assist investors to enable them to take balanced investment decisions. Not many advisers or sources of financial information are without knowledge gaps, interests or biases. Politicians also obviously have their own agendas. For most people and for most of the time we can say that following the consensus view is not only inevitable but a largely sensible course to take. But sometimes it isn't at all sensible.

We cannot possibly analyse everything, so we do have to rely on third party information but also views and analyses from others. Fortunately, a lot of the scenario-building work may already have been done for an investor by outside bodies including investment banks, asset management companies and consultants. Investors have to trust these outside providers to some extent, but there is a difference between taking the views of others in toto and sense-checking them or using them to stimulate or supplement one's own views. We should also, as many investors know, discount or weight the views of others by an appropriate amount; and we should weight our own views appropriately and expect our colleagues likewise to weight their own and our views. We can also assess where we fit in the information chain. Are we a simple meme receiver, very predictable? This may be a good thing for an investor – displaying consistency and reliability are prized qualities – but if so, the quality of the incoming memes is of heightened importance. Or are we a more complicated meme combiner and creator? In that case it may be important for us to receive ideas from many sources as the fodder for our invention. Discounting views is a normal process in much decisionmaking among people known well, and can be extended to those issues and people we are less familiar with. First we can get to know better their intelligence, skills and knowledge. A further common method to derive such weights is to consider track records: determining how far in line with later events views from a particular source have been in the past. We need to consider whether incentives may be affecting the views expressed, and we can observe behavioural traits and assess underlying character and reliability.

As we have shown, current investment theory has a tendency to focus on the past, find patterns and extrapolate. This can fail to recognise upcoming risks and opportunities, particularly when there are large structural shifts. We have mentioned David Swensen's 'Yale model' for portfolio investing, emphasising diversification. This aspect was and is clearly a major improvement in many respects on the more traditional view of institutional investing where the bulk of assets are deployed predominantly in domestic public equities and bonds. However, any investment process is vulnerable if it ignores or inappropriately belittles future structural shifts of a nature which has not been experienced in the available past data.

9.2   SCENARIO PLANNING

Scenario planning is a complement to more linear projections and a process which can inform investment thinking, particularly with regard to extreme risks. It admits uncertainty and the reality that history is path-dependent – that minor events can lead to large divergences. It considers numerous possible paths or narratives of how the future may unfold and explores the consequences of those scenarios, as well as different complementary interpretations of reality or 'mental maps'. It lacks much of the quantification and testability of models which extrapolate from the past, but helps us to compensate for the 'fat tails', the less predictable likelihoods, by conducting thought experiments about the future.

Once scenarios are identified, one should not always merely plan investments and asset allocation for the most likely scenario. One should assess how quickly one might shift from one scenario being most likely to another one, and what the lead indicators or triggers might be. How can one's portfolio cope with, or how quickly can it adapt to, the new scenario – at the minimum, how liquid are those investments most likely to suffer under new conditions, and how fast can decisions be made? In particular, if the answers are 'Not very' and 'Slowly', one should consider how one can mitigate damage through investments likely to act as insurance.

There is no simple answer to how and when to use scenario planning, but in this chapter we are going to give two examples of how one could think about investing today, both of which have strong scenario planning inputs. First are some thoughts about structuring a multi-asset class portfolio post-2008, given an environment of substantial structural shifts in the global macroeconomy and in perceptions of risk. Second is a description of how Ashmore invests in emerging market debt.

9.3   GLOBAL STRUCTURAL SHIFTS AHEAD?

Mandelbrot and Hudson (2005) list ten heresies of finance, the first of which is that markets are turbulent. They are more turbulent than most people appreciate. As Mandelbrot showed five decades ago, markets are not generally normally distributed. Power laws, common in networks, are more ubiquitous in financial markets than appreciated, yet few economic models have adopted power laws. Some distributions are however non-existent because, as Frank Knight originally coined it, events are 'one-off'.

Despite the major economic volatility in the 1970s, today's deleveraging problems in the US and in Western Europe are more severe than anything since the 1930s. This time, after three decades of financial deepening in the US and Western Europe – the last decade to excess – credit crunch is again a painful multi-year process of deleveraging and wealth destruction. With most of the deleveraging yet to occur at time of writing, it is far from over.

The best scenario for the credit crunch economies (US, Western Europe) is slow growth for a number of years, and managed currency depreciation (of the US dollar, euro and sterling) creating new competitiveness and export booms to emerging markets (the remaining hope for global aggregate demand), who manage to absorb a large amount of their own (and others') savings including through strong infrastructure investment and real estate development. However, there is significant risk of economic catastrophe in the US and Western Europe. The world is upside down, and the main reason to invest in emerging markets is to reduce risk by investing away from the catastrophe-prone developed countries or, as I call them, the crash zone or the HIDCs – heavily indebted developed countries.

Emerging markets are in very different economic cycles from the developed world. They do not have credit crunch. The emerging markets constituted at end 2012, according to IMF data, 49.6% of global GDP using purchasing power parity. In the worst scenario of US and European depression the emerging world will shift its trade and investment patterns more (this has already started) towards south-south trade and investment. Domestic demand in these economies is robust, and some countries (e.g. Brazil, India, Indonesia) are fairly insulated through being closed economies (low foreign trade/GDP). Others, more export-dependent, have diversified somewhat already away from EU and US dependence. There may be short-term market contagion but much less economic contagion. Above all, they have much more policy scope than Europe and the US, both in terms of dealing with inflation pressure and should the US/Western Europe descend into the abyss. This is because their debt levels are lower, achievable fiscal multipliers higher, public sectors smaller, central bank reserves higher and electorates more willing to support major policy change in times of crisis. Emerging policymakers and citizens have more experience of crisis and its consequences.

Political risk, as described in the second box in Chapter 5, has also reduced in emerging markets just as it has significantly increased in the credit-crunch countries. Poor electorates without strong welfare systems consistently vote very conservatively for growth and stability, whereas rich electorates have more propensity to believe what they want to believe. They have the luxury of ignoring reality and often vote for the economic story most attractive to them. And since 2008 they are in unfamiliar territory, which is why they have been particularly self-delusional – in denial of the multi-year consequences of deleveraging. Emerging countries which have strong mandates to control inflation and economic priorities (as opposed to social or other priorities) can be expected to continue to have the upper hand in driving key economic policies in times of economic stress.

We defined emerging markets in Chapter 2 by risk perception, not risk. All countries are risky. The emerging markets are where it is priced in. The developed world is where risk is not even perceived by a substantial portion of investors, and hence where sovereign risk markets tend to be dysfunctional. It is developed countries which face possible major disruption. So if there is substantial risk in parts of the developed world, possibly even depression in the US and Western Europe, even if this is not the main scenario, how should a pension fund or other large institutional investor allocate its portfolio?

Below are some rules, originally written by me (and so not as relevant now) as a note to investors in November 2010.

Asset allocation: some proposed new rules[1]

We know that our backward-looking finance theory is particularly bad at coping when we face structural shifts. So do we have major structural imbalances in the economy? Do we think policymakers may be out of their depth in trying to cope with them? Do we have massive investment herding? Might this herding suddenly change, causing major asset allocation shifts? Do we have major global rebalancing ahead? Is there a lot of soul searching and wealth destruction coming in the US and Western Europe? Is crisis management the order of the day in Western Europe and US; and with it potentially large policy shifts affecting investment returns? Are we entering a period of significant structural shifts affecting global investments? The answer to all the above questions may be 'Yes'. So perhaps we need to adopt some new rules for asset allocation as follows.

- **Pre-condition/Rule 0**: *Ask whether we are entering a period of significant structural shifts affecting global investments, and if so ditch, a lot of the conventional asset allocation methodology in favour of the rules below.*
- **Rule 1**: *If you are truly conservative in the prudential sense and worried about systemic risks, then do not invest in countries facing major deleveraging ahead.* In other words, do not invest in the crash zone of Western Europe or the US. Invest in emerging markets and possibly Japan, Australia, Canada and Scandinavia. If, possibly for reasons of liability structure, you consider that you have to have a non-zero exposure

---

[1] See disclaimer, p. 235.

to the US and Western Europe, then you are taking considerable risk and the other rules below become more important.

- **Rule 2**: *Employ scenario planning.* There may be a 65% likelihood that Bernanke's quantitative easing is successful and the US and Western Europe achieve recovery without catastrophe, but that leaves maybe 35% likelihood of some very unpleasant scenarios including dollar and euro crashes (maybe simultaneously) and, worst of all, developed world depression. Scenario planning involves first recognising these scenarios, and also needs to be ongoing in realtime (concomitant with the decision to take the risk of investing in the credit-crunch countries – see Rule 1). As part of one's ongoing scenario planning one needs to watch for structural shifts very carefully to gauge whether the main (perhaps most benign) scenario is becoming less likely, and indeed how the likelihoods of all scenarios are changing. If so one may need to change portfolio shape fast (in contrast to automatic portfolio rebalancing, which, in the face of structural shifts, is a loss-inducing strategy).
- **Rule 3**: *Re-consider liabilities.* Emerging markets are becoming more dominant in the global economy, are winning market share as a result of credit crunch and will increasingly be price-setters not price-takers in global goods as well as commodities markets. This means emerging markets will increasingly determine future liabilities for pensioners and savers today all over the world (as discussed in Chapter 8). For those credit-crunch countries with currency weakness ahead, this is particularly important, as it is for open economies. Having thought about Rule 3, one might want to revisit Rule 1 above.
- **Rule 4**: *Make efforts to insure your portfolio where possible against extreme negative risks associated with the worst-case scenarios.* Insuring against depression is difficult, but see Rule 1. Insuring against currency crashes in the US dollar and other deficit countries is easier as foreign exchange is a zero-sum game: all currencies are expressed in terms of each other. If deficit currencies go down, surplus ones must go up. Hence buy cash or other instruments in the emerging markets. Arguably the safest asset class in the world is short-duration emerging market local currency debt as it is in effect cash, only in a collection of safe currencies. It also has a yield cushion (unlike spot foreign exchange) and a highly heterogeneous investor base (because largely local in many different countries). To hedge against inflation risk (not the main concern at present it should be noted), one should buy real assets in emerging markets, inflation-linked bonds and commodities with limited supply. Oil is a better hedge in this regard than gold as it has more linkage with the real global economy. Gold has three other disadvantages: a highly homogenous investor base (in particular central banks), no yield and a contrast between its associated perception of safety and the reality that since 1971 – and for the first time in recorded history – gold is not part of the global monetary system. Belief in it could just evaporate, even though this is unlikely for a while.
- **Rule 5**: *Do not invest in any asset in the credit-crunch countries thinking they are safe.* There is no such thing as a risk-free asset, especially in Western Europe and the US. Indeed, in dangerous times assets perceived as safe may be more dangerous than ones where risk is priced in better. US Treasuries might be attractive if one believes yields are going to fall further, but they are certainly not safe and so should compete with equities and other assets for space in a portfolio mainly on the basis of anticipated return. Consider that the large holders (including emerging market central banks) may cut their losses at some point by selling Treasuries rather than pour good money after bad.

> ● **Rule 6**: *Do not invest in assets in the credit-crunch countries (unless supernormal returns are expected) which are illiquid.* There are two reasons: firstly, one may need to sell in a hurry; secondly, political risk for infrastructure investment in fiscally challenged credit-crunch countries may lead to significant investment risk even in the more benign macroeconomic scenarios.

9.4   INVESTMENT PROCESS IN EMERGING DEBT

When the team which became Ashmore started the first emerging debt fund in 1992, and already having long experience as a market maker in emerging debt,[2] the market was much riskier than today. Countries were more vulnerable to being cut off from external capital and thus to balance-of-payments crises, many investors were highly leveraged (as mentioned in Chapter 2) and there was risk of contagion from one country to another. The initial investor base for the fund was largely individuals – initially $19 million from the Middle East – though this changed to a predominantly institutional investor base after the fund established a three-year track record. These investors were willing to trust the team's judgement – up to a point. Consistent losses would not have been tolerated over the cycle – the cycle of dip and recovery in emerging markets can be shorter, but for major cycles is typically 18 months to three years.

The task was thus to design an investment process which reduced the risk of loss over the 18 month to three-year period, but which within this constraint maximised returns – i.e. risk considerations were always foremost, not an afterthought. The investment process arrived at has not changed substantially since, though it has responded differently to different market conditions and market developments, and more people are now part of the process.[3]

The monitoring of markets and the investment process are continuous, but there is a weekly meeting to formalise strategy and this starts with scenario planning. Taking a top-down view of global factors and then maybe also discussing in some detail perhaps 15 to 20 emerging countries, the most likely developments are considered, as well as triggers – events, data, policy decisions, market behaviour – which may lead to changed views. A change in view may lead to altered positions in the portfolios. The timeframe for these possible developments is most crucially, but not exclusively, between the current meeting and the following one a week later. By considering scenarios (largely over the following week until the next formal meeting) it can be ensured in portfolio construction that a fund is not too exposed to specific possible events. Say for example there is a chance that oil prices may fall dramatically: one does not want the largest three country positions all to be oil producers.

---

[2] Before the management buyout (MBO) establishing Ashmore in 1998/early 1999, the founders worked for ANZ Grindlays, which then became ANZ Investment Bank. Grindlays was an old British merchant bank: the largest foreign bank in India, one of the big three banks in Africa and with a substantial presence in the Middle East. Grindlays also had a large Latin American loan portfolio which became problematic in the early 1980s after the Mexico crisis in 1982. It was after this that the secondary market trading skills started to be developed within Grindlays (the genesis of Ashmore's skill set), leading to Grindlays becoming a major market maker in emerging debt. Grindlays' Latin American losses were also part of the reason for its acquisition by ANZ in 1984. Members of the emerging debt team, led by Mark Coombs, then helped build and run ANZ Investment Bank before the MBO establishing Ashmore.

[3] There are also now several different fund types: some for particular types of emerging debt, some for different emerging market asset classes altogether including emerging equities and some catering to those not comfortable with much deviation from standard-use index benchmarks.

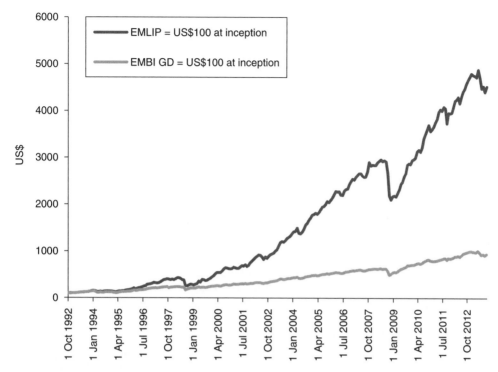

Figure 9.1 Active management (Ashmore's EMLIP) can outperform passive index investing. Source: Ashmore, JP Morgan gross data

The research input to this process emanates from constant dialogue with market participants all over the world. This involves visiting and assessing the views and positions of (as well as exchanging views with) local banks, investors and policymakers, but also political consultants, multilateral financial institutions and others. As mentioned in Chapter 7, the structure of the investor base is important, as are investors' different liabilities, incentive structures and perspectives. These factors impact our view of future behaviour, and so price movements, but also of future liquidity conditions. It is primarily through this direct research and contact that Ashmore builds a picture of possible future risks. Investment bank research is also a source of useful information and analysis, and a good measure of market sentiment.

At a time of particular market stress, such as just after Lehman Brothers collapsed in September 2008 and the interbank market seized up – and with it market making and bank-provided liquidity in many markets – our analysis of how liquidity conditions might change becomes more granular than normal. By that I mean that rather than considering overall liquidity conditions for types of securities, Ashmore considered possible future liquidity conditions for smaller sets of securities, even individual securities. To build scenarios of overall portfolio liquidity meant taking the time to think through how liquidity in different instruments might change in detail, adding several hours sometimes to our weekly investment meetings. That was what it was like in 2008: the most noticeable change to our routine was much greater time spent to assess instrument-specific liquidity.

Risk is not additive largely because it is not objectively measurable and different for different people: it cannot be budgeted like volatility. We expect different dynamics from various countries' bonds in different scenarios. We do not ascribe a uniform rating or risk measure to a country irrespective of specific scenarios, and then suppose a portfolio risk is the weighted sum of such risk measures over many countries. A weighted sum of supposed risk (as for many indices) would not tell us very much – it would be a simplistic, indeed misleading, summary of what we already know. In one scenario Russian debt might go up and Philippine debt down; in another the reverse. Yet a few weeks later both may go up or down together. Individually we may expect them to be more or less volatile, but we cannot simply observe past volatilities and extrapolate them, calling it 'risk'. Nor can we add the risks up, as prices may move in opposite directions as a result of the same event, and so, if several assets are owned, incorporate less risk than a simple addition would indicate. Nor can we assume that correlations between the price movements of different countries' bonds are stable. They might be for a while – and often are – but we cannot assume that to be the case for longer periods. Simple formulaic netting off of risk is thus also not sufficient. Emerging debt is a market (much like many others) in which correlations can form, and be observed by market participants who then trade as if the correlation will continue. Traders and other investors then arbitrage any deviation from the observed correlated relationship, so strengthening the correlation. Investment banks spread the news of the relationship via research or other media, further reinforcing the market behaviour. Then the relationship breaks down, often suddenly. Assessing risk is a full-time constant occupation, not simple, and highly dependent on the actions of others.

Having considered macroeconomic, political and technical factors,[4] these details are factored into the construction of the overall shape of the portfolio. Value is compared across countries and between specific assets in the context of market sentiment and liquidity. Typically, once the country decision is taken, the investment decision focuses on the most liquid assets (liquid now but also in the future). A great deal of thought goes into how the different scenarios impact portfolios as they currently stand. For some portfolios there is a bifurcated approach to liquidity: instruments are either highly liquid or offer extreme value. The highly liquid portion of the portfolio allows the overall risk exposure of the portfolio to be changed quickly if need be. Overall, asset allocation decisions are set by the clearly defined top-down scenario-based and liquidity-focused investment process, executed by the investment team, where individual positions are considered not only on their own merit but also in terms of the contribution to the overall characteristics of the portfolio – i.e. the expected portfolio performance under different scenarios. Position sizing and scaling are performed within the investment process, subject to the value proposition and liquidity.

This approach has been demonstrated to work well in emerging debt.[5] When thinking about the underlying complexity of emerging debt it is understandable that simpler, more

---

[4] Technicals or technical factors are facets of market structure, positioning and behaviour which may move the price of an asset. For instance, if foreign investors are overweight the index weight in Argentina this may lead to a more marked sell-off on bad news than if they had been underweight. If Mexican debt is included in a new investment grade index that may increase demand for Mexican debt – but not necessarily: if widely expected in advance such a move may already be 'priced in'. Rating agency moves in country weightings are also seen as technicals – the views of rating agencies are not considered particularly valuable by most specialised fund managers, except insofar as they drive the decisions of less well-informed investors and hence prices. Technicals should not be confused with 'technical analysis', which consists of rules of thumb extrapolating future price movements purely on the patterns of previous movements.

[5] When there is stability in the relationships between variables, then empirical approaches which estimate these relationships – for example using a regression analysis – and then extrapolate may be superior to non-quantitative approaches. The question is: Are the relationships stable? The UK marginal propensity to consume may be stable, but the dollar/yen exchange rate is not. This is not the same question as: Have they been stable?

formulaic approaches may not be as good at containing or side-stepping risks, especially extreme risks. Many emerging debt managers went out of business both in 1994/5 and in 1998. Others may have prospered since, mainly because risks are much less than they used to be. The mark-to-mark losses in 2008 following Lehman's collapse were understood to reflect poor liquidity being provided by market makers rather than serious default risks in emerging countries, and so only highly leveraged funds or those facing massive redemptions suffered more than temporarily.

9.5   CONCLUSION

North (2005, p. 126), in reviewing the difficulty of understanding institutions and organisations in the context of dynamic change, tells us we need 'more detailed knowledge than we currently possess of the institutional structure of an economy'. After such studies '… we are in a position to perceive the alterations in the opportunity costs of affected organisations and take that information into account in making policies. That hardly qualifies as anything like dealing with dynamic change properly; but is does make us more conscious of the issues we must deal with.'

I think we can do better than suggested by North. Even without such studies, and as investors and as policymakers, we can identify big misperceptions and errors in investment practice, together with structural changes already ongoing which may disrupt such misperceptions and errors. We can identify economies and markets which are becoming more important. Moreover, this is happening slowly, as people are highly resistant to ditching their models and prejudices, so we do have time to change before others, and prepare for more sudden and more negative scenarios. We can also do better by acting on information we do know, starting by recognising uncomfortable truths. A good example of where we can do better is quoted by Wadhwani in Turner *et al.* (2010, p. 139), talking of the post-Lehman credit crunch:

> 'A sad aspect of this crisis is that there were many policymakers who understood what was going on and voiced concerns, and yet our regulators did not respond. For example, a former governor of the Riksbank, Lars Heikensten (2009), writes of chairing a G10 working group which discussed provisioning in banks and measures to deal with the emerging housing bubble. He reveals that political opposition from the US and Britain led to the report of this group not even being published as a G10 report!'

Two main problems with strategic thinking are firstly that it is often simply not done – the big picture somehow is not anybody's responsibility and it falls through the cracks. Secondly, when it is done, it is too often seen as something to think through once a year or once every three years, not as a realtime vibrant part of managing a portfolio. It may be inconvenient, but if the world changes, then so should one's portfolio, and as soon as possible. In a world of only gradual change and mean/variance, allocation strategy may not need to be very dynamic. But if one does not normally change one's asset allocation more than once every five years, then perhaps one should at least have the option of making an exception when needed. Sometimes events get in the way.

10

A New Way to Invest

'It would be foolish, in forming our expectations, to attach great weight to matters which are very uncertain. It is reasonable, therefore, to be guided to a considerable degree by the facts about which we feel somewhat confident, even though they may be less decisively relevant to the issue than other facts about which our knowledge is vague and scanty. For this reason the facts of the existing situation enter, in a sense disproportionately, into the formation of our long-term expectations; our usual practice being to take the existing situation and to project it into the future, modified only to the extent that we have more or less definite reasons for expecting a change.'

Keynes (1936, Chapter 12, part II)

How should investors invest? There is clearly no easy answer to this question, whether we believe markets are efficient (in which case we cannot beat the market) or relatively inefficient. We have no credible theoretical framework. The goal of this chapter is not to unveil some new detailed and better method to make a fortune (I have no magic insight), but rather to help create a structure within which investment decisions can be made; and more specifically to raise a set of issues and questions to account for risks which may not have been taken fully into account before, and so to create a guide for thought.

Investment theory is still a young discipline trying to find its theoretical way. Moreover, markets are systems impacted by our investment behaviour and thus impossible to view completely objectively. We can identify various incentives, prejudices and other patterns which can help us invest. But reality is extremely complex. Thus we ask questions here rather than try to provide specific answers. Many of the practical consequences of what follows in this chapter are already practised by pragmatic investors. We present a checklist of general questions, arranged under 10 headings, to be adapted and added to depending on circumstance. It is hoped that following the conclusions drawn from asking these questions will establish new frameworks for investing, specific to individual and temporal circumstances: frameworks which may cope better with structural shifts and risk, yet which are easily explainable and justifiable and hence possible to implement in practice for an institutional investor. I hope to counter the tendency, identified by Keynes in the quote above, for existing facts to enter 'disproportionately' into our expectations.

There are other experienced investors who have also written on how to invest. Perhaps most influentially in recent years, and as mentioned in Chapter 8, David Swensen (2009) of Yale has written authoritatively in his book *Pioneering Portfolio Management* on how, from the perspective of an endowment, to find diversification and take a longer-term view. Various authors have written on how the world is changing, and how this should impact asset allocation, including for example Antoine van Agtmael (2007) in his book *The Emerging Markets Century*. Many have written on globalisation, many on the macroeconomic state of the world and many have criticised aspects of existing finance theory. Behavioural economics has observed and modelled many aspects of markets and investor behaviour inconsistent with previous theory. However, few of these approaches attempt to proffer an alternative framework for asset allocators, and when they have (as has Swensen), there is still so much more to be said. In general, where there is investment advice given it tends to be specific, not holistic. When a holistic view is given of the world, it tends not to translate into something easily usable for the asset allocator. As we have detailed throughout the book, much of what has been written still fails to incorporate macroeconomics and the state of the world, the importance of institutions and investor base structure. Financial market dynamics and self-reinforcing tendencies are often ignored or treated in a perfunctory way. Risk is a word constantly used but rarely thought through; our perceptions of risk and how they change are even more hazily factored in. We are constrained by conflicting and confused incentives, and by existing theory and practice. We fail to assess our liabilities or think strategically.

Portfolios face major avoidable losses in the event of sudden structural shifts. Portfolios managed by the likes of David Swensen have outperformed peers over some periods, but there are key moments when either perhaps they could do better, or they do indeed cope well, but precisely because there has been a suspension of the model in crisis – the model is known to be not suited to all situations. Investors can avoid problems by being alert and changing course quickly, but how this changed behaviour fits into the existing logic of asset allocation is a gap in the literature (if not always in practice) which needs filling. Frydman and Goldberg (2011), their imperfect knowledge economics and their contingent market hypothesis have started to explore the world in which investors change strategies in the face of a dynamic uncertain reality. The objective here is complementary to their work and the work of Swensen and others. We need to identify the occasions when an asset allocator should not merely supplement, but switch away from, traditional-backward looking models, and possibly not just for some of the portfolio in a mental accounting exercise but for the portfolio in its entirety. The task is thus a macro one: when to use traditional techniques, when to complement them with new approaches and when to abandon them completely. It is also a macroeconomic one: how and at what stage to introduce what we know from macroeconomics (and for that matter other disciplines) into asset allocation and investment decisions.

The ten items on my checklist start with assumptions, perhaps the most important of the ten, and from which much else follows.

10.1   SENSE-CHECKING ASSUMPTIONS

In debates and arguments it is the different starting points, and assumptions taken as given, which so often determine their contours and outcomes. If our starting assumptions are in error or are inappropriate, then our consequent reasoning may also lead us to distorted conclusions. Investors therefore need to be conscious of what their assumptions are – and something as simple as making a list is a good start. We also need to challenge some of them, and maybe go back further in the stages of collective human wisdom to re-evaluate some of the things we take for granted.

We can think of four areas in particular, commonly accepted as starting points for analysis, which we may want to re-examine: i) risk, uncertainty and information asymmetry assumptions; ii) investor psychology and behaviour assumptions; iii) structure, efficiency, equilibrium and market dynamics; and iv) asset class definitions.

10.1.1   Risk, uncertainty and information asymmetry assumptions

We have learnt how risk is often poorly analysed, seen as binary, with certain assets denoted 'risky' and others 'risk-free'. We have seen how it is confused with volatility. An example of the difference between the two is that risk can be impacted by information asymmetries in a way that volatility is not: specifically, more of the right type of information may lead to greater control and less risk. Thus having more information may correctly encourage an investor to take on more mark-to-market price volatility while taking less risk than a less well-informed peer.[1] We also mentioned how risk can be non-additive and so not possible to budget; and we discussed how uncertainty is often ignored in economic and investment theory. So, given these confusions and complications, perhaps investors should discipline themselves with greater clarity about what is meant when using the word 'risk'. To force ourselves to be more specific in our thoughts, we might stop ourselves every time we want to use the word 'risk' and try to replace it. Likewise, we should probably avoid using the terms 'risk-free' and 'benchmark risk', replacing them with 'perceived low risk' and 'benchmark deviation', respectively.

In any event it is worth distinguishing between: (a) past volatility; (b) the degree of risk perception – how much risk is priced in by others and ourselves; (c) the degree to which we are confronted with uncertainty rather than risk in the Knightian sense; and (d) the vulnerability of assets to future events of differing types and magnitudes and over various timeframes. We leave aside for the moment the more traditional classification of risk types: sovereign risk, basis risk, mark-to-market risk, counterparty risk, etc., in part because these classifications relate to the causes of risk rather than distinguish the areas where theory fails to account for them fully, which is our focus here. These risks should, however, inform what scenarios to consider under (d) and how we may expect our portfolios to fare under them.

By considering risk in this more comprehensive framework than typically assumed (see box on tabulation of risk and uncertainty) we may somewhat compensate for the well-researched psychological problem of investor overconfidence. Overconfidence may be caused in large part by the human habit of assigning probabilities only to the last stages of reasoning, with necessary preconditions in early stages of reasoning assumed in effect to be 100% likely.

This tabulation and framework presented in the box is admittedly a rather in-depth replacement for a past volatility measure. Using volatility is clearly much easier, and that is why it is so commonly used. But that does not mean it should always be preferred. Our framework is designed to challenge our standard assumptions about risk and tries to create a more complex and forward-looking perspective. The choice of events $E_{(N,T)}$ is also chosen to be illustrative, but there are many other events and scenarios which could and should be considered. For many comparisons past volatility may be a good proxy for the fuller picture, and if so we can revert in these instances to our convenient assumption equating risk with past volatility. It should be noted, however, that even where this is the conclusion at one point in time this may change. Hence thinking through risk in the framework may still be a useful exercise from time to time.

---

[1] Indeed, high volatility or tracking error (standard deviation of excess returns) displayed by a fund manager may even signal confidence based on competence and thus signal lower risk, as compared to a manager with lower volatility or tracking error.

A tabulation of risk and uncertainty assumptions

In order to provide a framework for analysis, it may be useful to tabulate our few aspects of risk as they relate to specific investment choices. Such tabulation could be purely descriptive or could attempt to include numerical scores. In an attempt to illustrate this we consider two investment choices for comparison: a portfolio of US Treasuries and one of emerging market dollar-denominated sovereign debt. The scoring is inevitably subjective and is illustrative only, pertaining to the particular view of the author at time of writing.

Our measure for (a) past volatility is the most straightforward, though the appropriate data frequency and time period for measurement even for this will vary with the type of investor. A pension fund with a 15-year liability structure is going to care less about short-term returns and more about the longer term than a day trader. For them daily volatility should thus probably be viewed as less relevant than monthly volatility, as measured by annualised standard deviation of monthly returns, SD_m.

The degree of risk perception (b) – how much risk is priced in by others and ourselves – is much more subjective (at least without extensive questionnaires and research on the issue). Risk perceptions could be estimated through behavioural surveys. These could possibly enable comparisons of the strengths of perceived risks with actual measures of risk, after the events. For example, historical default risks in a specified period could be compared with historical perceptions of default before the period. To be more forward-looking, we would then need to consider how such perceptions of risk and how actual risk may have subsequently changed. Thinking firstly of the risk perception of others, weighted by their influence on the investment opportunity, we could assign a 'risk perception' variable, $-1 < P_r < 1$, with a value of 0 indicating that risk is accurately estimated; and a lower value when it is underperceived. $P_r > 0$ could indicate a greater than actual perception of risks. However, this variable does need to be considered in the context of possible major shifts in perception in the future: the more likely a shift, the furthest from zero the measure should be. We may even like to multiply P_r by some variable denoting the chance of a major shift in risk perception in the future. To avoid increasing the notation we assume here that the chance of a major shift in the future is already factored in, multiplying P_r both above and below zero.

Relatively safe investments are often those where risk perception is poorest – at the extreme, so-called 'risk-free' investments. An investment being perceived as low risk may be consistent with widespread confidence in the investment and low attention to risk (which may or may not be justified). This contributes to predictability in the short term – the complacent behaviour of investors who are not perceptive of relevant risks can be counted on, at least for a while, in those cases where there is some significant risk. Risk-free status is thus partly self-justifying – we can say misperception of risk has self-reinforcing momentum. While such an investment may indeed be very low risk, on occasion it may not. Focus on short-term volatility may mean longer-term risks are being ignored by investors, yet for longer-term investors these are the most important, especially in the case where domestic sovereign bonds or so-called 'risk-free' assets are being invested in specifically in order to match long-term liabilities.

While generally speaking we can consider an investment with underperceived risk as inferior to one with well-perceived risk, there are caveats where there are good reasons to suppose one can observe risk perceptions of others and exit in advance of the crowd.

This is clearly not an appropriate strategy in all situations or for all types of investor. For this one's own risk perception needs to be estimated or guessed at. Hints include: whether one shares the view of the many; whether one can discern that the crowd's view is coming closer to yours over time (or the reverse); and whether you are likely to be able to change your view and act on it quicker or slower than others. In many senses this may be easier for an institution (provided such questions are asked and the answers taken due note of) than an individual, if that individual is not adept at, and does not have a conceptual structure to enable, rigorous self-criticism. In many other cases however, institutions are much slower at changing views than informed individuals. An assessment of one's own perception may help us gauge our own nimbleness – defined here as not just our speed of execution, but the speed at which our perception adapts to a new reality, relative to the speed of others, and then our ability to take consequent action. Psychological tests could be used to assess individual and collective group response times perhaps. Thus we could also divide P_r by a variable representing our own nimbleness relative to the nimbleness of the majority – if we are more nimble then we can weight market prejudices today as less of a concern. As with our multiplier factor for perception change, to save on notation we here assume this nimbleness is already factored into P_r.

The degree of uncertainty (c) as opposed to risk is important insofar as it alters the behaviour of other portfolio investors but also as it alters the behaviour of entrepreneurs and the amount of physical investment (as opposed to portfolio investment) in the wider economy (especially if an abundance of uncertainty causes a depression, as discussed in Chapter 4). Uncertainty is everywhere, but as investors we need a measure of what concerns us most. So we wish to assign a high value of uncertainty where there is the prospect of major permanent loss unrecognised by extrapolation from past data. In an assessment of the degree of uncertainty we need to be forward-looking. Moreover, the nature of uncertainty is that we cannot measure it even if we find some proxies. Any assessment should reflect if possible not just asset class or country specifics but more general and global considerations. It needs in particular to reflect the possibility of sudden change in investor base behaviour. Also, where we think we have a Knightian risk and an observable probability distribution, we need an estimate of the degree of certainty we have over the assumed probability distribution. As discussed in Chapter 5, risk and uncertainty may not be entirely distinct, and one person's uncertainty may be another person's risk.

Let us define $0 < U < 1$ where $U = 0$ denotes full knowledge of the probability distribution of random events and $U = 1$ denotes no knowledge of the distribution parameters, remembering that this is necessarily a subjective variable, giving high weightings to large permanent losses outside any standard estimates (if we have any) of the probability distribution.[2] To be clear, we are not here trying just to factor in fat tails or merely change our distribution from a normal distribution. We are guessing the degree to which we cannot measure what may happen, and in a quite separate consideration from our statistical measures of risk, including standard statistical confidence tests (which remember are estimated using past data). As with our measure of risk perception, we may also consider that we can typically be less certain the longer the time period. Consider a possible bubble in US Treasuries. We may ascribe a low value of U to a market with a long history and typically stable distribution pattern, such as US Treasuries, but the concentrated investor base and

---

[2] This approach can help frame a Bayesian analysis: we can change our assessments of the probability and risk as we learn more and our uncertainties reduce.

the prospect of a rush for the exit from central banks in a dollar crash similar to that in 1971 would indicate a high value. We clearly need to be forward-looking in coming up with our necessarily subjective value of U. In contrast, in markets where risk is understood and priced in by almost all investors, who are also highly heterogeneous, U should be low even where risk is high.

The vulnerability of assets to future events of differing type and magnitude and over various timeframes (d) is multidimensional – i.e. not a single variable but a matrix, possibly quite large. We can consider a number of events and scenarios, with $E_{(N,T)}$ the associated probabilities for N different scenarios and with different impacts over various time periods T in months.

Having looked at all these measures of risk and uncertainty, we can use the framework to develop a subjective view of the fairness or otherwise of using the simple numerical value (of past volatility) to represent risk in our subsequent cogitations. If volatility is a good proxy for all our other variables, we may reasonably employ the highly convenient shortcut of not thinking about risk and just substituting a volatility number, for a while at least. Then again, this is unlikely to be advisable when our other variables are at odds with volatility numbers, including when we consider likely major structural shifts ahead. Then our framework kicks in and can point us to those assumptions we need to be most thoughtful and careful about.

So for our example, we consider on the one hand US Treasuries and on the other hand emerging debt as in Table 10.1. This risk assessment is highly subjective and for illustrative purposes only. (In reality we would consider many other asset classes and investment opportunities at the same time.) It may be noted that the standard deviation of emerging debt is higher than that for US Treasuries, though not particularly high or approaching that of US equities. Yet here are two asset classes: one often seen as risky, the other risk-free. We capture that in the second variable, risk perception P_r, with scores indicating risk is significantly ignored for US Treasuries and somewhat overperceived for emerging debt. This perception in the short term might reduce US Treasury volatility (as a result of what we called momentum above) and amplify emerging debt volatility, but not in the longer term if perception distortions reduce, or should there be a major event risk. Our measure of uncertainty has, perhaps counterintuitively, allocated here the higher score to US Treasuries, indicating more uncertainty. This is in light of the concentrated holding structure, dominated by central banks, and global macroeconomic imbalances. Different scenarios are then considered in the right side of the table. Of interest perhaps here is that we might expect very different probabilities over one month, one year and five years. The likelihood for example of the dollar falling 30% in real terms over longer periods is quite significant, especially if one's liabilities are, say, in Asia. That amounts to a large permanent loss, i.e. a risk, even if it is gradual. In the other example shown, the risk of loss from US interest rate policy, emerging debt might be more vulnerable than Treasuries over one year (though not likely), but when at some point US interest rates rise decisively Treasuries are likely to be the big loser – emerging debt historically sometimes doing badly, but often doing well in such an environment.

Table 10.1   An example of risk parameters (US Treasuries and emerging debt)

	SD_m	P_r	U	$E_{(1,1)}$	$E_{(1,12)}$	$E_{(1,60)}$	$E_{(2,1)}$	$E_{(2,12)}$	$E_{(2,60)}$
UST	5.4	−0.8	0.7	0.01	0.1	0.3	0.001	0.02	0.5
EMD	9.2	0.4	0.5	0.005	0.05	0.005	0.001	0.05	0.005

SD_m Annualised monthly standard deviation of market index, 2000–2010
P_r Risk perception $(-1 > P_r > 1)$
U Uncertainty $(0 < U < 1)$
$E_{(1,T)}$ Likelihood of losing 30% in real terms (purchasing power) due to currency weakness
$E_{(2,T)}$ Likelihood of losing over 10% of investment due to US interest rate policy
...
$E_{(N,T)}$

10.1.2   Investor psychology and behaviour assumptions

Our knowledge of investor psychology and behaviour is substantial. It has not been the intention in this book to review the whole area, though we have discussed some features of what behavioural finance has uncovered in Chapter 4. Clearly, psychology affects investment decisions, and we should try to compensate, not least by thinking about how people think (metacognition) and not forgetting the bias bias – the tendency to perceive bias in others but not ourselves.

We can start by picking up on our measure of uncertainty introduced in the last section. Assessing the degree to which we face uncertainty as opposed to risk is not at all easy, a subjective function of several factors including the extent to which we assume past data can help model the future accurately (i.e. we can rely on probability distributions calculated from past observations) but also on how far we extend our horizons. We noted the work of Simon on bounded rationality in Chapter 4 – within a particular confined environment we can feel more confident about our decisions than if we consider factors further afield or in the future. The manner in which we do this is dictated, to some extent, by brain physiology and how our neural networks work. Investment is only one set of problems among many to solve in limited time. The brain thus thinks lexicographically, unless trained to do otherwise, and makes shortcuts. The result is mental framing, overconfidence and reliance on models and rules of thumb.

We ignore the possibility that the sun will not rise tomorrow – a fair assumption given its consistency in that regard in the past and our body of scientific knowledge about the universe.[3] By discarding the possibility that the laws of physics all change tomorrow, we are able to frame much of our physical analysis in terms of risk rather than uncertainty. Likewise, we often ignore extreme economic and investment scenarios, despite the fact that precedents have occurred in the past and despite our not possessing the same level of confidence in our understanding of markets as we have of planetary motion. Some of this is thought out, no doubt: there is justice in ignoring small uncertainties. But some decisions are taken by default, because we have neither time nor memory to estimate or even guess probabilities. We often think in binary terms: is it risky, or not? This leads us down decision paths which assign

---

[3] Though of course it stopped rising once we accepted a heliocentric solar system: since then it is the Earth which spins, not the Sun which rises!

probabilities of 1 to likely possibilities. The result is overconfidence and an underestimation of unlikely events.

We can do better. For example, is an earthquake a risk or an uncertainty? Quakes and tsunamis have major consequences and our knowledge of plate tectonics is insufficient to predict except in the very short term where and when an earthquake will occur (by observing the patterns of smaller advance quakes). However, we can observe the pattern of past quakes, and assess some rough probabilities from that. We do know which geographies are most at risk and, if we assume there are no major changes in the patterns and cycles of tectonic movement globally, we can estimate the sort of maximum impact associated with various probabilities (i.e. 1 in 100-year or 1 in 1000-year event size). Thus an individual living in a fault zone may ascribe zero probability to a quake in day-to-day decisions, while still being conscious of the risk; but an insurer takes past earthquake data into account when setting insurance premiums. Hence, to some extent, we can see that a wider scale of view can transform the ignored uncertainty of an individual into an insurable risk. If insurers can do this, so can investors, but it requires deliberation.

In investment and economics we likewise know some things at the macro level which are often not transferred to investment theory or practice (including earthquake risk). Our way of thinking, of dismissing minority scenarios, particularly in long decision chains, is understandable, but may lead to underestimation of low-probability major-impact events. As investors we can compensate for this by being conscientious about including probabilities into each stage of our thinking – working to understand how probabilities may combine to amplify or mitigate each other in a more Bayesian framework than often employed.

Akerlof and Shiller (2009) describe how confidence can cause feedback loops and hence bubbles. They also discuss at length how concerns about fairness frame the setting of wages and prices; the role of corrupt and antisocial behaviour on the economy; the impact of money illusion as the public does not see through the effects of inflation and deflation; and how stories about the economy drive behaviour. Shiller (2005) describes how psychological anchors can distort decisions, and how moral anchors take the form of stories which trump rational investment behaviour. Information cascades describe how small random events, when acted on by people wanting to be like others for rational or non-rational reasons, can lead to collectively irrational concentrations of investment behaviour (as seen in practice daily in the world's stock markets). The lack of ability to process all available information leads to shortcuts, including trusting the familiar (investments and people). Moreover, people cannot explain where their ideas come from or how their attention changes, giving false impressions of causality which often could do with being checked.

Another way to think about stories and other conclusions from Akerlof and Shiller's work is to consider memes, self-replicating ideas which evolve similarly to genes, and which we introduced in Chapter 7. For something to be a gene or a meme their algorithm (automatic mechanism) of replication requires three features: variation (so not all are identical); selection (so that some survive better in some environments than others); and retention (fidelity of characteristics or heredity). Memes are rife in the investment environment, including many which are not easily verifiable and many which appear contrary to objective observation. Memes include ideas such as 'US Treasuries are safe'. In the environment before the Lehman collapse such a meme was populous and secure. By being considered safe, Treasuries could be issued at low interest rates, making their serviceability attractively affordable to the US

Treasury. With the advent of quantitative easing, however, the risks have clearly risen, yet the meme remains intact, if less populous, at time of writing.

Investors can try to assess what stories or memes are currently in vogue: they can list them. They can assess which ones have been around a long time, which seem to be obviously wrong or distorted, which have recently grown rapidly or are declining and why, and what new environments might challenge them (like the end of and reversal of quantitative easing in the case of the US Treasury market for example).

False investment memes (by which I mean those which are not sustainable in the long term) can be classified under two different though non-exclusive categories. Firstly there are those which are the result of 'irrationality' on the part of the meme receiver (the investor who comes across the idea) and are falsifiable in some way. Much of the existing behavioural economics literature investigates these, and some types of investor may be able to resist them or instigate decision structures to resist them – most notably by being aware of behavioural finance literature and human biases, and then compensating. Then there are those memes which have an element of truth precisely because of others' belief in them and are not so easy to falsify given the initial data presented to the meme receiver. This includes various Ponzi schemes but also other patterns of behaviour with positive feedback loops. We can observe the dynamics of these memes – their life cycles (growth and aging), feeding grounds (susceptible investors and other relevant actors) and possible meme extinction risks (whether a new meme or event could gradually or suddenly destroy the idea).

The question for the investor is how much can they participate in analysing memes and take advantage of them – by avoiding some areas of investment, where the market appears to be experiencing an unsustainable meme epidemic; by employing hedge funds and others who may be able to take advantage; by getting ahead of the crowd through understanding one's peers or other classes of investor yet to be cured of, or infected by, a false meme. Are others suffering from reductionist fallacies like those at LTCM before it blew up? But first we need to drop the fiction of assuming investors are 'rational' in accordance with the rational expectations theory (RET).

10.1.3   Structure, market efficiency, equilibrium and market dynamics

As we need to consider whether volatility is a good proxy for risk, so we also need to consider whether our typical assumptions of continuing patterns of volatility, liquidity and correlations, but also market efficiency, are valid. In many circumstances they will be, but these conditions depend on the structure of investor bases and the incentives of market participants. Just as with our analysis of risk and uncertainty above, so there is no easy quick way to think about investor base structure. At a minimum we should challenge our assumptions that past patterns will continue into the future, and think about whether there are significant discontinuity risks ahead.

We should not stop there. Linked to investor base structure is overall market functioning and efficiency. Market efficiency is an area we now know a lot about, both in terms of the standard economic cases of market failure and distortions, but also from the discoveries of behavioural finance. The literature in this area is huge. Investors need to be aware of the broad characteristics of a particular market: how liquid it is (and is likely to be), and how regulations may impact access, transparency and liquidity provided by market makers now and in the future. How, in short, does the market behave and why, and will the same conditions remain, or change for better or worse? For example, concerning some emerging market equity markets, are our views up to date or representative of a less well governed, less transparent past which is now less valid? But also in the developed world, will interbank financing dry up again? Will new regulations to reduce systemic risk affect transaction costs and bank-provided liquidity?

10.1.4   Asset class definitions

Following our discussion in Chapter 8, we should review our assumptions about asset classes. Generally speaking, the wider our investment universe the better. We need to be careful about overlaps and the factors which define asset classes. We should understand what we are investing in; and, conscious that one definition of intelligence is the selective destruction of information, and that we are biased towards the familiar, we should also be clear about what details we do not need to know. As with Madoff's fund (a scam which one cannot believe could have lasted so long undetected had the underlying investments been perceived as risky), the asset classes we think we know well may also suffer from herding and misperceived risks precisely because they are so familiar. Our due diligence should as far as possible not only be thorough, but specific and equivalent across all investment opportunities which we assess.

Asset class distinctions, to be useful, should delineate different types of risk – they should have low future correlations. But risk is not straightforward. For example, depression in the US economy could make many different US asset classes, as traditionally defined, lose value permanently. Then again, on the upside these asset classes are likely to behave very differently, hence keeping the distinctions between all of them may be valid. Thinking of depression risk, though, we do need to add many more asset classes in our analysis than just those in highly leveraged economies.

The traditional criteria for the denotation of asset class include size, liquidity, ease of investment, measurability, but also widespread adoption by peers. Standard interpretations of these criteria may be questionable, as is the idea that one should have only a few asset classes. Considering the last in the list, determining the universe of asset classes may appear easy – it is what others use. Not only is this intellectually difficult to justify, as discussed in Chapter 8, but it ignores the trends determining what new asset classes there are going to be. Yet understanding what other investors think remains important. Getting in ahead of the crowd (buying early) has distinct and obvious advantages for any investor, as for example was the case for those early users of Swensen's 'Yale model'.

There is also the distinction to be made between 'investible' and 'easy to invest in' assets. The investible universe in the wider sense is set by the amount of economic activity. In practice much of this is not accessible, but a great deal of it is merely beyond the 'easy to invest in' criteria of publicly quoted assets. Moreover, there is reason to believe that more popular and crowded investments may provide less return and less diversification benefit to the investor. For example, there is now substantial research to show that simply capping the largest stocks in an equity market can help outperformance over time.

GDP investing may be a better way to allocate than any traditional index-weighted approach. But using a GDP index which is composed of the same underlying publicly listed instruments merely substitutes one bias for another by overweighting stocks from countries with a small stock market/GDP ratio. The objective, rather, is to invest in a fuller range of instruments in such countries. This takes more effort.[4]

So what should the set of asset classes look like, if not a mere facsimile of the existing collective norm? That is for each investor to decide, and to do so as a function of their desire to be comprehensive or selective in their search, and to the extent that they are bounded by peer pressure. It will also depend on their resources, and their view of how the world and the set of distinctive investment opportunities is changing and will change over a time period consonant with their liability structure. But we should not just assume that an asset class is a fixed entity with unchanging characteristics or relations to other asset classes, and we should not limit ourselves to the choices of others who have gone before us. We should not need the term 'alternative' as all the options should be alternatives to each other.

10.2   ASSESSING LIABILITIES

Understanding one's liabilities is a recognised and important stage in the management of institutional pools of capital, but all investors have liabilities, and different ones. University endowments have to balance the desire for fairly constant financial support for their university with preservation of the value, and growth of, the endowment. Swensen (2009) discusses the optimal endowment funding rule created at Yale by Tobin and others, involving a mixture of momentum in past spending and a percentage of the endowment's value. Specifically, the rule is that spending in a given year is the sum of 80% of the spending the previous year plus 20% of the long-term spending rate applied to the endowment's market value at the end of the previous fiscal year. For US foundations, however, the negative tax implications of not disbursing 5% of the endowment's value in a year motivates different spending rules to a college endowment.

Pension funds have long-term but not infinite liabilities. A typical liability structure is 15 years. In Chapter 8 we discussed the thinking behind matching this in the duration of portfolio investments. We also discussed how in practice a pension fund often creates a target rate of return from consideration of liabilities and then invests in order to achieve that return. This may be seen as a form of mental accounting, may also be encouraged if not mandated by the regulatory framework, but is hard to justify as optimal. If the fiduciary duty of pension fund trustees and, by extension, pension fund staff is to ensure as far as possible that future pension liabilities are met, then it is also important to maximise the buffer of overfunding today to insure against unforeseen loss tomorrow, and so to maximise returns within certain agreed risk parameters rather than try to reach full funding and then stop trying to make returns after that point – not least as liabilities are neither fixed nor perfectly measurable. It is a fiduciary responsibility to save up for a rainy day.

We also discussed in Chapter 8 how the techniques for working out future liabilities might be improved, at least in theory, through better understanding of preferences in the form of utility functions, and how possibly this could be achieved through carefully constructed questionnaire surveys. For instance, pensioners and pension fund trustees could be asked whether they prefer some combinations of more pension contributions, fewer benefits or

---

[4] One should also continue to make a distinction between the eligible universe for investing and one's actual portfolio. If a country in violent civil war has a non-zero GDP and it is eligible for investment using a GDP-weighted allocation approach, it does not follow that one should actually invest there. This is no different from saying that one should not invest in a bubble or bad investment in the US or elsewhere.

greater probability of underfunding or future erosion of pension benefits at various times in the future. Non-economic preference could also be assessed. Do pensioners want their pensions to be restricted from certain types of investments, or supportive of others? Surveys may not be effective in revealing these preferences, of course, as questions about the distant future are not fully rationalised by many people, the exact form of question are likely to have a significant impact on the answers, and preferences revealed by such questions may be intransitive (mutually incompatible). Also, there may be more information about external economic and other factors affecting future preferences of pensioners available to a well-resourced institutional investor than to a pension plan participant. We know average investors suffer from money illusion, for example, unable to discern real (inflation-adjusted) prices from nominal prices – see Shiller (2005).

In Chapter 8 we also discussed money illusion's simplification of perceived liabilities. The legal liability of a pension fund may be in dollars or another base currency, but what matters to pensioners is the future purchasing power of their pension. Insofar as trustees are mandated to represent their interests, this should also be the concern of the fund. Managing assets to produce a dollar or other base currency income stream in the future may appear to amount to the matching of liabilities, but in real terms and against the liabilities associated with purchasing power they may not. This is also true for individual savers.

The consequence is that thinking about future economic trends and how goods prices may change is important for assessing liabilities. As emerging countries are already of huge significance to global prices and this is highly likely to extend further, emerging markets are part of pension funds' and savers' and other investors' liabilities today at a scale many barely appreciate.

10.3   YOUR CONSTRAINTS

If this is to be a practical guide of how to invest then there needs to be reference to the investor's capabilities. We address here three types of constraint: the decision chain, institutional capabilities and psychological constraints.

10.3.1   The decision chain

Knowing the structure of the principal agent chain of an institutional investor helps map the information flow between agents and informs us who is able to make what types of decisions. Where one lies in the chain (or outside it) necessarily constrains and informs how one might improve investment performance.

The process of managing a large portfolio is often compartmentalised, and radical change is difficult to implement bureaucratically. For smaller investors multi-stage decisionmaking and agency problems should be less, but insofar as decisions are delegated to or advised by others, the status quo can still be overpowering. Hence many of those who do see major structural shifts ahead do not act.

From the perspective of someone working, say, on the investment staff of a large US public pension fund, one's constraints may be relatively easily described. Moreover, some of these constraints may seem not to be in the best interests of the pension plan participants. It is possible for example that there might be the following desirable improvements: (a) having more financially knowledgeable trustees, possibly with less turnover, to enable staff to widen the investment horizon and/or the portfolio's sophistication; (b) less fear of reputational damage from the press, leading to avoidance of sound investments about which the public or press may be prejudiced; (c) a less myopic review of performance which may not be in line with the longer-term liabilities of the fund; (d) less constant changing of investment objectives or strategy or other arrangements which result in investment strategies not being allowed the time to fulfil their intended roles in the portfolio; and (e) more resources to find and investigate investment opportunities. Trustees may of course have a very different perspective on some of these issues, as may, in turn, the pension plan participants and other principals in whose interests the trustees are supposed to act.

Thinking down the chain rather than up, while staff may consider themselves better informed on investment issues than trustees, and trustees may think themselves better informed than plan participants, they may both have less detailed investment knowledge than their outside managers hired to manage portions of the portfolio for them. Consultants may also be employed to assess liabilities and aid asset allocation and manager selection. Managers are motivated by the fees they receive for managing the money, and consultants, likewise, by their fees, posing a set of principal agent problems for staff. Is the decision chain fully understood, and how are you constrained within it?

10.3.2 Institutional capabilities

How knowledgeable are you or your institution? Can you identify your competitive advantages in the marketplace? Are you able to invest or change positions rapidly, quicker than others? What advantages or disadvantages does your size[5] or presence in particular markets give you? Do you have any informational advantages or disadvantages? How do counterparties and those with whom you deal perceive you and does this affect their transactions with you? What tasks are you demonstrably good and bad at? These are common questions for institutional investors, and indeed for individual investors.

10.3.3 Psychological constraints

Are you realistic about what you can achieve? Are you optimistic and overconfident or pessimistic and too conservative? Do you or your colleagues suffer from hindsight or confirmation bias or are you prone to money illusion? These questions, somewhat personal, are often difficult and impractical to pose or answer, but what one can do is have a rigorous staged analysis, starting with an examination of assumptions as already described at the start of this chapter. And the questions should be asked. Trust depends on internalisation of values and not just incentives, and sticking determinedly to professional values and approaches through thick and thin helps build trust. However, the same stubbornness can also blinker us, both individually and collectively.

---

[5] Woolley in Turner *et al.* (2010) lists ten items in an agenda for giant funds. I do not entirely agree with them. While they may reduce costs, they may also increase herding, and they still pander to conventional and static notions of what are acceptable asset classes.

10.4   CONSIDER CHANGING YOUR CONSTRAINTS: AGENCY ISSUES

Unless one manages all one's own money there will be some delegation and with it potential agency problems. The optimal degree of delegation will depend on the size of the portfolio, its liabilities and objectives and what skills may be already available. Changing the principal/ agent structure may be impractical, but then again in many cases the costs and benefits of change may not have been adequately considered in the past. The costs of various alternative structures, in both money and time, have to be weighed against the benefits. If we know the main risks for a fund, perhaps we should focus our attention on the main agency problems surrounding those risks. So, for example, for pension funds:

'The three main risks faced by a pension plan are: the asset-liability risk, or the risk incurred when the oversight committee selects a suboptimal benchmark to defease the liabilities; the tactical or benchmark risk taken by internal staff (such as over- or under-weighting asset classes, countries, capitalisation segments) in an attempt to add value over the investment benchmark; and the active risk taken by investment managers, who are overseen by internal staff, in an attempt to add value relative to the indices to which they are measured.'

Muralidhar (2001, p. 153)

So these are the three decision areas, but also the three associated sets of relationships which need careful consideration. The oversight committee or trustees may not understand the liabilities sufficiently. They or the staff may be advised externally on this, involving an agency problem, with one of the common results being no adjustment for money illusion. They may set inappropriate benchmarks and other fund targets, often motivated by the desire to be similar to peers. For a number of reasons, including political, they may not best represent the interests of the plan participants. They are also subject to a regulatory regime (they are agents to their regulator principals) and regulators in turn have their own principals, ultimately electorates. Trustees may also, as principals, not be able to monitor fully their agents, consultants, service providers and the staff, who may not be carrying out their instructions exactly, again for career or peer comparison reasons. The staff, in turn are principals to the external managers, service providers and consultants.

Individual investors, not just institutions, have to consider costs and benefits of various principal/agent structures. An individual may have investment objectives which include minimising their time spent thinking (and worrying) about investment. Formulating this may help in the choice of outsourcing decisions. However, the agency problems involved should always be borne in mind. If I take advice or even outsource discretionary management to a banker, wealth manager or fund manager, then I still need to have a view of their competence, incentives and conflicts. And I still need to understand what sort of advice they might be slow to give me (such as that they are about to be fired, or their employer is in serious difficulty). I need to understand their abilities and incentives with regards to uncommon risks in particular – whether they understand the bigger picture, and have good sources of information and analysis to draw on.

The same factors are true for institutional investors, and sometimes outside advice is taken with a degree of scepticism and some outside managers are given restricted mandates. Do large multifunctional institutions have credible separations of business activities? Are consultants paid by fund managers in any way? Are there commissions for anybody? Does anybody have a conflict of interest? But also, is recommending or doing the unorthodox a high risk strategy for someone's career? The presence of 'career risk' indicates a possible principal/agent problem. Are decisionmakers rewarded for good decisions and punished for bad ones? Or is there an asymmetry whereby poor investment performance resulting from orthodox allocations (similar to one's peer group) is not punished severely, losing from un-orthodox allocations can cost one's job, yet strong relative investment performance resulting from unorthodox allocations is not rewarded? Remembering that orthodoxy is not the same as safety, are staff in effect encouraged to gamble on the really big risks just like everybody else?

Not having incentive incompatibilities is better than having to cope with them. Character, ethical standards and reputation may reduce practical incentive incompatibility problems to a large extent. However, behaviour can still change in extreme circumstances. And heterodox opinions and approaches may be bad for a bank's, fund manager's or consultant's business. Particularly concerning out-sized possibilities those with fiduciary responsibility have to think for themselves.

10.5   BUILDING SCENARIOS

Predicting possible future structural shifts is not easy, but a good starting point is having a global view of large macro forces. Often these are not considered fully by asset allocators or, though analysed, not followed through appropriately in portfolio allocations and invest-ment management. This is not an area which can be just delegated to managers operating within specified asset classes. This may to some seem an unfair criticism of the investment industry, but how else to explain the lack of diversification away from key macroeconomic risks so often observed in institutional portfolios? This is set against the observation that the academic discipline of investment theory is still young, and much of it misleading.

In the last chapter we discussed strategic thinking and scenario planning. We also, in our section in this chapter on risk assumptions, started to introduce scenario planning by consid-ering the impact of various future scenarios on our proposed investments. In building sce-narios we first need to consider macroeconomic forces and imbalances. What global political shifts and scenarios might emerge? How are GDP dynamics and growth, savings, trade and investment patterns changing? What are the inflationary prospects for various economies and globally? What larger historical trends can we detect and what major policy developments might be brewing? While doing this we also need to bear in mind the appropriate timeframe, and be aware of current fashionable memes which may soon be gone and of others yet to mature.

Adjusting the whole portfolio so that it performs well in the main scenario, but is not caught out badly in the others, is perhaps an obvious approach. To do this involves thinking of ways to insure the portfolio against specific negative scenarios. It involves having the ability to spot structural shifts early and being able to adjust the portfolio in a timely manner, as discussed and illustrated in the last chapter; and if this is not possible, by giving up some expected returns through being prepared earlier. It may not simply mean engaging in a mental accounting exercise of having different portions of a static portfolio assigned to do well in different scenarios. The task is to develop portfolio management strategies for all the main scenarios: we should know what sort of decisions, if not the outcomes, need to be taken in specific scenarios, and what the triggers might be. This may involve changing overall return objectives and other targets, possibly rapidly, as well as major changes to portfolio construction.

10.6   UNDERSTANDING MARKET STRUCTURE

At a global but also asset class-specific level, understanding market structure can help us understand how market prices and liquidity conditions may react, including in ways not experienced before. In addition to understanding how investors are positioned and behave, we need also to factor in policy decisions by national monetary authorities (their reserve management policies are particularly key) and regulatory bodies, together with fiscal and political decisions by governments.

In addition to being generally aware of potential market risks due to investor base structure, we can be more specific about risks and opportunities if we can develop some maps of different investor bases. But rather like maps of 700 years ago, many of them will have uncharted territories. These maps, whether physical creations or merely in our minds, should aim to inform us what type of investors own an asset class, and indeed the sum of asset classes. Investor type categorisation should be organised around similarity of incentives and expected behaviour now and in the future under certain scenarios. What are their liabilities and how do they reach decisions? Do they have agency problems which slow them down or cause systemic and observable biases? What are their behavioural biases and prejudices and constraints, including regulatory, tax and other legal or government constraints? What do they believe about their own markets, global conditions and future scenarios? What memes infect them, and how; why and when might their views and prejudices change? Do they, for example, have core/periphery disease or other prejudices which might evaporate soon? Does our triple cocktail of a homogenous investor base, a vulnerable misperception of risk and leverage hold in certain asset classes?

Another useful subset of maps, for those who are peer conscious or peer constrained, would be peer maps. Understanding one's peers may not be enough to understand markets fully, but is a start, and may help identify major risks possibly not apparent to the wider market.

We also need to think of investor bases interactively and dynamically. Investors often do this in an informal way, thinking a few steps ahead.[6] To do this more formally one could model the institutions and networks of economic linkages in an asset class. More ideally still, one could try and understand the growth of such networks using simulations and maybe game theory to simulate their interactions with each other. Does a market display power laws, and do a few banks or other institutions constitute nodes of systemic importance to the network, facilitating substantial transaction cost reductions and efficiency increases, but at the risk of systemic failure should they come under attack? If we know the rough structure of a network we can draw some conclusions about its weaknesses.

As we know, news and sentiment have a significant impact on market expectations. We could also try to use simulations to model the impact of various types of events and memes, including global natural disasters, political shocks and Federal Reserve interest rate decisions, but also ideas such as that 'people power' can topple a domestic tyranny – an idea which spread across North Africa in early 2011 – or the belief that nuclear fusion, providing almost

---

[6] Thinking one or two steps ahead may be one more than other market participants, resulting in a clear market advantage.

limitless cheap energy, is within reach. Such exercises can indeed link into our scenario-planning process. We already know that seemingly unimportant news can be highly significant. Forbes (2010), commenting on Cutler *et al.* (1989), who studied large price movements in the US stock market from 1926–85, says:

> 'Combining all observable sources of news, Cutler *et al.* can explain less than half the variance in stock prices over the period by reference to observable news events. Indeed many major stock-market movements, such as the October 1987 crash, appear to be associated with only the most ephemeral news items.'

Such price movements may not last, of course, but they certainly provide investment opportunities, and for networks with strong nodality they can help us assess possible systemic vulnerabilities.

10.7 ASSET ALLOCATION

There is historical idiosyncrasy and arbitrariness in how asset classes have been accepted. One can perhaps instead start with GDP as a benchmark of economic activity, both globally for country allocations, but also for allocation weights within countries.[7] Then one can consider how one might be able to access under-represented income streams. One needs to think about the future growth of incomes, but also of capital markets and hence access to those incomes. One needs to try to identify new asset classes coming into fashion as well as those which are perhaps unsustainably fashionable. We need to work out ways to access private investments. We need to refer to our scenario planning in order to ensure diversification in the future, particularly in extreme situations.

We should also identify natural insurance characteristics of various asset classes against certain future risks: emerging surplus country currencies for a dollar crash; oil and real assets for inflation; large closed economies for scenarios of widespread global slowdown; countries with flexible, appropriate and timely policy response capabilities for a number of more extreme shocks; etc.

In terms of minimum size for an asset class, this is typically not very large, as it is primarily a function, as we have referred to Muralidhar (2001) saying, of whether an investor can invest, say, 5% of their portfolio. This is very different from being able to have everybody else in the world, or even one's own peer group, also invest the same proportion. Even for the really big funds, it should not constrain them much in the diversification they can achieve, but it does mean they cannot rely on copying each other.

Returns may be distinctive today, but we need to estimate how much of this is the result of investor behaviour which may alter radically in the future, and adjust accordingly. Also, as distinctive returns are important and these may be the result of the manager not just the set of underlying securities, so we can define asset classes by manager type.[8] How should we add to asset classes? I would say as often as practicable, so as to keep abreast of new opportunities as they arise, although avoiding being sucked into something unsubstantial.

---

[7] On this see for example Shiller (2003) p. 65; and Woolley p. 124 in Turner *et al.* (2010).

[8] We can call them investment opportunities if the definition of asset class is now becoming too strained from its original meaning for comfort.

This is a tall order. However, demand for research to facilitate such a shift in the eligible investment universe would create supply. The resources of the global institutional investment universe are quite sufficient to focus on finding new more diverse and representative asset classes, if only motivated to do so.

I recommend dispensing with the traditional juxtaposition of major asset classes and alternatives as it results in systematic overweighting of traditional as opposed to alternative asset classes. Instead, and as with any information processing problem, and as Gleick (2011, p. 409) says in his book *The Information: A History, a Theory, a Flood*: 'Strategies emerge for coping. There are many, but in essence they all boil down to two: filter and search.' We discuss two combinations: what I call the comprehensive approach has a lot of searching and then a lot of filtering, to whittle down the choices. The entrepreneurial approach does not try to be comprehensive in the search, but should try to compensate by being more selective and intelligent. By having a smaller universe the filtering is then also more straightforward, and less prone to error.

10.7.1   Route 1: Comprehensive

If one wants to optimise a portfolio's performance one may search for the best asset classes and investment opportunities, and try to be comprehensive in one's search, scouring all possibilities. Being comprehensive also helps if one wishes to step up to Roll's (1977) critique of the CAPM and standard allocation theory that the market portfolio has to include a weighted exposure to every asset in the world. The comprehensive route is the one many institutional investors aspire to, but do not manage to attain – including all possible investment opportunities into the universe from which an actual portfolio is subsequently chosen. An investment should not need to be in an accepted traditional asset class to be eligible, as all possible investments are eligible, not limited by number.

A comprehensive asset allocation process should arguably use GDP weightings, not public market capitalisation-weighted indices, to give us country exposure targets, and should make strenuous efforts to include less accessible investments. Where finding such investments is just too hard we should still not abandon GDP weighting, but adopt weights somewhere in between them and traditional market capitalisation weights. Emerging markets would become much more dominant, and would consist of many different asset classes. The universe of asset classes would change over time, with many not easily represented by indices. Characteristics for new asset classes would need to be estimated rather than calculated from past data, which may be a blessing in disguise if it forces forward- rather than backward-looking estimates including for asset classes with representative indices.

Many investors strive to implement this approach in practice, but often present the result in a more traditional framework. Systematic biases remain. Such biases include the home bias, low weights to emerging markets and high weights to public and older markets. Insofar as new asset classes are created and then sold by the financial industry, then so too there are biases determined by financial industry incentives and knowledge bases.

Being truly comprehensive in one's search for opportunities is onerous and costly. If the search is not only large, but carried out by many people then an organisation may layer the decisions, in effect risking the introduction of internal lobbies and other agency problems and hierarchies which can interfere with optimisation.

Investing in some assets and geographies is clearly not a good idea. But where does one draw the line? Arthur Conan Doyle's Sherlock Holmes employed a deductive method: 'Once you eliminate the impossible, whatever remains, no matter how improbable, must be the truth.' Similarly, we can see how asset allocation may start by looking at all possibilities and then exclude many due to unacceptable characteristics or insufficient knowledge (and too great an associated cost to acquire it). A weakness of such a deductive approach, however, is the assumption that one knows all the possibilities to start with. Doyle was a medical doctor, and it was accepted at the time as a matter of practice that there were a fixed number of known explanations for an ailment: hence the deductive method of Holmes would seem highly appropriate. Yet in many walks of life such a method is distinctively restricting in the search for new theories and explanations. If the only explanation, once the impossible has been excluded, is highly improbable, then maybe there is another explanation you have not thought of.

In investment, one could argue both ways. In practice there are a number of accepted asset classes. Many people do not see a strong desire to look much further and optimise their asset allocation choices from that accepted set. What we have tried to illustrate in this book is that the accepted universe, with its own limited ability to adjust to a changing reality, differs significantly from the current investment choices, notably in massive under-representation of emerging markets. It can thus be beneficial to think beyond traditional boundaries. The biggest limiting factor affecting many asset allocators is lack of imagination concerning the scope of the investment universe.

10.7.2 Route 2: Entrepreneurial

An entrepreneur typically does not use a comprehensive approach when considering an investment. Search may be limited. Rather, opportunities are examined one by one to see if they might work, to see what they might return and what the risks are. Consider an entrepreneur who does not scour the entire universe of possible opportunities before choosing an investment. Instead, he first tries to find opportunities, then once one has been found, assesses it against a set of criteria to see if it is attractive or not. Several, but not a huge number, of opportunities may be assessed and compared, or maybe only the one, before a decision is taken whether to invest or not.

Just as an entrepreneur may use such a strategy for selecting investments, so can a portfolio investor. The criteria may include the expected returns and risks of the opportunity and its expected correlations with other opportunities in the entrepreneur's existing or prospective portfolio. Assessment criteria are indeed similar to those using the comprehensive strategy.

Tversky (1972) observed what he calls 'elimination by aspects' as a filtering mechanism for making choices. Asset allocation is no exception. The result is a two-stage decision process, with the elimination criteria hugely important in determining the end result. If one changes one's mind about what criteria are desirable one can end up with non-optimal choices.[9] Thus the more restricted search function in the entrepreneurial approach needs to be carefully targeted in order to avoid significant bias.

However, this is possible. One can still look at a few opportunities while trying to look far afield. To do this effectively one's view of potential risks, including the risk that you end

---

[9] For example, say an institutional investor is new to an asset class and wants the first allocation to be conservative and low risk. They confuse low risk with low tracking error to a benchmark index. They eliminate more active managers with high tracking error. Then they work out that it is possible to reduce risk substantially below that of the index, yet they have already excluded the managers who could do this best for them.

up doing what everybody else is doing, should inform the selection process. Indeed, clear recognition of the inherent weakness of not being comprehensive, and so potentially missing opportunities, should focus the attention on the search so that it can be intelligent and targeted. Employing competent in-house staff is often preferred for this, and also for the related task of active manager selection, as outsourcing can create significant agency problems.[10] If this is achieved, then the entrepreneurial approach can be seen to have advantages over the comprehensive approach resulting from cost savings, flexibility and the absence of agency problems caused by too much internal bureaucracy, and outsourcing.

The problem for many investors is that they fall between these two approaches. Those believing themselves to be following the comprehensive approach are typically not comprehensive enough, and their search and filter processes are both liable to capture by interested parties, creating biases. Those not pretending to be comprehensive are often not compensating enough for a limited search by being more intelligent in deciding what they need to search for and where to look.

10.7.3   Asset allocation dynamics

The practical necessity, due to agency problems, to be in a herd may overwhelm the desire of an individual to break out of conventional asset class definitions, but there are compromises. Being aware of industry biases is something that the investor can take good advantage of. If one needs to be in the herd, but realises that a herd is a risky place to be, one can at least be on the edge closest to where ideally one would like to be. Peer pressure can be particularly important in defining the herd boundaries, so through action and persuasion an asset allocator, by pushing the boundaries, can also play a part in moving the herd. The cumulative effect is gradual change in herd direction.

Unfortunately, such a gradual approach can be inadequately responsive to new realities in a rapidly changing world. Indeed, investors have clearly significantly lagged behind the growth of emerging market opportunities, and also in avoiding developed world macroeconomic risks. Having one eye in the land of the blind may be great up to the point at which you need two eyes. Being a second quartile-performing pension fund in terms of investment performance may be acceptable in many instances, but not if 80% of your peers are in trouble, falling behind on their commitment to meet liabilities. One cannot eat relative return.

Slow decision-making may be a major impediment to investment performance. Most important is the ability to respond to major negative shocks. For many types of investor, liabilities change faster than they are measured, entry into new asset classes can take years, and decisions are timed to be regular and automatic rather than responsive to events. In particular a sense of history may help us work out whether and to what degree, and specifically in what ways, we live in extraordinary times.

---

[10] Swensen (2009, p. 298) says: 'The surest path to making effective active management decisions comes from engaging a highly qualified staff of professionals committed to serving the interests of the investment fund. A dedicated staff supplies the resources necessary to identify the exceedingly rare group of managers able to add value in the investment process. In addition, hiring a group of individuals to manage a particular investment fund reduces the severity of the principal/agent conflicts that pervade the money management industry, as the staff serves as a strong advocate for the institution's interests.'

10.8   META-ALLOCATION: TOOLSET CHOICE

We need to say a few more words about how to filter asset classes and choose the allocation. A lot of our quantitative tool set is of limited value if volatility is not a good proxy for risk; so too if other assumptions are in doubt; so too should large changes in investor perceptions or other structural shifts be around the corner. We showed in Chapter 9 an example of some alternative rules in times of structural shifts. So the first task is to assess our environment and then choose the tools for analysis and asset allocation, not the other way round: before allocation comes meta-allocation, the choice of allocation method.

Following the discussion in Chapter 8, given the statistical properties of asset classes and investments,[11] one can use a mean variance optimiser to recommend an asset allocation mix. One can then test the robustness of different portfolio combinations through multiple simulations. Alternatively, many portfolios are constructed in a pyramid with layers assigned for different goals in mental accounting exercises. One of the reasons for the popularity of mental accounting is that optimisations are so very sensitive to the data input, as simulations show, and the input data is phenomenally difficult to estimate. Then again, mental accounting is sub-optimal and static; however, dynamic mental accounting, if such is possible, may work much better than many alternatives.

My preference is to choose scenario planning for those periods where life is getting complex and structural shifts are in the air, allowing for more flexibility than just making adjustments to the allocation pyramid: instead potentially encompassing the use of the whole portfolio. If we go down this meta-allocation route, creating scenarios should be followed by thinking through the consequences of each scenario on specific portfolio combinations. While in theory this may sound like something which can be put through an optimiser or simulated, portfolio impacts from extreme negative events are often easier to assess without formal mathematical simulations. It is often easier for the human brain to keep a holistic view of a scenario's impact if it is not partially fed into a computer. We are also, many of us, more likely to believe the output.

For example, estimating the changing nature of the likely future correlations as the US sub-prime bubble built up was not possible with any degree of accuracy. However, accuracy was not necessary to inform asset allocation choice. Intelligent observers with understanding of the problem, including macroeconomists with some understanding of the structure of housing finance markets, could quite easily see that there was a systemic risk building. Those who had access to the ratings models and could see the correlation assumptions in them could also have come to the conclusion that the ratings agencies were using false assumptions. With such an insight the prudent investor could have exited the market. Knowing that there is significant unpriced major risk is enough: one does not need to know the exact size or even probability of the risk.

Likewise, assessing precisely when and how a country might default is much more difficult than working out that the country has a serious difficulty in avoiding the sort of crisis which may lead to default. Avoiding such major risk is the first task of an active manager in sovereign risk.

---

[11] At the minimum their mean expected returns, standard deviations and co-variances, and if one can reasonably assume a normal distribution.

As scenarios unfold one also needs mechanisms to adjust the portfolio appropriately, with possibly fast reactions to reduce exposures to risks in time of crisis. The capacity to change course (see 10.3 and 10.4 above) will be one of the determinants of which meta-allocation approach to choose: there is limited point in having a dynamic intelligent monitoring of events if it is not going to affect one's behaviour anyway.

10.9   FOLLOW THE SKILLSET

Deciding what and where to delegate is a function not only of incentives, but also of capabilities. Recall in Chapter 8 the emerging equity example of whether to employ tactical asset allocation (TAA) to emerging market equity, and the not necessarily correct implicit assumption that this would be at a level above that of the active emerging equity managers employed. It could be that tactical asset allocation to emerging markets can be made to work best by those close to developed markets, which in part may be because that is where the tactical decisions tend to be made. Even if true, however, this may change over time as emerging equity markets are driven increasingly by their own domestic considerations and by domestic capital. Conversely, an emerging equity manager may have less difficulty understanding the developed world equity markets than a developed economy equity manager does understanding emerging markets.

One suspects there is a strong desire to avoid regret by allocating in a traditional way. Regret avoidance might also be a partial factor behind institutional investors often employing several managers to manage to the same mandate. Initially, as a way to test which are more capable and able to deliver the level of service required, this may make sense. It also makes sense as a way to learn more about the asset class – obtaining a variety of market opinions. However, it can also be ill-advised where active managers are employed to do better than the benchmark but where some managers are just doing the opposite of others, in effect undoing each other's work – too many active managers can result in a more benchmark-like performance, but with higher fees.

Different managers should be employed for different jobs, and it is important to understand what their skillset is. Return streams may be firm-specific just as they may be asset class specific, and consequently one should see particular investment opportunities – managers and their specific products and asset classes as represented by indices – as interchangeable alternatives. The tendency to put managers in pre-defined categories, and select them after asset allocation, may result in underselection of good active managers (as well as those active outside traditional asset classes).

The entrepreneurial approach to asset allocation mentioned above may be more conducive in practice to following the skillsets of managers than the comprehensive strategy: there are simply less steps involved around which rigidity and agency problems can solidify in the decisionmaking process. Breaking down the line between the tasks of asset allocation and manager selection has already been done in practice many times, but remains at odds with the traditional dominant thinking that asset allocation comes first. The two tasks are intimately linked, and artificially separating them may result in sub-optimal allocations and the possible creation of agency problems.

10.10   PORTFOLIO CONSTRUCTION AND MONITORING

The problem of constructing and monitoring a portfolio in a static known world with clearly defined asset classes with clearly defined statistical characteristics is a very different one to constructing and monitoring a portfolio in a world full of uncertainty; prejudice; fluid and unclear asset class definitions, boundaries and characteristics; agency problems; and possible large structural shifts ahead in economics, investment returns, risks and risk perceptions.

One wants to avoid being a forced seller of assets in a falling market, for which one has to construct a portfolio carefully, and monitor overall liquidity, considering how this may change. But one does not want to forego illiquid investments, which may add return and diversification. One needs to be clear about causes of volatility, and anticipate the behaviour of others, including policymakers. Doing this well can build confidence and enable better overall investment performance.

Just because one needs to think constantly it does not necessarily follow that one should be changing one's portfolio constantly, adding to costs. The aim should be rather to have a decision process which is intelligent, allows thought to filtrate into the portfolio, but also preserves discipline and time consistency. The goal is to have a strategy for every contingency, which you have considered – not in detail maybe, but in outline.

Portfolio construction and monitoring should, I argue, be integrated. Having overarching reviews on portfolio shape only intermittently may not correspond to the underlying shifts in investment opportunities and risks. Swensen (2009, p. 315) says:

> 'Asset allocation targets ought to be reviewed once (and only once) per year. By concentrating the discussion of investment policy in one meeting, the most important investment decisions receive concentrated attention from both staff and committee. Perhaps equally important, limiting policy discussions to the assigned meeting diminishes the possibility of damage from ill-considered moves made in emotional response to the waves of gloom or euphoria that sweep over markets from time to time.'

This may look sensible at first glance, but one has to ask oneself what is appropriate for one's institution; and also whether you are an investor on top of global events, able to see scenarios unfold without huge surprise, or if you are prone to the waves of gloom and euphoria. Are you someone who panics or who finds the collective psychology of gloomy markets extremely interesting, stimulating even, as well as the policy choices that go with it? If (but it may be a big if) you can trust yourself not to get caught up by market sentiment, then you can probably afford to be more flexible than Swensen suggests. In any event, an exception should be made if events demand interim consideration before the annual review. The desire to avoid decisions is not just down to Swensen's 'emotional response', but also driven by aversion to future regret, and one should bear that in mind also. One can either accept this psychology and have occasional regular decisions, or try to correct for it – using what we know about behavioural biases – and have more timely ones.

Monitoring a portfolio is more than looking at returns and volatilities, and measuring managers against benchmarks, benchmarks against liabilities, and the effectiveness of strategic and tactical asset allocations. It is also about considering what might have been. If a manager takes precautionary action against a negative scenario which then does not come about, and underperforms another who gambled, this should be taken into account. As we are dealing with counterfactuals, we cannot simply push observed numbers into an algorithm. Monitoring is largely about establishing contact with the manager's views so that one can make sure, over time, one ends up with smart rather than merely lucky managers. It means understanding their view of the world and their scenarios, and preferably having managers who have similar awareness of major scenarios and risks as you do (which may mean learning from them as well as the other way round). All this necessitates dialogue. Just as scenario planning should help to avoid panic selling because problems are perceived in advance, so monitoring is also to a large extent something which occurs before the investment performance is known. It is an extension of due diligence and the conversation an investor has with their manager.

11
Regulation and Policy Lessons

If we want to understand how to regulate financial markets we need to start by understanding them – not just parts of them. We need to go beyond assuming that markets are naturally and perfectly competitive. We need government to help in the development and maintenance of efficient competitive markets, which do not necessarily come into being on their own. The huge volume of Benthamite legislation in 19th century Britain is a historical example of the amount of effort required to overcome anti-competitive tendencies. Yet much economic analysis has ignored institutions. It has been agnostic with regard to the role of property rights, law and government policy in creating the market competition whereby relative prices can express collective preferences and have a chance of forming other institutions and organisations.

> 'Institutions change, and fundamental changes in relative prices are the most important source of that change. To the noneconomist (and perhaps for some economists as well), putting such weight on changing relative prices may be hard to understand. But relative price changes alter the incentives of individuals in human interaction, and the only other source of such change is a change in tastes.'
>
> Douglass North (1990), p. 84

If relative prices are as important as Douglass North says, and given the likelihood they are going to be driven more and more by events in emerging markets, we need to think about how institutions may change as a result of the shifts in global economic power, including pricing power, to emerging markets. The end of the Cold War has meant the preferences of millions, previously constrained in their choices, are now moving prices. Over half the goods a European or US pensioner of tomorrow purchases may be priced if not produced in global markets dominated by emerging market producers and consumers.

Institutions that took centuries to grow in Western Europe we see evolving in decades in the emerging world. These changes are far faster than some of the ad hoc policy co-ordination of the recent past can cope with, particularly in our savings institutions. We need to fix the banks, but also the way we manage pensions and the international monetary system. We need to be on our guard for future global financial crises, which is hampered while we are still hostage to defunct finance theories.

Without repeating the arguments, some of the checklist items in the last chapter are also pertinent for the regulator and for the central banker. In particular the following:

- Assumptions about risk and uncertainty, market efficiency, and liquidity need to be challenged more often.
- Lessons from behavioural finance need to be taken on board – regulators and other policymakers could audit their own capabilities and constraints if they do not already do so.
- Agency chains need careful scrutiny, and indeed regulators and policymakers should also be aware of the agency effects which affect them.

- Some central bankers one suspects have been thinking the unthinkable and employing sce-
  nario- planning techniques already. Others could follow their lead, particularly in thinking
  through central bank reserve management policy and institutional savings regulation.
- Understanding market structure, and in particular its implications for systemic risk (including using network theory), is a task underway but in its infancy.
- Shifting toolsets – meta-allocation – is also absent in the more bureaucratic and entrenched
  areas of the public sector.

If nothing else, I hope this book will support healthy scepticism in regulators, central bankers
and other policymakers about markets, and also about their own practices and occasional
tendencies to both complacency and hubris.

This chapter lists lessons arising from a combination of my macroeconomic observations
at time of writing, and my critique of finance theory. We firstly identify some new general
lessons about regulating financial institutions, but also some old but forgotten lessons. We
then consider a further sub-set of such lessons – those concerning systemic risk (including
so-called 'macroprudential' regulation). Thirdly, I present an additional short policy wish list
for emerging market regulators and central banks. Fourthly, we discuss reform of the international monetary system and central bank reserve management in more detail. Fifthly, we
include a section for investors on what to expect from HIDC regulators, and sixthly, a list of
what investors might expect from emerging market policymakers, to be complemented in the
next chapter by a further list of other things investors might expect from emerging markets.

11.1   REGULATING FINANCIAL INSTITUTIONS: NEW AND OLD LESSONS

11.1.1   Fix the banks

We can start with banks. Banks are leveraged institutions at the heart of capitalist economies
which engage in credit creation and are vulnerable to deposit runs and crises of confidence.
The banking system of a country or of several countries can experience highly correlated
stresses as lack of confidence spreads rapidly across the system. Despite knowing how to
regulate banks for decades, regulators failed to prevent the superbubble from building and
then the crisis which broke in 2008. Some of this was due to the task having become more
difficult, not least due to the changes in incentives in investment banks as discussed in Chapter 3. With a partnership structure, the partners' capital and reputation were at risk in every
transaction, but with largely external public investor bases, major agency problems have led
to myopia inside the banks and a focus on quarterly and annual results over long-term health
and reputation.

The regulatory response can be to limit bank activities and/or try to address the agency
problems caused by widespread external ownership. Counter-cyclical capital buffers, for
instance by increasing bank capital requirements in rising markets and vice versa can be used
(as in Spain). This can help to reduce national asset bubbles. Turner in Turner et al. (2010,
p. 55), having discussed optimal liquidity, recommends shifting the bias in setting bank
capital requirements away from liquidity towards more conservatism (i.e. giving up more
market liquidity if necessary); the consideration of leverage limits to control speculation; and
possible financial transactions taxes. Such measures constitute ways to restrict the activity
of banks, and so curb excesses. But they do not address the incentive problems directly.

Addressing incentive problems is made difficult by the tacit nature of what is being regulated. Regulators need to be wary of focusing too much solely on quantifiable information, which may prove both inadequate to the task and create further mis-incentives. They face a trade-off between regulating what is observable in more detail at the potential cost of undermining reputation and trust further – crowding out the scope for reputation building.

Others have proposed splitting up the big global banks so none are too big to fail, splitting off commercial and other banking activities (the 'Volcker rule'), and 'living wills'. Such measures are probably the best way forward and may also help to reduce potential spillover from myopia within banks. The bank lobby against any reduction of their size is powerful, and arguably the main reason why more radical seizure and splitting of banks has not already occurred. Nevertheless, reducing the power of individual banks is only part of what is needed. Measures to clip banks' wings need to be complemented by incentive structures in which long-term reputation is prized by management above short-term profitability, and staff are also managed to behave towards this end.

In recognition that at least some of the problem lies with the move from partnerships, one could try to address incentives directly. One option is to try to recreate the past – foster partnership structures built on reputation. The difficulty is getting to such a structure from where we are. However, it is arguably much more relevant for emerging market regulators to consider this route. One of the consequences of the credit crunch is the weakened state of Western banks, and their higher borrowing costs and need to deleverage. As a result emerging market banks have been taking global market share. At time of writing some of the largest banks globally are now emerging market banks, but they have not yet entered much into cross-border investment banking activities. Given the dynamism of their economies and the rapid growth of their domestic capital markets, there are opportunities to build partnership investment banks with strong domestic and international reputations in several emerging markets.

Another course of action is to try to address agency problems in the publicly listed bank. Martin Wolf and others have argued for longer-term incentives for bank staff, linking remuneration to longer-term overall bank profitability through share options or similar structures. However, one could go further, as this on its own does not address the problem that public shareholders focus on the short term. The ownership of bank shares could come with measures to incentivise a longer-term view. Dividends could be announced as normal, but put aside to be paid out after several years – maybe a portion after one year, some after five and some after ten years. These pools of capital would be called on for recapitalisation in a crisis, but for no other reason, until the dividends are due to be paid to shareholders.

Another way to curb the potential for banking systems to cause mayhem, particularly in the emerging markets, is disintermediation – i.e. building bond markets and other institutions to do some of the job banks currently do, but without the leverage and liability mismatches (banks typically borrow short term and lend long term). Bank disintermediation is an ongoing process which accelerated from the birth of the Eurobond market in 1963. A bond market can replace bank loans, and in a nonleveraged format, transfer the long-term savings of pension funds and insurance companies and individual savers, via funds or directly, to governments, long-term investment projects and companies. The growth of corporate debt markets (which banks can sponsor and help build) is a major priority for many emerging markets as this can help deepen and diversify their financial markets, stimulate the growth of institutional savings and, together with the growth of public equity markets, reduce dependence on bank lending and retained earnings for corporate investment.

11.1.2   Non-banks: who holds what?

One can argue that the trend in the decades before 2008 was towards tougher regulation in securities but laxer rules for banks, but we have little reason to be complacent when it comes to non-banks. The bulk of financial fireworks has typically been the province of banking, from John Law in 1720 onwards. Institutional asset management is much newer than banking. But hedge funds like LTCM acquired enough assets to make their own pyrotechnic displays. Regulators have been concentrating mainly on the banks, where the leverage problems are demonstrably systematically important. It is clear, however, that reform of regulatory oversight should not be confined to banks. So called shadow banking is receiving attention, a term which for many indicates dangerous pools of leveraged unregulated capital. When he was chairman of the US Federal Reserve, Alan Greenspan was opposed to more regulation for derivatives. He gave more weight to their importance as a means to transfer risk to those able to bear it, than to their causing systemic risks. He also took the view that he was not able to spot bubbles and was better placed to clear up the mess after a bubble burst than to try to prevent it (a view which encouraged moral hazard and led to the term 'the Greenspan put'). Insofar as hedge funds and other holders of derivatives contract their derivatives with regulated investment bank counterparties, one view was that the regulator need only observe and regulate the bank counterparties. However, the growth of over-the-counter (OTC) derivatives not transacted or therefore registered on an exchange meant that the regulator(s) did not have an overall map of the structure of investor bases: they simply did not know where the pools of capital were. This may be fine in theory so long as markets are efficient, but not in practice.

I suggest we observe the structure of holdings in greater detail. Indeed, and by way of example, emerging market regulators have something to teach their developed world counterparts in this regard. In Brazil for example all derivatives are registered and so the central bank knows when, where and by how much to intervene in markets should systemic risks appear.

11.1.3   Reduce agency problems: trustee incentives

Well-established institutional investors like pension funds can and should be a major source of market stability, but they can also pose systemic risks to themselves and others. The largest problems with the regulation of pension funds and other institutional pools of capital are arguably principal/agent problems. Indeed, the reason asset allocators and investors put up with poor theory, use it and let others use it on their behalf is down to agency problems. There are strong tendencies to herd, to do what one's peers do. Agency problems are also created by regulations. For example, US ERISA legislation absolves pension funds from due diligence on every stock as long as there is plenty of diversification. The cumulative effect of US securities legislation since the 1930s was to create greater liquidity and near frictionless trading; but this was at the cost of mounting agency problems and reduced fiduciary oversight by both companies and investors.

I propose that it should be an established regulatory principle that a fiduciary, having made losses, should not be able to claim in their defence they were only doing what everybody else did. Indeed, offering such a defence should perhaps be seen as evidence of lack of due diligence having been carried out.

Money illusion, and its distorting impact on asset/liability management which we discussed in Chapter 8, is a substantial issue. Going even further, trustees and others could be encouraged to focus on future purchasing power rather than nominal or simple[1] inflation-adjusted liabilities. Western fiscal authorities have in the past, and for long periods, been reluctant to legislate to adjust for inflation, let alone purchasing powering, as nominal budgeting can be used to advantage in adjusting public expenditures downwards. Getting beyond denial, and recognising emerging markets as part of pensioners' liabilities, is an even greater challenge: it may mean domestic government funding costs would go up just as they would decrease in emerging markets. It is thus perhaps for the saver to become more enlightened on this point and lobby appropriately.

Regulation designed to reduce individual firm risk can create wider agency problems as it changes the incentives of regulated firms, and may create more uniformity of behaviour. A difference in regulatory approach between the US and UK has been between a rules-based and person-based focus. With a rules-based approach the letter of regulation may be followed rather than the spirit. A person-based focus can create regulatory uncertainty. But a problem facing both approaches is that if tacit contracts are forced into a regulatory structure demanding measurement, this can destroy relationships built on trust. For example, legislation to punish recalcitrant trustees may reduce their capacity and willingness to diversify away from their peer group averages. A regulatory approach which penalises mistakes heavily may discourage discretion. Self-regulation is generally preferable, but requires incentives to be appropriately aligned – e.g. such things as bank proprietary traders in universal banks not being allowed to play with taxpayer-insured retail deposits.

Indeed, this might have implications across a wide range of financial institutions. Take the specialist Lloyds insurance market, where tacit information and inter-personal trust are still integral. Forcing greater transparency on the Lloyds market (motivated by the desire to regulate individual firms better) may not be the optimal regulatory position if it reduces the relative price of tacit information compared to commoditised information. For example, 'treating customers fairly' may be interpreted in great detail yet allow egregious loading of fees onto end clients as long as these are declared in the small print.

So how does one best ensure effective self-regulation? We need some broad level guides on how to change rules. North (1990, p. 80) introduces the concept of adaptive efficiency to identify rules which help an economy adapt over time. One needs to look at incentives and the principal/agent chain. For pension funds, for example, the long-term interests of plan participants are not well served by incentives for short-termism. Appointing some young plan participants as trustees may be one way to compensate for such short-termism. Likewise, there could be deferred incentive pay for staff and for those providing advice on asset allocation. Such measures are often impractical, however. Either way, one needs to foster non-monetary incentives, traditionally the best defender of pensioners' interests.

11.1.4   Honour public service

Jane Jacobs (1992) compares the private and public sector syndromes as distinct. People are not merely motivated by money, and one way to cope with agency problems is to appeal to other motives than the pecuniary, and to avoid undue punishment for taking decisions in good faith. Trust can simply break down, and we need more than self-interest to foster and maintain trust. One needs to supplement pecuniary remuneration with honour and status and a public service ethos. Where this exists it should be nurtured – which may in some cases

---

[1] By 'simple' I mean not taking account of likely future relative price changes, particularly longer-term.

mean not introducing contradictory (arguably debasing) attempts to incentivise with money. Likewise, for regulators it means there are sensible limits to the desire to measure everything. Promotion of professional bodies and standards of professional ethics can play a part, as can the preservation of markets based on tacit knowledge and trust. This is very familiar ground for many finance professionals, but it may not always be clear to those same finance professionals how the maintenance of ethical standards links to our theories of market efficiency. The link is provided by an understanding of the fragility of competitive markets, the role of tacit information and trust in ensuring efficient allocation and the need for self-regulation. Character matters. Regulators should be constantly asking themselves the questions: does this measure distort incentives, but also does it erode the incentive to take ethical choices? Securitisation of sub-prime mortgages, for example, would have failed both tests.

11.1.5   Choice architecture

Ensuring a plurality of choice for voters, pension fund participants, savers, bank customers or retail investors is important to ensure competition by the providers of services, and this does not necessarily mean as many choices as possible. Swedish pension reform led to too many choices for plan participants in choosing their asset allocations. The majority of people, faced with a huge selection, went for the default option, defeating in practice the objective of competitive provision. To avoid crushes in sports stadia the appropriate policy response is to ensure density does not rise too high, and likewise in finance a competition of ideas and heterogeneous investors with different liabilities and views can be an effective technique to prevent bubbles. To quote Thaler and Sunstein (2008): 'In complex situations, the "Just maximise choices" mantra is not enough to create good policy. The more choices there are, and the more complex the situation, the more important it is to have enlightened choice architecture.' But who decides the choice architecture? This is not straightforward. The institutions of choice we inherit are also path-dependent (where we are depends on where we have been), and reform needs to work from an existing structure of choices in most instances.

Herding can on occasion be used to a regulator's advantage, by first finding an example of asset allocation done well and then show-casing it as best practice: 'If choice architects want to shift behaviour and to do so with a nudge, they might simply inform people about what other people are doing.'[2]

Lastly, improving the quality of demand for financial services is an important objective in improving provision. Transporting to financial services Hayek's insight that individuals are better allocators than the state, one can aim for greater discrimination by the end beneficial owner of the capital, and fewer agency problems distorting this demand in the agency chain.

11.2   WHAT TO DO ABOUT SYSTEMIC RISK?

People may not like volatility. Being at sea is disturbing for many landlubbers. But do we try to calm the oceans? Or do we encourage sea legs while at the same time avoid the roaring forties if at all possible? We need to be fully aware of our condition (transparency about the structure of the market) and we should avoid the instability caused by having our sails up (our assets leveraged) in a storm. Occasional loss is inevitable, even healthy, as is a bit of

---

[2] Thaler and Sunstein (2008, p. 65).

volatility. Risk is not the same as volatility. We may learn from crashes. We should care most about catastrophes. Yet it is the most frightening scenarios we prefer, collectively, to put out of our minds, and a convenient way to do this (consciously or subconsciously) is employ models which ignore them.

'What informed decisions in the run-up to the crisis was not the personal ideology of a few powerful individuals but a powerful collective psychology. A central tenet was the belief that it had become possible, using modern mathematical tools, to more effectively price and manage risk. Elegant mathematical formulae like the Black-Scholes model could be used to determine prices for options and other derivatives. Subject to the simplifying assumptions needed to render the model tractable, it was possible to give numerical estimate of the maximum loss ... The maximum loss that might be incurred ... was soon given its own name, Value at Risk (VaR).'

Eichengreen (2011, p. 106)

We have known for half a century that market prices are not distributed normally, yet we use VaR models which assume normal distributions. To follow up on Eichengreen's quote above, the Black-Scholes Merton model for pricing options assumes a bell-shaped distribution and that the parameters of the bell are known – yet neither assumption is valid. But the use of the Black-Scholes Merton model is not merely widespread, but uniform.[3] We know many of our assumptions are inaccurate or false, yet we put trust in our measurements of risk based on them. We have known at least since John Law nearly 300 years ago that banks are almost always central to large financial crises, yet we have been content to allow them to operate with huge leverage in the belief that risk management is strong. In large part this is because banks have successfully captured our political classes and regulators, allowing them to dismantle legal safeguards implemented after the previous crash. We also fell into the trap of the fallacy of composition. Yet the whole is not equal to the sum of the parts – regulating only the parts (still very necessary) can miss the build-up of systemic risks.

The task ahead to cope with systemic risk is not easy. While efforts are being made as of 2013 to increase international co-ordination of regulatory policy, it is an uphill struggle. The growth of markets and the technology enabling rapid global movement of capital is combined with the growth of different organisational forms of capital – different types of actor and market – to make the overall regulatory oversight more and more complex.

11.2.1 Avoid regulation that amplifies risk

Regulation of banks, together with the way they measure risk internally, creates self-reinforcing or reflexive swings because recently stable markets are wrongly equated with low risk, and this affects how much exposure a bank can take. Should volatility in 'safe' paper increase or associated ratings be cut, there is an amplified impact on a bank balance sheet, and indeed on a banking sector more widely. Bank selling to adjust balance sheets into regulatory compliance may push prices down even more, leading to even more required balance sheet shrinkage. One solution would be explicit adjustment in bank regulatory structures (internal

---

[3] Moreover, the model's widespread use has impacted market dynamics in a way which has deceived some observers into thinking it valid – see Bhidé (2010, p. 140). This in turn can create systemic risk.

and external) for major price swings or dynamics which do not conform to the assumption of normally distributed markets implicit in the standard value at risk (VaR) methodology. In effect, banks currently have an incentive to hold portfolios of paper which have displayed low volatility in the past, rather than more diverse portfolios which may be safer.

As well as regulators, the widespread use of rating agencies (including by regulatory bodies) can also distort investor base structures and so create systemic risks. Rating agencies often conflate volatility and risk, focus on backward-looking measureable data, err on the side of heavily discounting uncertainties (to be 'prudent'), do not present different scenarios to their clients[4] and ignore fallacies of composition. They typically overestimate the safety of recently non-volatile asset classes, and in so doing help attract safety-seeking investors who may add, in the short term, to low volatility price dynamics, while actually increasing the risk of the investment through contributing to greater investor concentration. This may be particularly marked for assets which are low-yielding and hence unattractive to a wider more return-seeking set of investors – the fictitiously named 'risk-free' assets. Rating agencies need to be more independent, and this involves reviewing how they get paid – i.e. not by entities being rated.

Suspensions of market activity, like official bailouts, and like a fixed exchange rate system such as Argentina's convertibility in the 1990s,[5] may give time to solve a problem, but are not themselves solutions. If mismanaged they can create more volatility elsewhere and exacerbate systemic risk. Generally, therefore, they may be ultimately effective only in concert with more fundamental policies. The alternative motives (other than to buy time) for suspending market mechanisms are often difficult to justify – i.e. when they are driven by short-term fear without a coherent analysis of the problem or solution, or when the proposer falsely thinks they know better than the market.

11.2.2   Beware market segmentation

We can think of major systemic events as paradigm shifts in the perception of risk. As mentioned in Chapter 7, this may follow a tell-tale period of market segmentation (as certain types of investors exit the market) and increased homogeneity of the views of the active investor base which remains.

The regulator should be on the lookout for warning signals: confused and very different explanations of events; market pricing not reflective of realistic price models; and market segmentation of the type described. These may indicate that there is a major risk misperception which is about to change. Courtesy of people being stubborn in their (collective) beliefs, such observations moreover are not hugely difficult to see once you know you what to look for.

11.2.3   Structure matters

There appears a remarkable absence of regulatory focus or even discussion of the structure of investor bases in the academic literature:

---

[4] Frydman and Goldberg (2011, p. 247).

[5] As discussed in Chapter 2, convertibility (involving a rigid fixed exchange rate to the US dollar) gave Argentina more time to resolve its fiscal imbalances. When these were not corrected, though, the system eventually collapsed spectacularly in December 2001 with sovereign default.

- Currency crises are described as unpredictable, which they are often not (remember the example of the Thai crisis and my segmentation theory).
- Macroeconomic vulnerabilities are often identified only in very general terms, without reference to investor base structure and who might do what. Information-gathering costs are posited as a reason for centralised international collection of more standardised international comparative data, which is fine in theory, but such comparative data is not often hugely useful except in predicting the behaviour of others using it.
- Groups of investors are sometimes considered ignorant by hubristic observers and policymakers, who characterise them as experiencing occasional sudden 'wake-up calls', without reference to more subtle incentives.
- Policy is directed to controlling markets and capital flows (often unrealistically) all without reference to the possibility of understanding the motives of investors in more detail.

Could this be a case of blind faith in the efficiency of competitive markets? Regulation of single institution risk can conflict with regulation of systemic risk; microeconomic theory, when extended economy wide, can contradict macroeconomic realities. An example is forcing institutional investors like EU-area insurers to be invested in highly rated, but high-risk low-return, developed world government bonds.[6] Aside from not placing sufficient value on the fallacy of composition we might suspect regulators of falsely assuming (either actively or by neglect):

1. There is a misallocation of assets by insurers which a regulator can correct, in a similar way to a misapplication of leverage seen in banks.
2. Past volatility is always the best proxy for risk.
3. There are such things as risk-free assets, and more specifically that EU sovereign bonds are very low risk or risk-free.
4. Market dynamics and risk are not impacted by the structure of an investor base.

All of these assumptions are wrong. The net effect of regulation may be to concentrate the structure of an investor base, and so create systemic risks.

By ignoring structure both investors and regulators can be fooled. For example, consider an investor wanting to control risk through hedging. The investor may buy a derivative to act as insurance, but with a counterparty who is not always making a market with another client wanting the opposite exposure. The counterparty, to lay off the risk, may then sell the underlying instrument, thus causing the asset price fall the original investor wanted to insure against. In this example the net effect of the hedge, though ostensibly effective in its task, may be close to zero. To counter this, a regulator may place restrictions on shorting, but this is unlikely to affect the longer- term asset price, but is likely to reduce market liquidity and efficiency. Regulators need to know the structure of financial markets in order to make intelligent choices. They should not assume that markets are efficient, or assume that their actions do not affect market structure, or neglect to consider the impact of market structure on systemic risk.

---

[6] Specifically Solvency II regulation.

11.2.4   Map perceptions of risk

Regulators could map not only risk, but the perception of risk. They need to try to ascertain those markets where there is a misperception of risk likely to be disillusioned at some time in the near future. This may sound like an impossible task – second-guessing the market. A lot of the time it will be. It may not be impossible, however, where a central bank or international agency has superior information, or where a misperception by some market participants, together with the explanations sustaining it, has already been identified by other market participants. That an investor base is fairly homogenous is a clue to this.

Tax, regulatory, agency or group misperceptions may keep some prices at artificial levels. By observing the views of different market participants, and how they are changing, regulators may at least be able to foresee some of the scenarios foreseen by other market participants. There may even be ways to encourage market participants suspicious of systemic risks or gross risk misperceptions to come forward. Having identified a misperception, regulators can also then ask themselves the question: What factors could break the misperception?

11.2.5   Detect and stop asset bubbles

Asset bubbles, as argued by many, including Smithers (2009), can be detected by central banks. Smithers makes the case for employing additional policy instruments than just interest rates to control bubbles, and specifically (p. 186) the regulation of bank minimum capital requirements. National housing markets in particular appear largely independent from those in other countries, hence national regulation efforts to control housing bubbles using bank minimum capital requirements may be effective without some of the side effects, including on currency valuation, which may occur through use of interest rates. The brief to control bubbles would need to be managed separately from the inflation control objective, but co-ordinated with it given the overlapping influence of policy measures on both objectives. The new structure at the Bank of England of having separate committees to address inflation and systematic risk but in the same institution would appear to follow his approach. Other central banks may follow suit.

Something as simple as low default rates may be an indication of bubble conditions building. Greenspan's view of letting bubbles build and then clearing up the mess afterwards is now accepted as imprudent given the salutary experience since 2008. Frydman and Goldberg (2011, p. 242) propose differential margin requirements in equity markets for bulls and bears, which may or may not be practicable given the need for an official guidance of what is and what is not a bull or a bear. A similar mechanism they propose for housing markets may be more implementable.

Pension funds and other large pools of institutional savings are, with the help of their consultants, rating agencies and principal/agent chains, also capable of contributing to bubble formation, aided and abetted by inappropriate regulatory structures. Exposures concentrated in a few economies or asset types – like the publicly-listed domestic securities of the home country – could cause sudden valuation shifts, possibly amplifying macroeconomic cycles. The key way to address much of these systemic problems is through addressing principal/agent problems better.

There are other structural policy proposals which would help reduce systemic problems in the future. Regulators may design measures to disincentivise peer group herding. Shiller (2005) argues in the case of the US for improved ethics and questions whether the government's pro-business stance can withstand further inequality and associated building resentment. He argues that investors should diversify more. He also argues that there should be a plan to increase savings, and private retirement plans and social security reformed. He also, like Frydman and Goldberg (2011) and many others, focuses on measures to reduce bubble development, arguing that monetary policy should 'gently lean against bubbles', that rules should be encouraged which prevent market bubbles and the public encouraged to hedge risks.

11.2.6   Preserve credibility

Many politicians and central banks understand the importance of retaining credibility. More difficult is to know how to react when that credibility is under threat. How can policy credibility crumble and what to do about it? Looking unprepared and reacting slowly as Northern Rock disintegrated may have been understandable but was far from optimal. The bond market can severely limit the choices policymakers can make if they are to steer the best (or least bad) course. Yet that is precisely why the concerns of the bond market should also be the concern of the regulator and why the regulator should try to understand how bond market views are capable of changing rapidly. Indeed, this is the reason why some central banks, concerned with systemic risk, already take considerable time and effort to familiarise themselves with market views on a wide range of issues.

Regulators are conscious of how market participants view them. Investors may be bad at looking ahead to new policy regimes, and markets penalise uncertainty. The consensus is thus normally for simple clear stable rules – something which monetary policymakers understand, but which does not always filter through to those responsible for other areas of regulation. Perceived regulatory competence, policy fashion, ideology, expected political interference, comprehensiveness and future reaction functions and bailout likelihoods and thus moral hazard, all affect a regulator's image. The structure of regulatory bodies matters, as does the degree of co-ordination between different policy objectives. Clear stable regulation is particularly important to reduce uncertainty over any threat to property rights, the bedrock of trust and incentive in an economy. Private contracts should not be interfered with. Policy with retroactive impact (normally an indication of prior policy failure) should be avoided except in extremis.

11.3   WISH LIST FOR EMERGING MARKET POLICYMAKERS

11.3.1   Allow markets to work

Equality before the law and strong property rights are the basis for economic incentives, and legislation and regulation should first strive to ensure these. With regulatory reform more and more economic activity in emerging economies is likely to enter the formal sector. As de Soto (2000, p. 240) says: '[m]uch behaviour that is today attributed to cultural heritage is not the inevitable result of people's ethnic or idiosyncratic traits but their rational evaluation of the relative costs and benefits of entering the legal property system.' De Soto has consulted governments across the developing world, helping them to establish property rights for the poor: clear transferable title against which debt can be raised to create jobs and wealth. It requires the correct policies and political will to fight the status quo. Changing institutions is not easy, as North tells us – more difficult than changing organisations. De Soto, echoing

Shakespeare's Dick the Butcher in *Henry IV*, even says of lawyers (p. 209): '[n]o group – aside from terrorists – is better positioned to sabotage capitalist expansion. And, unlike terrorists, the lawyers know how to do it legally.' The first job of the regulator is to avoid such statements being justified.

Then one needs to enable capital markets to work, which means more than just licensing some banks, but allowing financial entrepreneurship. As Shiller (2003, p. 2) says in introducing his book *The New Financial Order: Risk in the 21st Century*: 'Society can achieve a greater democratisation of finance and stabilisation of our economic lives through radical financial innovation. We must make this happen, given the economic uncertainty of our future at a time of global change and given the problems and inadequacies of today's financial arrangements.' He is thinking of the US, where arguably there has been too much of a good thing in some financial innovation. His sentiment is arguably of more potential impact in the developing world. A key priority is to build pension funds and banking systems without the problems in developed economies.

11.3.2   Proclaim and foster greater pricing power

After decades of movement the other way, one can ascribe the shift in terms of trade in favour of commodity producers starting in 2002 as largely a function of growing affluence and hence consumption in the developing world, principally in China and India. Increased incomes lead to greater meat and energy consumption, and more building, which is commodity-intensive. Urbanisation and industrialisation are increasing. These trends, moreover, are not likely to abate any time soon. The demographic transition is at different stages in different countries, but many emerging markets will retain young populations with low dependency ratios[7] for some decades. They will remain highly competitive in primary goods and simple manufacturing sectors, and in an increasing range of higher value-added sectors. The dominance of their own domestic markets for these goods – as well exports to other emerging markets not just to the developed world – means moreover that it will increasingly be the supply and demand conditions in the emerging markets which drive global goods prices.

The crisis in the HIDCs has probably accelerated the shift in pricing power to emerging countries. Emerging market companies are not merely cowering in the corner thinking how well they did to escape the worst of the financial crisis; they are taking global market share.

11.3.3   Promote EM global banks, south-south linkages

In terms of cross-border financial services, one might extrapolate from the brief history of investment banks in Chapter 3 that although Western incumbents have benefitted from strong barriers to entry for decades, this may be about to change (see Table 11.1). Emerging market banks may be able to enter and compete in the more commoditised financial services sectors as Western banks deleverage. In addition, one reason why US and European incumbents retained market share in the past was because of dominance in the areas of tacit knowledge, but as the partnerships have disappeared so too has the mechanism been weakened for passing this knowledge on to new generations.

---

[7] The ratio between the number of working age members of a population (typically assumed as those aged 15–64) to the total population.

Table 11.1   World's largest banks, (a) 2008 and (b) 2013. Source: relbanksinfo

(a) 31 December 2008

Number	Bank	Country	Total assets ($bn)
1	Royal Bank of Scotland	UK	3514.58
2	Barclays	UK	3004.33
3	Deutsche Bank	Germany	2895.50
4	BNP Paribas	France	2729.23
5	HSBC	UK	2527.47
6	JP Morgan Chase	US	2175.05
7	Credit Agricole	France	2173.89
8	Citigroup	US	1938.47
9	Mitsubishi UFJ Financial	Japan	1922.18
10	ING Group	Netherlands	1858.31
11	Bank of America	US	1817.94
12	UBS	Switzerland	1740.27
13	Mizuho Financial	Japan	1537.92
14	Societe Generale	France	1485.89
15	Banco Santander	Spain	1464.74

(b) 31 March 2013

Number	Bank	Country	Total assets ($bn)
1	Industrial & Commercial Bank of China (ICBC)	China	2953.85
2	HSBC Holdings	UK	2681.36
3	Deutsche Bank	Germany	2597.36
4	Credit Agricole Group	France	2582.42
5	BNP Paribas	France	2507.96
6	Mitsubishi UFJ Financial Group	Japan	2486.31
7	Barclays Plc	UK	2414.78
8	JP Morgan Chase & Co.	US	2389.35
9	China Construction Bank Corporation	China	2361.60
10	Japan Post Bank	Japan	2118.84
11	Agricultural Bank of China	China	2295.80
12	Bank of America	US	2174.61
13	Bank of China	China	2130.82
14	Royal Bank of Scotland Group	UK	1979.14
15	Citigroup Inc.	US	1881.73

More south-south trade, financial, investment and monetary links (already growing fast) should be encouraged, both to diversify economic linkages towards the fastest growing consumer markets in the world, but also to reduce global systemic risks. Greater cultural links can also foster business linkages and trust which are so integral to tacit knowledge in financial markets.

11.3.4   Build capital markets

Emerging countries are still relatively short of capital and need to build their capital markets as well as be satisfied that the capital is efficiently deployed. As markets expand, regulators need to ensure banks and other financial institutions are appropriately regulated, do not have large liability mismatches (including those which are assumed away by inappropriate risk model assumptions), are not excessively leveraged, and have agency problems identified and reduced or mitigated. Self-regulation should be encouraged but not simply assumed adequate – structure and incentives matter. Cross-border regulatory issues need to be co-ordinated and full domestic capital provisioning for foreign banks operating onshore considered in the light of future external pressures on foreign banks.

Foreign investors may be useful in domestic capital market development, not simply as a source of capital, but of expertise, and market heterogeneity and so liquidity, as well to verify to others market transparency, accountability and credibility.

Building domestic bond markets, starting with sovereign yield curves from which larger subsequent corporate issuance can price, can help disintermediate banks, and so reduce systemic risk in the financial system. Developing a local sovereign bond curve takes several years as described in Chapter 2, but reduces financing costs for the government and companies. The relative prices of information in these growing capital markets will determine institutional form and appropriate regulatory stance. For the larger economies building larger capital markets much tacit knowledge will be retained locally. The consequence may be dominant growth of local investment banks and boutiques, and the importance of local reputation in obtaining investment banking business. There may be a need for regulatory focus to encourage adequate self-regulation, as well as partnerships which can pass tacit knowledge on.

11.3.5   Fight core/periphery disease

If we reduce the distortions in our view of the economic planet – if we can mount a successful economic health programme against the devastating intellectual virus I call core/periphery disease – then we can perhaps reduce some of the risks of the most severe types which emanate from sudden and widespread risk perception changes. Hence emerging market policymakers should also think about policies which can counter core/periphery disease. This may include playing a responsible part in resolving global problems, as well as being more assertive in gaining recognition and voting rights in international bodies and forums. It also means fostering conditions allowing observers to make favourable parallels with developed world countries.

However, it most certainly means regulating domestic institutional savings pools without pandering to developed world conventions of 'risk-free' or the set of acceptable global asset classes. Emerging markets already have the bulk of global central bank reserves and are also experiencing rapid growth rates in institutionalised savings pools. As these pools of savings develop, so the logic of diversification of portfolios outside the national boundary is also asserting itself. However, this does not necessarily recommend allocation to the developed world, and certainly not exclusively. Yet the pattern so far is precisely that. Emerging market investors also suffer from core/periphery disease. Central banks would do well to lead by example, and stop squandering national resources by funding the US and Western Europe excessively cheaply. As investors and their regulators ponder investment abroad they will need to wean themselves off the core/periphery delusion just as their peers in the West also need to.[8]

This may, among other things, mean developing new rating agencies to assess sovereign risk and avoid Western efforts to bamboozle them into maintaining the core/periphery prejudice. China has already done this, establishing the Dagong rating agency. Others may follow, if only to guide their own pension funds away from the current deleveraging crash zone. This is no more than consistent with the already established growth in south-south trade and investment.

11.4   RESERVE MANAGEMENT AND THE INTERNATIONAL MONETARY SYSTEM

'The post-World War II recovery of Western Europe and Japan and now the emergence of China, India, and Brazil have reduced the economic dominance of the United States. It is not obvious why the dollar, the currency of an economy that no longer accounts for a majority of the world's industrial production, should be used to invoice and settle a majority of the world's international transactions. Nor is it clear why the dollar should still constitute a majority of the reserves of central banks and governments. As the world economy becomes more multipolar, its monetary system, logic suggests, should similarly become more multipolar.'

Eichengreen (2011, p. 121)

11.4.1   The dollar is your problem

In August 1971 at a conference in Rome US Treasury Secretary John Connally told European finance ministers that the dollar was 'our currency, but your problem'. This was the straw which broke the camel's back as far as European patience with the US was concerned, and heralded the collapse of confidence in the dollar and the end of dollar convertibility to gold. As mentioned in Chapter 1, the global monetary system set up in 1944 was, and remains, prone to the building of imbalances. Although, one way or another, the imbalances are likely to shrink over the next few years, if we do not reform the global monetary system we may yet experience a third post-WWII build-up of imbalances and a third crisis.

When the US held as dominant a share of global GDP as after WWII, the Triffin dilemma – the conflict faced when a central bank is central bank to both a single country and to the world – was nevertheless a problem. Today the US is still the largest and most influential economy, and likely to remain so for many years, but it no longer represents the approximately 50% of global GDP which it did in 1945. Since foreign exchange transactions no longer all go through central banks, and since the opening of not just current accounts in 1958 but capital

---

[8] This means for some central banks taking a loss on their existing portfolio of HIDC sovereign debt. But, rather like a losing trade, this is much better than denial, doing nothing and losing more.

accounts too since the Thatcher/Reagan era, the ability of central banks to compensate for building imbalances has dropped.

Until the growing importance of the emerging markets, optimists may have had reason to think that muddling through, characteristic since the creation of the gold pool, might suffice. The task of co-ordinating the central bank policies of a handful of European countries, the US and latterly Japan worked for a while, even when some major adjustments were required as with adjustments to the ERM[9] and the Plaza and Louvre Accords.[10] Despite events in 1971, one could argue that the lesson of that experience had been learned and the lack of dollar convertibility to gold after 1971 enabled the avoidance of major currency misalignments building. 1971 certainly represents a watershed, after which the era of unconstrained global fiat money began. However, the risk of imbalances building had not gone away, and without the discipline of fixity to gold or anything else except each other's currencies from time to time, central banks had both greater freedom to alter exchange rates and a harder job of persuading markets of their commitment to sound money. Since then, the policy history of hard and soft pegging to the deutschmark and dollar has been as much to anchor market expectations about the willingness to raise interest rates to defend currencies as it has been about maintaining foreign exchange stability for the sake of international trade.

The optimism that the world of fiat money since 1971 was being successfully navigated was encapsulated by the idea of the 'Great Moderation'. We may, more cynically with hindsight, ascribe the calm before the storm as largely due to the build-up of global imbalances as Asian savings pushed down Western yield curves, enabling current account deficits and profligacy, and creating artificial measurements of risk and a false and unsustainable sense of well-being.

The importance of emerging markets today means nobody should be in doubt any longer that we must tackle the Triffin dilemma – specifically the current dominance of the dollar in the international monetary system. Otherwise further imbalances will build and further crises develop. If the co-ordination of a handful of European central banks in the era of the gold pool proved impossible to sustain, what hope of co-ordinating so many more countries in the Dollar-is-King game, which fewer and fewer believe can work for much longer and which many find against their longer-term national interests?

Continued maintenance of the dollar as the central feature of the international monetary system would require not only a reduction of current global imbalances, but measures to avoid a repeat – i.e. a credible commitment by the US Federal Reserve to subjugate the domestic interests in determining monetary policy to the global interests. This seems politically inconceivable.

11.4.2   Alternatives to the dollar

To avoid Triffin's dilemma, global reserves should be issued as needed into the global economy, not all into one country which may or may not be moving in line with the global economy. Moreover, it should be the correct amount of liquidity for the global economy, not what is convenient for a few – as with quantitative easing. The task is not therefore to find

---

[9] The Exchange Rate Mechanism of the European Monetary System, precursor to the euro.

[10] In both occasions these accords were successful because they were pushing an open door – the adjustments targeted may have happened soon anyway. The fortuitous combination of factors enabling success cannot be counted on to occur. See Lawson (2010) for an illuminating inside account.

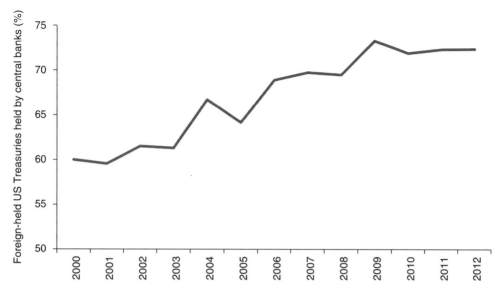

Figure 11.1   Percentage of foreign-held US Treasuries held by central banks. Source: IMF

an alternative existing national currency to the dollar, but to find a true global alternative for reserve managers.

A traditional stumbling block to progressing towards this is concern about liquidity. As discussed, this can change suddenly, always negatively, and is a function of the collective behaviour of many different actors. There is no easy way to establish what future liquidity may be, but there are our three warning signals: investor homogeneity/segmentation; vulnerable misperception of risk; and leverage. The US Treasury market displays the first two characteristics, having central banks as the dominant foreign holders (see Figure 11.1) and being perceived as 'risk-free' in an environment where this is becoming increasingly seen as a misnomer. The wider US economy, but not US Treasuries, at least partially fulfils the third. Central banks are aware of their own herding in 1971, creating the downfall of the dollar then, as well as their collective rush out of gold in 1999. Financial repression can add to the risks by increasing the homogeneity of an investor base – corralling some types of investor to buy keeps yields unattractive for others. In a Treasury buyers' strike the Federal Reserve might step in to provide some temporary liquidity, but this may not be sustainable or conducive to restoring private sector demand. It could not on its own stop the dollar sliding, which is the likely scenario should central banks be selling their Treasuries into other currencies.

So while the US Treasury market has been liquid, this may not be the case in all future scenarios. Yet the motive for central banks investing in liquid assets is that they be liquid when most needed: in a crisis when many other central banks are also potential sellers. Excluding some scenarios from one's assessment because they are unpleasant can be a false economy. So it is with a US Treasury liquidity/dollar crash scenario.

It is an unpleasant thought that US Treasuries may not provide the necessary liquidity for the world's now very large stock of reserves. Were reserves lower, as in the past, this might not be such a problem. Were significantly less reserves in dollars, illiquidity scenarios might also be less of a concern. Given the unpleasant thought, however, it does not answer to simply consider another single national currency as a viable alternative. The argument to remain wedded to the dollar because no other currency is as liquid is a 'straw man' argument. Instead one needs either a new currency which is not a national one but represents better the weights of the global economy, so avoiding the Triffin dilemma, or a multi-currency reserve system.

A desirable feature to look for in a new global currency would be high liquidity. There are two alternatives: a commodity (presumably gold) or a basket of existing currencies. The inconvenience of returning to the gold standard for most countries (the majority of which have neither a domestic supply nor a significant stockpile) is likely to make this course almost impossible to agree, even if one could overcome the paucity of supply which was one of the objections to its readoption in 1944.

Alternatively, a new currency could be a basket of existing currencies, such as an augmented SDR.[11] However, I am highly sceptical about there being the necessary political will to make the SDR a global currency. The level of international agreement to establish widespread use of a new global currency should be seen in the context of the consistent inability to adjust shareholding in the IMF to something vaguely representative of global economic and trading weights. The IMF's SDR was originally a broader basket of 16 currencies, but this was reduced to four – the US dollar, sterling, euro and yen – in large part to assist in its de facto main role as the IMF's unit of account. Though there have been countries which have pegged their currencies to the SDR, the SDR itself needs to be converted into the underlying currencies before wider use. It has very poor liquidity, and even were its issuance expanded significantly, this structural feature would need to be addressed. For its widespread adoption its component weights would need to be seen as legitimate representations of global economic activity. Yet the IMF is an institution perceived by many emerging countries as an exclusive US/European club, the principal services of which they do not expect to use again. It is hard to see the SDR becoming liquid enough as a reserve currency to pose a threat to the dollar or be its successor.[12]

A much more likely alternative to the dollar, and one which does not require international agreement on relative weights, or involve using any central body as some sort of adjudicator is a multi-currency system. Countries should choose to weight their reserves holdings more broadly, and to a large extent in accordance with their trade weights with other countries, or even future expected trade weights.

This entails less liquidity than desired, but may not in practice mean a reduction in liquidity attainable today in the most stressed scenarios central banks need to plan for. It needs to be recognised that the liquidity central banks have been habitually assuming they could rely on in the US Treasury market is probably unobtainable. The consequence is that central banks also need to think through scenarios as I have already recommended for investors; and in doing so they need to reassess their objectives for reserve management and reduce the

---

[11] The IMF Special Drawing Right (SDR) is a basket currency used for internal IMF accounting but which was originally intended also as a potential reserve currency.

[12] In April 2009 the G20 approved a further 250 billion of SDR issuance (subsequently distributed in proportion to IMF shareholdings). The events leading up to this however are open to interpretation. One credible explanation is as follows. Not wanting to be blamed for causing a dollar crash should they exit the dollar, the Chinese proposed the SDR issuance. If the US rejected the proposal (as they initially intimated) then they could hardly blame the Chinese for what might follow. The relatively small issuance of SDR250 billion was not a substantive threat to the dollar, and so the US dropped its objection. The SDR should perhaps not be interpreted (as it has been by many) as a realistic long-term alternative to the dollar because of this 2009 decision.

priority given to (past or theoretical) liquidity. Stiglitz (2010, p. 234) is one of those who predicts a multi-currency system is likely without an agreement on a new global reserve system. He is not alone in worrying that it may create a 'regime more unstable than the current system in the long term' – maybe so, but one probably less likely to cause the occasional global financial crisis as in 2008. Things which look stable may give rise to building pressures which then explode – let us have the more unstable system Stiglitz worries about if it avoids more occasional global financial catastrophes.

The final defences of the use of the dollar amount largely to a combination of habit and money illusion. The psychological desire to avoid change is strong but needs to be overcome by reason. The argument against adoption that a multi-currency system is more complex mathematically to administer is contradicted by the ease of use of computers. That exporters invoice in dollars, and so demand dollars from the central bank can be changed by persuading them to invoice in other currencies.

That liquidity or access is limited in some alternative currencies is also likely to change. If central banks invest more in each other's currencies, these will become both more stable and more liquid. It is often thought that full currency convertibility is a pre-requisite for reserve currency status. Yet this is contradicted by the experience of the deutschmark, which was a reserve currency before it was convertible. The key is access for other central banks, not necessarily for the wider market. Wider private market access can follow. And this need not preclude greater liquidity either. Market liquidity can remain in offshore non-deliverable forward markets (common for countries with capital controls) but then switch into new onshore forwards markets. This policy transformation can be executed gradually. Eichengreen (2010, p. 97) refers to Japan's experience when he says:

> '[t]his history does not suggest that it is necessary to finish liberalising the capital account and developing the interbank forward market before moving to a more flexible exchange rate. It suggests that corporations can hedge at least some of their exposures despite the maintenance of residual capital controls. It suggests that the development of forward-market liquidity is, at least in part, endogenous to the monetary regime; greater flexibility will help to produce the larger volume of transactions desired by the authorities.'

11.4.3   Too many reserves

In 2013 we have imbalances in the global macroeconomy, following the build-up of large emerging market central bank reserves. These reserves not only need to be diversified away from the dollar; they are also unnecessarily large in some cases. Eight reasons why central banks should sell dollars and allow their currencies to appreciate were presented in Chapter 3. At time of writing there has been some movement by emerging market central banks to buy each other's bonds and so diversify reserves, but this was limited and slow after 2008. There has been no discernible reduction in the size of reserves. Why?

There was a strong desire to maintain the status quo and not disrupt the dollar initially after 2008 – it was widely understood that the US Federal Reserve needed time and stability to recapitalise banks and large currency movements could have dented fragile market confidence, and so investment and growth. Also, until the end of 2010 there was very little inflation in emerging countries, which of the eight earlier listed motives is the one requiring prompt action. And when inflation did come in the form of food price inflation, there was uncertainty over its permanence and pass-through effects on inflation expectations. Then in August 2011 there were concerns about the US debt ceiling and from September major uncertainties in Europe which kept central banks from bold changes in reserve policy – again to avoid unnerving fragile global market sentiment. Meanwhile inflation pressure had abated.

So-called 'currency wars', though ostensibly north-south, are arguably mostly south-south. As emerging market trade flows and rivalry for third markets shift more towards each other, most notably towards China, and in the growing acknowledgment by central banks that the dollar is likely to depreciate over time to redress global imbalances, so the focus is on the timing of the moves by other emerging central banks. Brazil, for example, is a substantially closed economy, but one whose principal exports are commodities. Manufacturers may be uncompetitive, due to domestic infrastructure deficiencies as much as the exchange rate, but they are also capable of lobbying the government and the media to complain about the exchange rate. Yet the competitive pressure they face is largely from Asian economies such as South Korea. So if the central bank wishes to placate them, the exchange rates with Asian economies would seem more apt as targets than the dollar. Indeed, Brazil's trade with China alone is around double what it is with the United States. The Brazilian central bank could purchase Korean won, for example, thus exerting upward pressure on the won. This could be funded by selling dollars. The Koreans could reciprocate by buying Brazilian reals. In similar fashion, many emerging markets could buy each other's currencies to maintain competitiveness, and fund such purchases mostly by selling dollars. In this way a gradual global rebalancing may be achieved without much formal co-ordination. Emerging market currency liquidity will increase, mitigating current liquidity concerns. Central banks maybe want others to show the way in allowing appreciation, but also don't want to be the last to hold a concentrated portfolio of devaluing HIDC currencies.

Too many emerging markets are now massive net creditors but still thinking like debtors; worried about cross-border flows which they do nothing to counter when they should be using reserves to create stability; worrying about current account deficits when they should be importing capital; thinking about macroeconomic balances which pose little threat when they should be focusing on how supply-side structural reforms can aid entrepreneurship, growth and employment. They also have too many reserves.

The task of globally responsible and co-ordinated central banks and other policymakers is to ensure these imbalances reduce gradually without sudden, possibly catastrophic, adjustments. It is to avoid a similar scenario to 1971, whether by gradual modification of reserve holdings as just outlined or more explicit (G20) co-ordination.

11.5   WHAT INVESTORS CAN EXPECT FROM HIDC POLICYMAKERS

We list here some possible policy measures coming principally from HIDC policymakers. At the time of writing these should be considered scenarios rather than predictions.

11.5.1   Financial repression

We should expect more measures to capture domestic savings, including pension, insurance and bank regulations to force buying of 'risk-free' assets, and if the ratings agencies downgrade HIDC sovereign bonds, we can expect regulators to come up with new definitions of what is 'risk-free' to ensure the bonds are still bought. There have even been noises in Brussels about creating a new rating agency should the existing ones have the temerity to downgrade EU sovereigns.

The prospect of financial repression means negative real interest rates in HIDC countries for a while and no early increase in short-term interest rates – or not unless or until financial repression fails to work effectively. The desire to control inflation is not the same as before; inflation is intended to be higher than interest rates so as to erode the real value of government debt.

Financial repression is thus not in the interests of savers – the owners of the capital being repressed. Capturing savings and keeping interest rates artificially low results in lower savings rates. It can also divert savings into equity and housing-market asset bubbles. The resulting concentration of exposures in overbought developed market government securities increases risk. It increases the concentration of portfolios. A wider awareness of the financial repression characteristics of various policy measures is the first step to trying to reduce the repression. Investors may be advised to avoid financial repression through exiting certain markets and savings pools affected or at risk.

For foreign investors there is a small risk of future capital controls being imposed (on those not persuadable using tax, regulatory actions and threats) to prevent capital repatriation and 'bail in' foreign investors on the same terms as domestic ones. Emerging market central banks are at risk of having their arms twisted to help the HIDCs. It behooves them to be alert to developments which may end with them facing policies to tax or prevent repatriation of their investments, or more likely, reputational damage should they do so. Better to reduce holdings gradually and early, realise and use bargaining power to gain concessions for staying invested, and start voicing concerns both to lobby against financial repression, but also to reduce the risk of future reputational damage should they pull the plug on the Eurozone or the US at a later date.

11.5.2   Consequences of financial repression for banks

Western banks wanting to deleverage often prefer to do so at home and not to lose market share in the emerging markets, which they rightly see as more promising markets longer term. That some have withdrawn anyway from emerging markets is evidence that financial repression is biting hard, forcing them to do so. A consequence is that non-HIDC banks can take market share in emerging markets.

This withdrawal was preceded by another distortion caused by the need to raise capital back home: in Central Europe post-2008 some Western European banks, desperate for short-term funds at home, were offering unsustainably large deposit rates for depositors at their Central European subsidiaries, thus displacing local bank competition and distorting the domestic savings market. A greater focus on local branch bank capitalisation is a likely response.

11.5.3   No early exit from quantitative easing?

The endgame for quantitative easing is unclear, but it is linked to the ability to sustain financial repression. Stopping further growth of quantitative easing is not too problematic, but as discussed earlier, exit from quantitative easing might be botched should bonds held by central banks not prove liquid enough to sell before interest rates rise. I suspect the preference for many policymakers is to continue rolling quantitative easing for many years in conjunction with financial repression which gradually erodes the real value of government debt.

11.5.4   Bond crash

Keeping inflation a couple of percentage points above interest rates for a decade or so is not likely to prove easy. Financial markets are more complex and less controlled than after World War II. There is a risk that markets will at some point respond en masse to negative real interest rates, and will demand higher returns on HIDC sovereign debt. Quantitative easing was designed to repair bank balance sheets. At some point these banks may feel healthy enough to pump credit into the economy again in volume. A growth spurt might then put central banks on the spot and lead to clearer evidence of reluctance to fight inflation while national indebtedness (but also central bank balance sheets) are so high. Thus a major steepening of HIDC yield curves could occur, so reducing governments' abilities to finance themselves. A steeper yield curve indicates higher replacement cost of debt, and potentially reduced creditworthiness, further raising bond yields. In other words the bond market yields could 'blow out' in a bond market crash.

11.5.5   Inflation

Should HIDC central banks not raise interest rates sufficiently when inflationary pressure rears its head, and should central bank credibility in the fight against inflation be damaged, the resultant pattern of inflation could look similar to that in the 1970s. With that comes the possibility of increased volatility and uncertainty in markets, myopic and short-lived policies, vociferous politics over relative goods and labour prices, currency devaluation and even bottlenecks and shortages. The task of government and monetary authorities alike will be to sanction some inflation, but not let it get carried away. A greater role of the state in controlling prices is possible, as is protectionism.

11.5.6   Appeals to foreign investors

We can expect more attempts by HIDC governments to promote foreign inward investment, especially into infrastructure projects otherwise starved of government funding due to fiscal tightening. Foreign investors who have been burnt before, buying into HIDC banks in particular post-2008, should be wary about future tariff and other policy changes – though deals may be there to be made at the right prices.

11.5.7   Regulatory muddle-through

The greater focus on systemic risk is likely to lead to more regulation, but some of this will conflict with existing (and in aggregate pro-cyclical) regulation applied to individual financial institutions. Regulators may try to protect non-expert investors, but in doing so pander to existing prejudices of what is and what is not safe. Regulation of insurance companies and pension funds should be less of a copy of bank regulation – though the logic of financial repression is pushing in the other direction for now. Cross-border regulatory co-ordination will likely continue to be more a dream than a reality, leading to more country-specific regulation, including full local bank capitalisation of foreign banks.

11.5.8   Pension reform

At some point it is to be hoped that pension funds will be regulated differently so that pensioners' interests are better looked after. More financial repression followed by a decade of inflation in particular may focus minds. Unfortunately it will probably take that, and that long. Liabilities need to be assessed in terms of future purchasing power. Pension funds need to be aware well in advance of such a change – which could arrive in a single piece of legislation at any time should public awareness of the issue grow.

Regulation also needs to allow if not encourage: the use of a much broader investment universe; less reliance on traditional asset class definitions; and less use of indices for asset allocation. Incentives and behavioural biases should instruct regulatory policy more. Anti-herding incentives should be adopted – following the herd should not be a usable defence for those who have lost money.

11.5.9   Pension regulatory conflict may only abate once EM investors exit

At some point central banks and other emerging market investors will stop subsidising HIDCs by investing so heavily in US Treasuries and other HIDC government bonds, which currently pushes down HIDC governments' costs of capital. Emerging market-owned capital will be redeployed back home and to other emerging markets, and so reduce their cost of capital while that for HIDCs rises (other things being equal).

When this happens, and trying to attract emerging markets capital back to HIDCs becomes futile (once you are convinced you are being robbed, albeit slowly, you are not easily prepared to resubmit yourself to the same treatment again), the conflict in the HIDCs between funding the state cheaply and looking after pensioners may reduce. HIDC policymakers may be more inclined to reform their concepts of risk and encourage longer-term pensions to be benchmarked against probable future (purchasing power defined) liabilities. This is not to say that the conflict between looking after tomorrow's pensioners and financing the government cheaply today disappears, but that the balance in the trade-off will shift once the additional reason for keeping government funding costs super-low (at the cost of reducing pensioners' future incomes) disappears. In other words, as HIDC governments find it more difficult to pull the wool over the eyes of emerging market investors, so it may be in their interests to stop trying so hard to do the same to their own future retirees.

11.5.10   Rating agencies

The credibility of rating agencies has been damaged by the sub-prime crisis, yet their sovereign ratings are being used by regulators for financial repression. At some point, however, reform is likely. The obvious reform is to re-establish that ratings not be paid for by the rated.

11.5.11   Intellectual reassessment

Instead of despairing about the parlous state of finance theory but using it anyway, we should expect some movement towards the use of some of the ideas in this book. This will happen only gradually, as prejudice often dies only with the holder of the prejudice.

With this comes the realisation that the emperor's new clothes are not as fabulous as advertised: that policymakers have not done enough to control banks, and have been saying one thing and thinking another about quantitative easing, financial repression and inflation.

11.6   WHAT INVESTORS CAN EXPECT FROM EMERGING MARKET POLICYMAKERS

Prediction is always hazardous, but drawing together what we have said in the book so far, the following is a brief summary of what investors can perhaps expect from emerging market policymakers:

1. Emerging market central banks are likely to be more active in their use of reserves and key to global exchange rates in the medium term.
2. Emerging market central banks with large reserves may continue to be complacent and allow their currencies to be impacted by modest external events, but if faced with a large shock they can be expected to act to defend their currencies, possibly causing significant dollar weakness.
3. Central banks are most likely to change reserve allocations by diversifying away from the dollar. In so doing they will reduce the systemic risk in the global monetary system. They are likely to diversify more towards emerging market currencies and more in line with relative weights in global GDP. This will result in increased liquidity and stability in larger emerging market currencies.
4. Reserve diversification in many emerging markets will probably follow China's lead. Reserve managers are loath to appreciate faster than their export competitors, but equally do not want to be left behind holding all the devaluing currencies. China and others seem to be already moving towards matching foreign currency reserves to better represent their trade flows, but they are likely to go beyond this as perceptions of risk change further.
5. Countries will encourage invoicing in their own currencies and those of export partners, reducing the use of the dollar, and so the call on central bank-held dollars in crises.
6. South–South monetary flows, including bilateral and multilateral central bank swap lines, will expand.
7. Moving to a multi-currency international monetary system as a result of this action will reduce global monetary systemic risk through reducing the Triffin dilemma problem – i.e. by reducing dependence on US domestic monetary policy.
8. Emerging markets may become more assertive in international economic issues and politics, and less tolerant of under-representation in international bodies. As the benefits become clearer they are also likely to co-ordinate their actions more. If reform of existing international bodies is not forthcoming, I expect more exclusively emerging market international institutional initiatives (such as the BRICS bank and Asian Monetary Fund initiatives).
9. The tendency in some emerging markets, including China, will (continue) to be to move away from export-led growth to more domestic consumer demand-led growth.
10. Should HIDC protectionism rear its head, emerging markets are likely to retaliate but foster greater free trade with each other, as well as move faster to domestic consumer-demand-led models of growth.

11. While there may be more examples of 'macroprudential' regulations to insulate domestic markets from flighty foreign capital, capital controls to alter exchange rates are not expected to become more popular with policymakers – largely because they do not work and may cause unwanted side effects.

12. Foreign investment from developed countries will be welcomed not solely because of the need for capital, but also to help transparency in local capital markets and catalyse domestic investors. Regulators are also likely to start paying more attention to the sources of capital – the structure of investor bases – and to favour longer-term unleveraged sources of capital. Strategic foreign direct investment involving skills or technology transfers will continue to be welcomed, but so will liquidity-enhancing portfolio investment of the right type.

13. Substantial aid recipients in sub-Saharan African countries may continue to have difficulty in attracting cheap corporate overseas debt funding until they develop liquid sovereign yield curves. It is hoped aid donors recognise this in their attempts to help catalyse inward private investment.

14. I anticipate more actions to facilitate private infrastructure investment, given the needs are far greater than can be met by traditional government-led investment.

15. In order to attract more catalytic foreign capital I expect more focus on appropriate competition and merger and acquisition regulations, transparent stock market rules, and domestic consumer protection/advertising standards.

16. Emerging market regulators have greater motive and so may be the first to counter core/periphery disease in asset allocation, and we may see new sovereign ratings agencies, less biased towards high ratings for HIDCs.

12

Conclusion

12.1 A FINAL LIST...

Below is another brief concluding list, complementary to the one at the end of Chapter 11, predicting some non-policy-driven trends which may be of interest to investors. They are very general and I am not brave (or foolhardy) enough to attach detailed numbers with time-frames: continuous scenario planning requires that such matters be constantly reassessed.

1. Investors can expect emerging economies to continue their trend towards a greater share in the global economy, with all that that entails.
2. Globalisation will continue to open up opportunities for emerging markets and be viewed more ambiguously in the developed world. Emerging market labour will compete with developed country workers either directly (subject to immigration policies) or indirectly via global goods markets. This may pressure the financing of Western welfare states, and stimulate higher productivity growth and innovation in many Western economies. There will also, however, be a combination of complacency and resistance to this competition.
3. As emerging market economic production enters higher-technology product areas, so developed countries will continue to specialise in international export markets in the highest value-added sectors. But even finance, higher education and film and media industries (industries with high barriers to entry and incumbent market power) will face increased competition from emerging markets as the emerging market middle-class consumers grow. To be successful may increasingly require partnering with emerging markets, even in high technology sectors, as we have already started to see with, for example, outsourcing of software writing and medical trials.
4. Emerging market demographics, and in particular the rapid growth of young middle classes with discretionary income, will have a large influence on global relative prices in commodities and a wide range of goods. We can expect more housing-related purchases as young populations enter the housing market in large numbers for the first time, and similarly in telecoms, media and mass consumption goods.
5. South–South trade and investment are set to continue to grow rapidly, approaching proportions more in line with relative global GDP weights.
6. Infrastructure investment is likely to increase substantially in many emerging markets, together with affordable housing. Such investment has the potential scale to boost economic growth at a global level. Implementation may involve capital and experience in some emerging markets being deployed in others, and a far greater reliance on private capital than in the past.
7. Should large-scale infrastructure investment take place, this is likely to support the upward trend in terms of trade for energy and commodities.

8. Institutional saving will increase rapidly, and emerging market pension funds, which are starting to invest overseas, will eventually match and then surpass developed world pension funds in size.

9. The rapid growth in pension funds and other institutional savings pools, once these invest in more than domestic emerging market government debt, will help build domestic emerging market corporate debt markets, mortgage markets, derivatives markets and equity markets.

10. Capital markets will grow faster than GDP in many emerging markets, with rapid further near-term growth in local currency-denominated corporate debt markets in particular. Both domestic and international demand for listed stocks will enable rapid expansion of listed entities, whereas corporate debt markets will also be driven by the desire to disintermediate banks.

11. Private equity opportunities are likely to attract more international interest, particularly as investors move towards GDP weighting in their portfolio allocations. I suspect the successful private equity models will be more focused on working with local partners and less dependent on leverage than the traditional US private equity model. We may see models develop of private equity investing helping to accelerate stock market listing pipelines.

12. Emerging market banks will also grow rapidly domestically. Some will take international market share, either through organic growth or through buying developed world banks.

13. Investors will discriminate more between different countries and different asset classes within them. Whether a country has a strong local investor base will be seen as an important dividing line between the more and less prone to external shocks.

14. Behavioural finance will expand further as a discipline and, together with further focus on agency problems, will have greater impact on the institutional arrangements of how money is managed and how markets are regulated.

15. Concepts of risk may change rapidly, particularly for those already engaging in double-think. The exclusive focus on volatility and on concepts of 'risk-free' and 'investible' and even the perceived usefulness of 'spreads' will give way to ideas of relative risk, and risk being different from investor to investor, greater focus on extreme events leading to permanent loss, and the distinction between risk and uncertainty. This will engender much more complexity in the investment world – complexity which through its diversity can help create greater robustness and reduce global systemic risks.

16. The structures of investor bases, and their links to liquidity crises, will receive more attention from investors, and policymakers focused on reducing systemic risk. Again, this will help increase market complexity and robustness.

17. Investor liability assessments will focus more on future purchasing power, particularly should high inflation become a likely scenario.

18. Core/periphery disease will change gradually, and patterns of changing perceptions will continue to create many opportunities for investors who perceive them.

19. Investment will continue to be hazardous, but investors thinking more strategically and employing investment processes which include the full sum of available knowledge including macroeconomics, politics and history, will continue to have a potential advantage over those who do not. Macroeconomic analysis in particular should be at the forefront of asset allocation.

20. With greater adherence to the ideas in this book, it may be that investors better appreciate the huge diversity of risks as well as opportunities in emerging markets, and be more

comfortable in taking those risks: in the process employing more people and more productively than otherwise would be the case.

12.2 ... FOR AN UPSIDE DOWN WORLD

'Taking a new step, uttering a new word, is what people fear most.'

Dostoevsky, *Crime and Punishment* (1866)

A reason for wanting to write a book both practical and theoretical is that the two seem so disjointed today. To write a book criticising investment practice is not novel, and neither is one criticising finance theory; but one criticising both is an attempt to make both criticisms more meaningful.

This book has covered a lot of ground. It includes a history of emerging markets, reasons to invest in them, a description of how asset management is currently conducted, a critique of finance theory, my own assessment of some of the major global economic issues at time of writing, and some policy recommendations and predictions. Many of the predictions will no doubt soon look outdated and wrong. However, they form part of my thinking, as do the other components just listed – all are interconnected.

I do not have any simple formula for investing. But I am sure that current orthodoxy is often not just unhelpful, but deeply misleading. I am sure that there is no substitute for thinking investment and asset allocation through in much more detail than is often the case. I am sure that investors are unjustifiably biased against emerging markets. And I am sure of the power of ideas to change this, not least as so much is built on misperception and prejudice.

Those who associate my name with emerging markets and bought the book on the strength of it are, I hope, not disappointed by the broader threads I have woven. My aim is to insist that emerging markets are central to many wider issues, not to be categorised as peripheral or separate from mainstream international and global debates. Emerging markets have ever greater impact on developed economies and markets. Even for those stubbornly uninterested in investing in emerging markets, they are ever more important for understanding the risks in the markets they do invest in.

The world is upside down. As I said in Chapter 2, I define emerging markets not by risk but by risk perception. All countries are risky: the emerging markets are those where this is priced in. Developed countries have more dysfunctional markets – in which a significant portion of the investor base does not even think about their own sovereign risk. Because prejudice is so powerful, this reality may be eroded but will not disappear for decades. In the meantime we can expect highly attractive investment opportunities in emerging markets to continue. It takes more than a few years to replace a prejudice as strong as what I have called 'core/periphery disease' with a more balanced view of the planet. In the meantime, those who understand that the world is upside down and can act on this knowledge will have an advantage over those who do not.

Further Research

Further research avenues present themselves, many already identified. A brief list of some avenues is provided below:

- Further research could be conducted on when volatility may be a good proxy for risk and when not.
- There is need for more research on investment choice and choice architecture. How does the availability of products on offer affect the choice of eligible asset classes?
- How does one adjust for biases? How do we incorporate into asset allocation the range of behavioural biases we know of? How can we use our knowledge of these biases to structure decisionmaking, and change institutional structures and incentives so as to make better investment decisions?
- There is scope for considerably more research on principal/agent chains in the investment industry, and how these may be improved.
- Regulating agency problems from a systemic risk point of view is also an avenue worthy of study, starting with something as simple as training and incentives for fiduciaries. If a fiduciary invests in the equivalent of a Madoff investment or Icelandic bank without proper due diligence it should not be an acceptable excuse, as in practice it largely is today, that others did the same.
- There is scope for research on the benefits of non-pecuniary incentives such as honour and duty as a means to combat principal/agent distortions.
- There is also ample scope for research into the design of dynamic rules for definition and acceptance of new asset classes into an investor's universe of eligible investments – an area that currently appears largely ad hoc and momentum driven.
- How to improve on the staged investment process of asset allocation followed by manager selection and mental accounting deserves more research. The consequences of allocating in a world with an unknown 'market portfolio' could be investigated further, building on prospect theory and my 'entrepreneurial' approach to asset allocation.
- Asset/liability management would be aided both by making the measurement of liabilities more dynamic, and from better understanding of utility functions, possibly acquirable through questionnaires designed to reveal the trade-offs in preferences between different scenarios – for example, do trustees prefer, say, a 2% increase in contributions now or a 20% chance of becoming underfunded in 5 years.

- Asset/liability management is beset by money illusion – more research into this may be a prelude to reducing it.
- The structure of an investor base can be researched at various levels – knowing who holds what is not as useful as also knowing their liabilities and behavioural traits. Knowing leverage levels is also important for both investors and regulators.
- Structural change may occur in perceptions of risk and of the world (in the prejudice layer), not just in the domains of macroeconomic aggregates and policy dynamics. Therefore we also need to map and understand investment prejudices better and what may change them.
- From various mapping exercises into the structure of investor bases (including ones emphasising principal/agent chains – incentive maps), research could focus on the dynamics of financial market networks and how resilient they are to macroeconomic shocks, systemic deleveraging, new memes or other changed conditions. Better maps could be used to test models using network, game and other theories in more satisfactory ways than at present.
- More research to understand investor base structure may also be focused on combating systemic risk by identifying priority areas for international co-ordination.
- In general, how should macroeconomic dynamics and structural changes be incorporated into asset allocation? I have suggested some ideas which may loosely be called a framework for this, but some empirical identification of key imbalances and leading indicators may be possible.
- I favour strategic thinking as a continuous process, not an exercise to carry out once every few years only. Scenario planning should perhaps be more widely used. Consultants and advisers could do more to emphasise this. Rating agencies might be encouraged to offer scenarios, or at least more sophisticated views concerning timescales. Better frameworks could be researched and developed to enable investors to consider a range of scenarios in their decisionmaking.
- Another subject worthy of more research is how to re-foster self-regulation in finance, particularly in the investment bank. This should be a clearer objective than perhaps the existing emphasis on limiting the amount of dynamite they can each have.
- For emerging market regulators the optimal path of development of capital markets should be researched and thought through carefully on a country-specific basis, as in many instances it already is.

Disclaimer

Glossary

Asset class – A grouping of financial securities (assets) with similar characteristics.

BIS – The Bank for International Settlements (BIS), which serves as a bank for central banks, helping foster both international co-operation and monetary and fiscal stability of individual central banks.

Bonds – A bond is a debt security, under which the issuer owes the holders a debt and, depending on the terms of the bond, is obliged to pay them interest (the coupon) and to repay the principal at a later date (the maturity). Interest is usually payable at fixed intervals, typically semi-annual or annual. The ownership of the bond can be transferred in the secondary market.

Brady bond – Brady bonds were dollar-denominated Eurobonds issued in sovereign debt restructurings in exchange for existing debt – mostly distressed short-term bank loans. They were issued mostly by Latin American governments from the late 1980s in accordance with national Brady plans (named after then US Treasury Secretary Nicholas Brady). A Brady plan also entailed new official lending to the country, conditional on macroeconomic and structural reforms.

Bretton Woods – Bretton Woods in 1944 was the setting for the construction of a new global monetary architecture that included the initiation of the World Bank and the IMF.

BRIC – The term BRIC is an acronym for four major emerging market economies: Brazil, Russia, India and China.

Call option – A call option gives the holder the right, but not the obligation, to buy an agreed quantity of a particular commodity or financial instrument from the seller of the option at a certain time for a certain price.

Capital controls – Capital controls restrict cross-border capital inflows or outflows to or from an economy's domestic capital markets. Changing rules to restrict capital outflows strongly discourages future inflows. Policy debate more typically focuses on using capital controls to restrict inflows which might be destabilising.

CAPM – The capital asset pricing model (CAPM) is a standard model for assessing if a security should be included in a portfolio. It does this through calculating the rate of return for the security and comparing this to expected rates of return for securities of similar 'risk'. The CAPM is based upon modern portfolio theory and highly sensitive to assumptions of comparable risk.

CDO – A collateralised debt obligation (CDO) is an asset-backed legal entity which finances purchases of assets through issues of various tranches of debt with different seniorities. In the event of a series of defaults in the underlying securities, more senior tranches are repaid in full before more junior ones receive any repayments. This effectively provides greater security for the more senior tranches (which are often given high credit ratings as a result) and leverage to the potentially higher-performing junior tranches. Defaulting mortgaged-backed CDOs were a major source of financial contagion during the 2008 financial crisis.

CDS – A credit default swap (CDS) is a financial derivative which is referenced to an underlying security. The holder pays the issuer a sum at the start of the contract and is paid a specified sum by the issuer if the underlying security defaults. In theory, the CDS price should thus move with a similar dynamic to the underlying security, except the underlying security may have a non-zero recovery value post-default.

CEMENT – Countries in emerging markets excluded by new terminology is a term used to describe emerging markets other than the BRICs (Brazil, Russia, India and China). Why invest in four countries when one can invest in 64?

Co-variance – Co-variance is related to correlation. The co-variance between two variables, x and y, $S_{xy} = r.S_x.S_y$ where r is their coefficient of correlation and S_x and S_y the standard deviations of x and y, respectively.

Credit crunch – A credit crunch is systemic crisis characterised by many significant lending institutions facing major reductions in access to credit, which in turn reduces their ability to extend credit to others. Being cut off from credit lines by each other, the affected financial institutions in turn also cut credit to their non-lending clients, and may become insolvent.

CTA – A commodity trading fund (CTA) is either a hedge fund, or their adviser, regulated by the US Commodity Futures Trading Commission (CTFC), typically investing in a wide range of commodities and futures and often employing automated quantitative trading strategies.

Duration – Duration is the average term of the payments of a bond, expressed in years, and weighted by the size of the payments. A discount rate (the interest rate) is applied across the life of a bond to estimate the current price – the sum of the net present values of the bond's stream of future payments. A bond's duration is thus also the percentage change (one year equating to one percent) in the value of the bond caused by a one percent move in the discount rate.

Dutch disease – Dutch disease, named after events in the Netherlands following the discovery of natural gas, refers to the policy problem of a natural resource boom putting upward pressure on the exchange rate. This can squeeze other domestic exporters and import-competing sectors as they find it more and more difficult to compete in international markets.

Economic rent – Economic rent is payment made beyond that necessary to produce a good or service.

Efficiency frontier – An efficiency frontier is a locus of points where each point represents a possible portfolio. Based upon an investor's utility function, these points can be used to calculate an efficient portfolio of assets.

EMH – After assuming rational expectations theory, the efficient market hypothesis (EMH) postulates that market prices at all times fully reflect all available information. The EMH model assumes that investors' behaviour is collectively unpredictable and distributed normally.

Equity – Equity can be a stock or other security that represents an ownership interest.

ESF – The US Exchange Stabilisation Fund (ESF) is a US Treasury-controlled fund for emergency protection of the US dollar, and was used to assist Mexico in their 1994 crisis. This support took the form of short- and medium-term currency swaps and guarantees.

ETF – An exchange traded fund is a security that tracks an index, a commodity or a basket of assets, like an index fund. ETFs are traded like stocks on an exchange and thus experience price changes throughout the day as they are bought and sold.

Eurobond – A Eurobond is a bond issued in a jurisdiction and in a currency other than that of the country in which the issuer is based.

Excess return – The excess return of a security or portfolio, E, is the geometric difference between the security's percentage return, r, and that of a benchmark security or index, b, in the same period: $E=(1+r)/(1+b)-1$.

Fallacy of composition – The fallacy of composition occurs when one infers that something is true of the whole when it is true merely for some small part.

Financial repression – Financial repression is government policy which channels captive domestic savings to finance the government, and at lower cost than would otherwise be the case.

G20 – The Group of Twenty Finance Ministers and Central Bank Governors (G20) is a group of finance ministers and central bank governors from 20 major economies. Nineteen members are individual countries and the twentieth is the European Union.

Gambler's fallacy – When there are repeated independent random events, the gambler's fallacy is the belief that after a series of trials with a similar deviation from the expected result, deviation in the opposite direction is more likely.

GATT – The General Agreement on Tariffs and Trade was established in 1947 to promote international trade. It was replaced in 1995 by the World Trade Organization.

Gold pool – The gold pool was an agreement in 1961 whereby the US and seven European central banks co-ordinated sales of gold in the London gold market, buying dollars, which they then invested in US Treasuries.

Hedge fund, long-short hedge fund – Hedge funds are funds or limited partnership structures which employ hedging – i.e. they buy some assets but also short others (sell others which are borrowed). They may short to reduce investment risk, or (more typically) to allow greater capital to be released for effective leveraging, as by shorting they receive monies which can be put back into the market. They may employ high levels of such leverage and other borrowing. They may provide limited liquidity for investors in the fund to exit. They typically charge investors high fees, and may not be very transparent about their exposures.

HIDC – Heavily indebted developed countries, coined in contrast to HIPC (see below).

HIPC – Heavily indebted poor countries is a termed coined by the IMF/World Bank for countries in receipt of official debt relief under a programme of the same name.

IFC – The International Finance Corporation is the private sector lending arm of the World Bank Group.

IMF – The International Monetary Fund (IMF) was one of the institutions set up at Bretton Woods at the end of WWII. Its purpose is to monitor international monetary conditions, and prevent and assist in managing balance of payments crises.

Indices – Indices of sets of financial assets are commonly used in investment management to benchmark investment manager performance. They are also commonly used to define, and as proxies for, asset classes in asset allocation exercises.

Institutional investor – Institutional investors are organisations which pool large sums of money on behalf of third-party owners and invest them. They include pension funds, insurance companies, endowments and foundations, corporate treasury monies and some bank-owned or managed funds.

Investment grade – Rating agencies rate company, security and country credit-worthiness; one such possible rating is 'investment grade'. Ratings above investment grade are considered (by regulators) without major default risk, and appropriate for banks and the most conservative institutional investors to invest in. Sub-investment grade ratings levels are sometimes denoted speculative grade. Below that are issuers in default.

ISI – Import substitution industrialisation (ISI) is a set of policies promoted by Raúl Prebisch, Hans Singer and others in Latin America from the 1950s to the 1980s, focused on protection and incubation of domestic infant industries so they may emerge to compete with imported goods and make the local economy more self-sufficient.

Law of large numbers – The law of large numbers states that when a trial is repeated many times, the average result will move closer to the expected result.

Lender of last resort – A lender of last resort is a source of near-term funding to prevent default for a borrower in difficulty. For the banking sector this responsibility is often taken on by the central bank.

Leverage – The use of borrowed capital or other financial instruments to simulate the economic effect of borrowing.

LOOP – The law of one price (LOOP) states that in an efficient market identical things will have the same price.

LTCM – Long Term Capital Management (LTCM) was a large hedge fund management firm, employing very high levels of leverage, which collapsed in the late 1990s. LTCM posed such a significant systemic risk to US financial markets because of amounts owed to US banks that the New York Federal Reserve organised a private sector bailout to enable an ordered winding-up.

Macro-hedge fund – A hedge fund which primarily bases its holdings on overall macroeconomic principles and views.

Money illusion – Money illusion is the phenomenon whereby individuals do not adjust valuations for inflation. For example, people often remember the nominal prices of houses more than other goods over long periods, giving them the false impression of house price appreciation when in real term prices may not have gone up.

Moral hazard – Moral hazard is the incentive to take on additional risk when one has insurance.

MPT – Modern portfolio theory (MPT) is an asset selection theory which selects, from all allowable combinations, the optimal combination of assets or asset classes to produce a portfolio which maximises return for a given level of risk or minimises risk for a given level of return.

NAFTA – The North American Free Trade Agreement (NAFTA) is a trilateral trade block between the United States, Canada and Mexico, created in January 1994.

NDF – A non-deliverable forward (NDF) contract is a cash-settled derivative on a currency's value at a future specified date. At maturity the difference is paid between the actual currency value and the value specified in the contract, typically but not necessarily expressed versus the US dollar. Fully convertible currencies tend not to have NDF markets as market liquidity passes to onshore currency forward (deliverable) markets instead.

OPEC – The Organisation of the Petroleum Exporting Countries (OPEC) is an oil cartel, intended to co-ordinate the output policies of oil-producing member countries in order to control the price.

Paradigm shift – In his book *The Structure of Scientific Revolutions* Thomas Kuhn coined the phrase 'paradigm shift' to describe the relatively sudden change in beliefs following a long period of slow acceptance of a new idea, or paradigm. After the consensus of which paradigm to employ has shifted, it is followed by a second long period of gradual acceptance by those retaining belief in the earlier paradigm.

Portfolio rebalancing – Portfolio rebalancing assumes that market valuations revert to longterm means. In an attempt to meet target asset allocations, it involves the periodic selling of asset classes which have performed well over the previous period and buying of those which have performed poorly.

Preferred creditor status – Official lenders use the term 'preferred creditor status' to describe themselves in the context of their ideal that they should be the priority creditor when a borrowing country does not have the means to repay all creditors. However, if such a status exists, in practice it is the borrower who decides who has preferred creditor status as they decide whom and whom not to pay. This is likely to be the creditor most expected to extend the next loan – in many cases an official rather than a private lender, but not always. It is also sometimes the case that political or other pressures come into play to encourage priority repayment to the official lenders, and that the use of the term itself may sometimes blind borrowers away from their own best interests in who to repay first.

Prisoners' dilemma – The prisoners' dilemma, from game theory, describes two criminals being interviewed in separate cells by police who suspect them jointly of a crime, but have little evidence. The prisoners cannot communicate with each other. Both are offered deals of a light sentence if they give evidence against the other, but not if they both implicate each other, in which case they get only slightly shorter sentences than if they don't talk but are implicated. The best solution for them is to remain silent, in which case they both go free. Assuming no loyalty between thieves though, if one prisoner assumes the other will talk, then he also has an incentive to talk, so they both talk and both go to prison for a long, if not the longest, stretch.

Prospect theory – Prospect theory, developed by Daniel Kahneman and Amos Tversky, describes decisions between risky alternatives: people have been observed, using experimental data, to base decisions on potential losses and gains rather than expected outcomes. In a two-stage process, people first edit the choices: they order them, determine a neutral outcome and consider those with better outcomes as gains and those with worse outcomes as losses. In the second stage, evaluation, people behave as if they have computed utilities associated with different outcomes' gains and probabilities, and then maximised their utility. Beyond certain points they value additional losses and gains less. They also weight gains less than losses.

QE – Quantitative easing (QE) is the central bank's purchasing of bonds – and thus increasing the monetary base – once interest rates are at near zero and cannot be reduced further.

RET – Rational expectations theory (RET) assumes that, on average, economic agents (individuals and firms) are not systematically wrong in their decisions over long periods of time.

Rent seeking – Rent seeking is the process of obtaining economic rent through influencing institutional arrangements.

Risk-free rate – The risk-free rate is the expected rate of return on assets that theoretically pose no default, or other type of risk.

SDR – The IMF special drawing right is a basket currency used for internal IMF accounting but which was originally intended also as a potential reserve currency.

SDRM – The sovereign debt restructuring mechanism was a process suggested by the IMF to provide a specific mechanism for dealing with sovereign defaults in the early 2000s. It has subsequently been proposed again for potential European Union bond restructurings.

Sharpe ratio – The Sharpe ratio of a portfolio is the expected excess return divided by the portfolio's standard deviation.

Shorting – Shorting, or taking a short position, is the sale of a borrowed asset with the expectation that the asset will fall in value.

Spread – The spread is the amount of additional yield above the 'risk-free rate' which the market requires from an investment due to its default and other risks.

Stagflation – Stagflation is the condition of high and persistent unemployment in combination with inflation.

Stand-by agreement – A stand-by agreement is an IMF lending facility that provides loans to overcome short-term or cyclical balance of payments difficulties. These loans are usually conditional upon performance criteria and allow both parties to assess the borrower's progress in implementing the agreed upon conditions.

Technicals – Technicals, or technical factors, are facets of market structure, positioning and behaviour which may move the price of an asset.

Time value of money – The time value of money expresses the difference between having money now versus money in the future. Inflation erodes the real value of money, while interest earnings compensate for this erosion. Government budgeting often ignores the time value of money.

Variance – The variance of a data set is normally defined as the average squared difference from the expected value of the variable, where the expected value is normally the mean.

Washington Consensus – Coined by John Williamson with reference to Latin America, the Washington Consensus is a set of 10 economic policies which were deemed desirable in the late 1980s and early 1990s. From a loose description of policies which had worked, some of them became more dogmatically and prescriptively employed, used to frame conditionality in multilateral support programmes for developing countries.

World Bank – The International Bank for Reconstruction and Development and its soft-loan sister organisation the International Development Association are collectively called the World Bank. Founded at Bretton Woods in 1944, its initial purpose was lending to governments for the reconstruction of war-torn Europe, but subsequently its main purpose has been to promote economic and social progress in developing countries.

Yield curve – A yield curve is a curve showing several yields or interest rates across different contract lengths for the same government or other issuer. The curve shows the relation between the interest rate and the time to maturity.

Bibliography

Acemoglu, D., Robinson, J. A. (2012) *Why Nations Fail: The Origins of Power, Prosperity, and Poverty*. London: Profile Books.

Adler, G., Castro, P., Tovar, C. E. (2012) Does Central Bank Capital Matter for Monetary Policy? *IMF Working Paper.* WP/12/60.

Adler, G., Tovar, C. E. (2012) Riding Global Financial Waves: The Economic Impact of Global Financial Shocks on Emerging Market Economies. *IMF Working Paper.* WP/12/188.

Agtmael, A.V. (2007) *The Emerging Markets Century: How a New Breed of World-Class Companies is Overtaking the World.* New York: Free Press, Simon & Schuster.

Akerlof, G. A., Kranton, R. E. (2010) *Identity Economics: How Our Identities Shape Our Work, Wages, and Well-being.* Woodstock: Princeton University Press.

Akerlof, G. A., Shiller, R. J. (2009) *Animal Spirits: How Human Psychology Drives The Economy, and Why It Matters for Global Capitalism.* Princeton, NJ: Princeton University Press.

Albert, M. (1993) *Capitalism Against Capitalism.* London: Wurr Publishers.

Alesina, A., Giavazzi, F. (2006) *The Future of Europe: Reform or Decline.* Cambridge, MA: MIT Press.

Allen, L. (2005) *The Global Economic System Since 1945.* London: Reaktion Books.

Arner, D. W. (2007) *Financial Stability, Economic Growth, and the Role of Law.* New York: Cambridge University Press.

Authers, J. (2011) *Research finds a reason for active fund managers.* Available: http://www.ft.com/cms/s/0/2575b69a-3b9c-11e0-a96d-00144feabdc0.html#axzz2hiH9RgO3. Last accessed 14 October 2013.

Authers, J. (2011) *We need new models in an uncertain world.* Available: http://www.ft.com/cms/s/0/3cf4bd28–4c2e-11e0–82df-00144feab49a.html#axzz2hiH9RgO3. Last accessed 14 October 2013.

Axelrod, R. (1984) *The Evolution of Cooperation.* New York: Basic Books.

Aylward, L., Thorne, R. (1998) An Econometric Analysis of Countries' Repayment Performance to the International Monetary Fund. *IMF Working Paper.* WP/98/32.

Baba, C., Kokenye, A. (2011) Effectiveness of Capital Controls in Selected Emerging Markets in the 2000s. *IMF Working Paper.* WP/11/281.

Bagehot, W. (1873) *Lombard Street: A Description of the Money Market.* London: Henry S. King and Co. Library of Economics and Liberty [online]. Available: http://www.econlib.org/library/Bagehot/bagLom1.html.

Barabási, A. L. (2003) *Linked: How Everything is Connected to Everything Else and What It Means for Business, Science, and Everyday Life.* London: Plume.

Bayoumi, T., Brockmeijer, J., Cashin, P. *et al.* (2012) *Pilot External Sector Report.* Available: http://www.imf.org/external/np/pp/eng/2012/070212.pdf. Last accessed 3 November 2013.

Batini, N., Callegari, G., Melina, G. (2012) Successful Austerity in the United States, Europe and Japan. *IMF Working Paper*. WP/12/190.

Bauer, P. T. (1984) *Reality and Rhetoric: Studies in the Economics of Development*. London: Harvard University Press.

Beck, U. (2000) *What Is Globalization?* Cambridge: Polity Press.

Berlin, I. (1953) The originality of Machiavelli. In Berlin, I. (1979) *Against the Current: Essays in the History of Ideas*. London: Pimlico.

Bethell, T. (1998) *The Noblest Triumph: Property and Prosperity Through the Ages*. New York: St Martin's Press.

Bhidé, A. (2010) *A Call for Judgement: Sensible Finance for a Dynamic Economy*. New York: Oxford University Press.

Blackmore, S. (1999) *The Meme Machine*. Oxford: Oxford University Press.

Blanchard, O., Leigh, D. (2013) Growth Forecast Errors and Fiscal Multipliers. *IMF Working Paper*, January, WP/13/1.

Bobbitt, P. (2002) *The Shield of Achilles: War, Peace and the Course of History*. London: Penguin.

Booth, J. (1992) *Protectionism and agricultural commodity trade: an investigation into world wheat trade using spatial equilibrium modelling*. Available: http://ethos.bl.uk/OrderDetails.do?uin=uk. bl.ethos.333334. Last accessed 2 November 2013.

Booth, J. (2002) Argentina: The case for a permanent end to fiscal transfers. *Cambridge Review of International Affairs* 15 (3).

Boughton, J. M., Lombardi, D. (eds) (2009) *Finance, Development, and the IMF*. Oxford: Oxford University Press.

Botterill, L., Mazur, N. (2004) Risk and risk perception: A literature review. *Rural Industries Research and Development Corporation*. Publication No 04/043, Project No BRR 8A.

Braudel, F. (2000) *The Mediterranean and the Mediterranean World in the Age of Philip II*. Emended from 2nd edn. Translated from French by S. Reynolds, 1972–3. London: The Folio Society.

Brinson, G. P., Hood, L. R., Beebower, G. L. (1986) Determinants of portfolio performance. *Financial Analysts Journal* 42 (4), 39–44.

Brinson, G. P., Singer, B. D., Beebower, G. L. (1991) Determinants of portfolio performance II: An update. *Financial Analysts Journal* 47 (3), 40–48.

Buchan, J. (1998) *Frozen Desire: An Inquiry into the Meaning of Money*. London: Picador.

Buiter, W. (2009) *The unfortunate uselessness of most 'state of the art' academic monetary economics*. Available: http://www.voxeu.org/article/macroeconomics-crisis-irrelevance. Last accessed 4 October 2012.

Burger, D., Warnock, F., Warnock, C.E. (2010) Investing in Local Currency Bond Markets. *National Bureau of Economic Research*. Working Paper 16249.

Calderisi, R. (2006) *The Trouble with Africa: Why Foreign Aid Isn't Working*. New Haven, CT: Yale University Press.

Caplen, B. (2000) Paris Club comes under attack. *Euromoney*, September.

Cassen, R. and Associates (1986) *Does Aid Work?* New York: Oxford University Press.

Chakotin, S. (1940) *The Rape of The Masses: The Psychology of Totalitarian Political Propaganda*. London: George Routledge & Sons.

Chang, H. (ed.) (2003) *Rethinking Development Economics*. London: Anthem Press.

Chang, H. (2003) *Kicking Away the Ladder: Development Strategy in Historical Perspective*. London: Anthem Press.

Chang, H. (2007) *Bad Samaritans: The Guilty Secrets of Rich Nations & the Threat to Global Prosperity*. London: Random House Business Books.

Chen, J., Dai, D., Pu, M., Hou, W., Feng, Q. (2010) The trend of the Gini coefficient of China. *BWPI Working Paper 109, January*. Manchester, UK: Brooks World Poverty Institute, University of Manchester.

Chen, S., Liu, P., Maechler, A., Marsh, C., Saksonovs, S., Shin, H. (2012) Exploring the Dynamics of Global Liquidity. *IMF Working Paper.* WP/12/246 .

Clarke, W. K. (2001) *Waging Modern War.* New York: Public Affairs.

Coase, R. H. (1937) The nature of the firm. *Economica* 4 (16), 386–405.

Collier, P. (2008) *The Bottom Billion: Why the Poorest Countries Are Failing and What Can Be Done About It.* New York: Oxford University Press.

Collier, P. (2009) *Wars, Guns and Votes: Democracy in Dangerous Places.* London: The Bodley Head.

Collier, P. (2010) *The Plundered Planet: How to Reconcile Prosperity with Nature.* London: Allen Lane.

Collier, P., Gunning, J. W. (1999) Explaining African economic performance. *Journal of Economic Literature* 37 (1), 64–111.

Cooper, G. (2008) *The Origin of Financial Crises: Central Banks, Credit Bubbles and the Efficient Market Fallacy.* Petersfield, Hampshire: Harriman House.

Coyle, D. (2010) *The Soulful Science: What Economists Really Do and Why It Matters.* Princeton, NJ: Princeton University Press.

Cutler, D., Poterba, J. Summers, L. (1989) What moves stock prices? Moves in stock prices reflect something other than news about fundamental values. *Journal of Portfolio Management* 15, 4–12.

Davidson, P. (2009) *Efficient Market Theory vs. Keynes's Liquidity Theory.* Available: http://www.progressive-economics.ca/2009/06/11/davidson-efficient-market-theory-vs-keynes%E2%80%99s-liquidity-theory/. Last accessed 14 October 2013.

Davies, H., Green, D. (2008) *Global Financial Regulation: The Essential Guide.* Cambridge: Polity Press.

Dawkins, R. (1976) *The Selfish Gene.* Oxford: Oxford University Press.

De Bock, R., Demyanets, A. (2012) Bank Asset Quality in Emerging Markets: Determinants and Spillovers. *IMF Working Paper.* WP/12/71.

De Bondt, W., Muradoglu, G., Shefrin, H., Staikouras, S. K. (2008) Behavioral finance: Quo vadis? *Journal of Applied Finance* 18 (2), 7–21.

De Soto, H. (2000) *The Mystery of Capital: Why Capitalism Triumphs in the West and Fails Everywhere Else.* London: Black Swan.

Dehn, J. (2000) The Effects on Growth of Commodity Price Uncertainty and Shocks. *World Bank Policy Research Working Paper,* September, WPS-2455.

Della Croce, R., Steward, F., Yermo, J. (2011) Promoting longer-term investment by institutional investors: Selected issues and policies. *OECD Journal: Financial Market Trends* 1, 145–164.

Deutsche, K. W. (1963) *The Nerves of Government: Models of Political Communication and Control.* New York: Free Press.

Diamond, J. (1999) *Guns, Germs and Steel: The Fates of Human Societies.* New York: W. W. Norton & Company.

Dixit, A. K., Pindyck, R. S. (1994) *Investment Under Uncertainty.* Princeton, NJ: Princeton University Press.

Dodd, N. (1994) *The Sociology of Money: Economics, Reason and Contemporary Society.* New York: Continuum.

Dostoyevsky, F. (1866) *Crime and Punishment.* Moscow: The Russian Messenger.

Dunn, J. (2000) *The Cunning of Unreason: Making Sense of Politics.* London: HarperCollins.

Easterly, W. (2006) *The White Man's Burden: Why the West's Efforts to Aid the Rest Have Done So Much Ill and So Little Good.* New York: Oxford University Press.

Eaton, J., Gersovitz, M. (1981) Debt with potential repudiation: Theoretical and empirical analysis. *Review of Economic Studies* 48 (February), 289–309.

Eichengreen, B. (2010) *Global Imbalances and the Lessons of Bretton Woods.* Cambridge, MA: MIT Press.

Eichengreen, B. (2011) *Exorbitant Privilege: The Rise and Fall of the Dollar.* Oxford: Oxford University Press.

Eichengreen, B., Gupta, P., Kumar, R. (eds) (2010) *Emerging Giants: China and India in the World Economy*. Oxford: Oxford University Press.

Eichengreen, B., Park, D., Shin, K. (2011) When Fast Growing Economies Slow Down: International Evidence and Implications for China. *National Bureau of Economic Research*. Working Paper 16919.

Eichengreen, B., Wyplosz, C., Park, Y. C. (eds) (2008) *China, Asia, and the New World Economy*. Oxford: Oxford University Press.

El-Erian, M. (2008) W*hen Markets Collide: Investment Strategies for the Age of Global Economic Change*. New York: McGraw-Hill.

Eocjner, A. S. (ed.) (1983) *Why Economics Is Not Yet a Science*. London: Macmillan Press.

Fama, E. (1998) Market efficiency, long-term returns, and behavioural finance. *Journal of Financial Economics* 49(3), 283–306.

Farmer, R. E. A., (2010) *How the Economy Works: Confidence, Crashes and Self-fulfilling Prophecies*. New York: Oxford University Press.

Ferguson, N. (2001) *The Cash Nexus: Money and Power in the Modern World, 1700–2000*. New York: Basic Books.

Ferguson, N. (2006) *The War of the World: History's Age of Hatred*. London: Penguin Group.

Ferguson, N. (2008) *The Ascent of Money: A Financial History of the World*. London: Allen Lane

Ferri, G. (2004) More Analysts, better ratings: Do ratings agencies invest enough in less developed countries? *Journal of Applied Economics* 7 (1), 77–98.

Findlay, R., O'Rourke, K. H. (2007) *Power and Plenty: Trade, War, and the World Economy in the Second Millennium*. Princeton, NJ: Princeton University Press.

Fligstein, N. (2001) *The Architecture of Markets: An Economic Sociology of Twenty-First-Century Capitalist Societies*. Princeton, NJ: Princeton University Press.

Forbes, W. (2009) *Behavioural Finance*. Chichester: John Wiley & Sons.

Freedman, D. H. (2011) *A Formula For Economic Calamity*. Available: http://www.scientificamerican.com/article.cfm?id=a-formula-for-economic-calamity. Last accessed 14 October 2013.

French, K. R., Poterba, J. M. (1991) Investor diversification and international equity markets. *National Bureau of Economic Research*. Working Paper 3609.

Frenkel, M., Nickel, C., Schmidt, G., Stadtmann, G. (2001) The Effects of Capital Controls on Exchange Rate Volatility and Output. *IMF Working Paper*, November, WP/01/187.

Friedman, M., Schwartz, A. J. (1963) *A Monetary History of the United States, 1867–1960*. Princeton, NJ: Princeton University Press for NBER.

Frydman, R., Goldberg, M. D. (2011) *Beyond Mechanical Markets: Asset Price Swings, Risk, and the Role of the State*. Princeton, NJ: Princeton University Press.

FSB, IMF, BIS (2011) *Macroprudential Policy Tools and Frameworks, Progress Report to G20*. Available: http://www.imf.org/external/np/g20/pdf/102711.pdf. Last accessed 9 August 2013.

Fukuyama, F. (1992) *The End of History and the Last Man*. New York: Free Press.

Gai, P., Kapadia, S. (2010) Contagion in financial networks. *Proceedings of the Royal Society A: Mathematical, Physical and Engineering Science* 466 (2120), 2401–2423.

Galbraith, J. K. (1961) *The Great Crash 1929*. Harmondsworth, Middlesex: Pelican.

Galbraith, J. K. (1975) *Money: Whence it Came, Where it Went*. Harmondsworth, Middlesex: Penguin Books.

Gardner, D. (2008) *Risk: The Science and Politics of Fear*. London: Random House.

Gardner, D. (2012) *Future Babble: How to Stop Worrying and Love the Unpredictable*. London: Virgin Books

Gladwell, M. (2005) *Blink: The Power of Thinking Without Thinking*. London: Penguin Books.

Gleick, J. (2011) *The Information: A History, a Theory, a Flood*. London: Fourth Estate.

Gonzáles-Páramo, J. M. (2011) *The challenges of the European financial sector.* European Central Bank: speech given to conference at the Spanish National Council of the Urban Land Institute, Barcelona, 26 May 2011.

Goodhart, C. A. E. (2011) The changing role of central banks. *Financial History Review* 18 (2), 135–154.

Gould, S. J. (1981) *The Mismeasure of Man*. New York: Norton

Gowers, A. (ed.) (2012) *Investing In Change: The Reform of Europe's Financial Markets*. London: AFME.

Goyal, R., Marsh, C., Raman, N., Wang, S., Ahmed, S. (2011) Financial Deepening and International Monetary Stability. *IMF Staff Discussion Note.* SDN/11/16

Grossman, S. J., Stiglitz, J. E. (1980) On the impossibility of informationally efficient markets. *The American Economic Review* 70 (3), 393–408.

Habermeier, K., Kokenyne, A., Baba, C. (2011) The Effectiveness of Capital Controls and Prudential Policies in Managing Large Inflows. *IMF Staff Discussion Note.* SDN/11/14.

Haldane, A. (2009) Rethinking The Financial Network, speech delivered at the Financial Student Association, Amsterdam, April.

Haldane, A., May, R. (2011) Systemic risk in banking ecosystems. *Nature* 469 (7330), 351–355.

Harris, S. (2010) *The Moral Landscape: How Science Can Determine Human Values.* London: Transworld Publishers.

Hayek, F. A. (1944) *The Road to Serfdom*. Abingdon: Routledge Classics.

Heikensten, L. (2009) Inflation Targeting 20 Years On. Presentation at Norges Bank Conference. Oslo, June 12.

Heiner, R.A. (1983) The origin of predictable behavior. *The American Economic Review* 73 (4), 560–595.

Hersh, S. M. (1983) *The Price of Power: Kissinger in the Nixon White House*. New York: Summit Books.

Hirschman, A. O. (1970) *Exit, Voice, and Loyalty. Responses to Decline in Firms, Organisations and States*. Cambridge, MA: Harvard University Press.

Hobsbawm, E. J. (1990) *Nations and Nationalism Since 1780*, 2nd edn. Cambridge: The Press Syndicate of the University of Cambridge.

Hobsbawm, E. J. (2007) *Globalisation, Democracy and Terrorism*. London: Abacus.

Hunt, D. (1989) *Economic Theories of Development: An Analysis of Competing Paradigms*. London: Harvester Wheatsheaf.

Huntington, S. P. (1996) *The Clash of Civilizations and the Remaking of the World Order*. London: Simon & Shuster.

Ibbotson, R. G., Kaplan, P. D. (2000) Does asset allocation policy explain 40, 90, or 100 percent of performance? *Financial Analysts Journal* 56 (1), 26–33.

Ilzetzki, E., Mendoza, E. G., Végh, C. A. (2011) How Big (Small?) are Fiscal Multipliers? *IMF Working Paper*, March, WP/11/52.

Isard, P. (2005) *Globalization and the International Financial System.* Cambridge: Cambridge University Press.

Jacobs, J. (1992) *Systems of Survival: A Dialogue on the Moral Foundations of Commerce and Politics*. New York: Random House.

Jacobs, J. (2000) *The Nature of Economies*. New York: The Modern Library.

Jeffrey, R., Doron, A. (2013) *The Great Indian Phone Book: How the Cheap Cell Phone Changes Business, Politics, and Daily Life*. London: C. Hurst & Co.

Jo, J.H. (2012) Managing systemic risk from the perspective of the financial network under macroeconomic distress. Bank for International Settlements. Working Paper, JEL Classification G21, G28 .

Johnson, S. (2009) The quiet coup. *Atlantic Monthly*, May. Available: http://www.theatlantic.com/magazine/archive/2009/05/the-quiet-coup/307364/. Last accessed 15 January 2014.

Judt, T. (2010) *Ill Fares the Land*. London: Penguin Books.

Kahneman, D. (2011) *Thinking, Fast and Slow*. London: Allen Lane.

Kahneman, D., Slovak, P., Tversky, A. (eds) (1982) *Judgement under Uncertainty: Heuristics and Biases*. New York: Cambridge University Press.

Kahneman, D., Tversky, A. (1979) Prospect theory: An analysis of decision under risk. *Econometrica: Journal of the Econometric Society* 47 (2), 263–291.

Kaminsky, G., Schmukler, S. (2003) Short-Run Pain, Long-Run Gain: The Effects of Financial Liberalization. *IMF Working Paper*, February, WP/03/34.

Kaplinsky, R. (2005) *Globalization, Poverty and Inequality*. Cambridge: Polity Press.

Kawai, M., Newfarmer, R., Schmukler, S. (2003) *Financial Crises: Nine Lessons from East Asia*. Available: http://siteresources.worldbank.org/DEC/Resources/Kawai-Newfarmer-Schmukler-EEJ-9May2003.pdf. Last accessed 1 October 2013.

Kay, J. (2003) *The Truth About Markets: Their Genius, Their Limits, Their Follies*. London: Penguin Group.

Kay, J. (2010) *Obliquity: Why Our Goals Are Best Achieved Indirectly*. London: Profile Books.

Kenny, C. (2011) *Getting Better: Why Global Development is Succeeding – and How We Can Improve the World Even More*. New York: Basic Books.

Keppler, M. (1990) *Risk is Not the Same as Volatility*. Available: http://www.kamny.com/load/publications/p03_eng.pdf. Last accessed 7 October 2013.

Keynes, J. M. (1919) *The Economic Consequences of the Peace*. New York: Harcourt, Brace, and Howe.

Keynes, J. M. (1936) *The General Theory of Employment, Interest and Money*. Cambridge: Macmillan Cambridge University Press, for Royal Economic Society.

Kiff, J., Nowak, S. B., Schumacher, L. (2012) Are Rating Agencies Powerful? An Investigation into the Impact and Accuracy of Sovereign Ratings. *IMF Working Paper.* WP/12/23.

Kim, J. I. (2008) Sudden Stops and Optimal Self-Insurance. *IMF Working Paper.* WP/08/144

Kondratiev, N. D. (1925) The major economic cycles. *Voprosy Konjunktury* 1 (1), 28–79.

Koo, R. C. (2009) *The Holy Grail of Macroeconomics: Lessons from Japan's Great Recession*. Singapore: John Wiley & Sons (Asia).

Korinek, A. (2011) The New Economics of Capital Controls Imposed for Prudential Reasons. *IMF Working Paper.* WP/11/298.

Krueger, A. O. (1974) The political economy of the rent-seeking society. *The American Economic Review*, 64 (3), 291–303.

Krugman, P. (2008) *The Return of the Depression Economics and the Crisis of 2008*. London: Penguin.

Lawson, N. (2010) *Memoirs of a Tory Radical*. London: Biteback.

Lawson, N. (2011) *Five Myths and a Menace*. Available: http://standpointmag.co.uk/features-janfeb-11-five-myths-and-a-menace-ligel-lawson-adam-smith-economics. Last accessed 15 October 2013.

Levi, M. (1988) *Of Rule and Revenue*. Berkeley, CA: University of California Press.

Lewis, C. M. (2002) *Argentina: A Short History*. Oxford: Oneworld Publications.

Lewis, C. S. (1964) *The Discarded Image: An Introduction to Medieval and Renaissance Literature*. Cambridge: Cambridge University Press.

Li, J., Rajan, R. S. (2011) *Do Capital Controls Reduce the Volatility of Gross Capital Inflows and Outflows? Intended and Unintended Consequences*. March draft. Available: http://cemp.gmu.edu/files/pdfs/Annual_Research_Forum/2012/Impact_of_Capital_Controls_of_Capital_Volatility_Revisited.pdf

Leijonhufvud, A. (1968) *On Keynesian Economics and the Economics of Keynes*. New York and Oxford: Oxford University Press.

Lo, A. W. (2005) Reconciling Efficient Markets with Behavioral Finance: The Adaptive Markets Hypothesis. *Journal of Investment Consulting* 7 (2), 21–42.

Lo, A.W. (2011) *Reading About the Financial Crisis: A 21-Book Review*. Available: http://www.argentumlux.org/documents/Lo__2011__-_Reading_About_the_Financial_Crisis__JEL_.pdf. Last accessed 8 October 2013.

Louge, D.E. Rader, J.S. (1997) *Managing Pension Plans: A Comprehensive Guide to Improving Plan Performance*. New York: Oxford University Press.

Lucas, R. (1976) Econometric Policy Evaluation: A Critique. In: Brunner, K., Meltzer, A., *The Phillips Curve and Labor Markets*. Carnegie-Rochester Conference Series on Public Policy, 1. New York: American Elsevier, pp. 19–46, ISBN 0–444–11007–0.

Mackintosh, J. (2011) *Better models alone won't avert crises*. Available: http://www.ft.com/cms/s/0/070946f0–68d7–11e0–9040–00144feab49a.html#axzz2hiH9RgO3. Last accessed 14 October 2013.

Mackintosh, J. (2011) *Reward for risk seems to be a chimera*. Available: http://www.ft.com/cms/s/0/8c39b7a6–5194–11e0–888e-00144feab49a.html#axzz2hiH9RgO3. Last accessed 14 October 2013.

Maddison, A. (2007) *Contours of the World Economy, 1–2030 AD: Essays in Macro-Economic History*. Oxford: Oxford University Press.

Magud, N., Reinhart, C., Rogoff, K. (2007) Capital Controls: Myth and Reality A Portfolio Balance Approach to Capital Controls. *Federal Reserve Bank of San Francisco Working Paper Series*. Working Paper 2007–31.

Mahbubani, K. (2008) *The New Asian Hemisphere: The Irresistible Shift of Global Power to the East*. New York: Public Affairs.

Malik, K. (2013) *Human Development Report 2013, The Rise of the South: Human Progress in a Diverse World*. Available: http://hdr.undp.org/en/media/HDR_2013_EN_complete.pdf. Last accessed 1 November 2013.

Manasse, P., Roubini, N., Schimmelpfennig, A. (2003) Predicting Sovereign Debt Crises. *IMF Working Paper*, WP/03/221.

Mandelbrot, B., Hudson, R. L. (2005) *The (Mis)Behaviour of Markets: A Fractal View of Risk, Ruin and Reward*. London: Profile Books.

Mandeng, O. (2011) The G-20 and the dollar: what's new? *Central Banking* 22 (2).

Mankiw, N. G., Reis, R. (2001) Sticky information: A model of monetary nonneutrality and structural slumps. *National Bureau of Economic Research*. Working Paper 8614.

Markowitz, H. M. (1959) *Portfolio Selection: Efficient Diversification of Investments*. Cowles Foundation for Research in Economics at Yale University, Monograph 16. New York: John Wiley & Sons.

Marsh, D. (2009) *The Euro: The Politics of the New Global Currency*. London: Yale University Press.

Matthews, R. C. O. (1968) Why has Britain had full employment since the war? *The Economic Journal* 78 (311), 555–569.

Maziad, S., Farahmand, P., Wang, S., Segal, S., Ahmed, F. (2011) Internationalization of Emerging Market Currencies: A Balance between Risks and Rewards. *IMF Staff Discussion Note*. SDN/11/17.

McCloskey, D. (1994) *Knowledge and Persuasion in Economics*. Cambridge: Cambridge University Press.

Meier, G. M. (ed.) (1991) *Politics and Policy Making in Developing Countries: Perspectives on the New Political Economy*. San Francisco, CA: ICS Press.

Micklethwait, J.,Woolridge, A. (2000) *A Future Perfect: The Challenge and Hidden Promise of Globalisation*. London: William Heinemann.

Miller, P. (2010) *Smart Swarm: Using Animal Behaviour to Change Our World*. London: Collins.

Mishkin, F. S. (2006) Weissman Center Distinguished Lecture Series, Baruch College, New York, 12 October 2006.

Montier, J. (2002) *Behavioural Finance: Insights into Irrational Minds and Markets*. Chichester: John Wiley & Sons.

Morrison, A. D., Wilhelm, W. J., Jr (2007) *Investment Banking: Institutions, Politics, and Law*. Oxford: Oxford University Press.

Mosley, P., Harrigan, J., Toye, J. (1991) *Aid and Power: The World Bank & Policy-based Lending Volume 1*. London: Routledge.

Moyo, D. (2009) *Dead Aid: Why Aid is Not Working and How There is Another Way for Africa*. London: Allen Lane.

Muradoglu, G. (2002) Portfolio managers' and novices' forecasts of risk and return: are there predictable forecast errors? *Journal of Forecasting* 21 (6), 395–416.

Muralidhar, A. S. (2001) *Innovations in Pension Fund Management*. Stanford, CA: Stanford University Press.

Naba, M. (2011) Targets, Interest Rates, and Household Savings in Urban China. IMF Working Paper, September, WP/11/223.

Nier, E. W., Osiński, J., Jácome, L. I., Madrid, P. (2011) *Institutional Models for Macroprudential Policy*. Available: http://www.imf.org/external/pubs/ft/sdn/2011/sdn1118.pdf. Last accessed 8 October 2013.

Nofsinger, J. R. (2011) *The Psychology of Investing*, 4th edn. Boston, MA: Prentice Hall.

Nofsinger, J. R. Sias, R. W. (1999) Herding and feedback trading by institutional and individual investors. *The Journal of Finance* 54 (6), 2263–2295.

North, D. (1981) *Structure and Change in Economic History*. New York: W.W. Norton.

North, D. C. (1990) *Institutions, Institutional Change and Economic Performance*. New York: Cambridge University Press.

North, D. C. (2005) *Understanding the Process of Economic Change*. Princeton, NJ: Princeton University Press.

OECD (2011) Getting the most out of international capital flows. OECD Economic Outlook, Volume 2011/1. Available: http://www.oecd.org/eco/outlook/47836248.pdf. Last accessed 7 October 2013.

Olson, M (1965) *The Logic of Collective Action: Public Goods and the Theory of Groups*. Cambridge, MA: Harvard University Press.

Omerod, P. (1994) *The Death of Economics*. London: Faber and Faber.

Omerod, P. (1998) *Butterfly Economics*. London: Faber and Faber.

Ostry, J. D., Ghosh, A. R., Habermeier, K., Chamon, M., Qureshi, M. S., Reinhardt, D. B. S. (2010) *Capital Inflows: The Role of Controls*. Available: http://www.imf.org/external/pubs/ft/spn/2010/spn1004.pdf. Last accessed 8 October 2013.

Pakenham, T. (1991) *The Scramble For Africa*. London: Weidenfeld & Nicolson.

Paris, E. (2000) *Long Shadows: Truth, Lies and History*. Toronto: Vintage Canada .

Patterson, S. (2010) *The Quants: How a Small Band of Maths Wizards Took Over Wall Street and Nearly Destroyed It*. New York: Random House.

Peter, M. (2002) Estimating Default Probabilities of Emerging Market Sovereigns: A New Look at a Not-So-New Literature. *The Graduate Institute of International Studies, Geneva: HEI Working Paper*, 06/2002.

Phillips, K. (2002) *Wealth and Democracy: A Political History of the American Rich*. New York: Broadway Books.

Polanyi, M. (1958) *Personal Knowledge: Towards a Post-Critical Philosophy*. Chicago, IL: University of Chicago Press.

Popper, K. (1976) *Unended Quest: an Intellectual Autobiography*. La Salle: Open Court.

Postman, N. (1985) *Amusing Ourselves to Death: Public Discourse in the Age of Show Business*. New York: Penguin.

Postman, N. (1992) *Technopoly: The Surrender of Culture to Technology*. New York: Vintage Books.

Pozsar, Z., Singh, M. (2011) The Nonbank-Bank Nexus and the Shadow Banking System. IMF Working Paper. WP/11/289.

Putnam, R. D. (2000) *Bowling Alone: The Collapse and Revival of American Community*. New York: Touchstone.

Rajan, R. G. (2005) Has financial development made the world riskier? National Bureau of Economic Research. Working Paper 11728.

Rajan, R. G. (2010) *Fault Lines: How Hidden Fractures Still Threaten the World Economy*. Princeton, NJ: Princeton University Press.

Rajan, R. G., Zingales, L. (2003) *Saving Capitalism from the Capitalists: How Open Financial Markets Challenge the Establishment and Spread Prosperity to Rich and Poor Alike*. London: Random House Business Books.

Reinhart, C. M., Reinhart, V. R., Rogoff, K. S. (2012) Debt overhangs: past and present. National Bureau of Economic Research. Working Paper 18015.

Reinhart, C. M., Rogoff, K. S. (2009) *This Time is Different: Eight Centuries of Financial Folly*. Princeton, NJ: Princeton University Press.

Richards, T. (1990) *The Commodity Culture of Victorian England: Advertising and Spectacle, 1851–1914*. Stanford, CA: Stanford University Press.

Ridley, M. (2010) *The Rational Optimist: How Prosperity Evolves*. London: Fourth Estate.

Rifkin, J. (2009) *The Empathic Civilization: The Race To Global Consciousness In A World In Crisis*. New York: Penguin Group.

Roberts, J. (1998) Inflation expectations and the transmission of monetary policy. Federal Reserve Board FEDS Paper. 98–43.

Robinson, J. (1962) *Economic Philosophy*, 2009 reprint. New Brunswick, NJ: Aldine Transaction.

Roll, R. (1977) A Critique of the asset pricing theory's tests. Part I: On past and potential testability of the theory. *Journal of Financial Economics* 4 (2), 129–176.

Roubini, N. (2001) Debt Sustainability: How to Assess Whether a Country is Insolvent. Stern School of Business, New York University, mimeo.

Roxburgh, C., Lund, S., Daruvala, T. *et al.* (2012) *Debt and deleveraging: Uneven progress on the path to growth*. Available: http://www.mckinsey.com/insights/global_capital_markets/uneven_progress_on_the_path_to_growth. Last accessed 4 October 2012.

Roxburgh, C., Lund, S., Wimmer, T. *et al.* (2010) *Debt and deleveraging: The global credit bubble and its economic consequence*. Available: http://www.mckinsey.com/insights/global_capital_markets/debt_and_deleveraging_the_global_credit_bubble_update. Last accessed 4 October 2012.

Santos-Paulino, A. U., Wan, G. (eds) (2010) *Southern Engines of Global Growth*. Oxford: Oxford University Press.

Sanyal, S. (2012) *Mapping the World's Financial Markets*. Available: http://www.euromoney.com/downloads/3/DB_RandomWalk_2013–02–13_0900b8c08653e545.pdf. Last accessed 4 October 2012.

Schelling, T. C. (2006) *Micromotives and Macrobehaviour*. New York: Norton.

Seabright, P. (2010) *The Company of Strangers: A Natural History of Economic Life*. Princeton, NJ: Princeton University Press.

Sedlacek, T. (2011) *Economics of Good and Evil: The Quest for Economic Meaning from Gilgamesh to Wall Street*. New York: Oxford University Press.

Sen, A. (1981) *Poverty and Famines: An Essay on Entitlement and Deprivation*. New York: Oxford University Press.

Sen, A. (1999) *Development As Freedom*. New York: Anchor Books.

Sharpe, W. (1990) Asset allocation. In: Magin, J., Tuttle, J. (eds), *Managing Investment Portfolios – A Dynamic Process*. New York: Warren, Gorham and Lamont.

Shefrin, H. (2002) *Beyond Greed and Fear: Understanding Behavioral Finance and the Psychology of Investing*. New York: Oxford University Press.

Shefrin, H., Statman, M. (2000) Behavioral portfolio theory. *Journal of Financial and Quantitative Analysis* 35 (2), 127–151.

Shell, M. (1982) *Money, Language, and Thought: Literary and Philosophic Economies from the Medieval to the Modern Era*. Berkeley and Los Angeles, CA: University of California Press.

Shiller, R. J. (2003) *The New Financial Order: Risk in the 21st Century*. Princeton, NJ: Princeton University Press.

Shiller, R. J. (2005) *Irrational Exuberance*, 2nd edn. Princeton, NJ: Princeton University Press.

Shiller, R. J. (2008) *The Subprime Solution*. Princeton, NJ: Princeton University Press.

Shi, X. J. (2012) *Reform the International Rating System to Promote the World Economic Recovery (four)*. Available: http://en.dagongcredit.com/content/details20_5102.html. Last accessed 4 October 2012.

Siedentop, L. (2000) *Democracy in Europe*. London: Penguin.

Simmel, G. (1990) *The Philosophy of Money*, 2nd English edn. London: Routledge.

Skidelsky, R. (1995) *The World After Communism: A Polemic for our Times*. London: Macmillan.

Smith, A. (1776) *An Inquiry into the Nature and Causes of the Wealth of Nations*. London: J. M. Dent & Sons.

Smith, R. (2005) *The Utility of Force: The Art of War in the Modern World*. London: Penguin Group.

Smithers, A. (2009) *Wall Street Revalued: Imperfect Markets and Inept Central Bankers*. Chichester: John Wiley & Sons.

Soros, G. (2008) *The New Paradigm for Financial Markets: The Credit Crisis of 2008 and What it Means*. London: Public Affairs.

Spilimbergo, A., Schindler, M., Symansky, S. A. (2009) Fiscal multipliers. *IMF Staff Position Note*. SPN/09/11.

Statman, M. (1987) How many stocks make a diversified portfolio? *Journal of Financial and Quantitative Analysis* 22 (3), 94.

Statman, M. (1999) Behavioural finance: Past battles and future engagements. *Financial Analysts Journal* 55 (6), 18–27.

Statman, M. (2011) *What Investors Really Want*. New York: McGraw-Hill.

Stern, F. (1977) *Gold and Iron: Bismarck, Bleichröder, and the Building of the German Empire*. New York: Knopf.

Stewart, F. (1997) Comment on John Williamson and the Washington Consensus Revisited. In: Emmerij, L. (ed.) (1997) *Economic and Social Development into the XXI Century*. Washington, DC: Inter-American Development Bank, pp. 62–69.

Stiglitz, J. (2002) *Globalization and Its Discontents*. London: Allen Lane.

Stiglitz, J. (2006) *Making Globalization Work: The Next Steps to Global Justice*. London: Allen Lane.

Stiglitz, J. (2010) *Freefall: America, Free Markets, and the Sinking of the World Economy*. New York: W. W. Norton & Company.

Suskind, R. (2004) *The Price of Loyalty: George W. Bush, the White House, and the Education of Paul O'Neill*. New York: Simon & Shuster.

Swensen, D. F. (2009) *Pioneering Portfolio Management: An Unconventional Approach to Institutional Investment*. New York: Free Press.

Taleb, N. N. (2007) *The Black Swan: The Impact of the Highly Improbable*. London: Penguin Books.

Tett, G. (2009) *Fool's Gold*. London: Little, Brown.

Tett, G. (2012) *Anthropologists join actuaries on risk*. Available: http://www.ft.com/cms/s/0/faea0bda-dcb5–11e1–99f3–00144feab49a.html#axzz2hiH9RgO3. Last accessed 14 October 2013.

Thaler, R. H., Sunstein, C. R. (2008) *Nudge: Improving Decisions About Health, Wealth, and Happiness*. New Haven, CT: Yale University Press.

Thirsk, J. (1978) *Economic Policy and Projects: The Development of a Consumer Society in Early Modern England*. New York: Oxford University Press.

Toynbee, A. J. (1946) *A Study of History*. Oxford: Oxford University Press.

Turner, A., Haldane, A., Woolley, P. *et al.* (2010) *The Future of Finance: The LSE Report*. London: London School of Economics and Political Science.

Tversky, A. (1972) Elimination by aspects: A theory of choice. *Psychological review* 79 (4), 281.

Vayanos, D., Woolley, P. (2008) An institutional theory of momentum and reversal. *Review of Financial Studies* 26 (5), 1087–1145.

Volcker, P. A. (2011) *Financial Reform: Unfinished Business*. Available: http://www.nybooks.com/articles/archives/2011/nov/24/financial-reform-unfinished-business/?pagination=false.   Last accessed 14 October 2013.

Vujanovic, P. (2011) Understanding the Recent Surge in the Accumulation of International Reserves. OECD Economics Department Working Papers. No. 866. OECD Publishing.

Waldrop, M. (1992) *Complexity*. London: Penguin Group.

Wells, L. T., Ahmed, R. (2007) *Making Foreign Investments Safe: Property Rights and National Sovereignty*. New York: Oxford University Press.

Wessel, D., Vogel, T. (1993) *Market Watcher: Arcane World of Bonds is Guide and Beacon To a Populist President*. Available: http://snapshot.factiva.com/Article/Print. Last accessed 28 January 2013.

Williamson, J. (ed.) (1990) *Latin American Adjustment: How Much Has Happened?* Washington, DC: Institute for International Economics.

Wolf, M. (2004) *Why Globalization Works: The Case for the Global Market Economy*. London: Yale University Press.

Wolf, M. (2009) *Fixing Global Finance: How to Curb Financial Crises in the 21st Century*. London: Yale University Press.

Wolf, M. (2010) *Why rising rates are good news*. Available: http://www.ft.com/cms/s/0/b129a644–07b5–11e0-a568–00144feabdc0.html?siteedition=uk#axzz2hiH9RgO3. Last accessed 14 October 2013.

Wolfram, S. (2002) *A New Kind of Science*. Champaign, IL: Wolfram Media.

Index